Serenity™

宁静 FIREFLY CLASS 03-K64

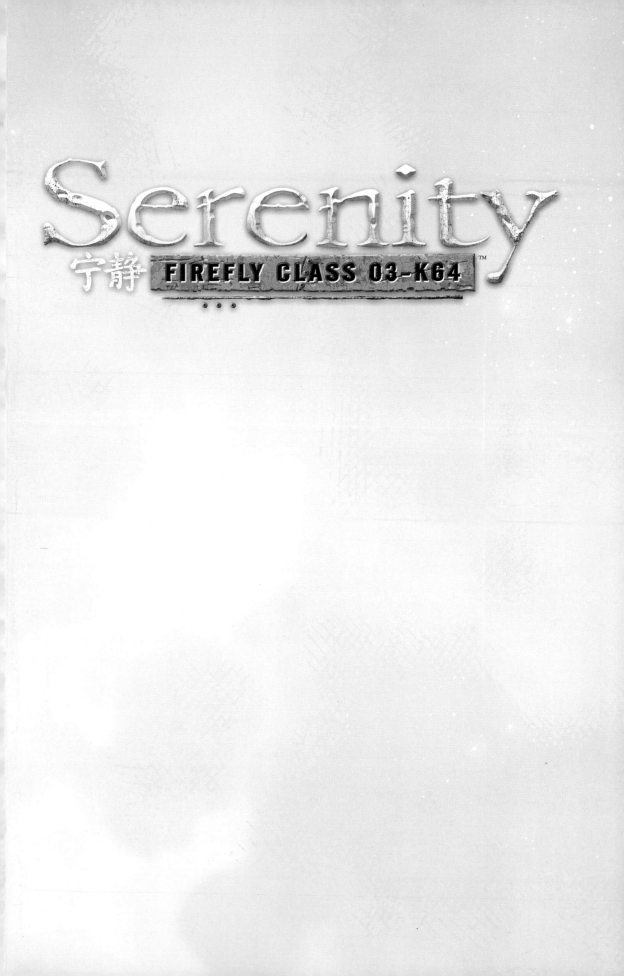

Serenity

宁静 FIREFLY CLASS 03-K64 ™

— LEAVES ON THE WIND —

ZACK WHEDON
GEORGES JEANTY
FÁBIO MOON

EXECUTIVE PRODUCER
JOSS WHEDON

FRONT COVER AND CHAPTER BREAK ART
DAN DOS SANTOS

DARK HORSE BOOKS

PRESIDENT & PUBLISHER
MIKE RICHARDSON

EDITOR
SCOTT ALLIE

ASSISTANT EDITOR
FREDDYE LINS

COLLECTION DESIGNER
JUSTIN COUCH

"IT'S NEVER EASY" EDITED BY SCOTT ALLIE AND SIERRA HAHN

SPECIAL THANKS TO SIERRA HAHN, LAUREN WINARSKI AND JOSH IZZO AT TWENTIETH CENTURY FOX, DANIEL KAMINSKY, CHRIS HARBERT, BRIANNA BARCUS AND RICHARD BROOKS, ADAM BALDWIN, AND JEWEL STAITE.

———————

NEIL HANKERSON Executive Vice President • TOM WEDDLE Chief Financial Officer • RANDY STRADLEY Vice President of Publishing • MICHAEL MARTENS Vice President of Book Trade Sales • ANITA NELSON Vice President of Business Affairs • SCOTT ALLIE Editor in Chief • MATT PARKINSON Vice President of Marketing • DAVID SCROGGY Vice President of Product Development • DALE LaFOUNTAIN Vice President of Information Technology • DARLENE VOGEL Senior Director of Print, Design, and Production • KEN LIZZI General Counsel • DAVEY ESTRADA Editorial Director • CHRIS WARNER Senior Books Editor • DIANA SCHUTZ Executive Editor • CARY GRAZZINI Director of Print and Development • LIA RIBACCHI Art Director • CARA NIECE Director of Scheduling • TIM WIESCH Director of International Licensing • MARK BERNARDI Director of Digital Publishing

Serenity: Firefly Class 03-K64 Volume 4—Leaves on the Wind

This volume collects the miniseries *Serenity: Leaves on the Wind* #1–#6 and the short story "It's Never Easy," from *Free Comic Book Day 2012: Serenity/Star Wars.*

Published by Dark Horse Books
A division of Dark Horse Comics, Inc.
10956 SE Main Street
Milwaukie, OR 97222

DarkHorse.com

To find a comics shop in your area, call the
Comic Shop Locator Service toll-free at (888) 266-4226.
International Licensing: (503) 905-2377

First edition: November 2014

ISBN 978-1-61655-489-7

1 3 5 7 9 10 8 6 4 2
Printed in China

LEAVES ON THE WIND

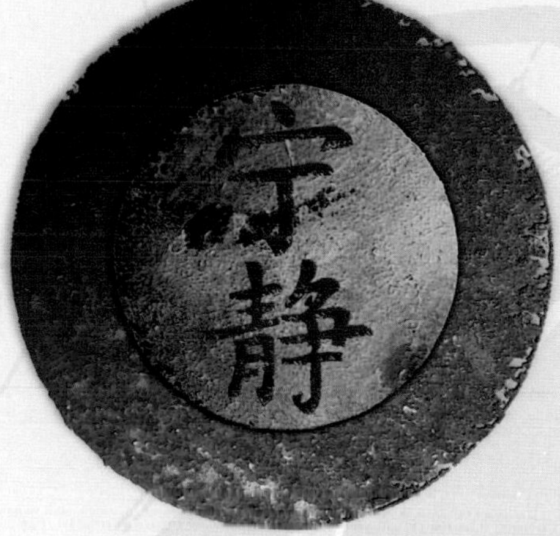
宁静

SCRIPT
ZACK WHEDON

PENCILS
GEORGES JEANTY

INKS
KARL STORY

COLORS
LAURA MARTIN
COLORS FOR CHAPTER 6 BY LAURA MARTIN AND LOVERN KINDZIERSKI

LETTERS
MICHAEL HEISLER

The galaxy still reels from the Unification War, in which the Alliance cemented its dominance, crushing the Browncoat resistance. Deep in the blackness of space, a Firefly-class vessel named *Serenity* shuttles between planets, taking odd jobs, both legal and otherwise. The captain of the ship, Malcolm Reynolds, and first mate Zoe Washburne remain Browncoats at heart, dodging bounty hunters and making friends and enemies throughout the 'verse. Among *Serenity*'s crew is Dr. Simon Tam, who rescued his genius sister River from Alliance experiments and found refuge on *Serenity*. River, prized and feared by the Alliance for her psychic abilities, has been pursued relentlessly across the 'verse. In their fight to elude the Alliance, Mal Reynolds and his crew revealed that the Reavers, an interstellar breed of cannibal pirates, were the result of another Alliance experiment. In a bloody last stand, Mal broadcast this revelation to the 'verse, proving it to the operative sent to kill River. As the outlaw crew try to cope with the loss of two of their own, the Alliance and the rebels both ask . . . where is *Serenity*?

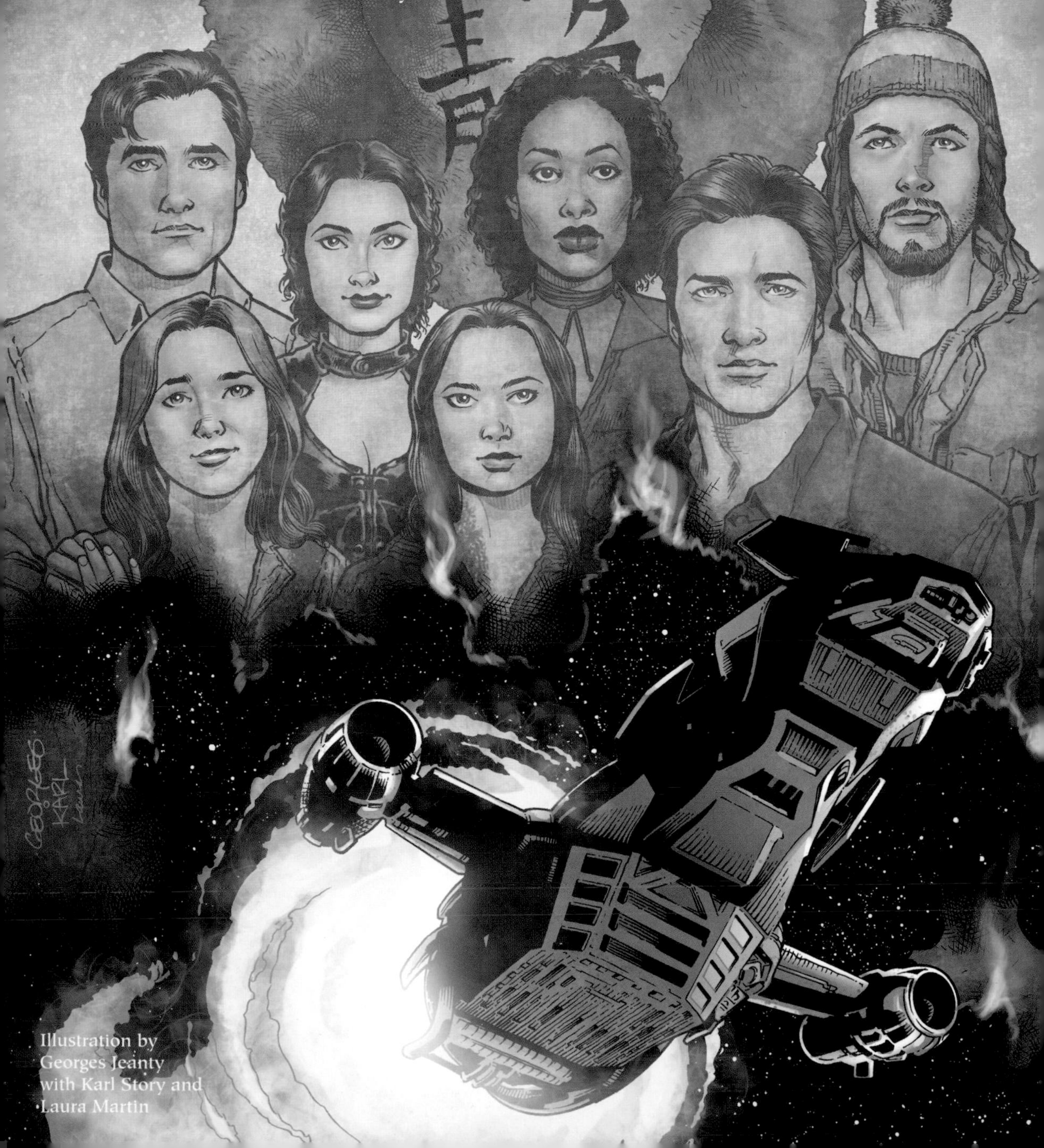

Illustration by Georges Jeanty with Karl Story and Laura Martin

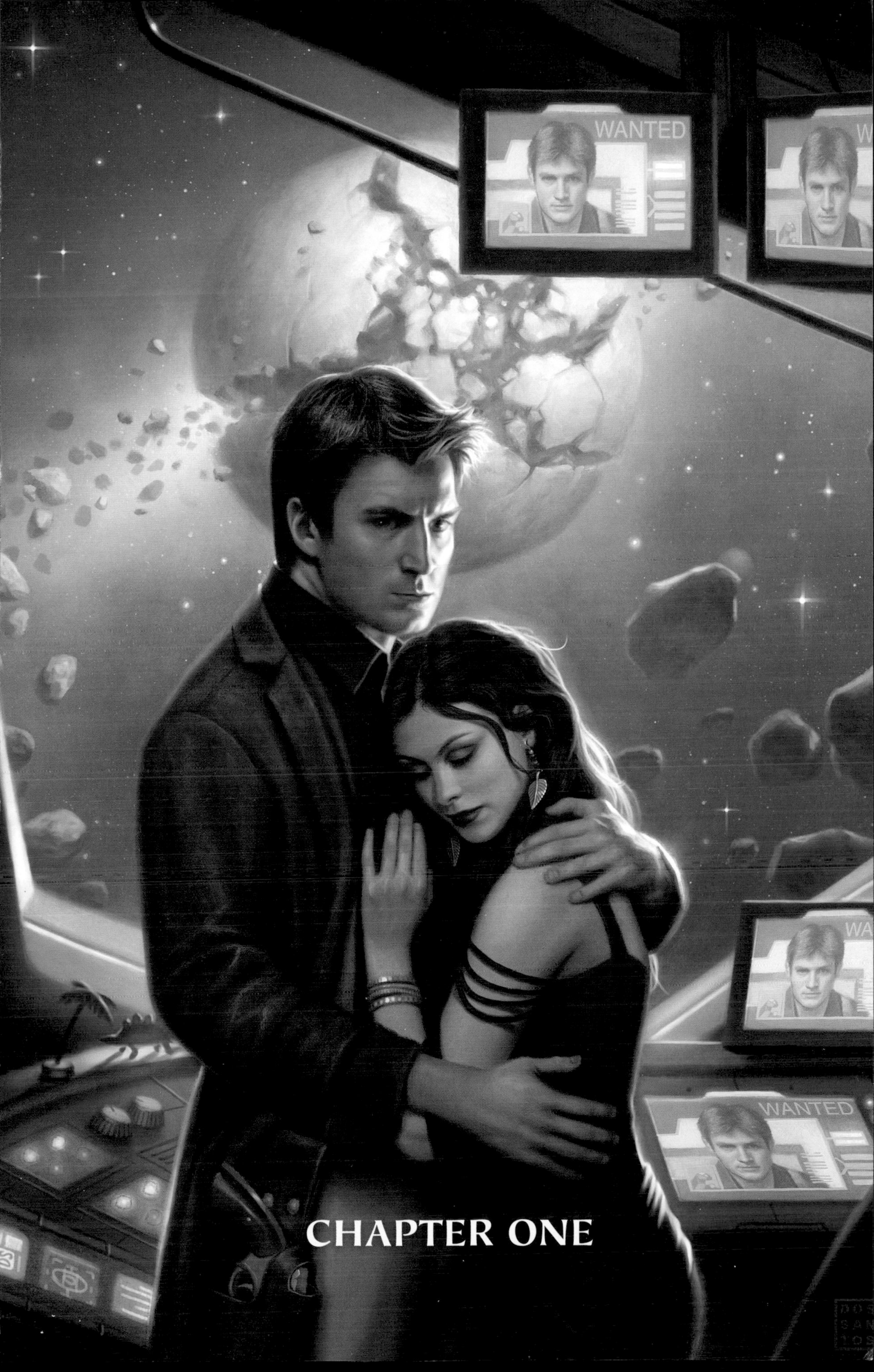
WANTED
WANTED

CHAPTER ONE

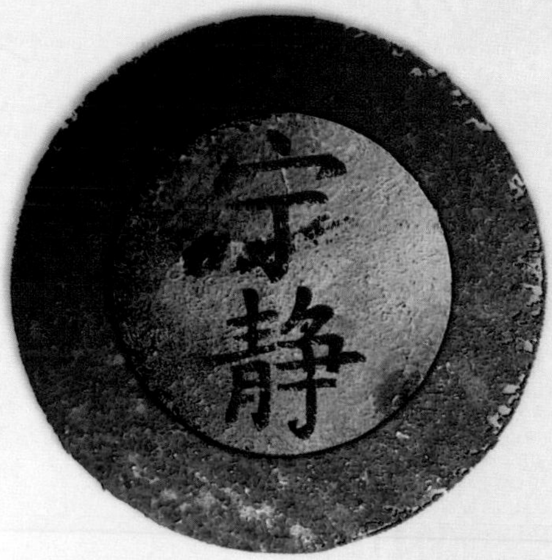
守静

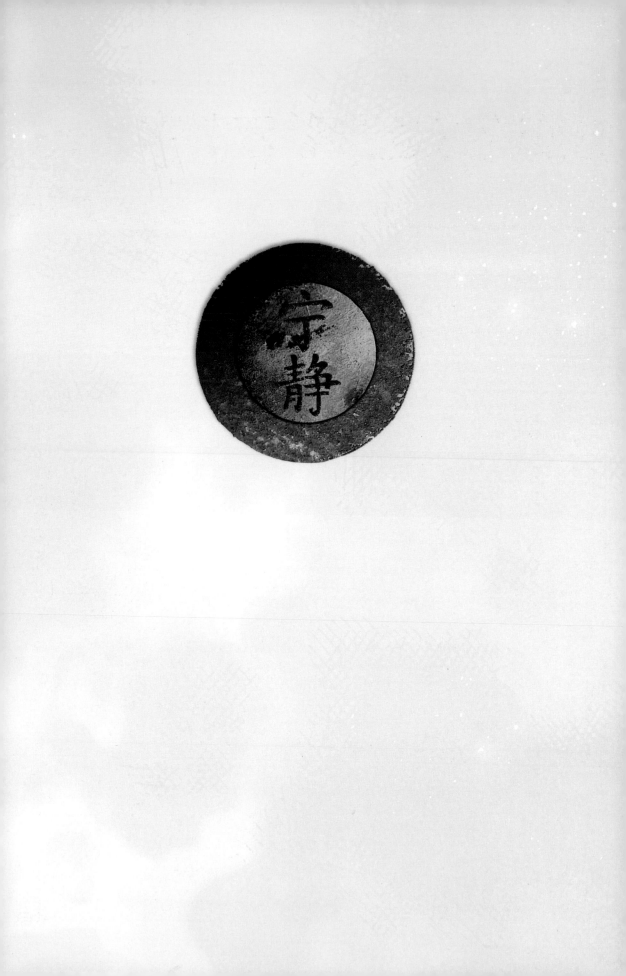

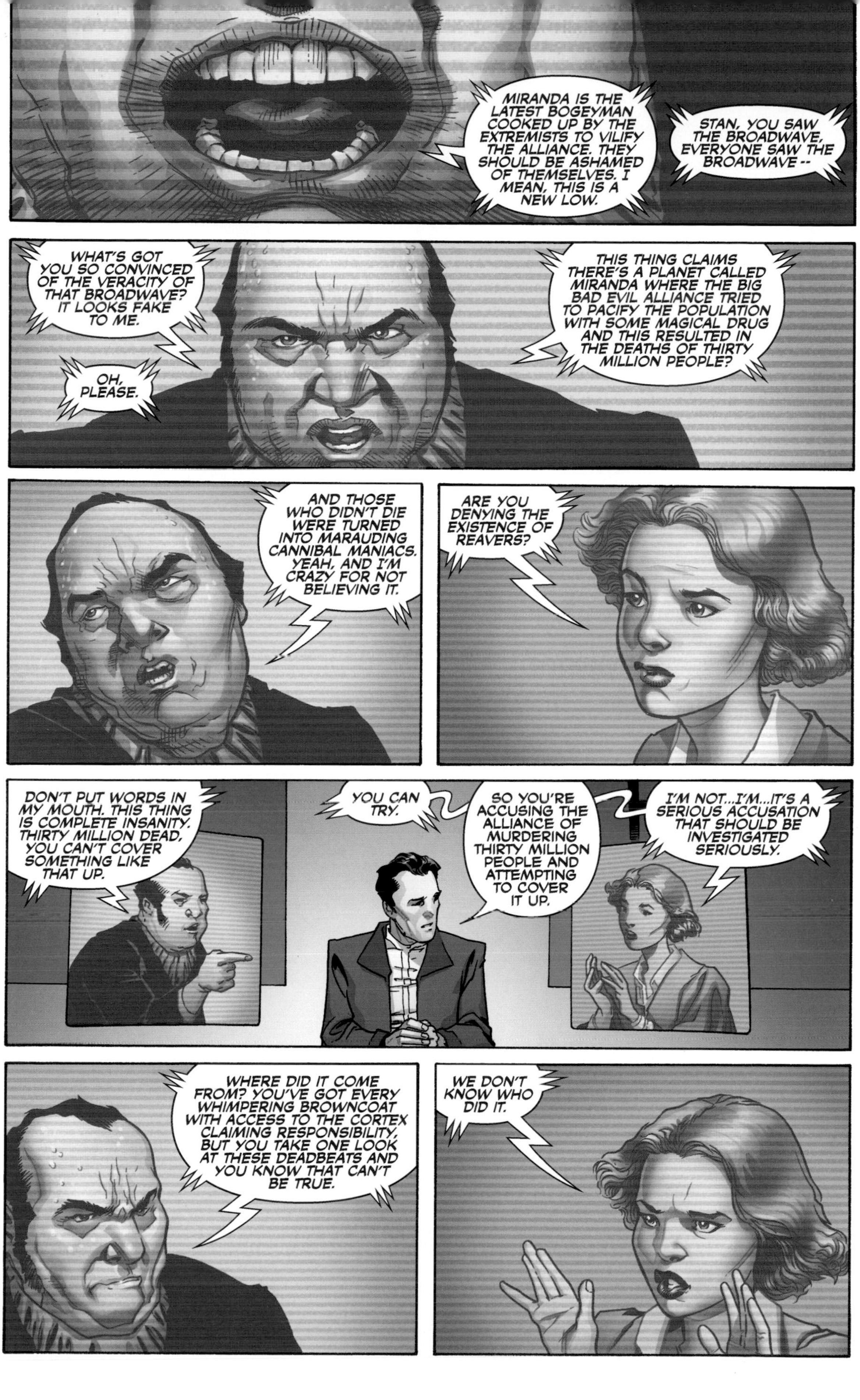
MIRANDA IS THE LATEST BOGEYMAN COOKED UP BY THE EXTREMISTS TO VILIFY THE ALLIANCE. THEY SHOULD BE ASHAMED OF THEMSELVES. I MEAN, THIS IS A NEW LOW.
STAN, YOU SAW THE BROADWAVE, EVERYONE SAW THE BROADWAVE --
WHAT'S GOT YOU SO CONVINCED OF THE VERACITY OF THAT BROADWAVE? IT LOOKS FAKE TO ME.
OH, PLEASE.
THIS THING CLAIMS THERE'S A PLANET CALLED MIRANDA WHERE THE BIG BAD EVIL ALLIANCE TRIED TO PACIFY THE POPULATION WITH SOME MAGICAL DRUG AND THIS RESULTED IN THE DEATHS OF THIRTY MILLION PEOPLE?
AND THOSE WHO DIDN'T DIE WERE TURNED INTO MARAUDING CANNIBAL MANIACS. YEAH, AND I'M CRAZY FOR NOT BELIEVING IT.
ARE YOU DENYING THE EXISTENCE OF REAVERS?
DON'T PUT WORDS IN MY MOUTH. THIS THING IS COMPLETE INSANITY. THIRTY MILLION DEAD, YOU CAN'T COVER SOMETHING LIKE THAT UP.
YOU CAN TRY.
SO YOU'RE ACCUSING THE ALLIANCE OF MURDERING THIRTY MILLION PEOPLE AND ATTEMPTING TO COVER IT UP.
I'M NOT...I'M...IT'S A SERIOUS ACCUSATION THAT SHOULD BE INVESTIGATED SERIOUSLY.
WHERE DID IT COME FROM? YOU'VE GOT EVERY WHIMPERING BROWNCOAT WITH ACCESS TO THE CORTEX CLAIMING RESPONSIBILITY, BUT YOU TAKE ONE LOOK AT THESE DEADBEATS AND YOU KNOW THAT CAN'T BE TRUE.
WE DON'T KNOW WHO DID IT.

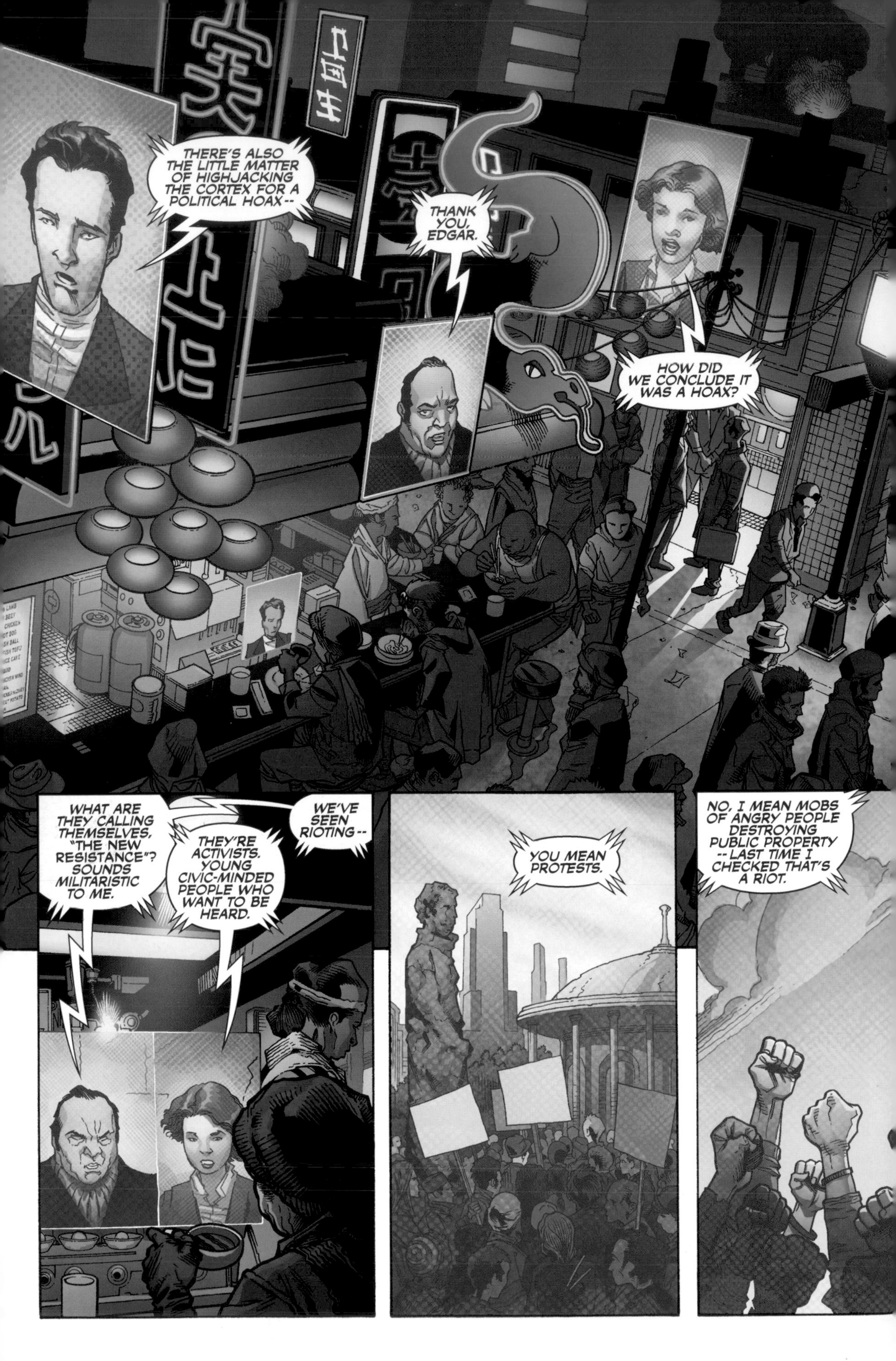
THERE'S ALSO THE LITTLE MATTER OF HIGHJACKING THE CORTEX FOR A POLITICAL HOAX--
THANK YOU, EDGAR.
HOW DID WE CONCLUDE IT WAS A HOAX?
WHAT ARE THEY CALLING THEMSELVES, "THE NEW RESISTANCE"? SOUNDS MILITARISTIC TO ME.
THEY'RE ACTIVISTS. YOUNG CIVIC-MINDED PEOPLE WHO WANT TO BE HEARD.
WE'VE SEEN RIOTING--
YOU MEAN PROTESTS.
NO, I MEAN MOBS OF ANGRY PEOPLE DESTROYING PUBLIC PROPERTY --LAST TIME I CHECKED THAT'S A RIOT.

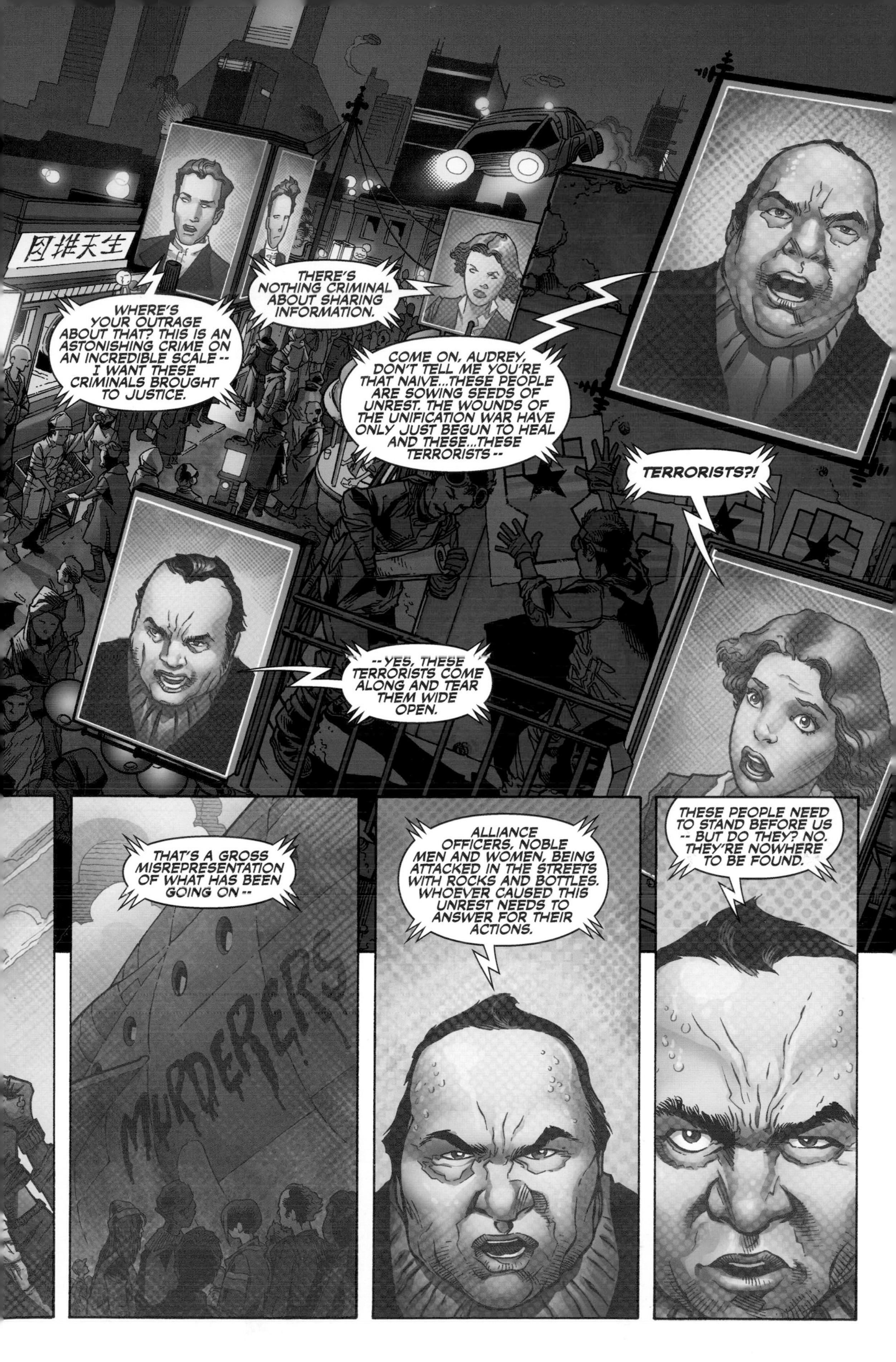

因排天生
WHERE'S YOUR OUTRAGE ABOUT THAT? THIS IS AN ASTONISHING CRIME ON AN INCREDIBLE SCALE -- I WANT THESE CRIMINALS BROUGHT TO JUSTICE.
THERE'S NOTHING CRIMINAL ABOUT SHARING INFORMATION.
COME ON, AUDREY, DON'T TELL ME YOU'RE THAT NAIVE...THESE PEOPLE ARE SOWING SEEDS OF UNREST. THE WOUNDS OF THE UNIFICATION WAR HAVE ONLY JUST BEGUN TO HEAL AND THESE...THESE TERRORISTS --
TERRORISTS?!
-- YES, THESE TERRORISTS COME ALONG AND TEAR THEM WIDE OPEN.
THAT'S A GROSS MISREPRESENTATION OF WHAT HAS BEEN GOING ON --
MURDERERS
ALLIANCE OFFICERS, NOBLE MEN AND WOMEN, BEING ATTACKED IN THE STREETS WITH ROCKS AND BOTTLES. WHOEVER CAUSED THIS UNREST NEEDS TO ANSWER FOR THEIR ACTIONS.
THESE PEOPLE NEED TO STAND BEFORE US -- BUT DO THEY? NO. THEY'RE NOWHERE TO BE FOUND.

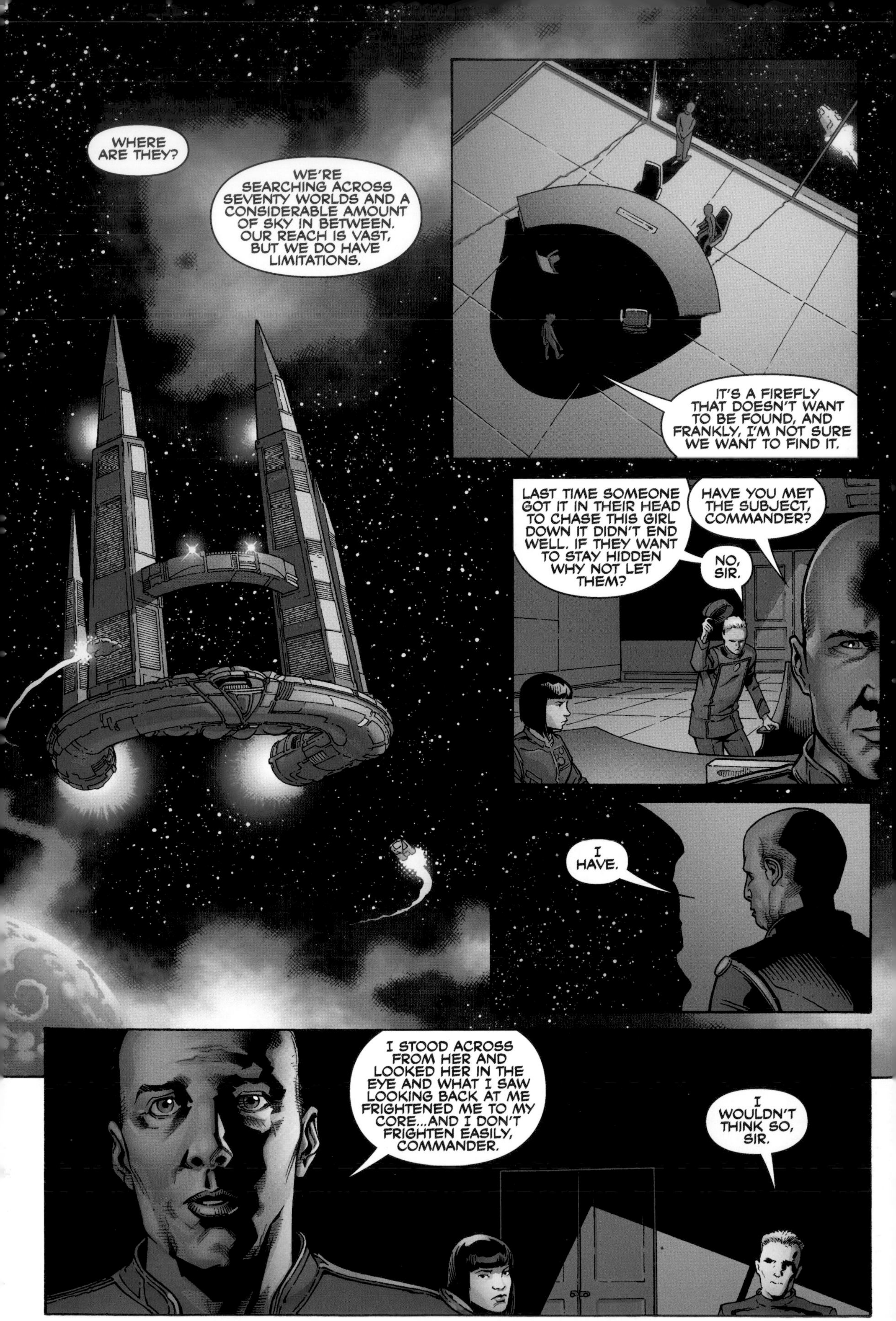
WHERE ARE THEY?
WE'RE SEARCHING ACROSS SEVENTY WORLDS AND A CONSIDERABLE AMOUNT OF SKY IN BETWEEN. OUR REACH IS VAST, BUT WE DO HAVE LIMITATIONS.
IT'S A FIREFLY THAT DOESN'T WANT TO BE FOUND, AND FRANKLY, I'M NOT SURE WE WANT TO FIND IT.
LAST TIME SOMEONE GOT IT IN THEIR HEAD TO CHASE THIS GIRL DOWN IT DIDN'T END WELL. IF THEY WANT TO STAY HIDDEN WHY NOT LET THEM?
HAVE YOU MET THE SUBJECT, COMMANDER?
NO, SIR.
I HAVE.
I STOOD ACROSS FROM HER AND LOOKED HER IN THE EYE AND WHAT I SAW LOOKING BACK AT ME FRIGHTENED ME TO MY CORE...AND I DON'T FRIGHTEN EASILY, COMMANDER.
I WOULDN'T THINK SO, SIR.

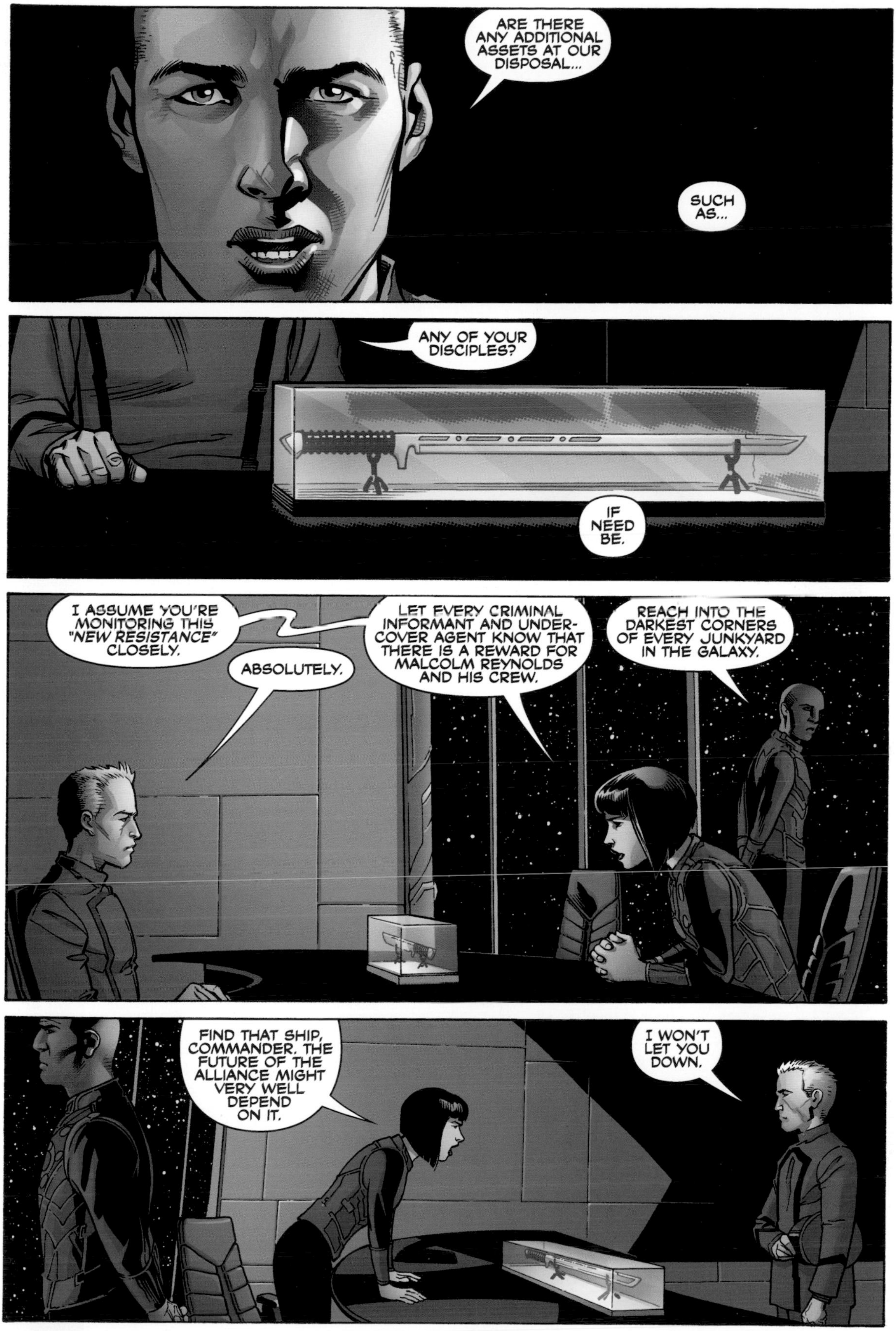
ARE THERE ANY ADDITIONAL ASSETS AT OUR DISPOSAL...
SUCH AS...
ANY OF YOUR DISCIPLES?
IF NEED BE.
I ASSUME YOU'RE MONITORING THIS "NEW RESISTANCE" CLOSELY.
ABSOLUTELY.
LET EVERY CRIMINAL INFORMANT AND UNDER-COVER AGENT KNOW THAT THERE IS A REWARD FOR MALCOLM REYNOLDS AND HIS CREW.
REACH INTO THE DARKEST CORNERS OF EVERY JUNKYARD IN THE GALAXY.
FIND THAT SHIP, COMMANDER. THE FUTURE OF THE ALLIANCE MIGHT VERY WELL DEPEND ON IT.
I WON'T LET YOU DOWN.

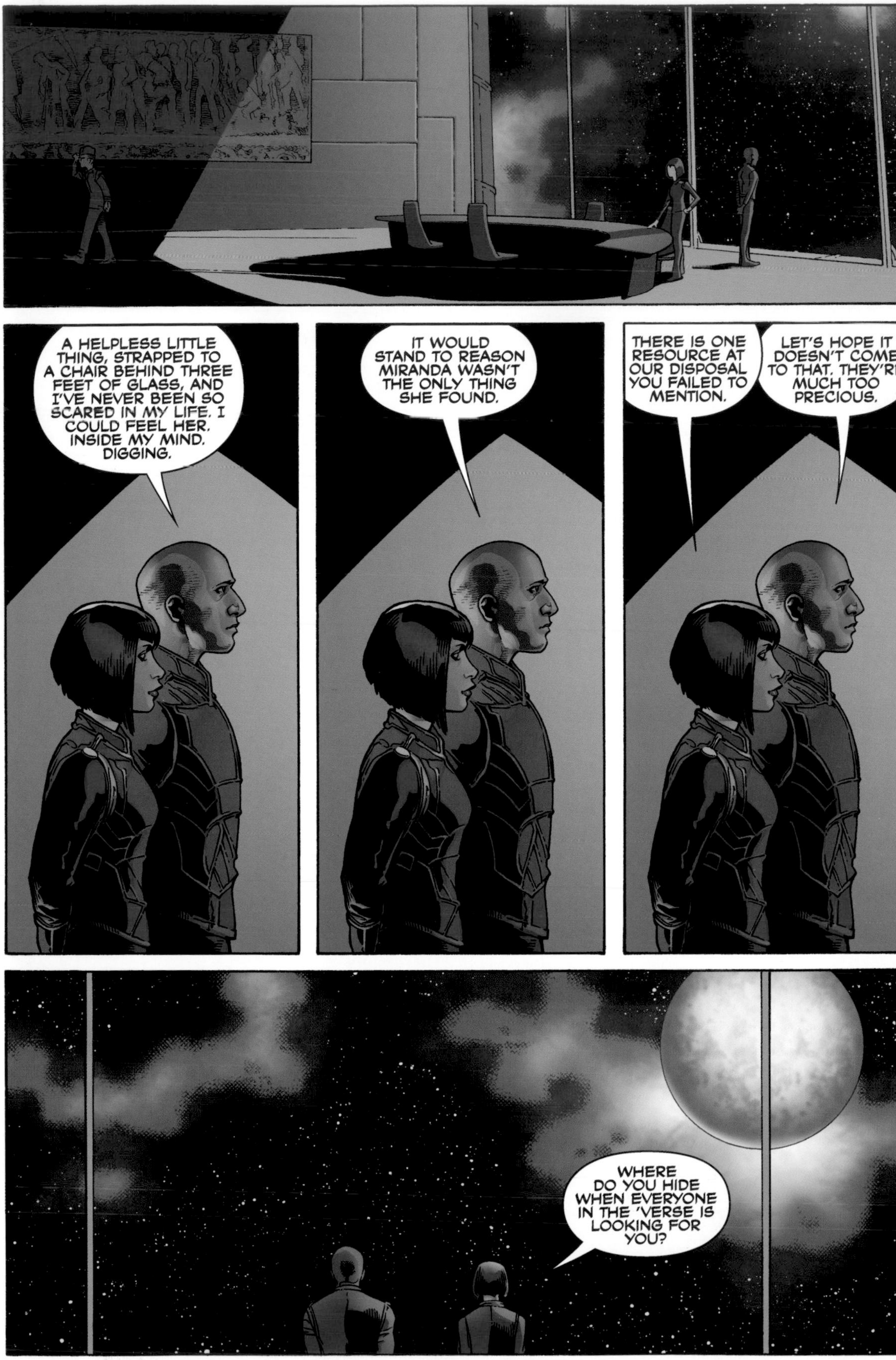

A HELPLESS LITTLE THING, STRAPPED TO A CHAIR BEHIND THREE FEET OF GLASS, AND I'VE NEVER BEEN SO SCARED IN MY LIFE. I COULD FEEL HER. INSIDE MY MIND. DIGGING.
IT WOULD STAND TO REASON MIRANDA WASN'T THE ONLY THING SHE FOUND.
THERE IS ONE RESOURCE AT OUR DISPOSAL YOU FAILED TO MENTION.
LET'S HOPE IT DOESN'T COME TO THAT. THEY'RE MUCH TOO PRECIOUS.
WHERE DO YOU HIDE WHEN EVERYONE IN THE 'VERSE IS LOOKING FOR YOU?

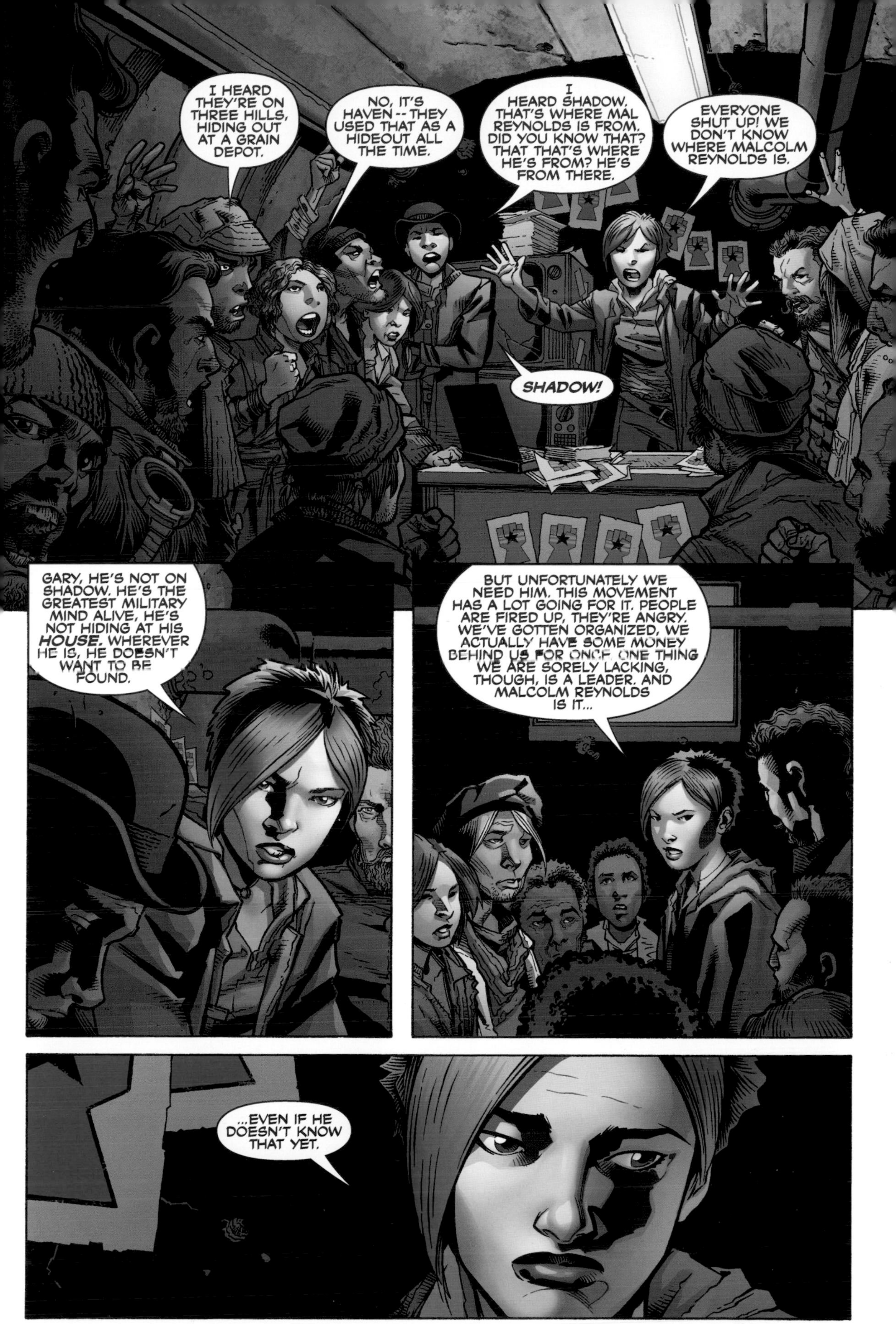
I HEARD THEY'RE ON THREE HILLS, HIDING OUT AT A GRAIN DEPOT.
NO, IT'S HAVEN -- THEY USED THAT AS A HIDEOUT ALL THE TIME.
I HEARD SHADOW. THAT'S WHERE MAL REYNOLDS IS FROM. DID YOU KNOW THAT? THAT THAT'S WHERE HE'S FROM? HE'S FROM THERE.
EVERYONE SHUT UP! WE DON'T KNOW WHERE MALCOLM REYNOLDS IS.
SHADOW!
GARY, HE'S NOT ON SHADOW. HE'S THE GREATEST MILITARY MIND ALIVE, HE'S NOT HIDING AT HIS HOUSE. WHEREVER HE IS, HE DOESN'T WANT TO BE FOUND.
BUT UNFORTUNATELY WE NEED HIM. THIS MOVEMENT HAS A LOT GOING FOR IT. PEOPLE ARE FIRED UP, THEY'RE ANGRY. WE'VE GOTTEN ORGANIZED, WE ACTUALLY HAVE SOME MONEY BEHIND US FOR ONCE. ONE THING WE ARE SORELY LACKING, THOUGH, IS A LEADER. AND MALCOLM REYNOLDS IS IT...
...EVEN IF HE DOESN'T KNOW THAT YET.

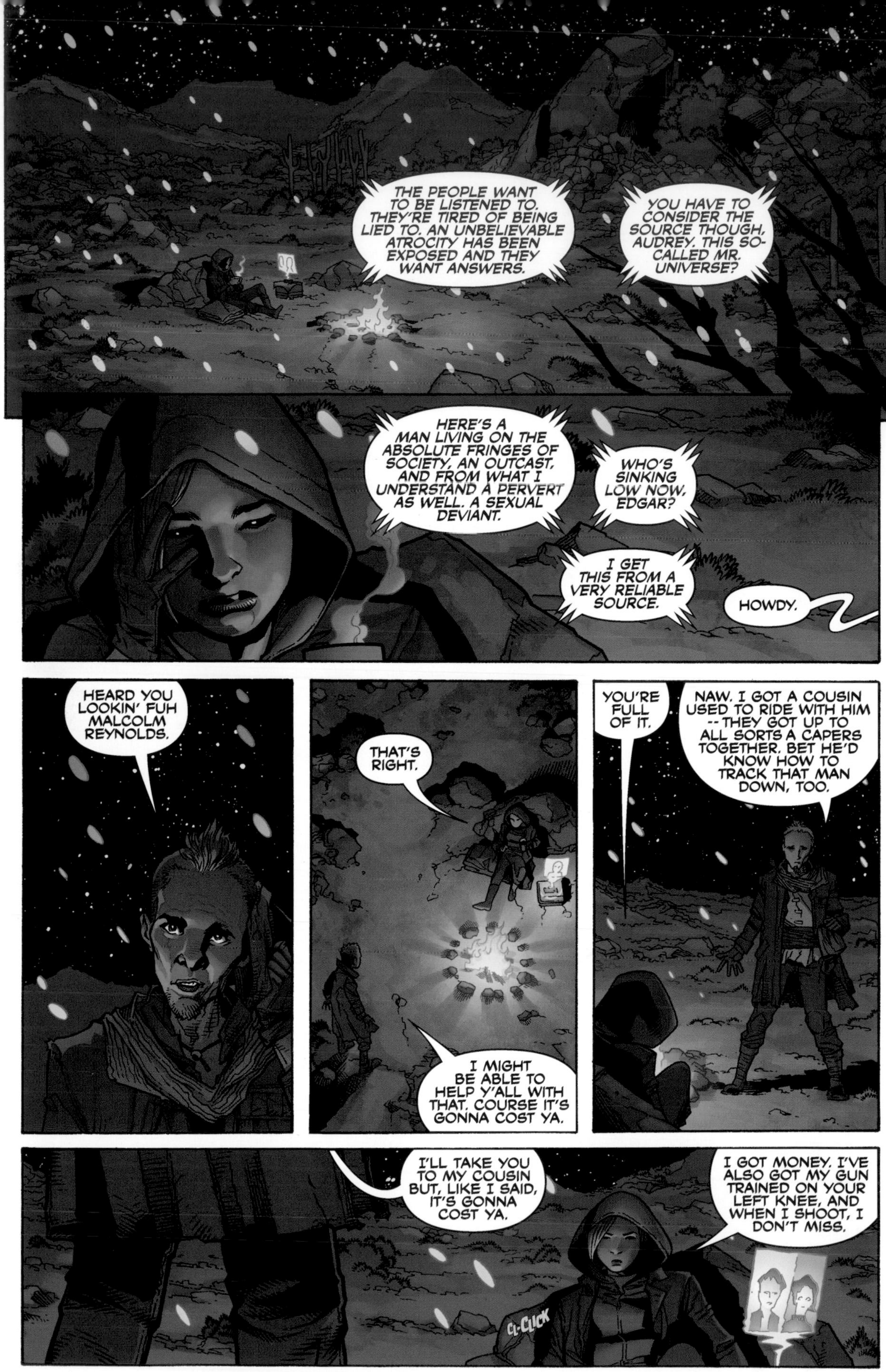
THE PEOPLE WANT TO BE LISTENED TO. THEY'RE TIRED OF BEING LIED TO. AN UNBELIEVABLE ATROCITY HAS BEEN EXPOSED AND THEY WANT ANSWERS.
YOU HAVE TO CONSIDER THE SOURCE THOUGH, AUDREY. THIS SO-CALLED MR. UNIVERSE?
HERE'S A MAN LIVING ON THE ABSOLUTE FRINGES OF SOCIETY, AN OUTCAST, AND FROM WHAT I UNDERSTAND A PERVERT AS WELL. A SEXUAL DEVIANT.
WHO'S SINKING LOW NOW, EDGAR?
I GET THIS FROM A VERY RELIABLE SOURCE.
HOWDY.
HEARD YOU LOOKIN' FUH MALCOLM REYNOLDS.
THAT'S RIGHT.
I MIGHT BE ABLE TO HELP Y'ALL WITH THAT. COURSE IT'S GONNA COST YA.
YOU'RE FULL OF IT.
NAW. I GOT A COUSIN USED TO RIDE WITH HIM -- THEY GOT UP TO ALL SORTS A CAPERS TOGETHER. BET HE'D KNOW HOW TO TRACK THAT MAN DOWN, TOO.
I'LL TAKE YOU TO MY COUSIN BUT, LIKE I SAID, IT'S GONNA COST YA.
I GOT MONEY. I'VE ALSO GOT MY GUN TRAINED ON YOUR LEFT KNEE, AND WHEN I SHOOT, I DON'T MISS.
CL-CLICK

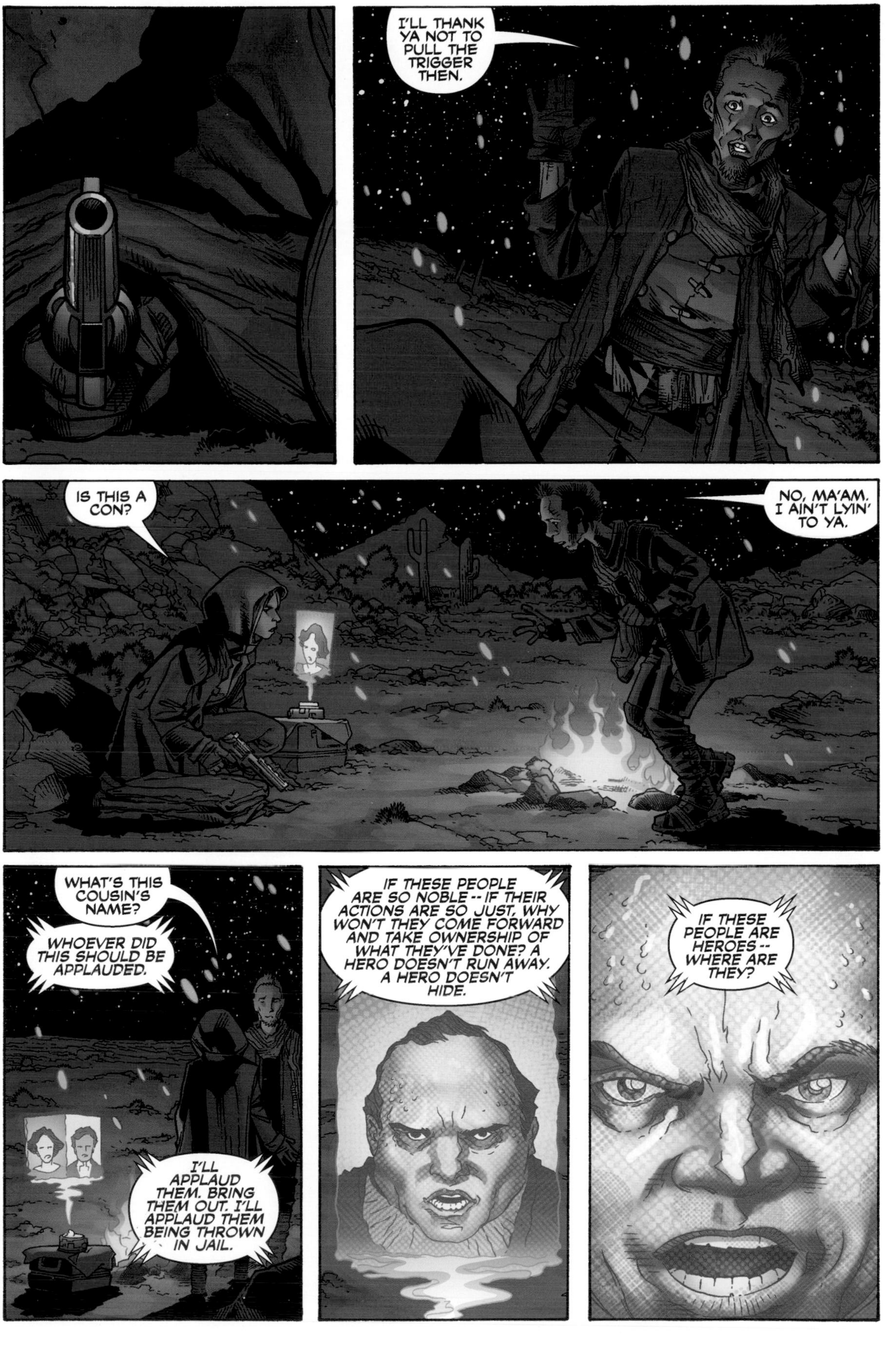
I'LL THANK YA NOT TO PULL THE TRIGGER THEN.
IS THIS A CON?
NO, MA'AM. I AIN'T LYIN' TO YA.
WHAT'S THIS COUSIN'S NAME?
WHOEVER DID THIS SHOULD BE APPLAUDED.
I'LL APPLAUD THEM. BRING THEM OUT. I'LL APPLAUD THEM BEING THROWN IN JAIL.
IF THESE PEOPLE ARE SO NOBLE -- IF THEIR ACTIONS ARE SO JUST, WHY WON'T THEY COME FORWARD AND TAKE OWNERSHIP OF WHAT THEY'VE DONE? A HERO DOESN'T RUN AWAY. A HERO DOESN'T HIDE.
IF THESE PEOPLE ARE HEROES -- WHERE ARE THEY?

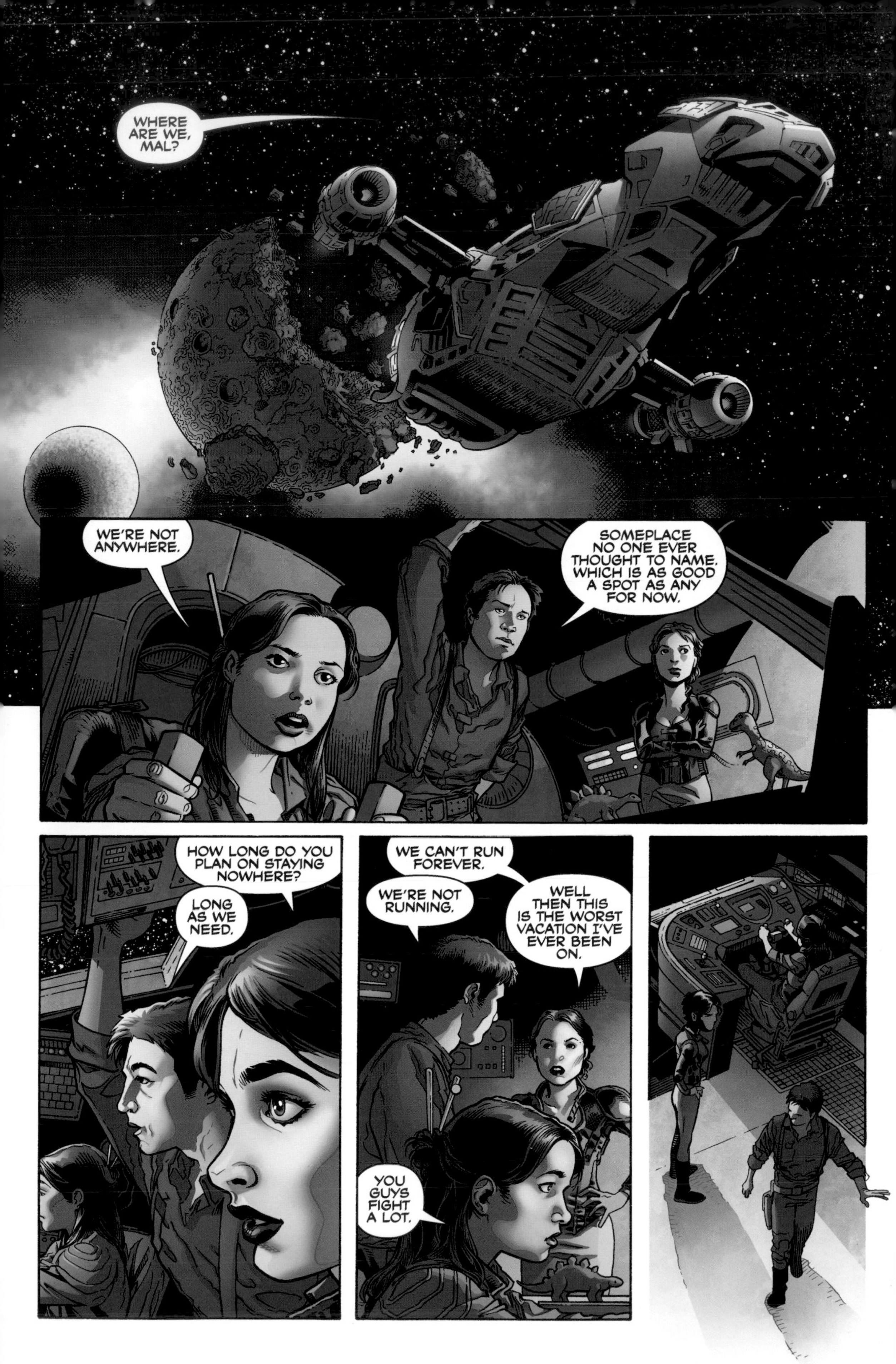
WHERE ARE WE, MAL?
WE'RE NOT ANYWHERE.
SOMEPLACE NO ONE EVER THOUGHT TO NAME. WHICH IS AS GOOD A SPOT AS ANY FOR NOW.
HOW LONG DO YOU PLAN ON STAYING NOWHERE?
LONG AS WE NEED.
WE CAN'T RUN FOREVER.
WE'RE NOT RUNNING.
WELL THEN THIS IS THE WORST VACATION I'VE EVER BEEN ON.
YOU GUYS FIGHT A LOT.

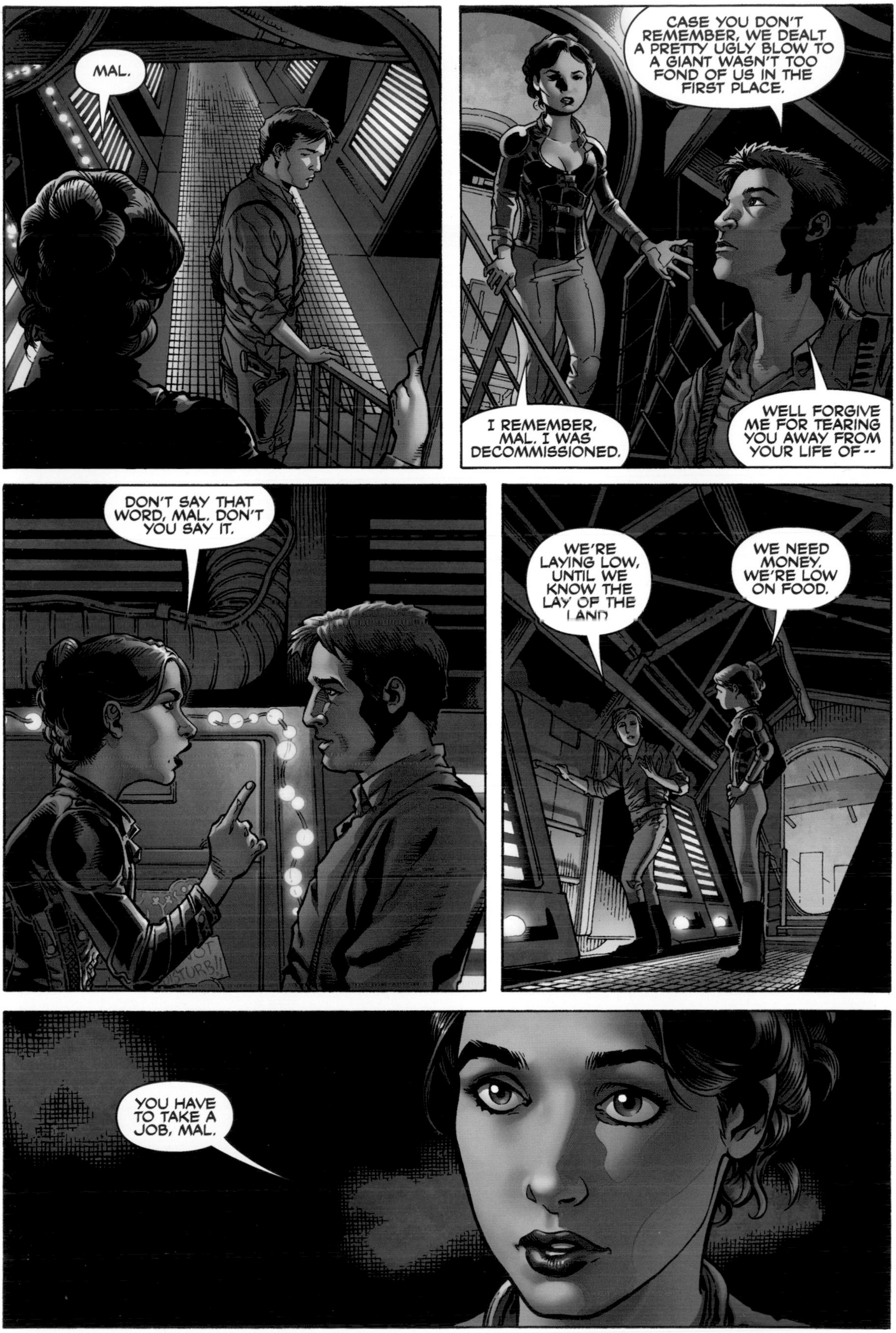
MAL.
CASE YOU DON'T REMEMBER, WE DEALT A PRETTY UGLY BLOW TO A GIANT WASN'T TOO FOND OF US IN THE FIRST PLACE.
I REMEMBER, MAL. I WAS DECOMMISSIONED.
WELL FORGIVE ME FOR TEARING YOU AWAY FROM YOUR LIFE OF --
DON'T SAY THAT WORD, MAL. DON'T YOU SAY IT.
WE'RE LAYING LOW, UNTIL WE KNOW THE LAY OF THE LAND
WE NEED MONEY. WE'RE LOW ON FOOD.
YOU HAVE TO TAKE A JOB, MAL.

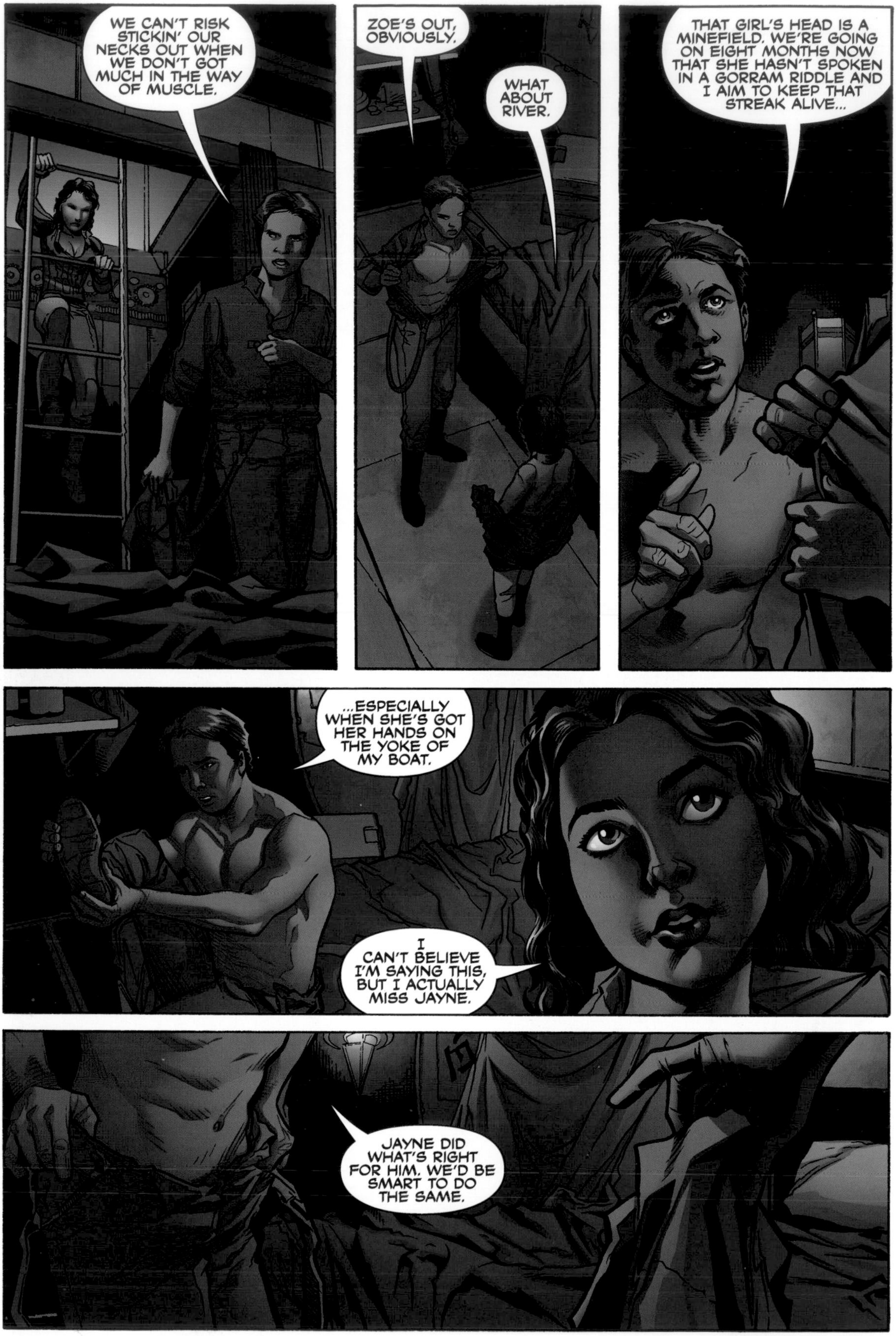
WE CAN'T RISK STICKIN' OUR NECKS OUT WHEN WE DON'T GOT MUCH IN THE WAY OF MUSCLE.
ZOE'S OUT, OBVIOUSLY.
WHAT ABOUT RIVER.
THAT GIRL'S HEAD IS A MINEFIELD. WE'RE GOING ON EIGHT MONTHS NOW THAT SHE HASN'T SPOKEN IN A GORRAM RIDDLE AND I AIM TO KEEP THAT STREAK ALIVE...
...ESPECIALLY WHEN SHE'S GOT HER HANDS ON THE YOKE OF MY BOAT.
I CAN'T BELIEVE I'M SAYING THIS, BUT I ACTUALLY MISS JAYNE.
JAYNE DID WHAT'S RIGHT FOR HIM. WE'D BE SMART TO DO THE SAME.

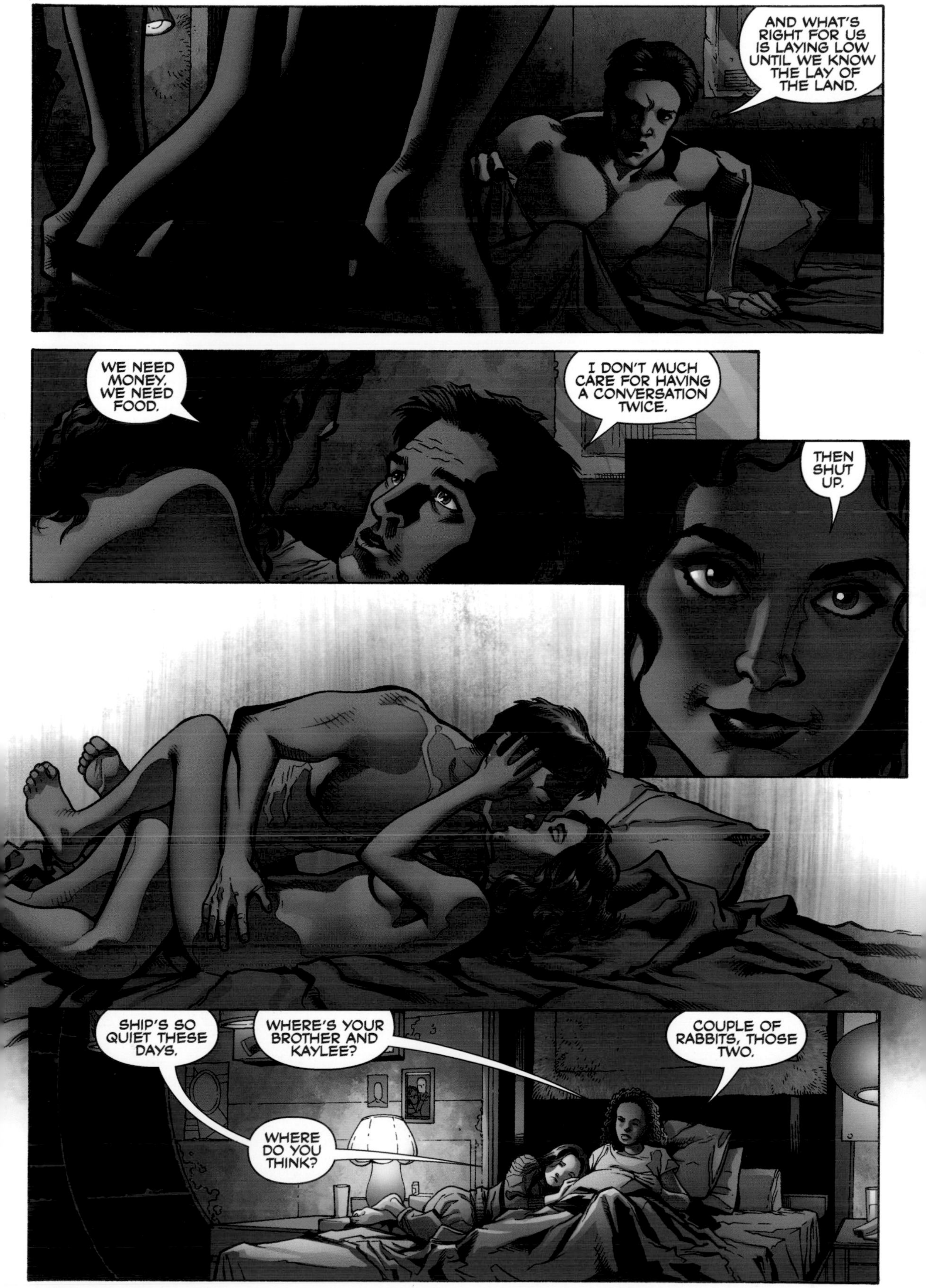
AND WHAT'S RIGHT FOR US IS LAYING LOW UNTIL WE KNOW THE LAY OF THE LAND.
WE NEED MONEY. WE NEED FOOD.
I DON'T MUCH CARE FOR HAVING A CONVERSATION TWICE.
THEN SHUT UP.
SHIP'S SO QUIET THESE DAYS.
WHERE'S YOUR BROTHER AND KAYLEE?
WHERE DO YOU THINK?
COUPLE OF RABBITS, THOSE TWO.

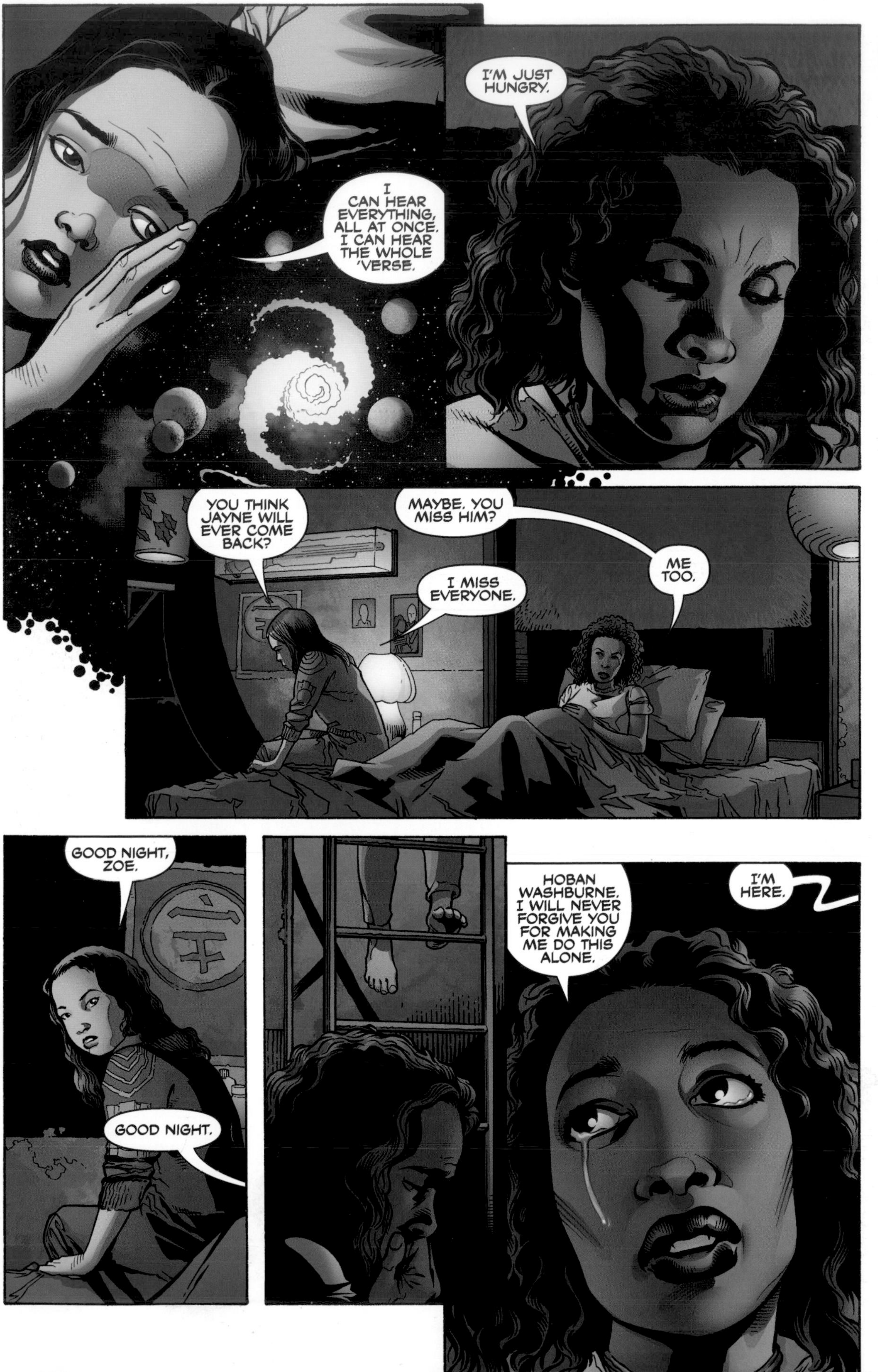
I CAN HEAR EVERYTHING, ALL AT ONCE. I CAN HEAR THE WHOLE 'VERSE.
I'M JUST HUNGRY.
YOU THINK JAYNE WILL EVER COME BACK?
MAYBE. YOU MISS HIM?
I MISS EVERYONE.
ME TOO.
GOOD NIGHT, ZOE.
GOOD NIGHT.
HOBAN WASHBURNE, I WILL NEVER FORGIVE YOU FOR MAKING ME DO THIS ALONE.
I'M HERE.

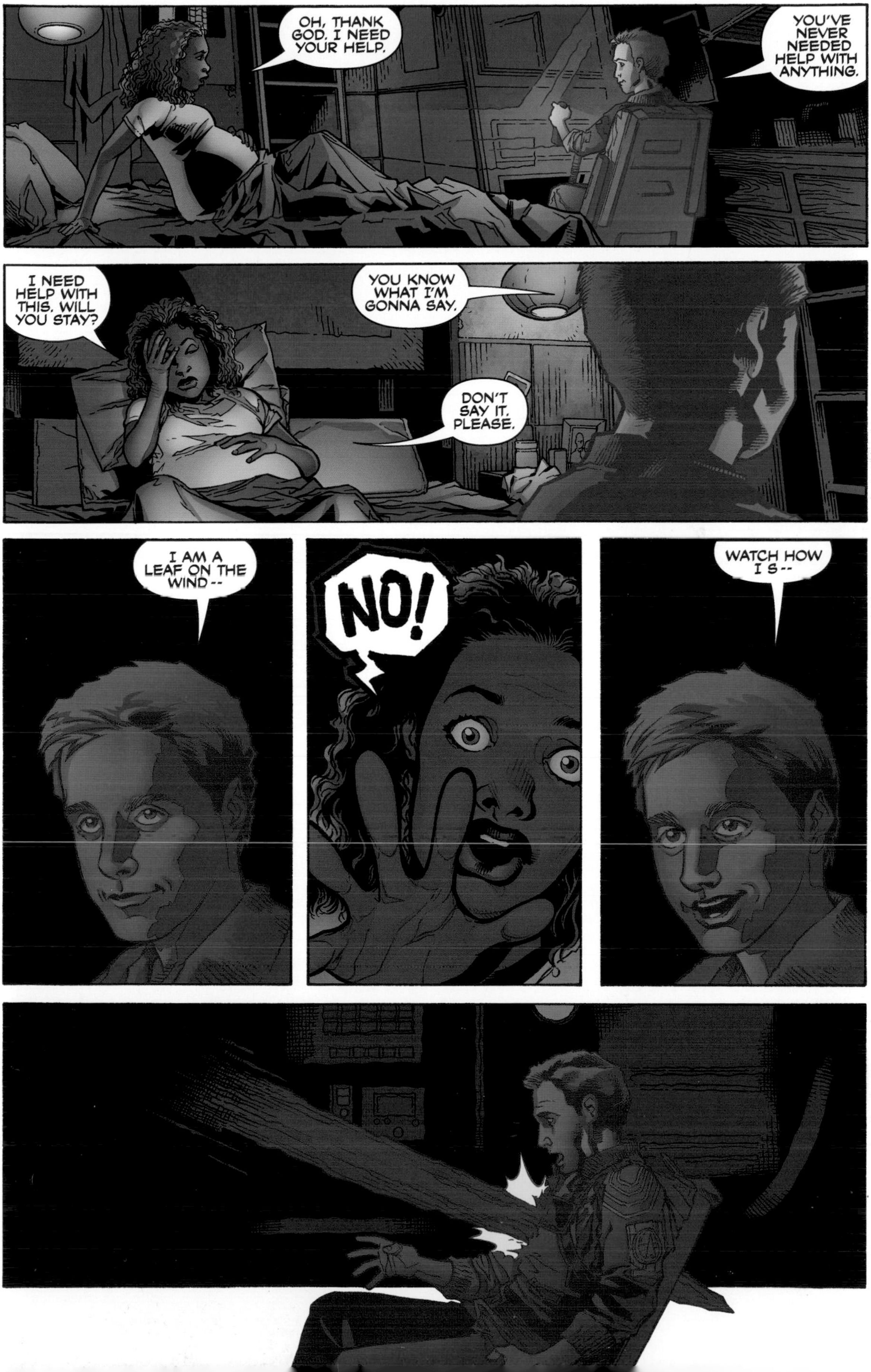
OH, THANK GOD. I NEED YOUR HELP.
YOU'VE NEVER NEEDED HELP WITH ANYTHING.
I NEED HELP WITH THIS. WILL YOU STAY?
YOU KNOW WHAT I'M GONNA SAY.
DON'T SAY IT. PLEASE.
I AM A LEAF ON THE WIND --
NO!
WATCH HOW I S --

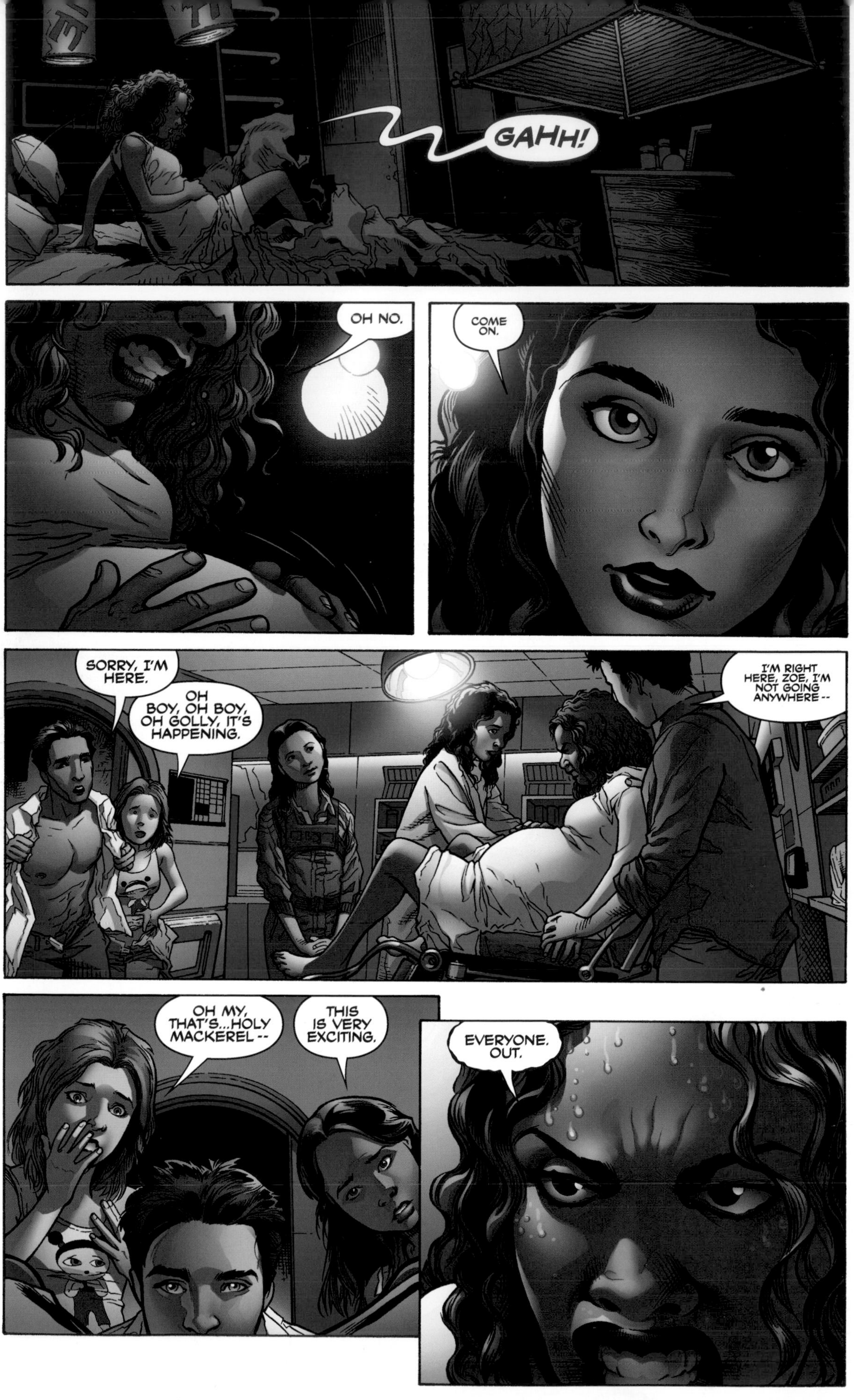
GAHH!
OH NO.
COME ON.
SORRY, I'M HERE.
OH BOY, OH BOY, OH GOLLY, IT'S HAPPENING.
I'M RIGHT HERE, ZOE, I'M NOT GOING ANYWHERE --
OH MY, THAT'S...HOLY MACKEREL --
THIS IS VERY EXCITING.
EVERYONE. OUT.

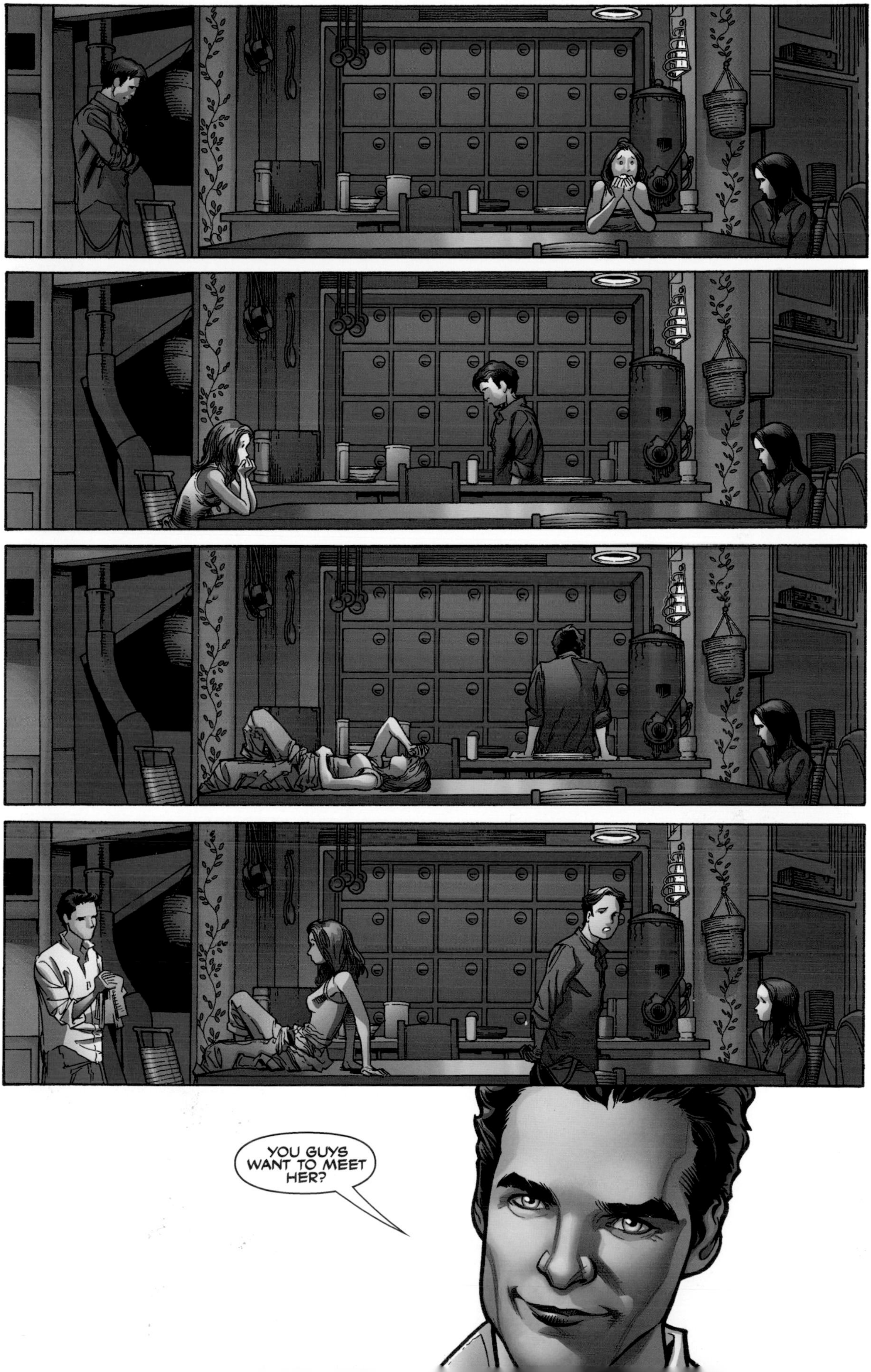
YOU GUYS WANT TO MEET HER?

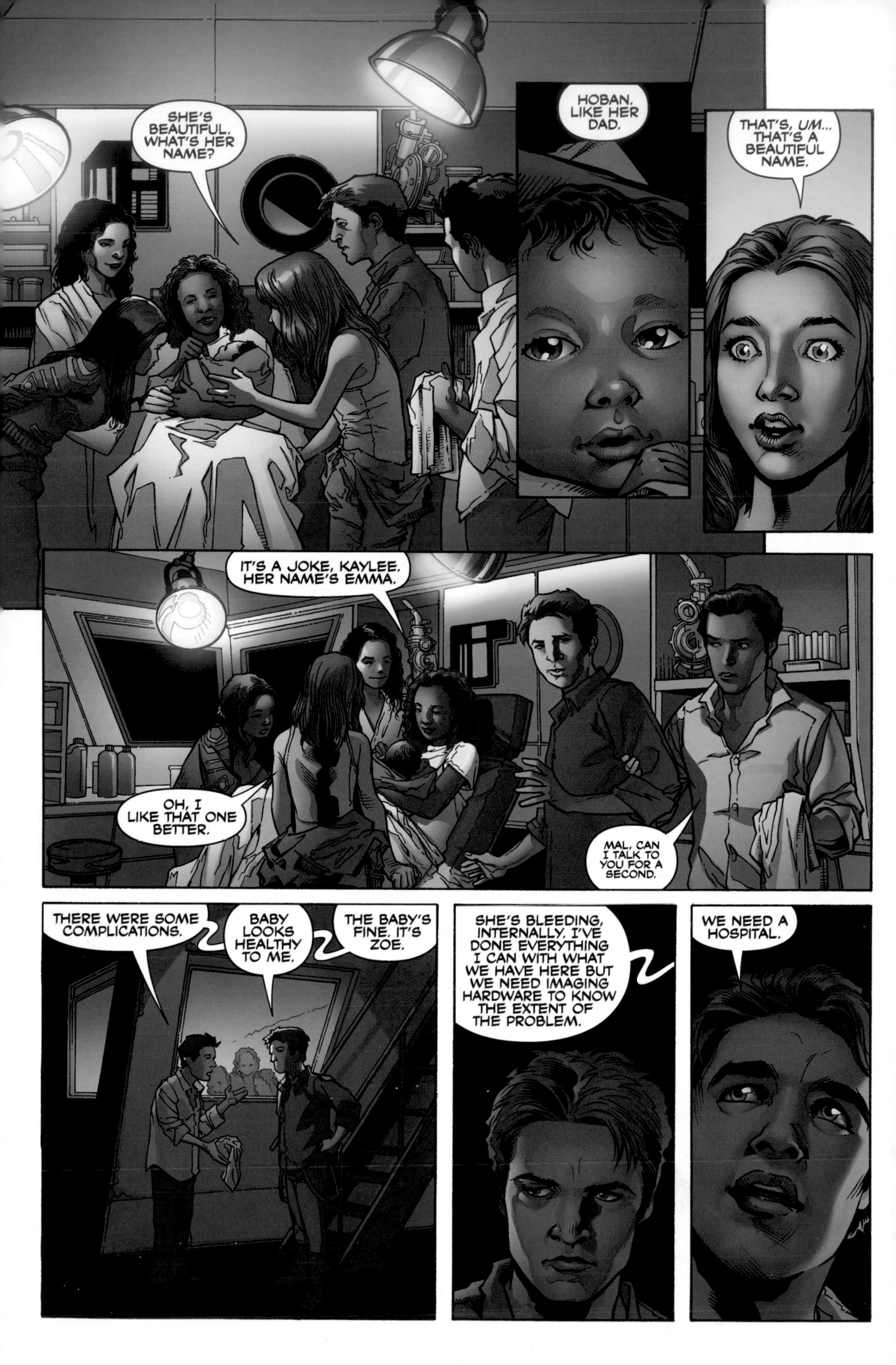
SHE'S BEAUTIFUL. WHAT'S HER NAME?
HOBAN. LIKE HER DAD.
THAT'S, UM... THAT'S A BEAUTIFUL NAME.
IT'S A JOKE, KAYLEE. HER NAME'S EMMA.
OH, I LIKE THAT ONE BETTER.
MAL, CAN I TALK TO YOU FOR A SECOND.
THERE WERE SOME COMPLICATIONS.
BABY LOOKS HEALTHY TO ME.
THE BABY'S FINE. IT'S ZOE.
SHE'S BLEEDING, INTERNALLY. I'VE DONE EVERYTHING I CAN WITH WHAT WE HAVE HERE BUT WE NEED IMAGING HARDWARE TO KNOW THE EXTENT OF THE PROBLEM.
WE NEED A HOSPITAL.

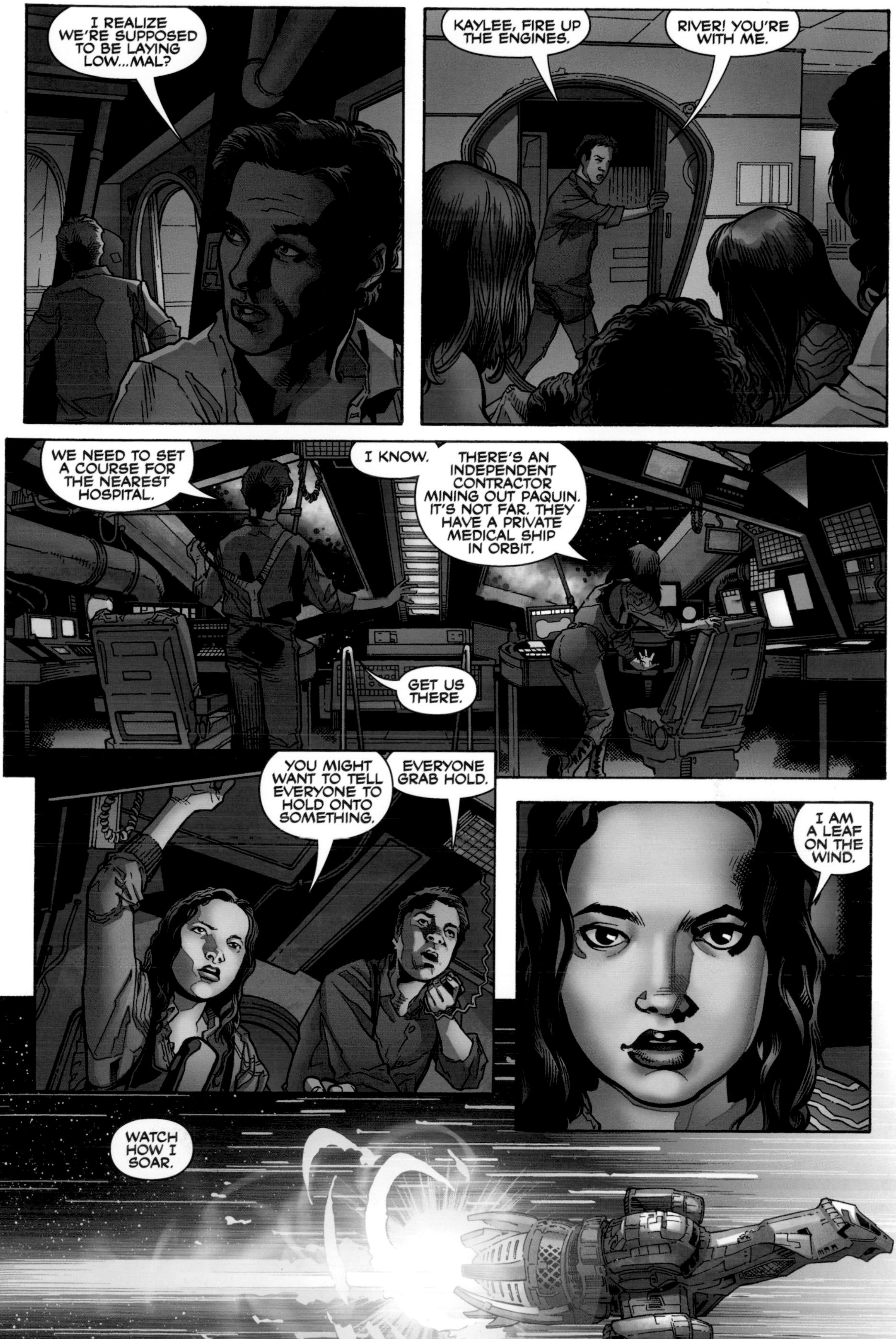
I REALIZE WE'RE SUPPOSED TO BE LAYING LOW...MAL?
KAYLEE, FIRE UP THE ENGINES.
RIVER! YOU'RE WITH ME.
WE NEED TO SET A COURSE FOR THE NEAREST HOSPITAL.
I KNOW.
THERE'S AN INDEPENDENT CONTRACTOR MINING OUT PAQUIN. IT'S NOT FAR. THEY HAVE A PRIVATE MEDICAL SHIP IN ORBIT.
GET US THERE.
YOU MIGHT WANT TO TELL EVERYONE TO HOLD ONTO SOMETHING.
EVERYONE GRAB HOLD.
I AM A LEAF ON THE WIND.
WATCH HOW I SOAR.

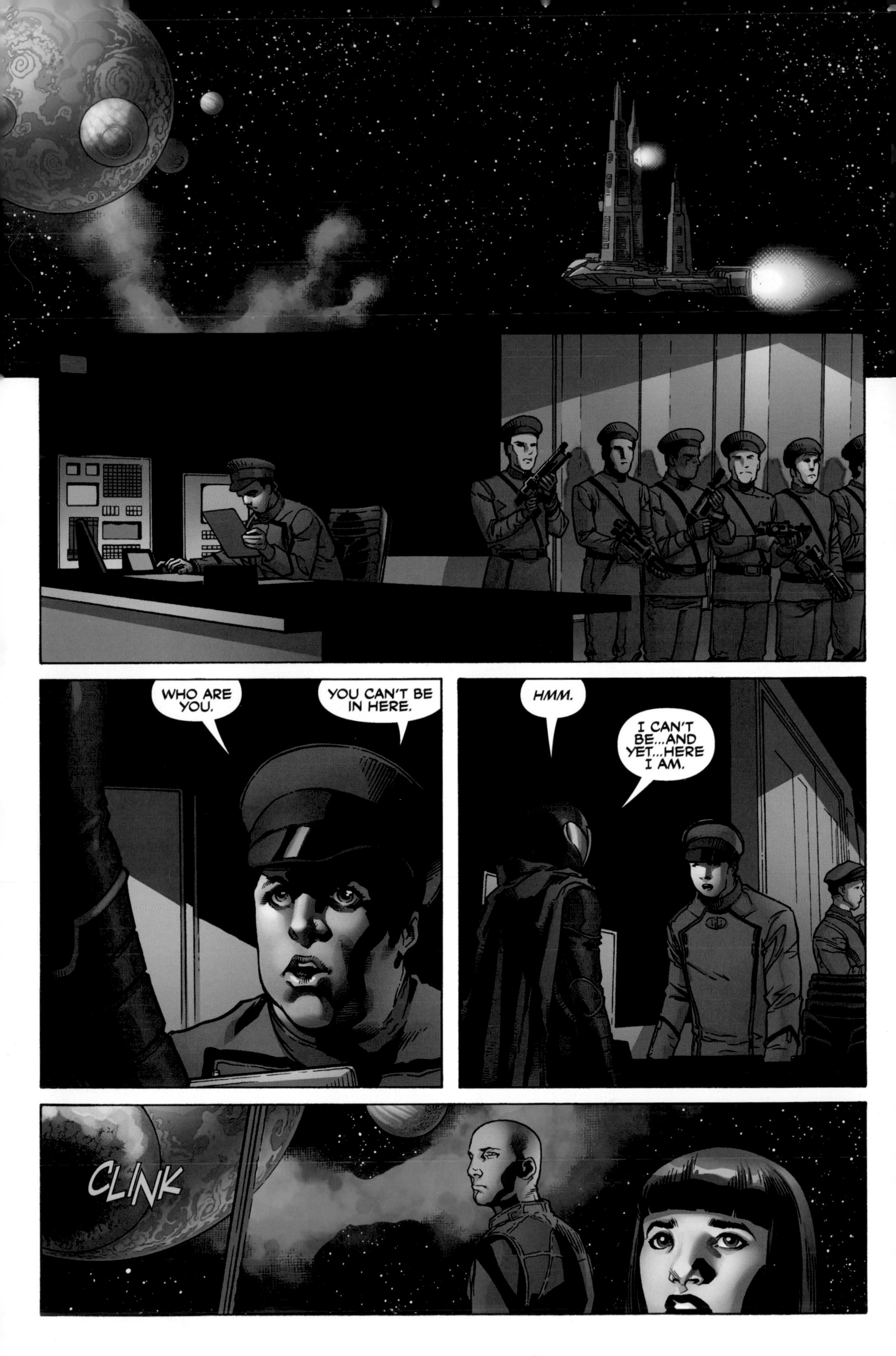
WHO ARE YOU.
YOU CAN'T BE IN HERE.
HMM.
I CAN'T BE...AND YET...HERE I AM.
CLINK

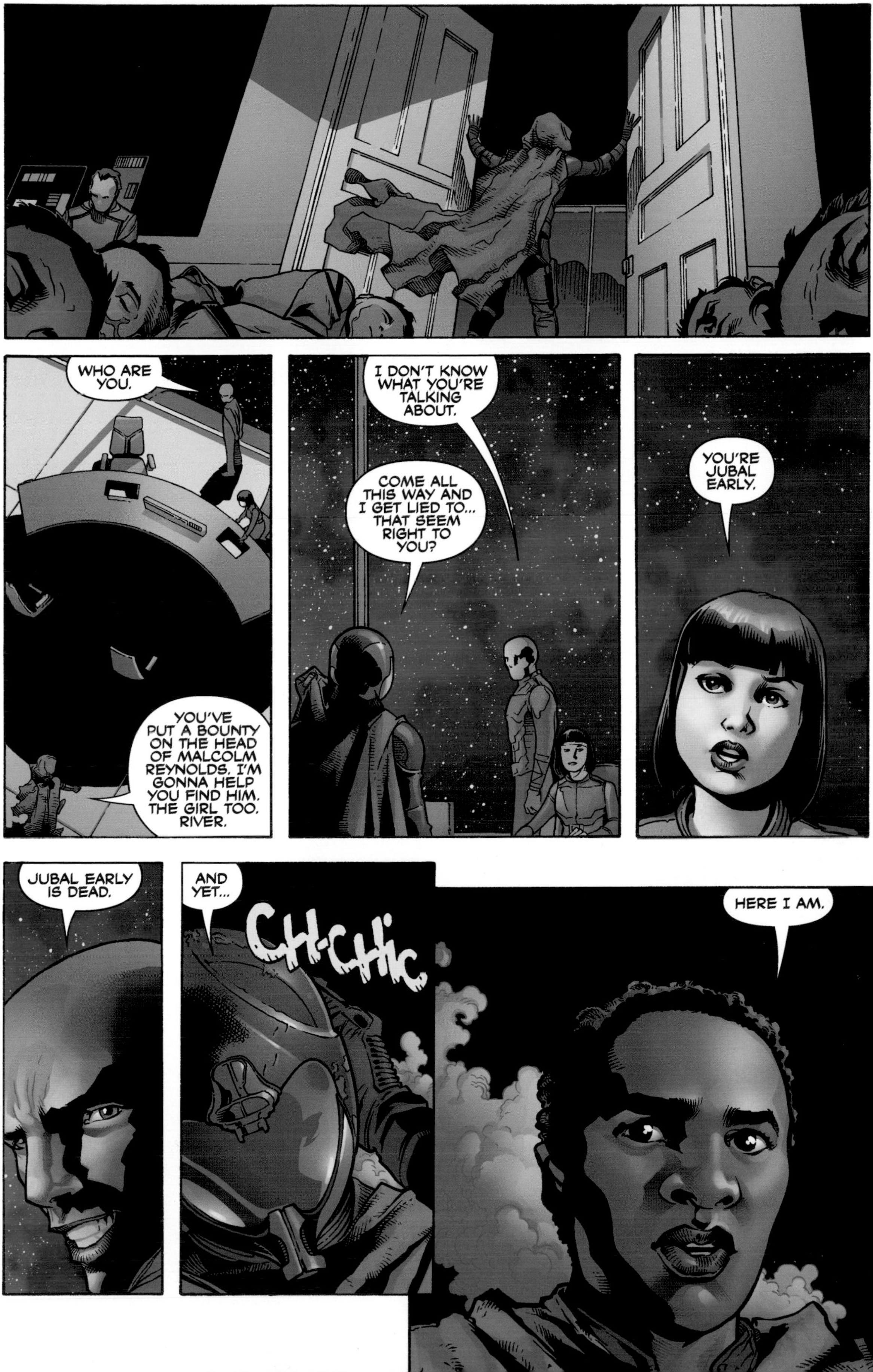
WHO ARE YOU.
YOU'VE PUT A BOUNTY ON THE HEAD OF MALCOLM REYNOLDS. I'M GONNA HELP YOU FIND HIM. THE GIRL TOO. RIVER.
I DON'T KNOW WHAT YOU'RE TALKING ABOUT.
COME ALL THIS WAY AND I GET LIED TO... THAT SEEM RIGHT TO YOU?
YOU'RE JUBAL EARLY.
JUBAL EARLY IS DEAD.
AND YET...
CH-CHIC
HERE I AM.

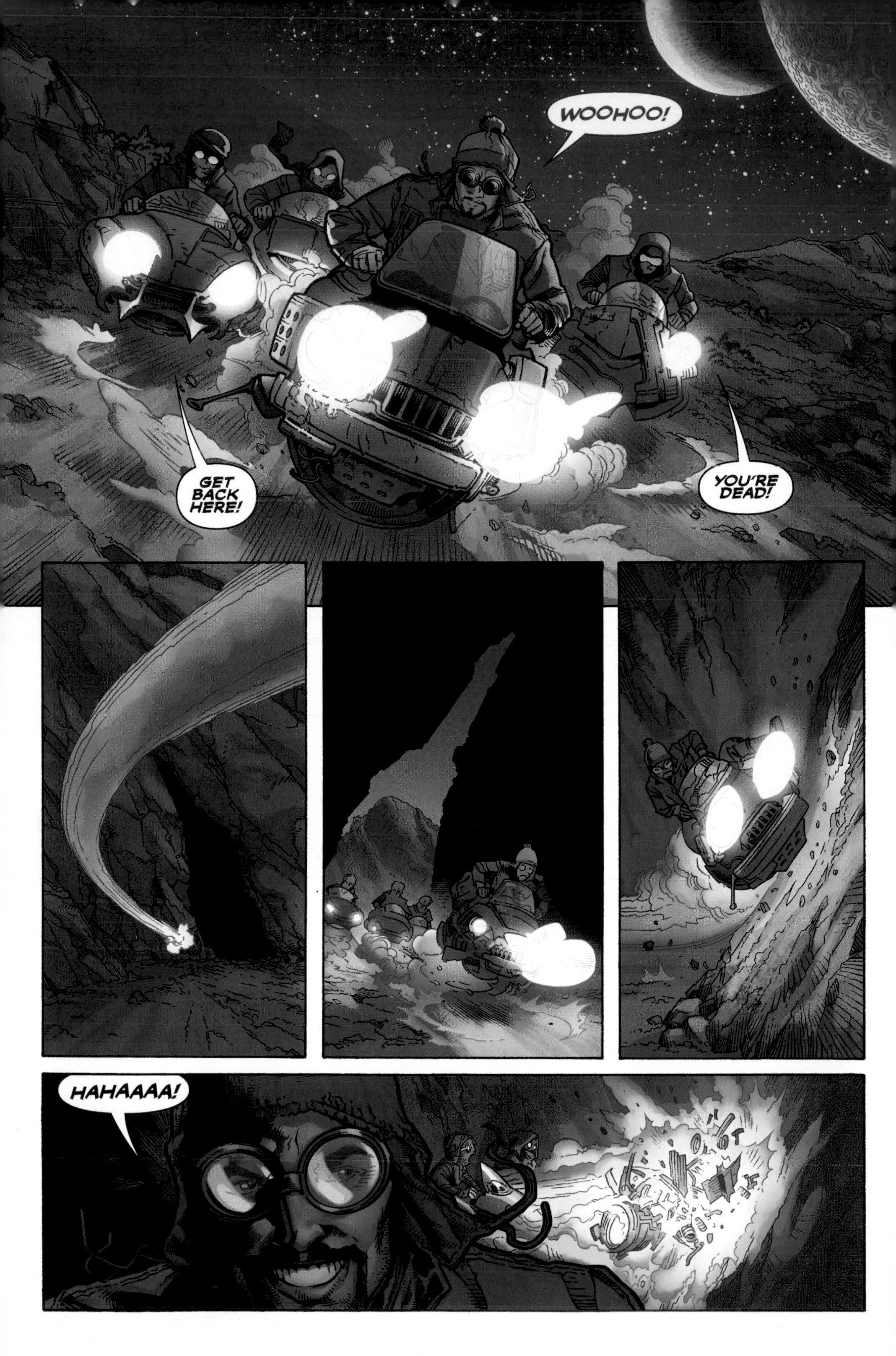
WOOHOO!
GET BACK HERE!
YOU'RE DEAD!
HAHAAAA!

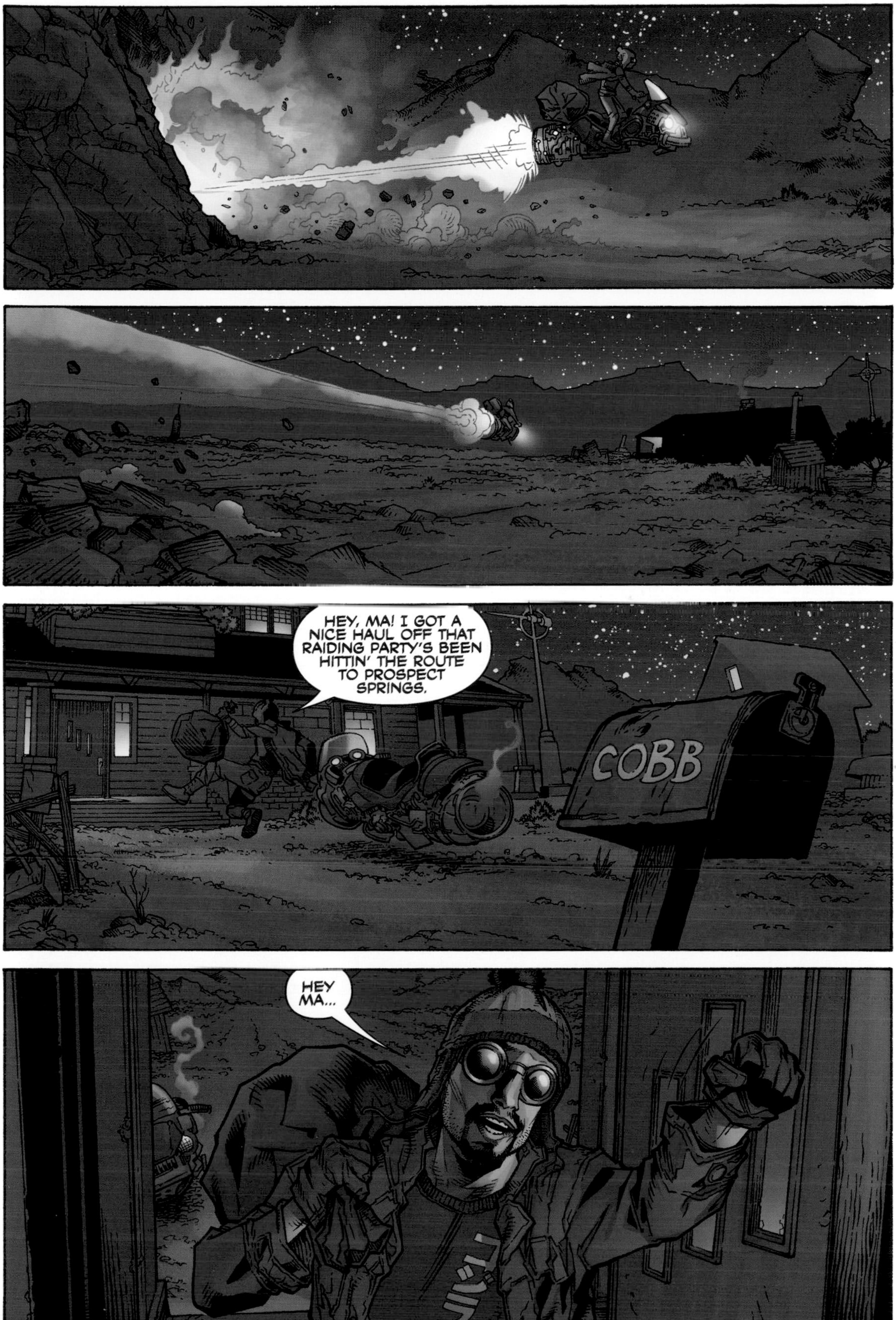
HEY, MA! I GOT A NICE HAUL OFF THAT RAIDING PARTY'S BEEN HITTIN' THE ROUTE TO PROSPECT SPRINGS.
COBB
HEY MA...

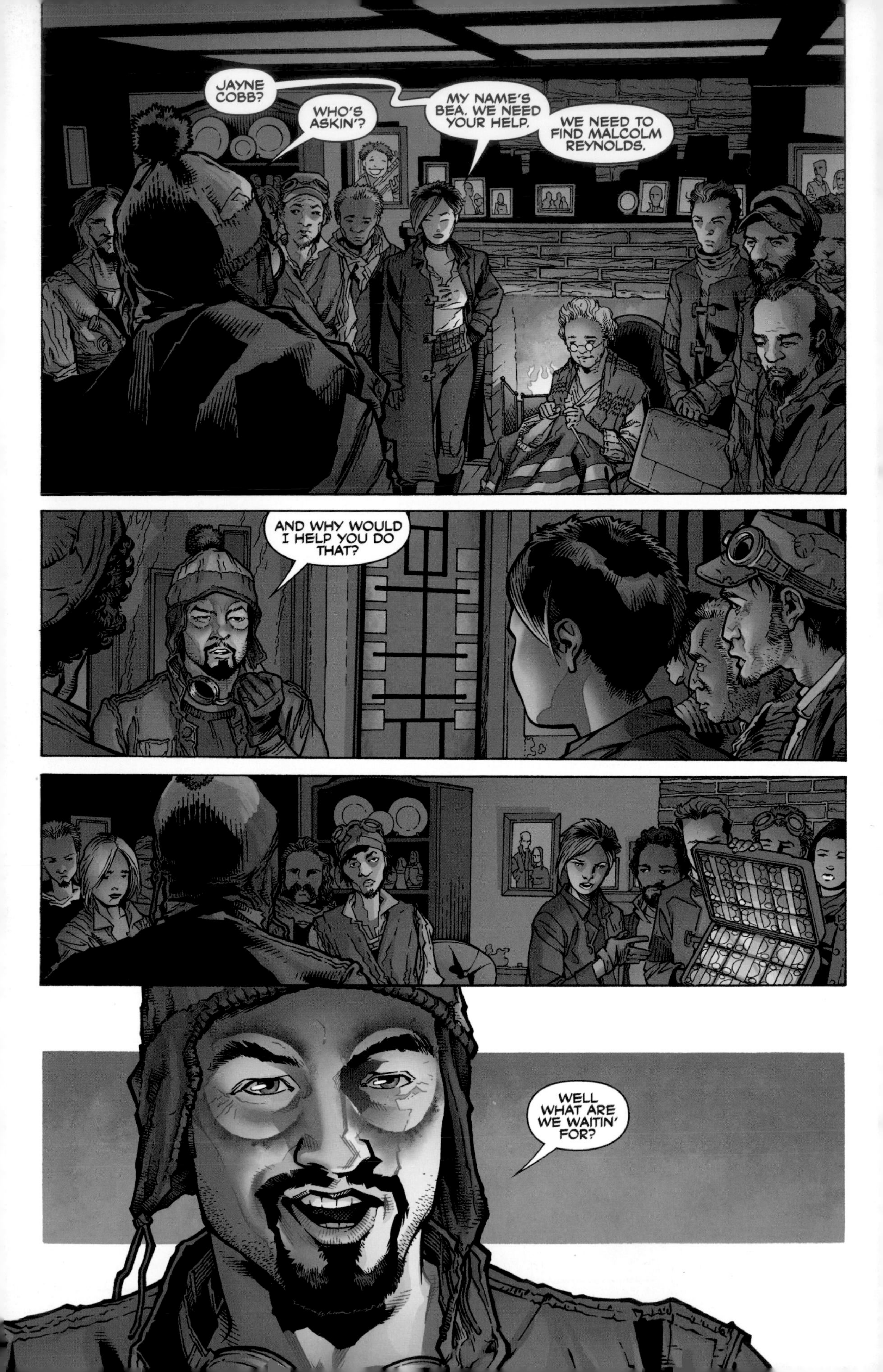
JAYNE COBB?
WHO'S ASKIN'?
MY NAME'S BEA. WE NEED YOUR HELP.
WE NEED TO FIND MALCOLM REYNOLDS.
AND WHY WOULD I HELP YOU DO THAT?
WELL WHAT ARE WE WAITIN' FOR?

CHAPTER TWO

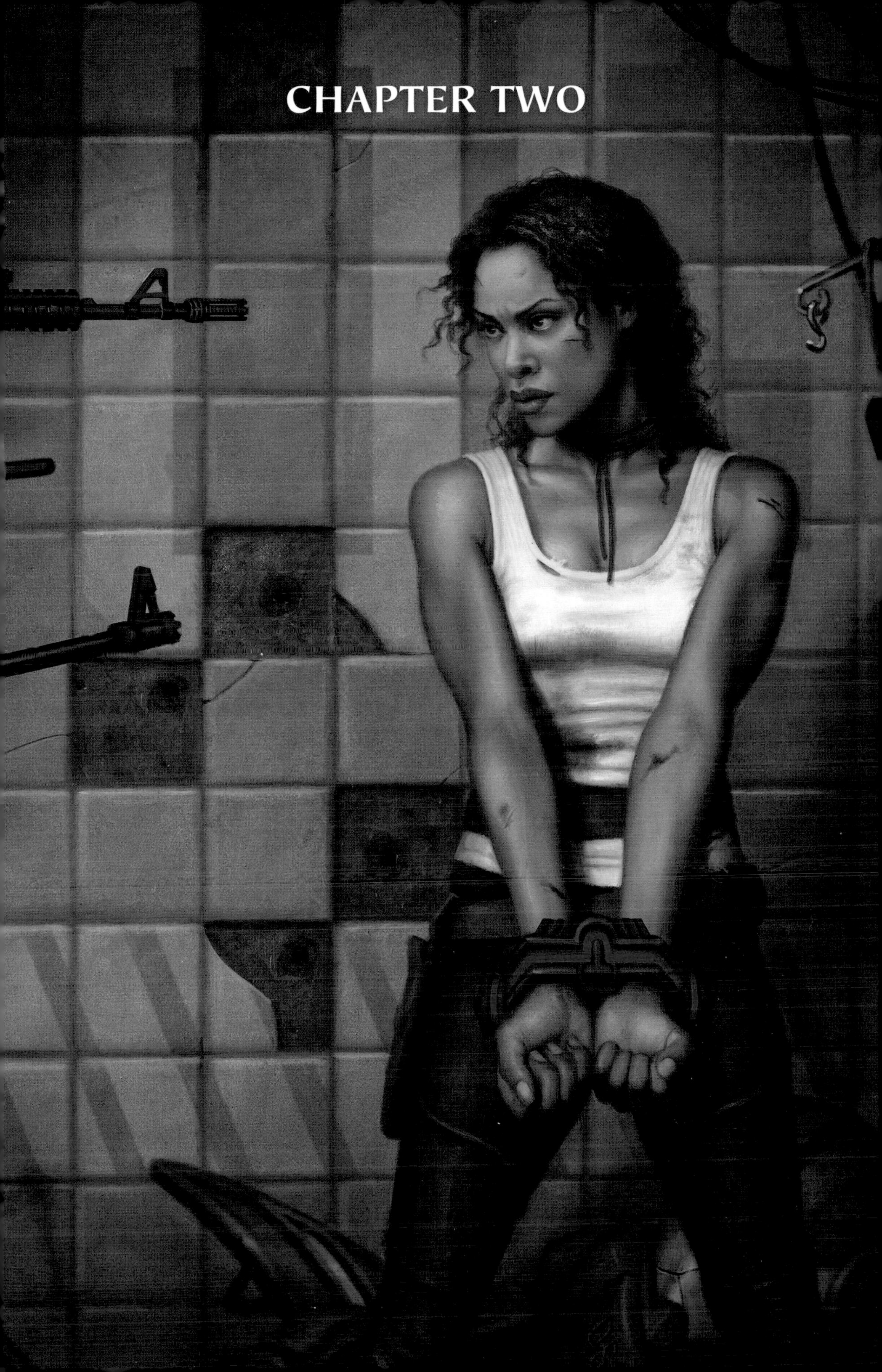

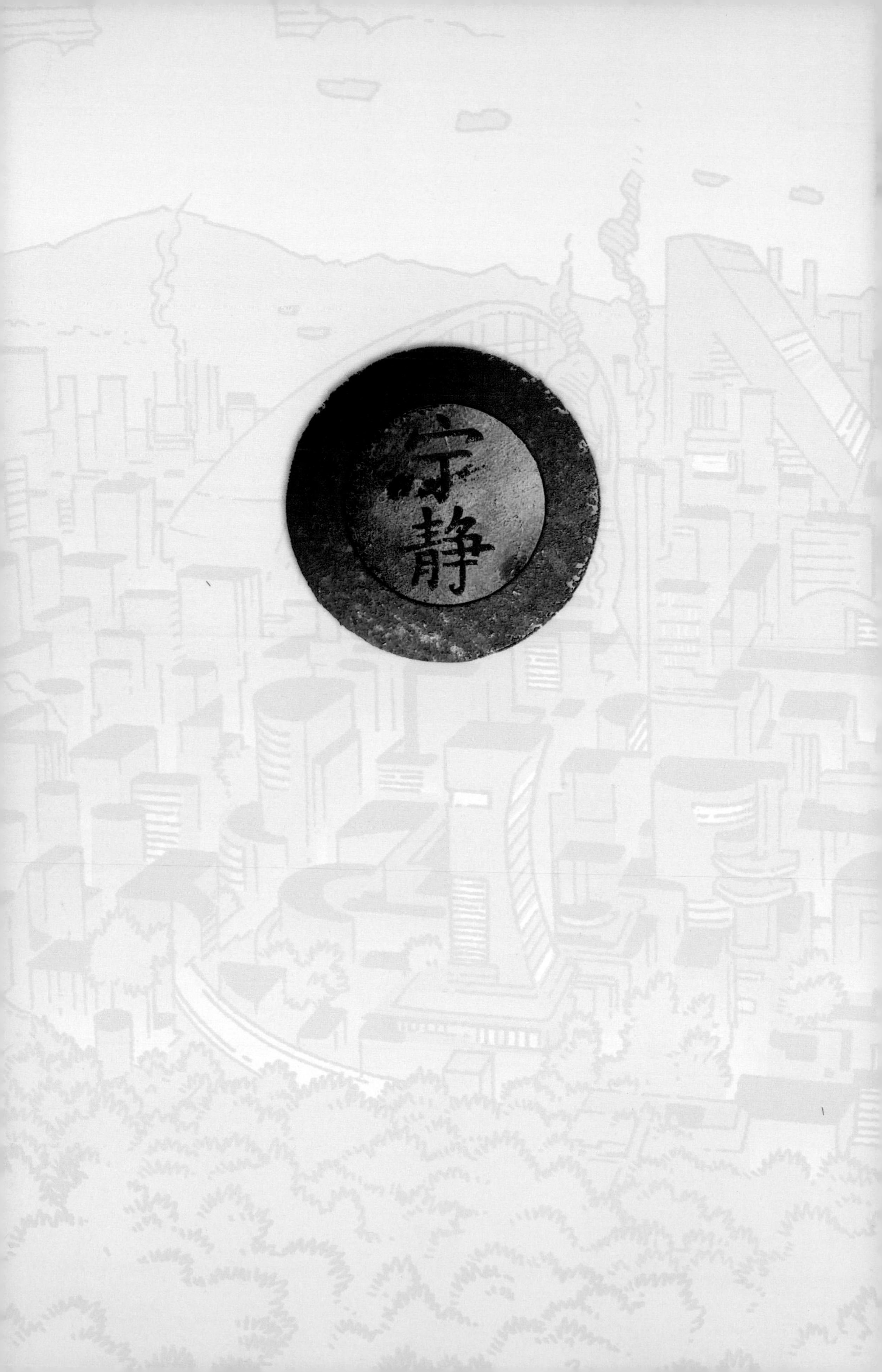
宁静

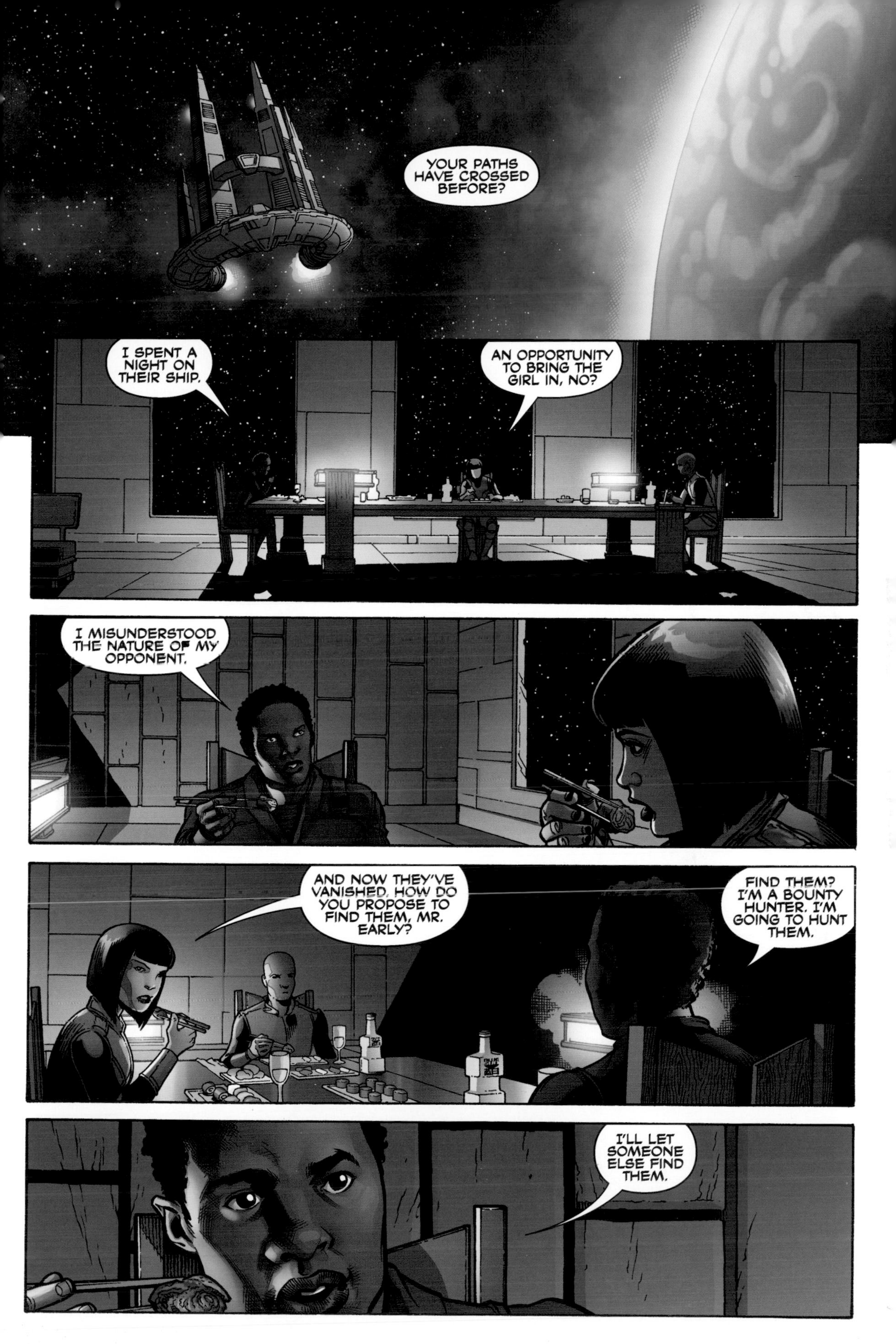
YOUR PATHS HAVE CROSSED BEFORE?
I SPENT A NIGHT ON THEIR SHIP.
AN OPPORTUNITY TO BRING THE GIRL IN, NO?
I MISUNDERSTOOD THE NATURE OF MY OPPONENT.
AND NOW THEY'VE VANISHED. HOW DO YOU PROPOSE TO FIND THEM, MR. EARLY?
FIND THEM? I'M A BOUNTY HUNTER. I'M GOING TO HUNT THEM.
I'LL LET SOMEONE ELSE FIND THEM.

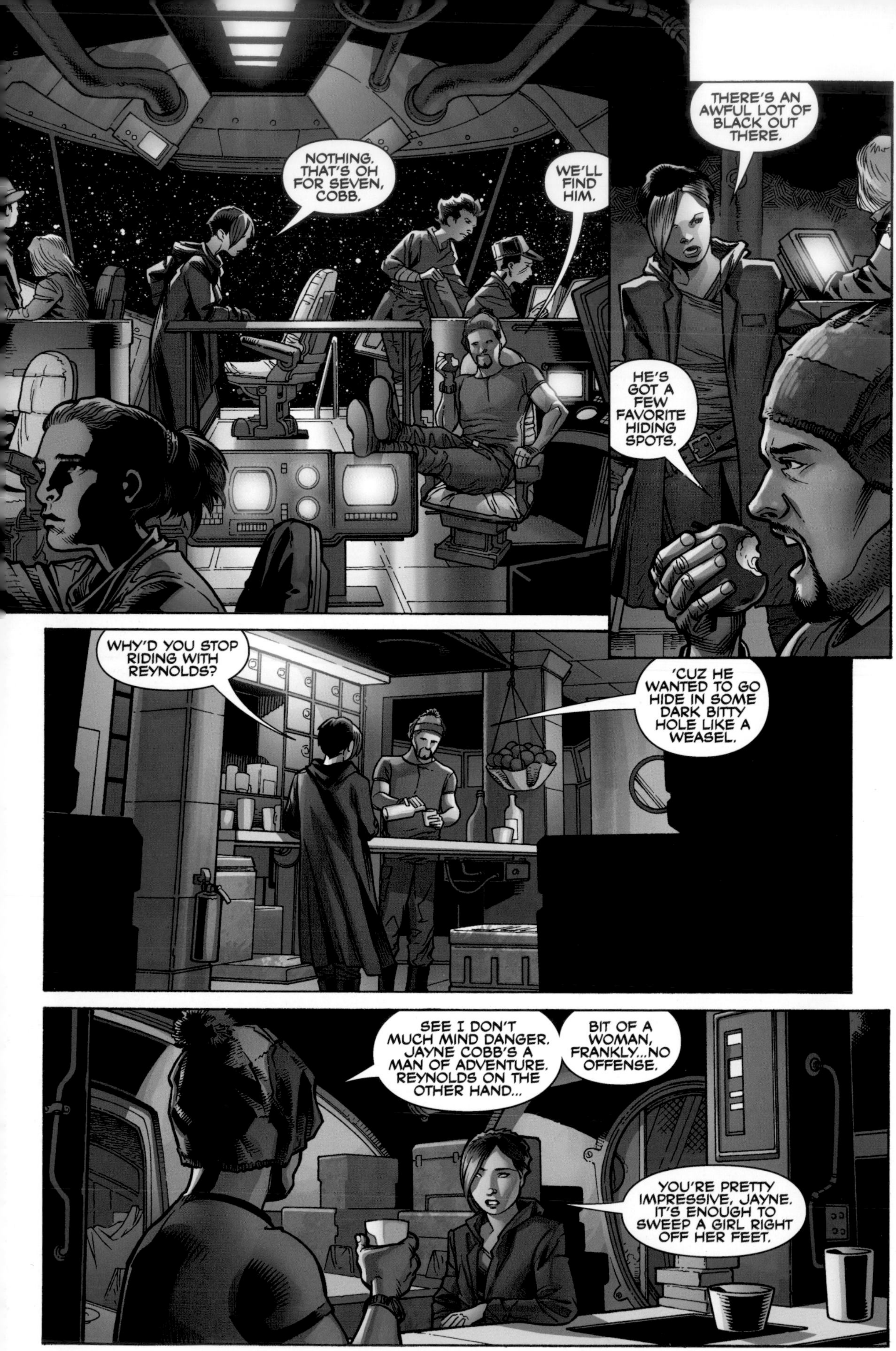
NOTHING. THAT'S OH FOR SEVEN, COBB.
WE'LL FIND HIM.
THERE'S AN AWFUL LOT OF BLACK OUT THERE.
HE'S GOT A FEW FAVORITE HIDING SPOTS.
WHY'D YOU STOP RIDING WITH REYNOLDS?
'CUZ HE WANTED TO GO HIDE IN SOME DARK BITTY HOLE LIKE A WEASEL.
SEE I DON'T MUCH MIND DANGER. JAYNE COBB'S A MAN OF ADVENTURE. REYNOLDS ON THE OTHER HAND...
BIT OF A WOMAN, FRANKLY...NO OFFENSE.
YOU'RE PRETTY IMPRESSIVE, JAYNE. IT'S ENOUGH TO SWEEP A GIRL RIGHT OFF HER FEET.

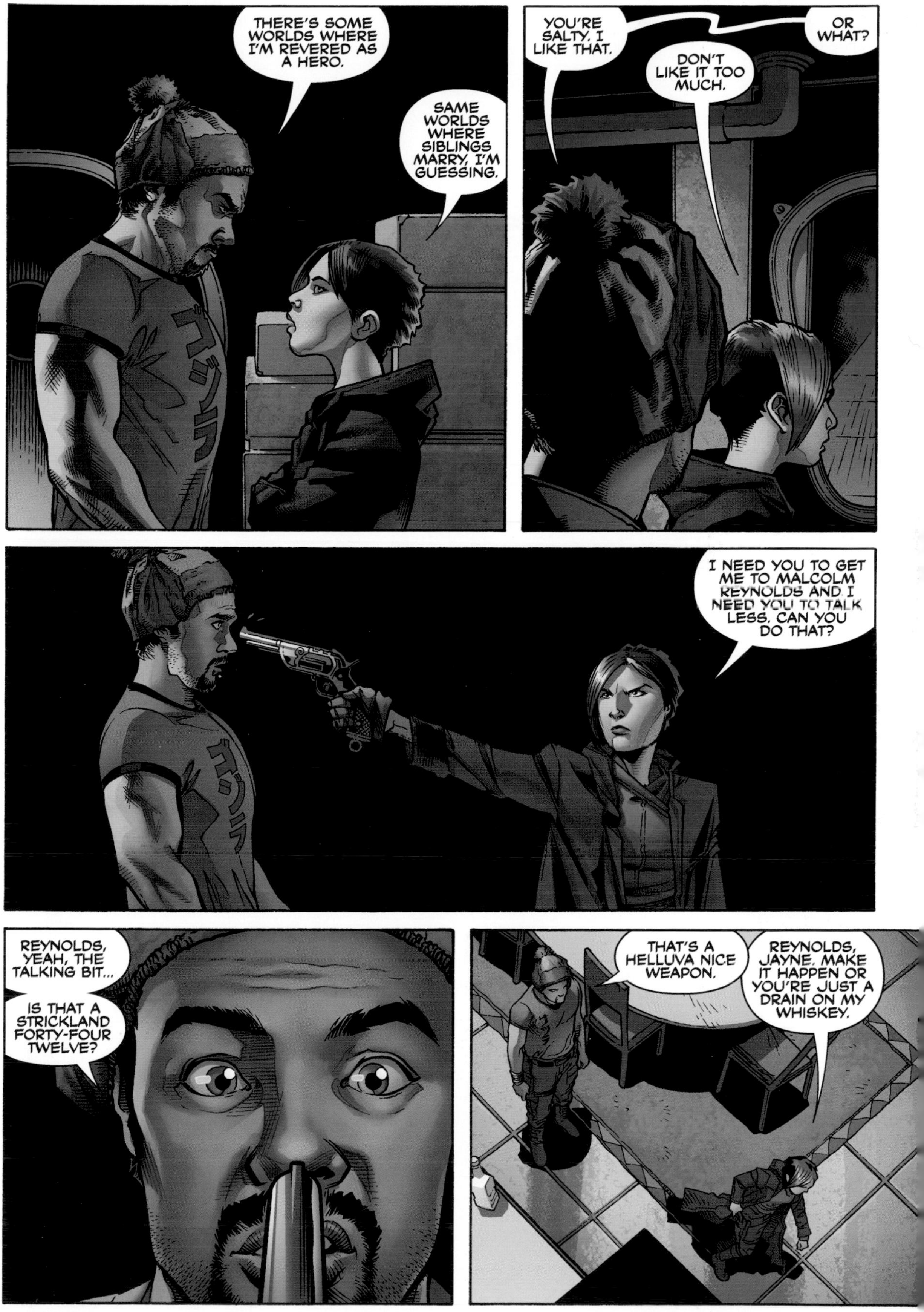
THERE'S SOME WORLDS WHERE I'M REVERED AS A HERO.
SAME WORLDS WHERE SIBLINGS MARRY, I'M GUESSING.
YOU'RE SALTY. I LIKE THAT.
DON'T LIKE IT TOO MUCH.
OR WHAT?
I NEED YOU TO GET ME TO MALCOLM REYNOLDS AND I NEED YOU TO TALK LESS. CAN YOU DO THAT?
REYNOLDS, YEAH, THE TALKING BIT...
IS THAT A STRICKLAND FORTY-FOUR TWELVE?
THAT'S A HELLUVA NICE WEAPON.
REYNOLDS, JAYNE. MAKE IT HAPPEN OR YOU'RE JUST A DRAIN ON MY WHISKEY.

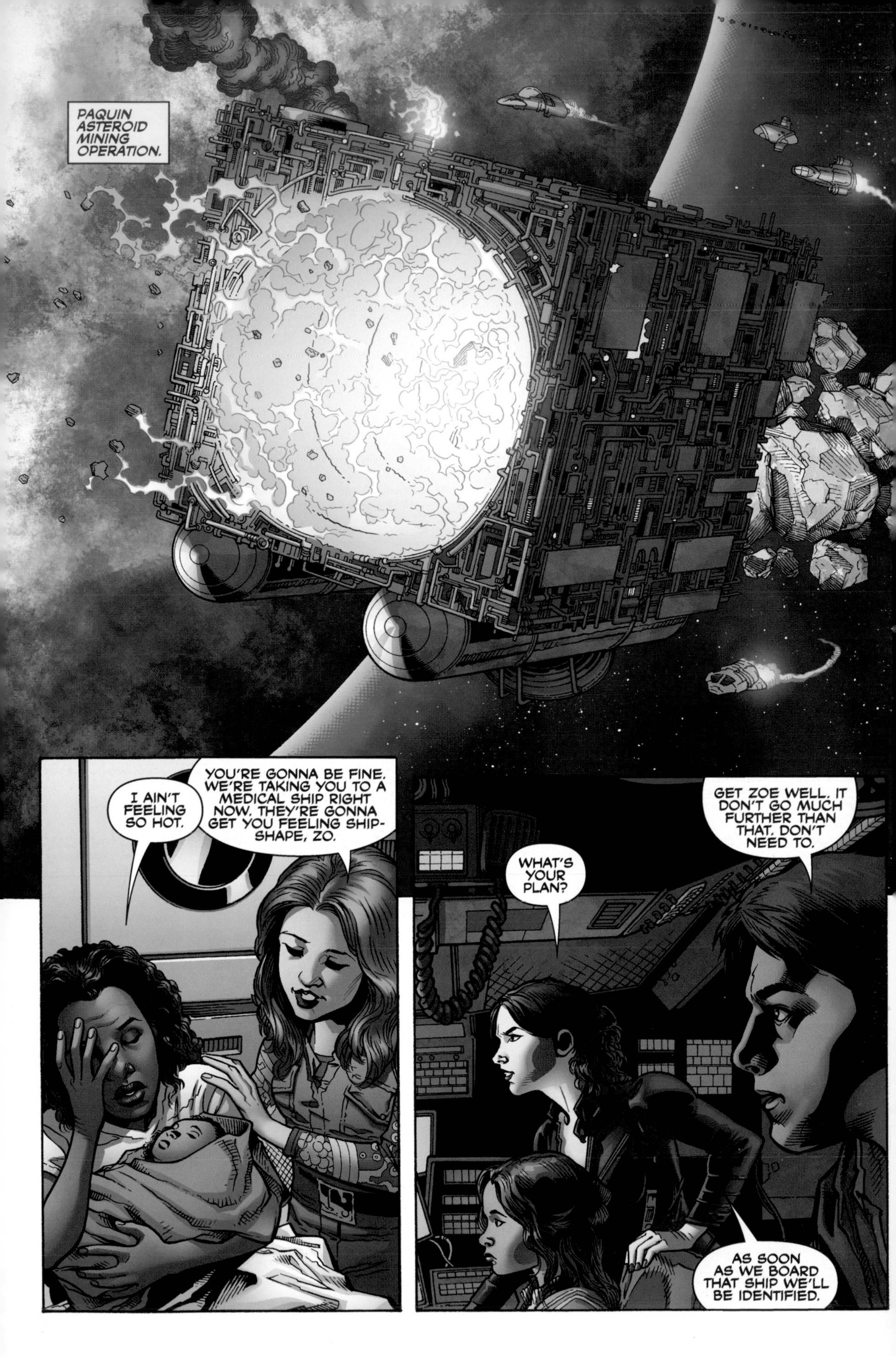
PAQUIN ASTEROID MINING OPERATION.
I AIN'T FEELING SO HOT.
YOU'RE GONNA BE FINE. WE'RE TAKING YOU TO A MEDICAL SHIP RIGHT NOW. THEY'RE GONNA GET YOU FEELING SHIP-SHAPE, ZO.
WHAT'S YOUR PLAN?
GET ZOE WELL. IT DON'T GO MUCH FURTHER THAN THAT. DON'T NEED TO.
AS SOON AS WE BOARD THAT SHIP WE'LL BE IDENTIFIED.

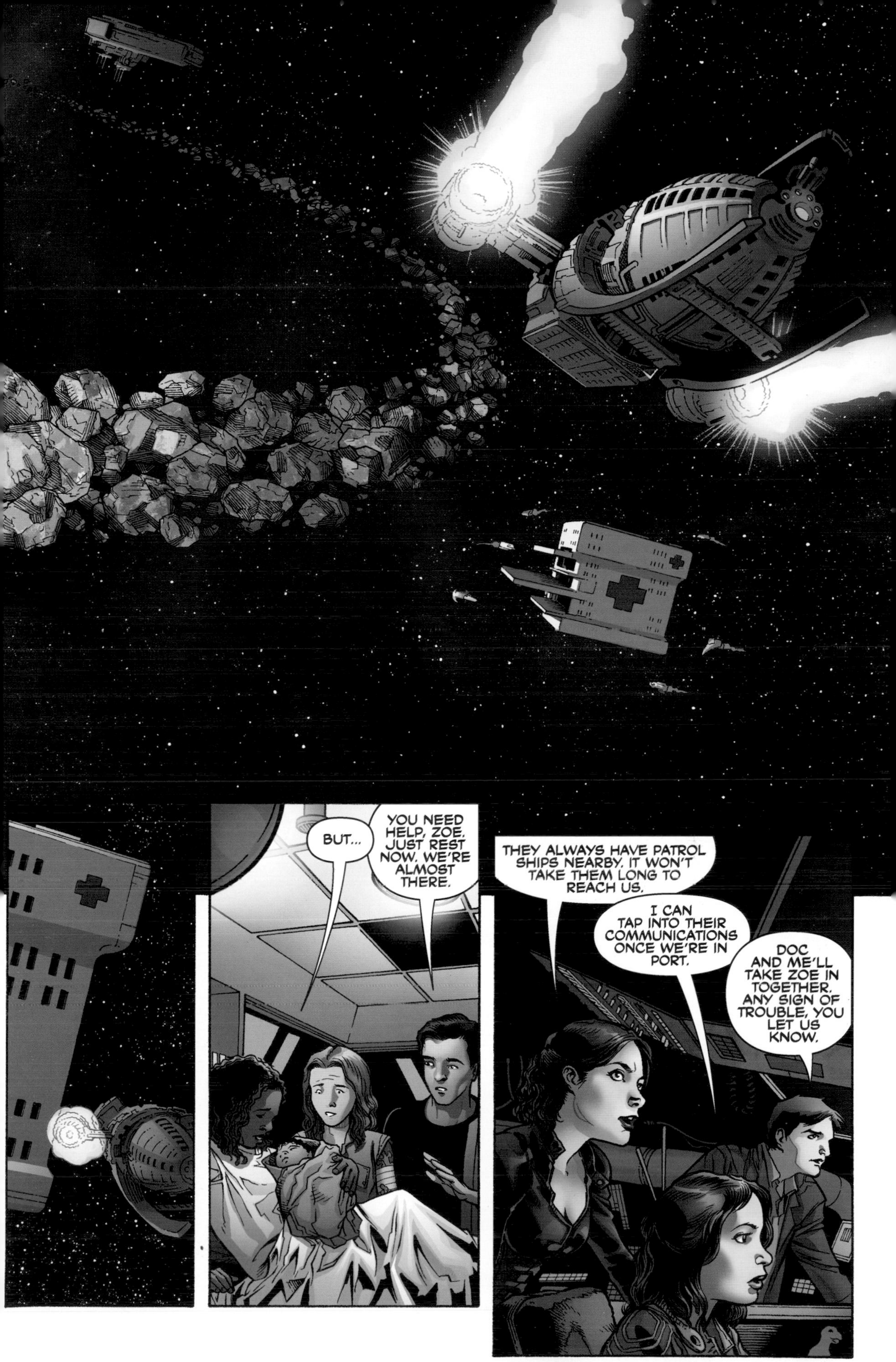
BUT...
YOU NEED HELP, ZOE. JUST REST NOW. WE'RE ALMOST THERE.
THEY ALWAYS HAVE PATROL SHIPS NEARBY. IT WON'T TAKE THEM LONG TO REACH US.
I CAN TAP INTO THEIR COMMUNICATIONS ONCE WE'RE IN PORT.
DOC AND ME'LL TAKE ZOE IN TOGETHER. ANY SIGN OF TROUBLE, YOU LET US KNOW.

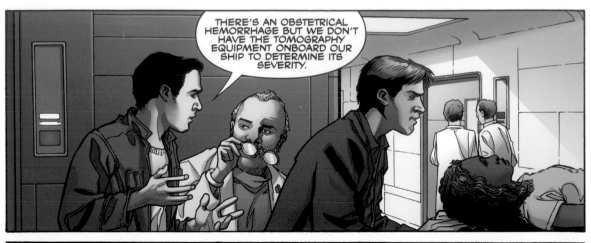

THERE'S AN OBSTETRICAL HEMORRHAGE BUT WE DON'T HAVE THE TOMOGRAPHY EQUIPMENT ONBOARD OUR SHIP TO DETERMINE ITS SEVERITY.

GOOD NEWS IS WE'RE GOING TO BE ABLE TO SAVE HER, BUT WE NEED TO OPERATE RIGHT AWAY.

HOW LONG TILL SHE'S BACK ON THE SHIP?

WE DO NEED TO ACT FAST THOUGH. A TRAUMA TEAM IS ON THEIR WAY UP NOW.

NOT TOO LONG, MAYBE FIVE DAYS?

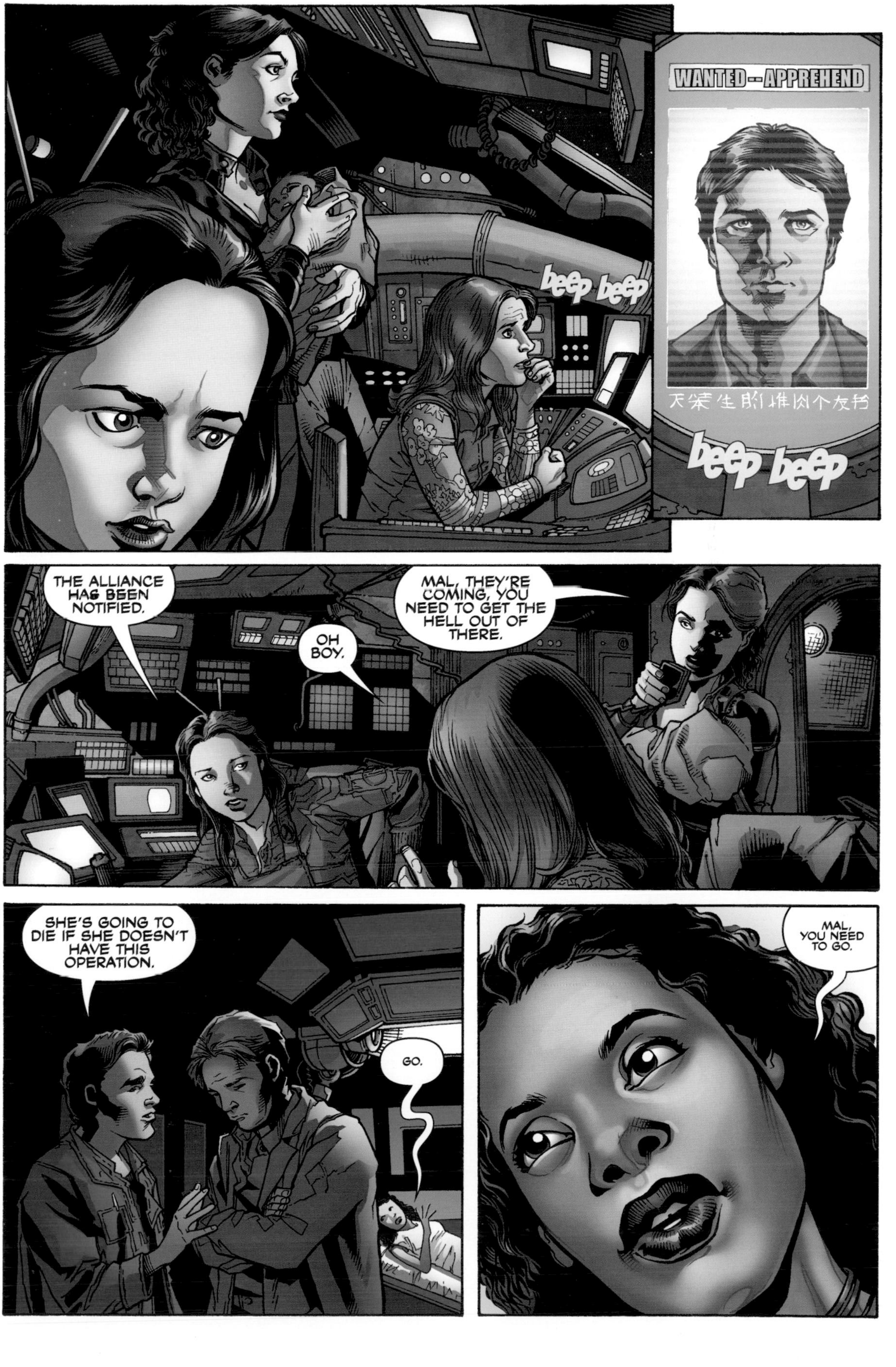

WANTED -- APPREHEND
beep beep
beep beep
THE ALLIANCE HAS BEEN NOTIFIED.
OH BOY.
MAL, THEY'RE COMING, YOU NEED TO GET THE HELL OUT OF THERE.
SHE'S GOING TO DIE IF SHE DOESN'T HAVE THIS OPERATION.
GO.
MAL, YOU NEED TO GO.

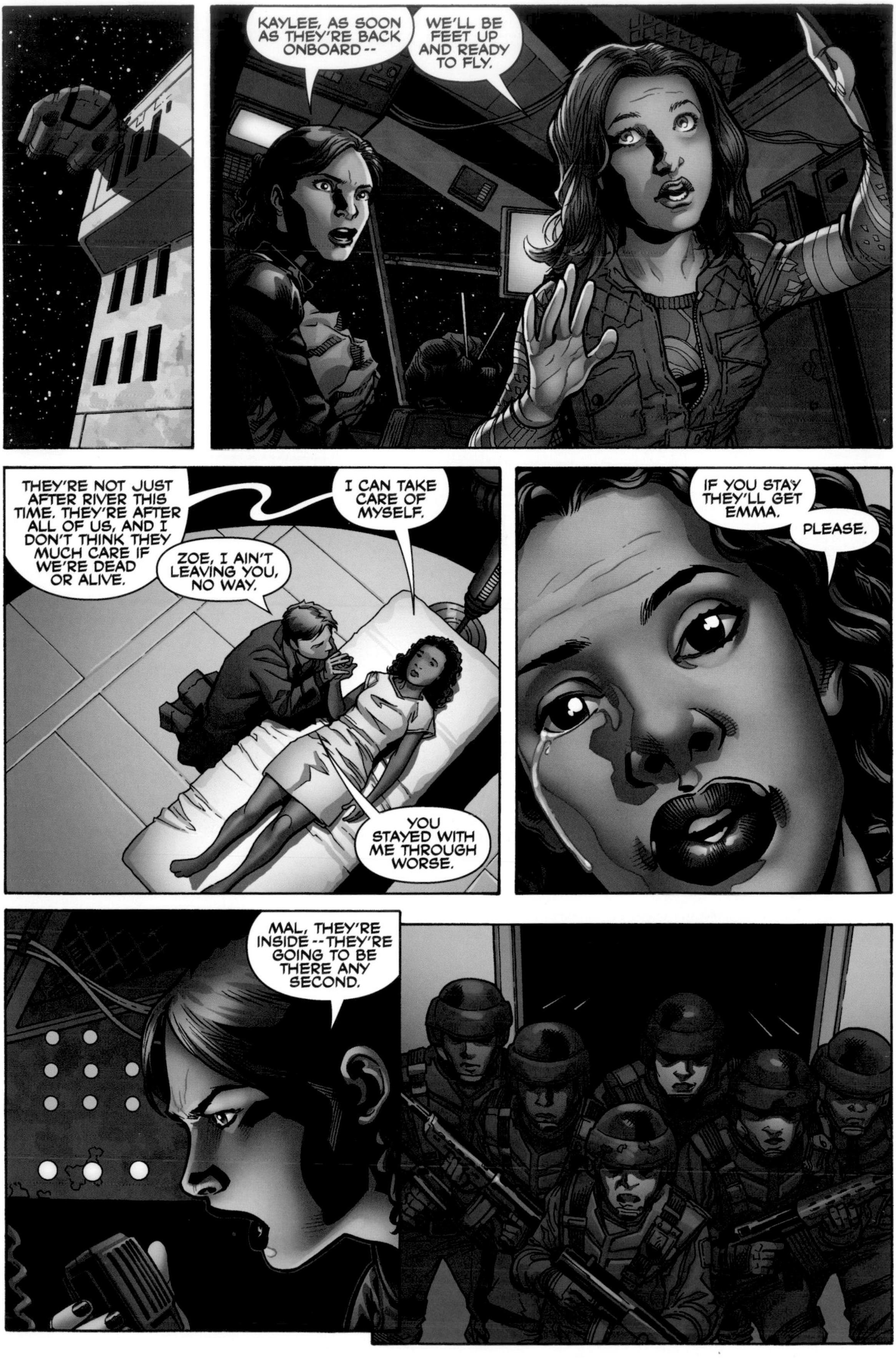
KAYLEE, AS SOON AS THEY'RE BACK ONBOARD --
WE'LL BE FEET UP AND READY TO FLY.
THEY'RE NOT JUST AFTER RIVER THIS TIME. THEY'RE AFTER ALL OF US, AND I DON'T THINK THEY MUCH CARE IF WE'RE DEAD OR ALIVE.
I CAN TAKE CARE OF MYSELF.
ZOE, I AIN'T LEAVING YOU, NO WAY.
YOU STAYED WITH ME THROUGH WORSE.
IF YOU STAY THEY'LL GET EMMA.
PLEASE.
MAL, THEY'RE INSIDE -- THEY'RE GOING TO BE THERE ANY SECOND.

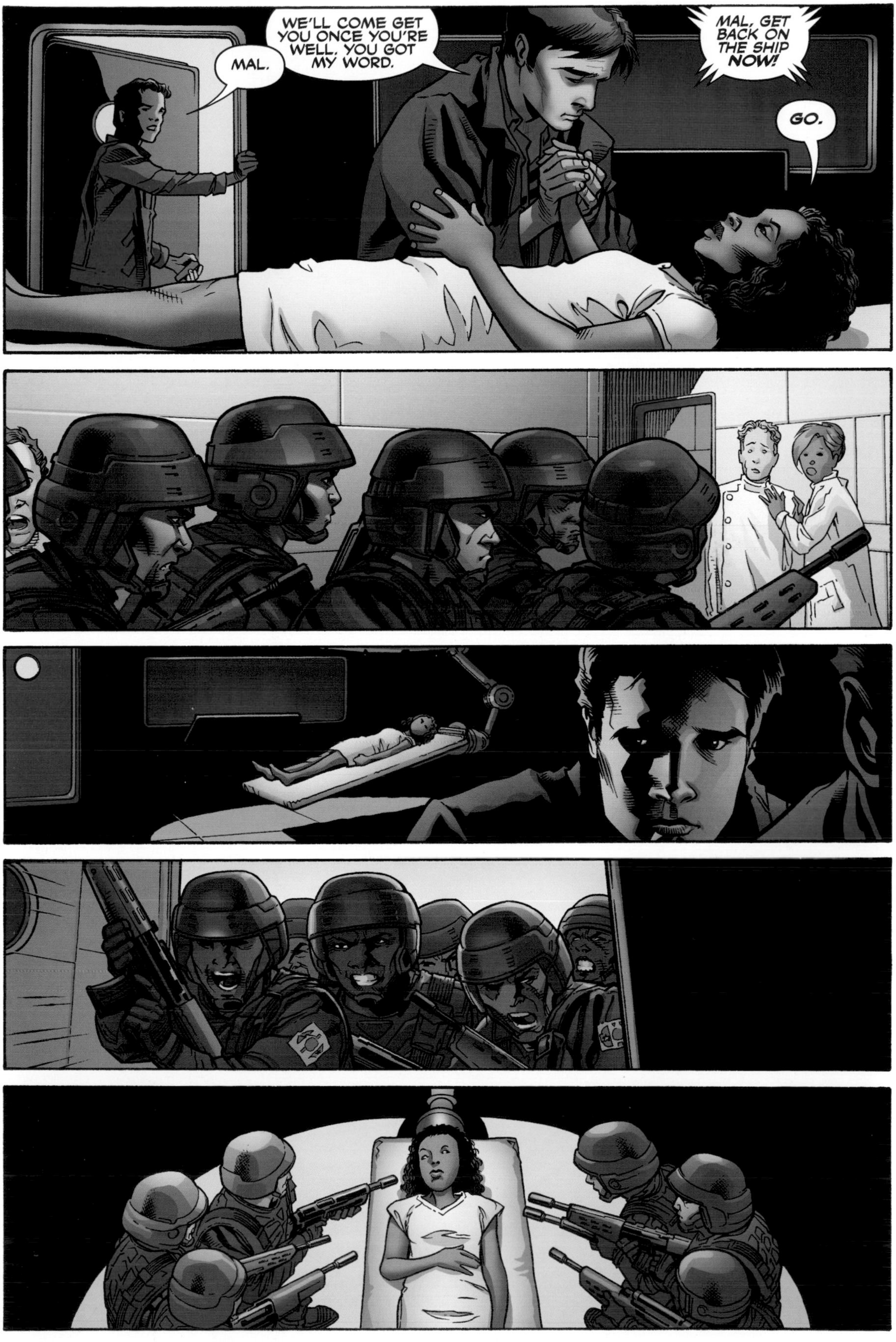
MAL.
WE'LL COME GET YOU ONCE YOU'RE WELL. YOU GOT MY WORD.
MAL, GET BACK ON THE SHIP NOW!
GO.

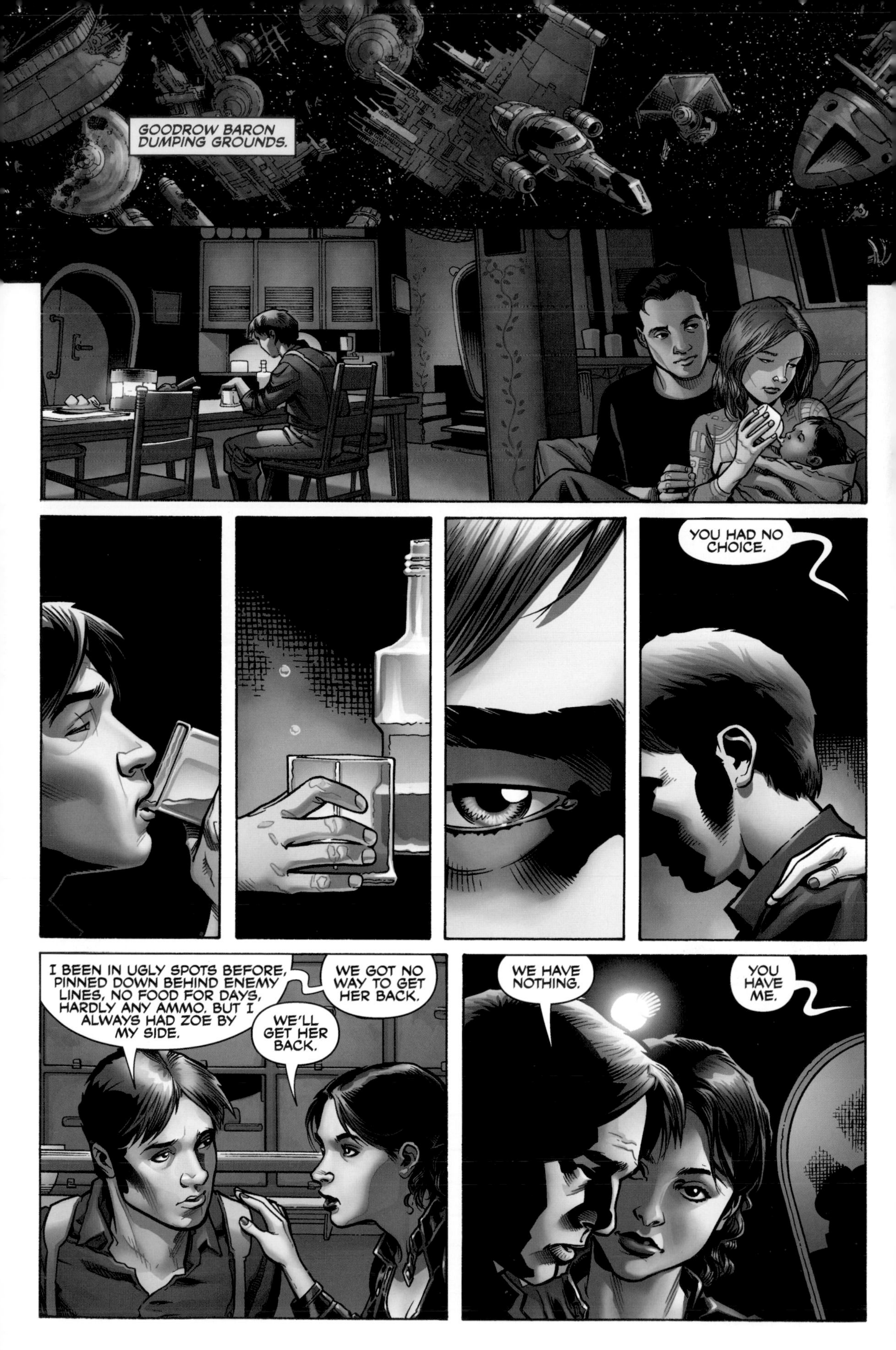
GOODROW BARON DUMPING GROUNDS.
YOU HAD NO CHOICE.
I BEEN IN UGLY SPOTS BEFORE, PINNED DOWN BEHIND ENEMY LINES, NO FOOD FOR DAYS, HARDLY ANY AMMO. BUT I ALWAYS HAD ZOE BY MY SIDE.
WE GOT NO WAY TO GET HER BACK.
WE'LL GET HER BACK.
WE HAVE NOTHING.
YOU HAVE ME.

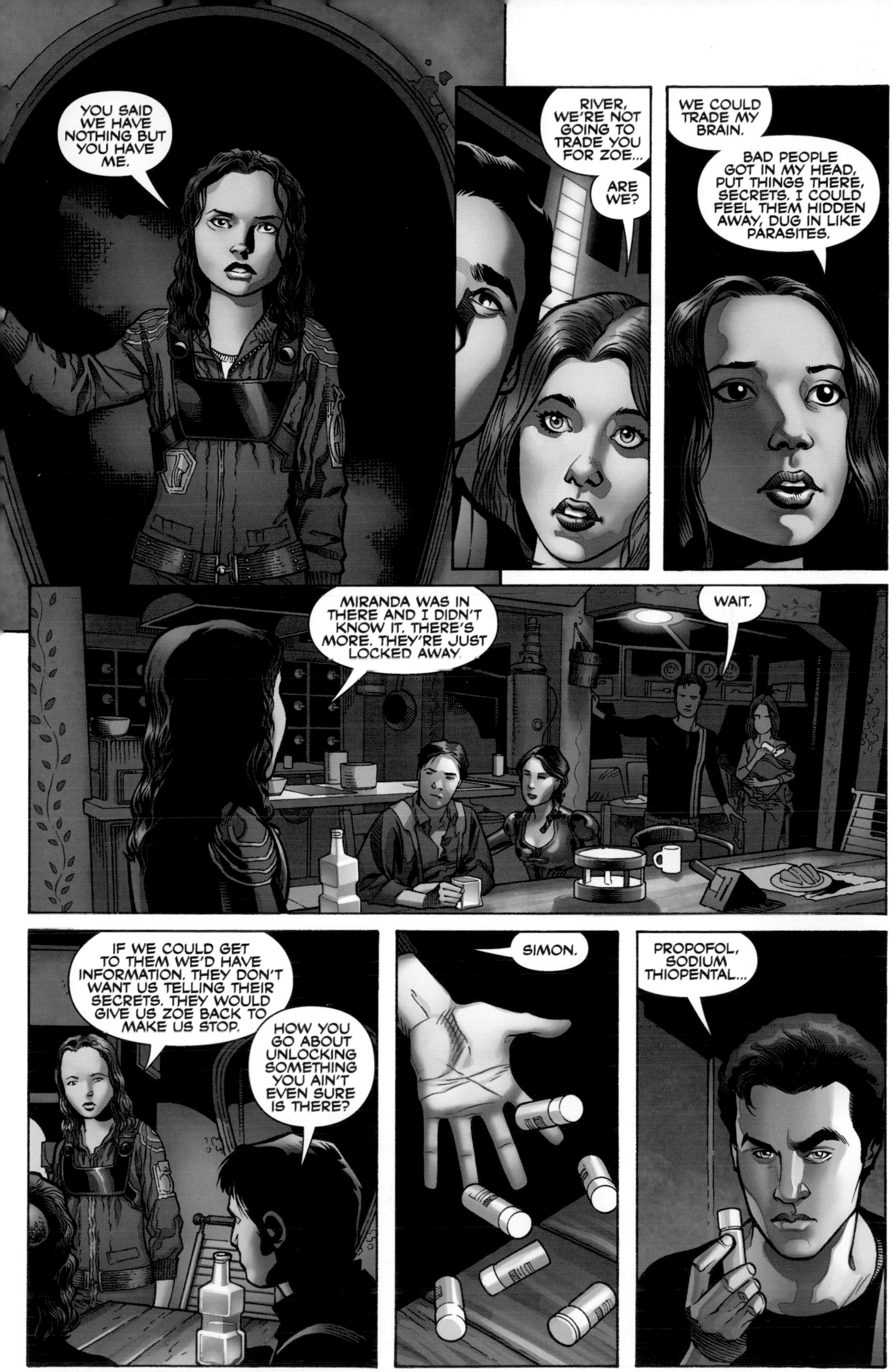
YOU SAID WE HAVE NOTHING BUT YOU HAVE ME.
RIVER, WE'RE NOT GOING TO TRADE YOU FOR ZOE...
ARE WE?
WE COULD TRADE MY BRAIN.
BAD PEOPLE GOT IN MY HEAD, PUT THINGS THERE, SECRETS. I COULD FEEL THEM HIDDEN AWAY, DUG IN LIKE PARASITES.
MIRANDA WAS IN THERE AND I DIDN'T KNOW IT. THERE'S MORE. THEY'RE JUST LOCKED AWAY.
WAIT.
IF WE COULD GET TO THEM WE'D HAVE INFORMATION. THEY DON'T WANT US TELLING THEIR SECRETS. THEY WOULD GIVE US ZOE BACK TO MAKE US STOP.
HOW YOU GO ABOUT UNLOCKING SOMETHING YOU AIN'T EVEN SURE IS THERE?
SIMON.
PROPOFOL, SODIUM THIOPENTAL...

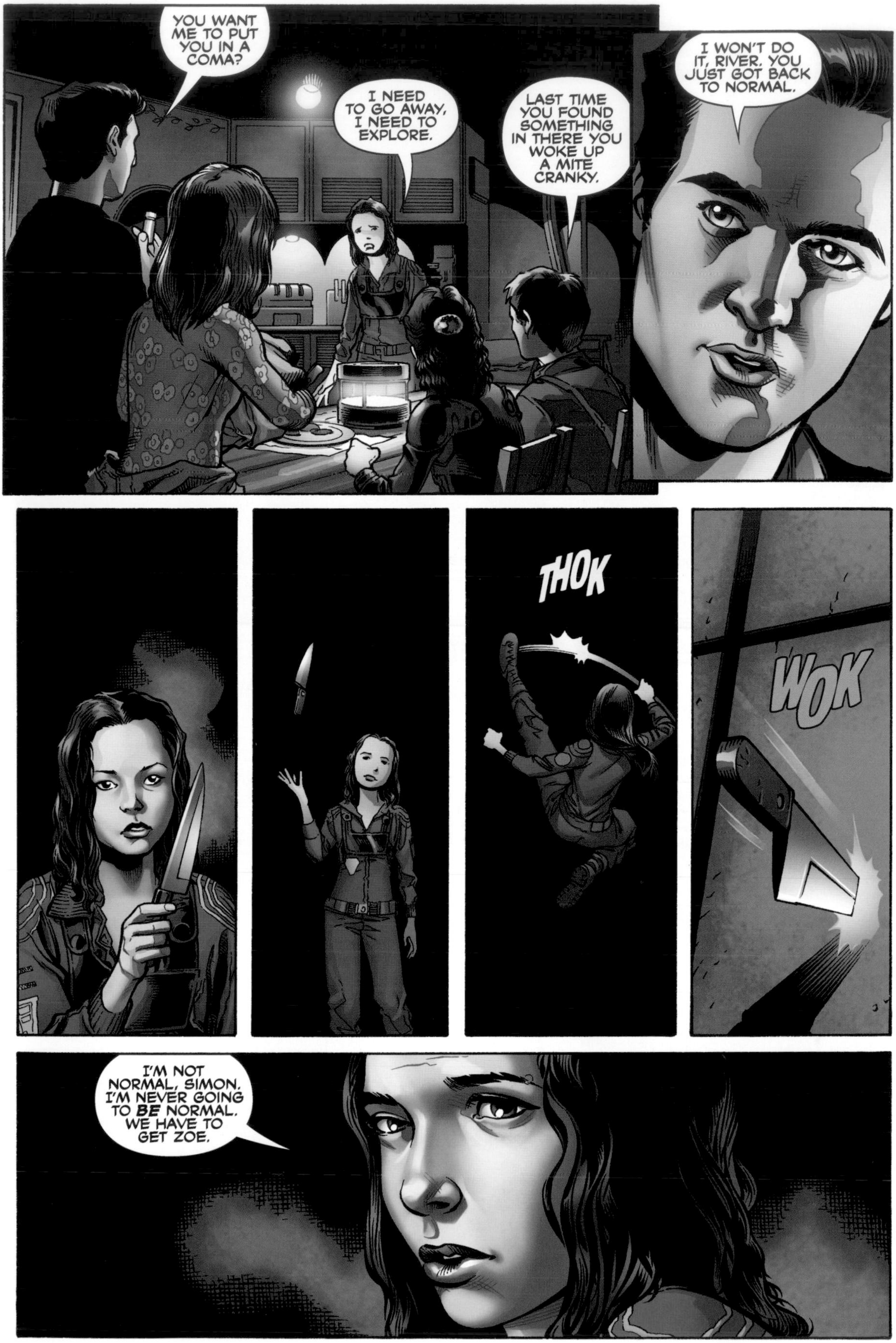
YOU WANT ME TO PUT YOU IN A COMA?
I NEED TO GO AWAY, I NEED TO EXPLORE.
LAST TIME YOU FOUND SOMETHING IN THERE YOU WOKE UP A MITE CRANKY.
I WON'T DO IT, RIVER. YOU JUST GOT BACK TO NORMAL.
THOK
WOK
I'M NOT NORMAL, SIMON. I'M NEVER GOING TO BE NORMAL. WE HAVE TO GET ZOE.

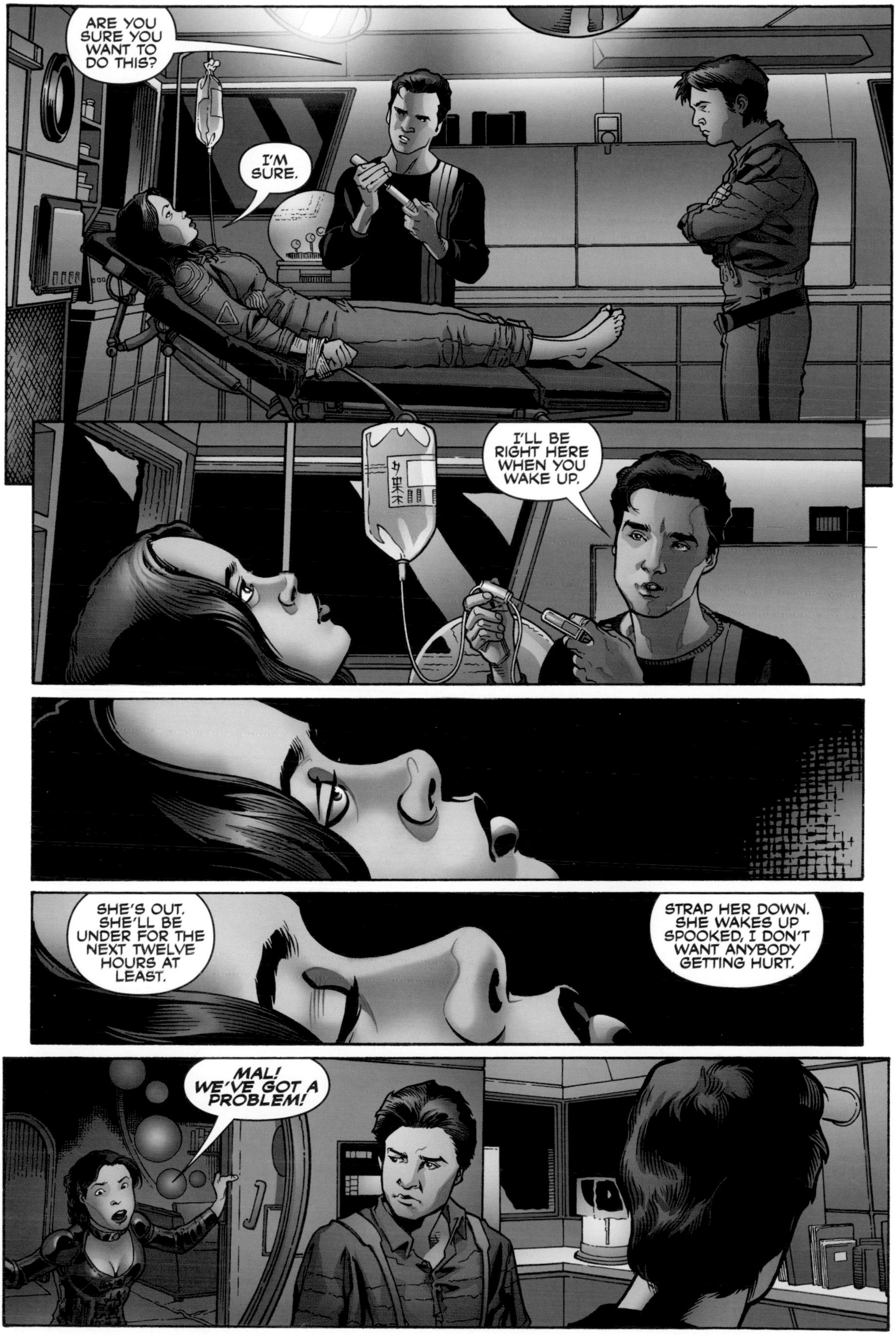
ARE YOU SURE YOU WANT TO DO THIS?
I'M SURE.
I'LL BE RIGHT HERE WHEN YOU WAKE UP.
SHE'S OUT. SHE'LL BE UNDER FOR THE NEXT TWELVE HOURS AT LEAST.
STRAP HER DOWN. SHE WAKES UP SPOOKED, I DON'T WANT ANYBODY GETTING HURT.
MAL! WE'VE GOT A PROBLEM!

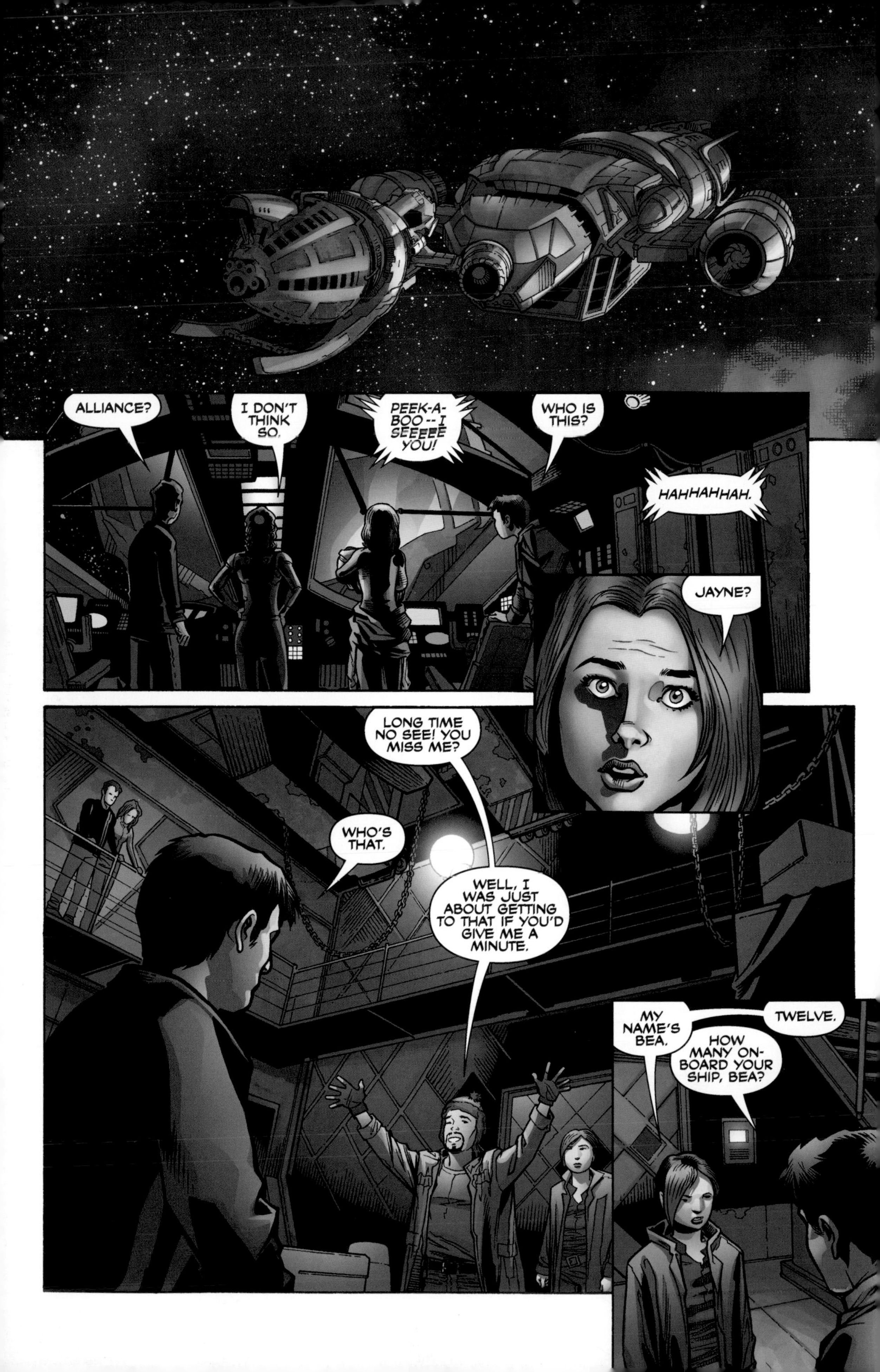
ALLIANCE?
I DON'T THINK SO.
PEEK-A-BOO-- I SEEEEEE YOU!
WHO IS THIS?
HAHHAHHAH.
JAYNE?
LONG TIME NO SEE! YOU MISS ME?
WHO'S THAT.
WELL, I WAS JUST ABOUT GETTING TO THAT IF YOU'D GIVE ME A MINUTE.
MY NAME'S BEA.
TWELVE.
HOW MANY ON-BOARD YOUR SHIP, BEA?

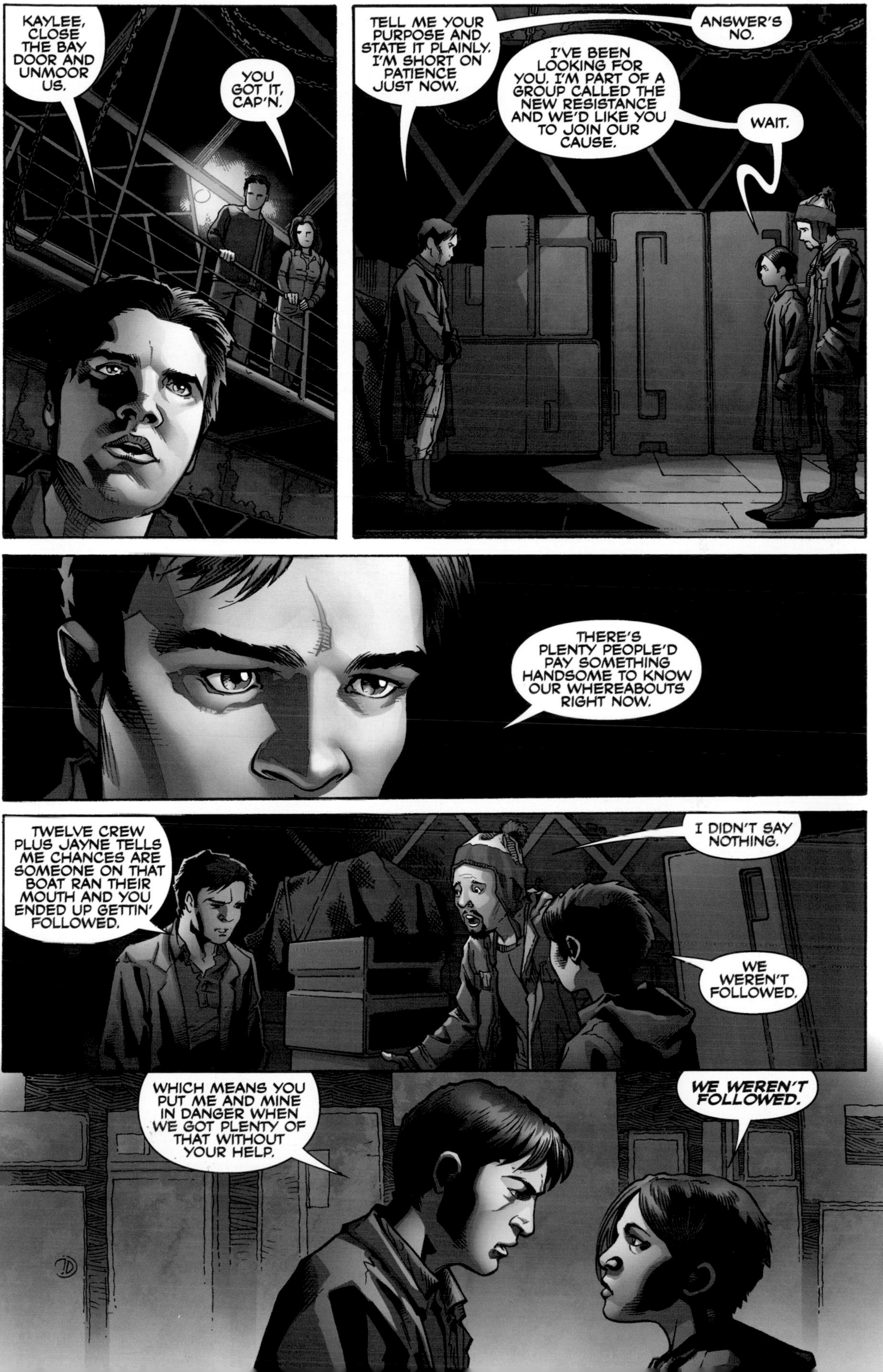
KAYLEE, CLOSE THE BAY DOOR AND UNMOOR US.
YOU GOT IT, CAP'N.
TELL ME YOUR PURPOSE AND STATE IT PLAINLY. I'M SHORT ON PATIENCE JUST NOW.
I'VE BEEN LOOKING FOR YOU. I'M PART OF A GROUP CALLED THE NEW RESISTANCE AND WE'D LIKE YOU TO JOIN OUR CAUSE.
ANSWER'S NO.
WAIT.
THERE'S PLENTY PEOPLE'D PAY SOMETHING HANDSOME TO KNOW OUR WHEREABOUTS RIGHT NOW.
TWELVE CREW PLUS JAYNE TELLS ME CHANCES ARE SOMEONE ON THAT BOAT RAN THEIR MOUTH AND YOU ENDED UP GETTIN' FOLLOWED.
I DIDN'T SAY NOTHING.
WE WEREN'T FOLLOWED.
WHICH MEANS YOU PUT ME AND MINE IN DANGER WHEN WE GOT PLENTY OF THAT WITHOUT YOUR HELP.
WE WEREN'T FOLLOWED.

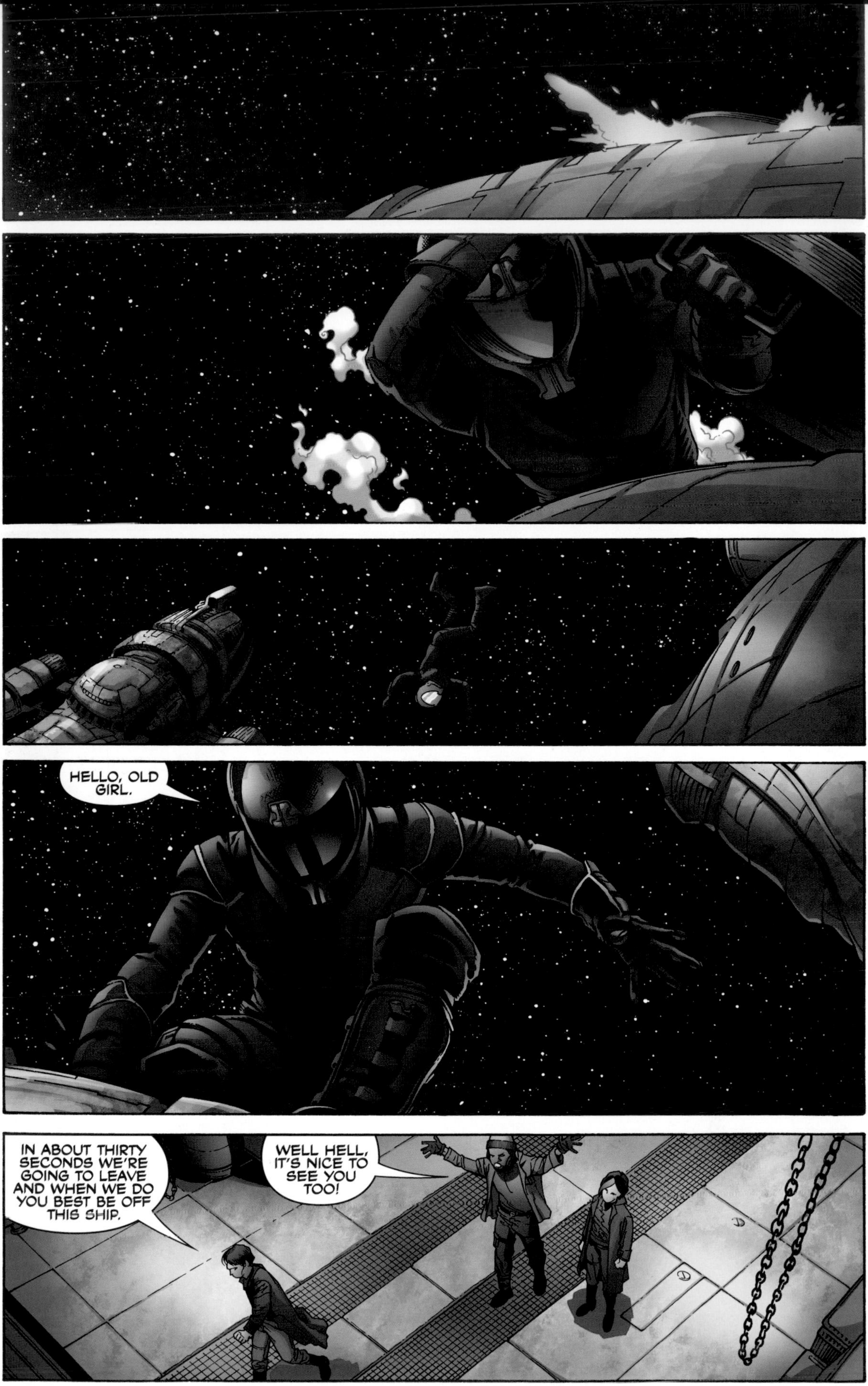
HELLO, OLD GIRL.
IN ABOUT THIRTY SECONDS WE'RE GOING TO LEAVE AND WHEN WE DO YOU BEST BE OFF THIS SHIP.
WELL HELL, IT'S NICE TO SEE YOU TOO!

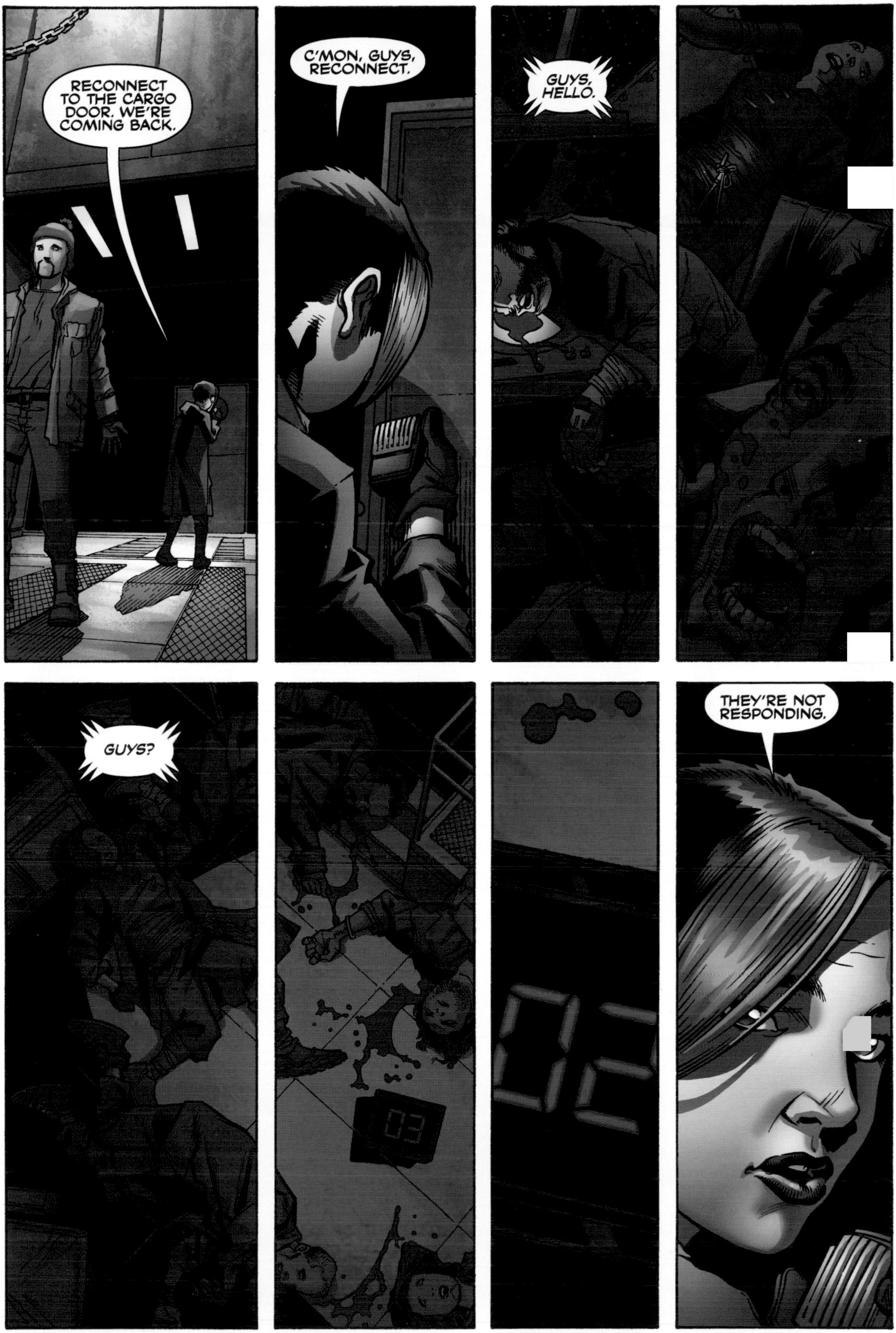
RECONNECT TO THE CARGO DOOR. WE'RE COMING BACK.
C'MON, GUYS, RECONNECT.
GUYS, HELLO.
GUYS?
THEY'RE NOT RESPONDING.

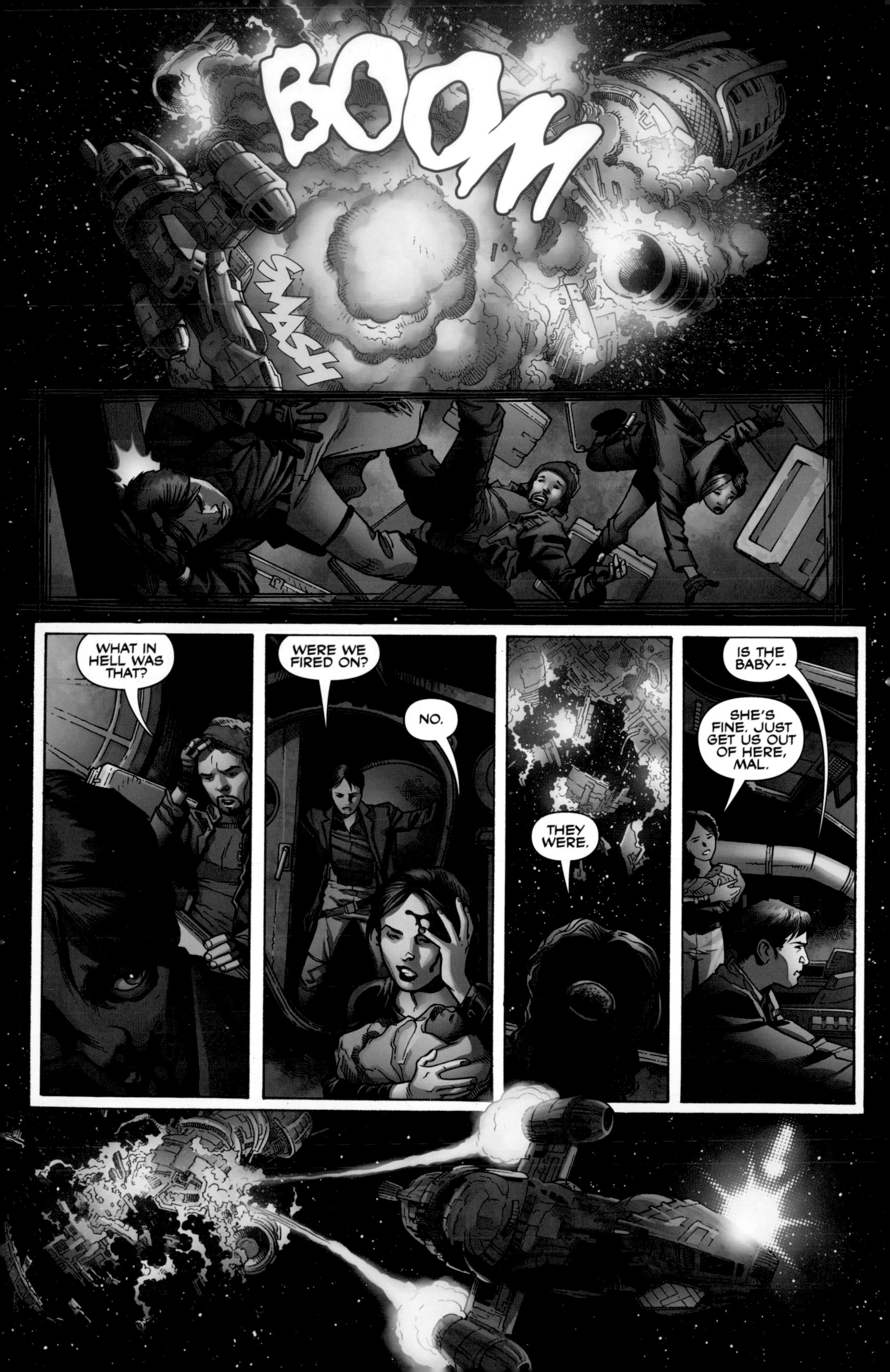
BOOM
SMASH
WHAT IN HELL WAS THAT?
WERE WE FIRED ON?
NO.
THEY WERE.
IS THE BABY--
SHE'S FINE. JUST GET US OUT OF HERE, MAL.

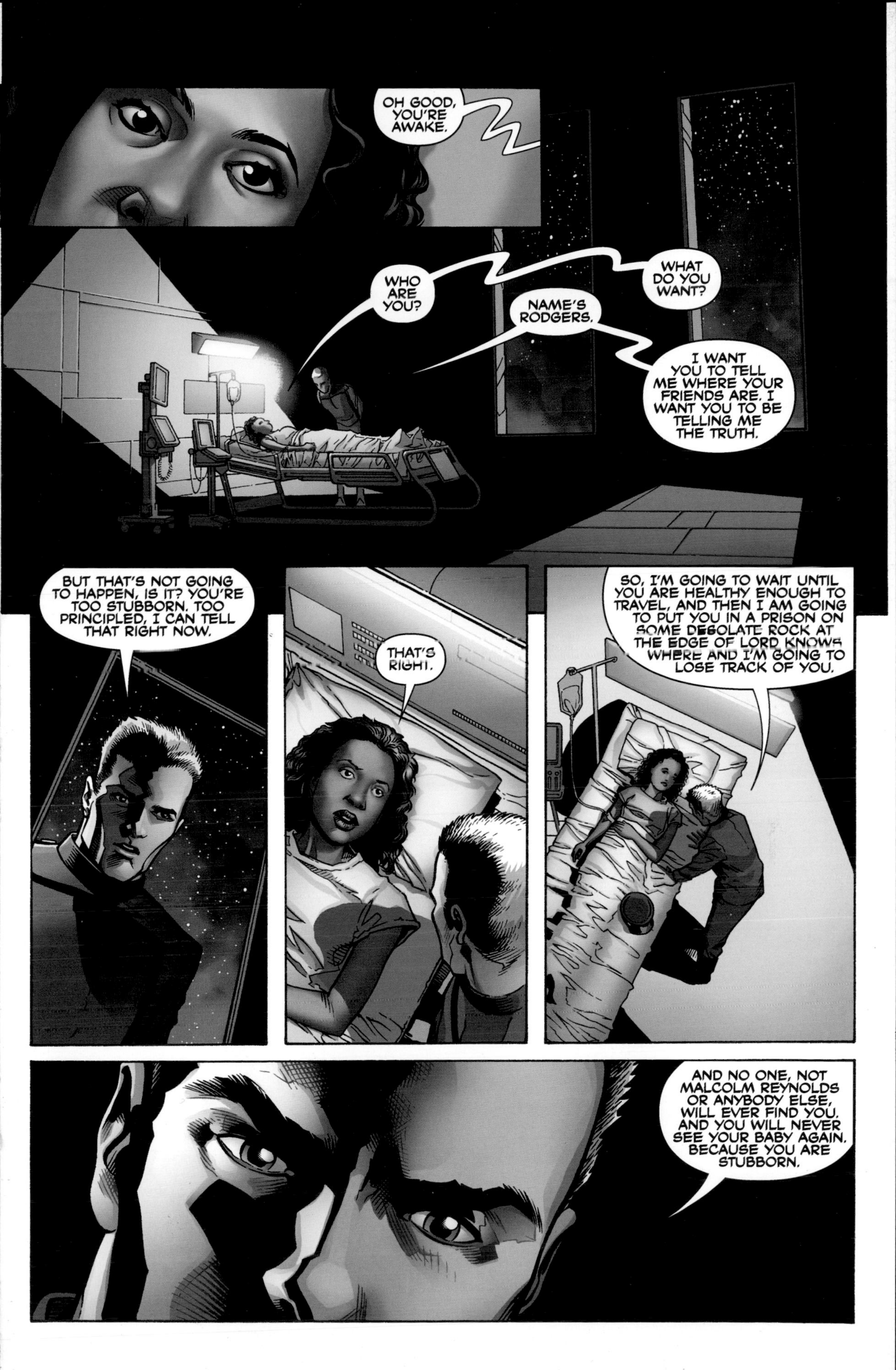
OH GOOD, YOU'RE AWAKE.
WHO ARE YOU?
WHAT DO YOU WANT?
NAME'S RODGERS.
I WANT YOU TO TELL ME WHERE YOUR FRIENDS ARE. I WANT YOU TO BE TELLING ME THE TRUTH.
BUT THAT'S NOT GOING TO HAPPEN, IS IT? YOU'RE TOO STUBBORN, TOO PRINCIPLED. I CAN TELL THAT RIGHT NOW.
THAT'S RIGHT.
SO, I'M GOING TO WAIT UNTIL YOU ARE HEALTHY ENOUGH TO TRAVEL, AND THEN I AM GOING TO PUT YOU IN A PRISON ON SOME DESOLATE ROCK AT THE EDGE OF LORD KNOWS WHERE AND I'M GOING TO LOSE TRACK OF YOU.
AND NO ONE, NOT MALCOLM REYNOLDS OR ANYBODY ELSE, WILL EVER FIND YOU. AND YOU WILL NEVER SEE YOUR BABY AGAIN. BECAUSE YOU ARE STUBBORN.

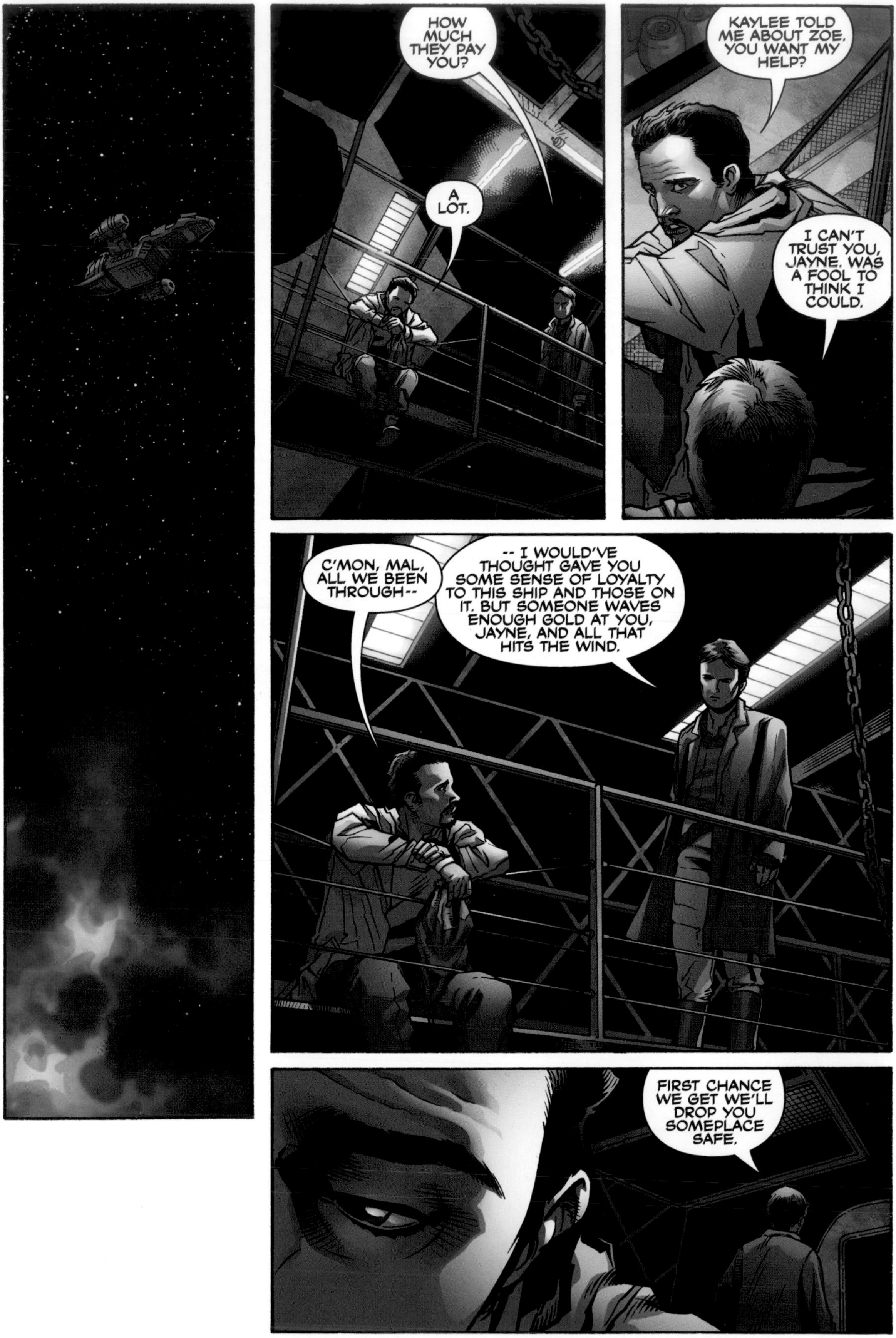
HOW MUCH THEY PAY YOU?
A LOT.
KAYLEE TOLD ME ABOUT ZOE. YOU WANT MY HELP?
I CAN'T TRUST YOU, JAYNE. WAS A FOOL TO THINK I COULD.
C'MON, MAL, ALL WE BEEN THROUGH--
-- I WOULD'VE THOUGHT GAVE YOU SOME SENSE OF LOYALTY TO THIS SHIP AND THOSE ON IT. BUT SOMEONE WAVES ENOUGH GOLD AT YOU, JAYNE, AND ALL THAT HITS THE WIND.
FIRST CHANCE WE GET WE'LL DROP YOU SOMEPLACE SAFE.

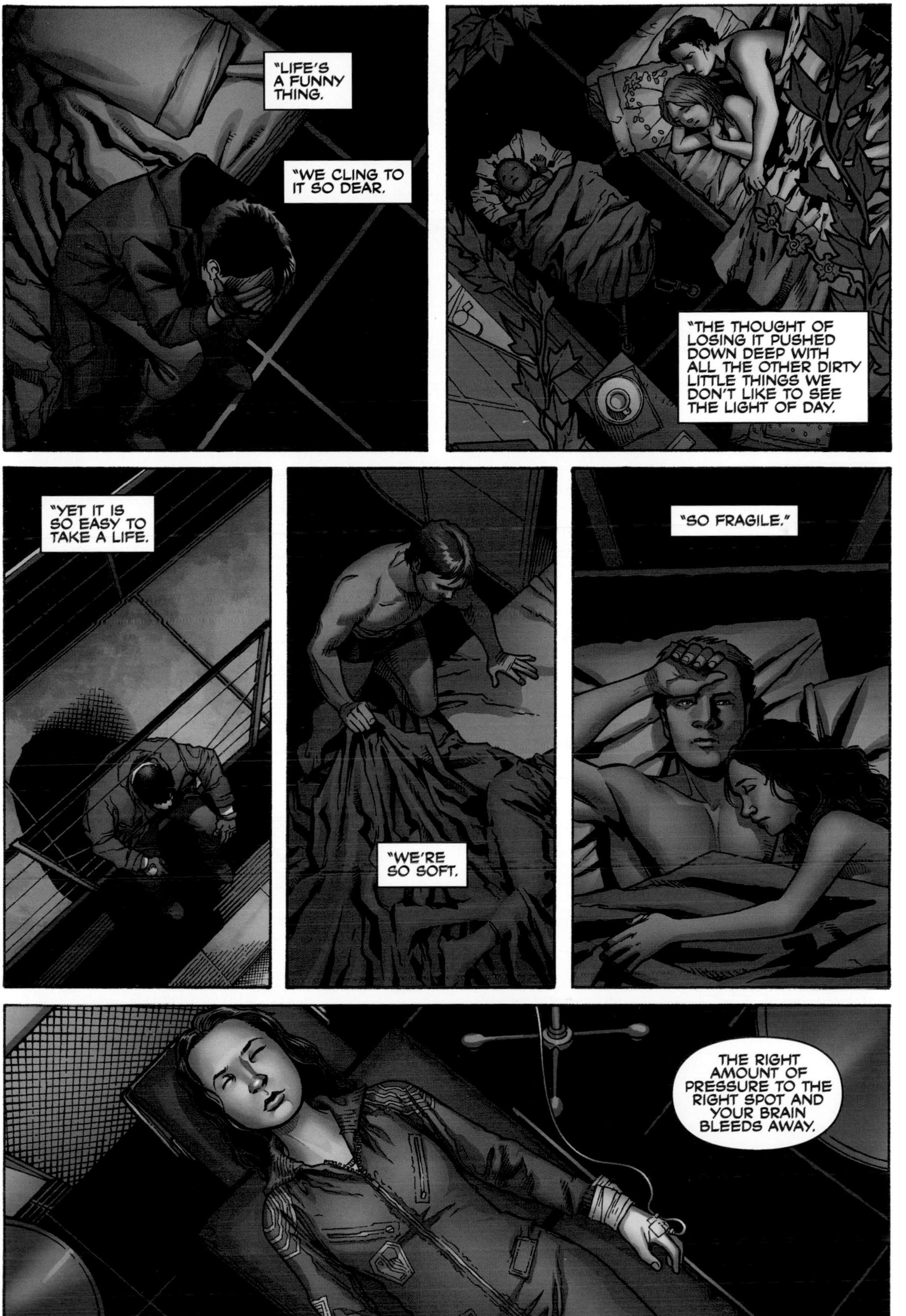
"LIFE'S A FUNNY THING.
"WE CLING TO IT SO DEAR.
"THE THOUGHT OF LOSING IT PUSHED DOWN DEEP WITH ALL THE OTHER DIRTY LITTLE THINGS WE DON'T LIKE TO SEE THE LIGHT OF DAY.
"YET IT IS SO EASY TO TAKE A LIFE.
"WE'RE SO SOFT.
"SO FRAGILE."
THE RIGHT AMOUNT OF PRESSURE TO THE RIGHT SPOT AND YOUR BRAIN BLEEDS AWAY.

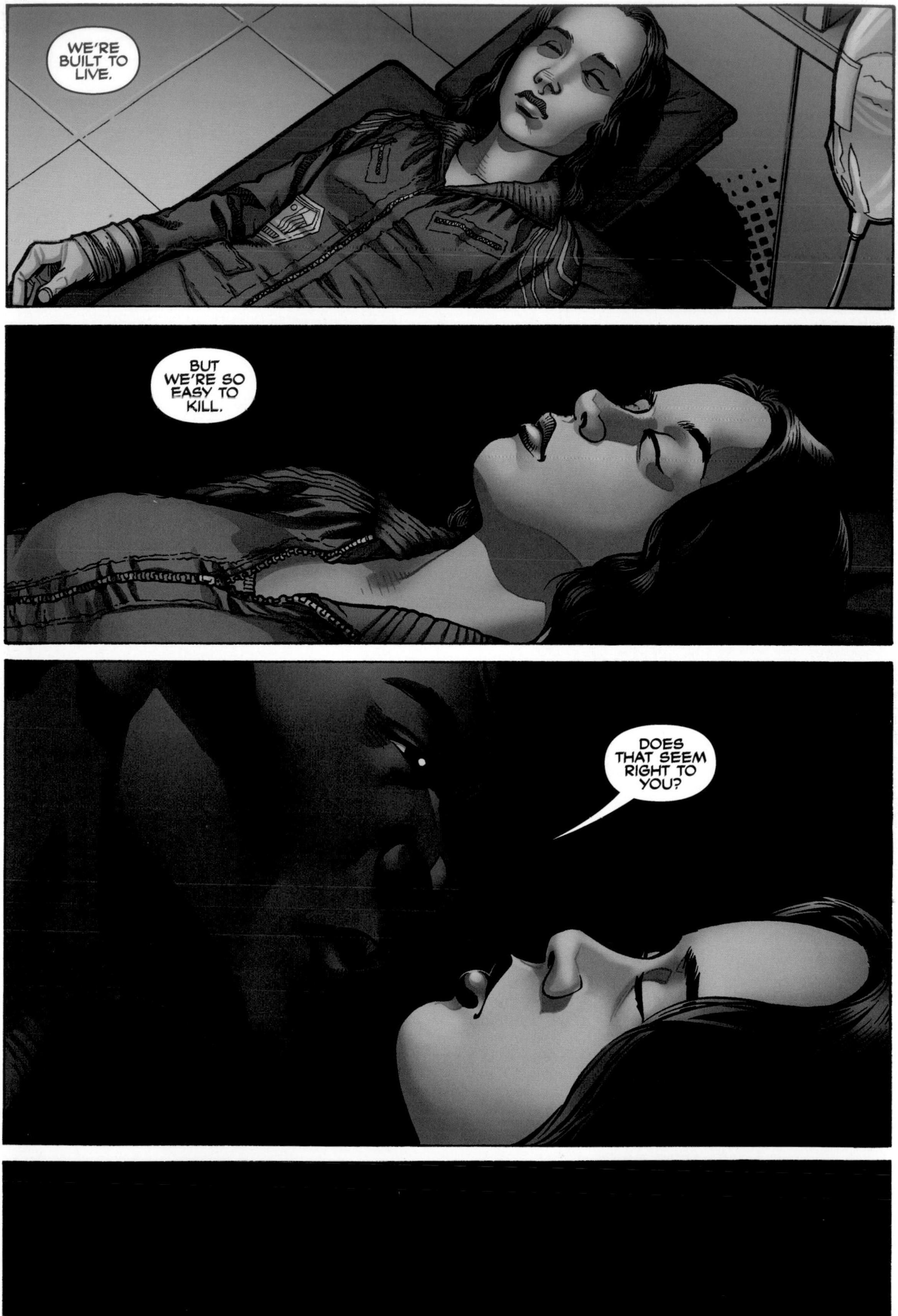
WE'RE BUILT TO LIVE.
BUT WE'RE SO EASY TO KILL.
DOES THAT SEEM RIGHT TO YOU?

CHAPTER THREE

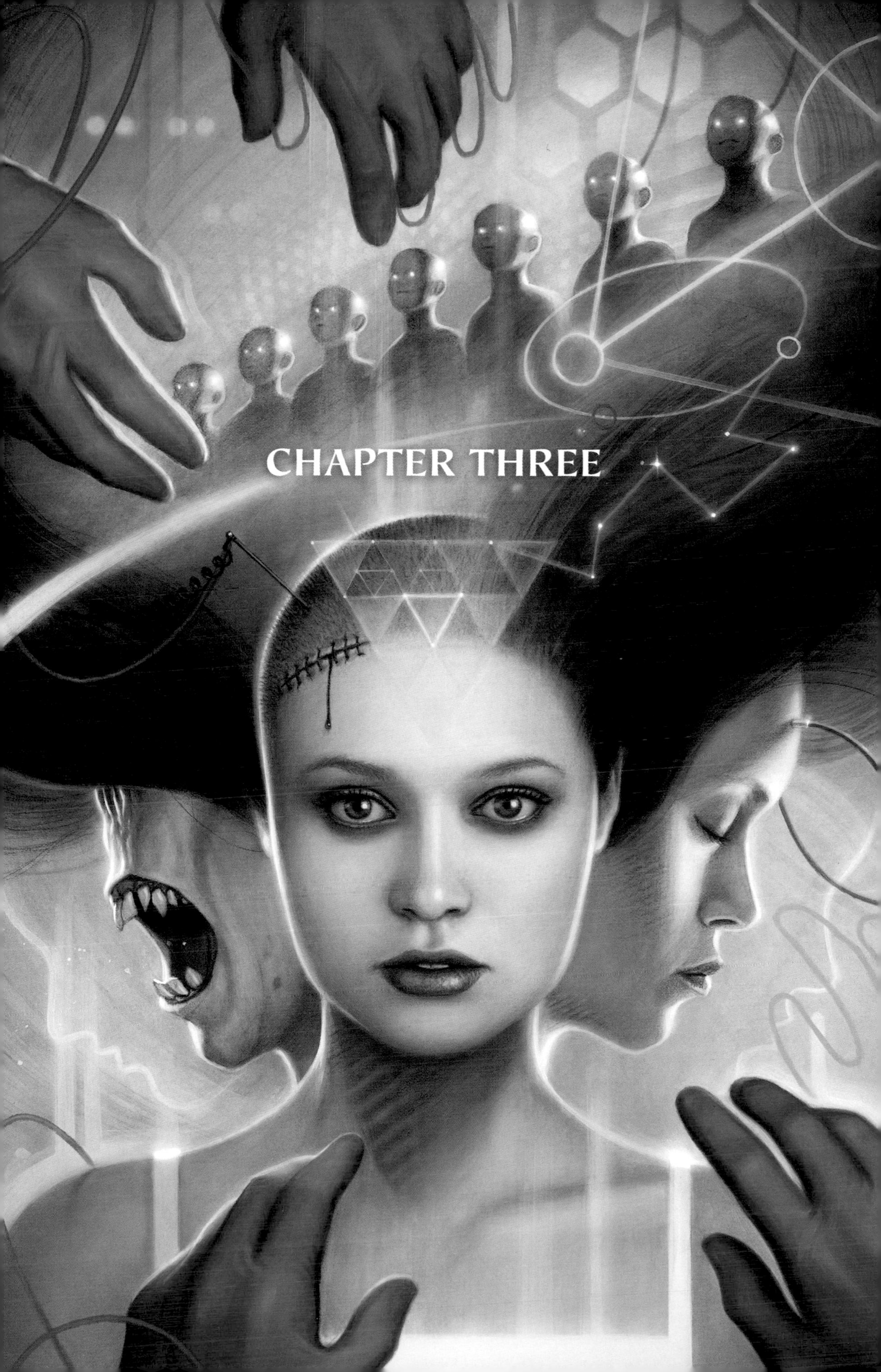

静

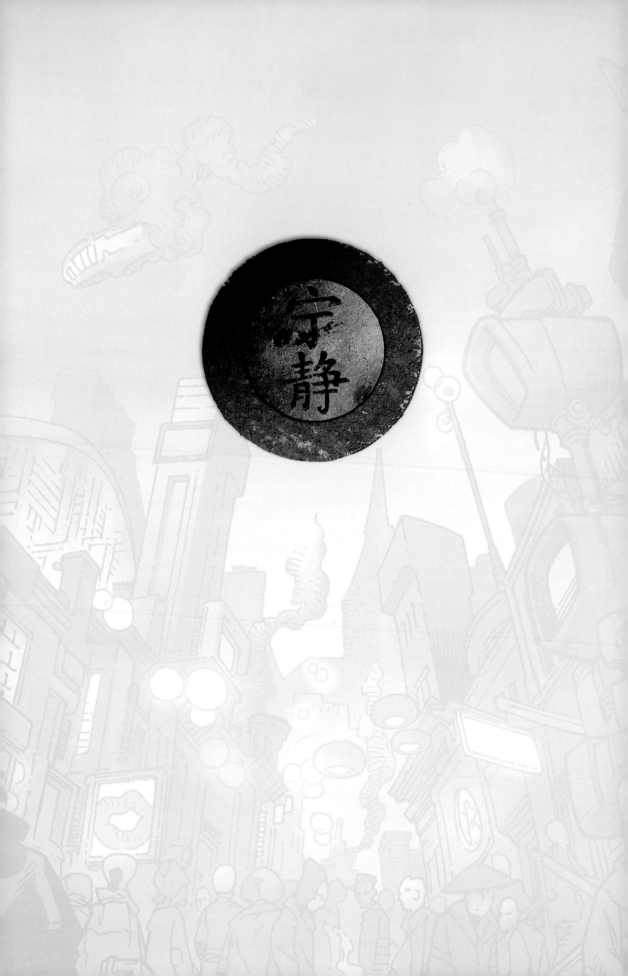

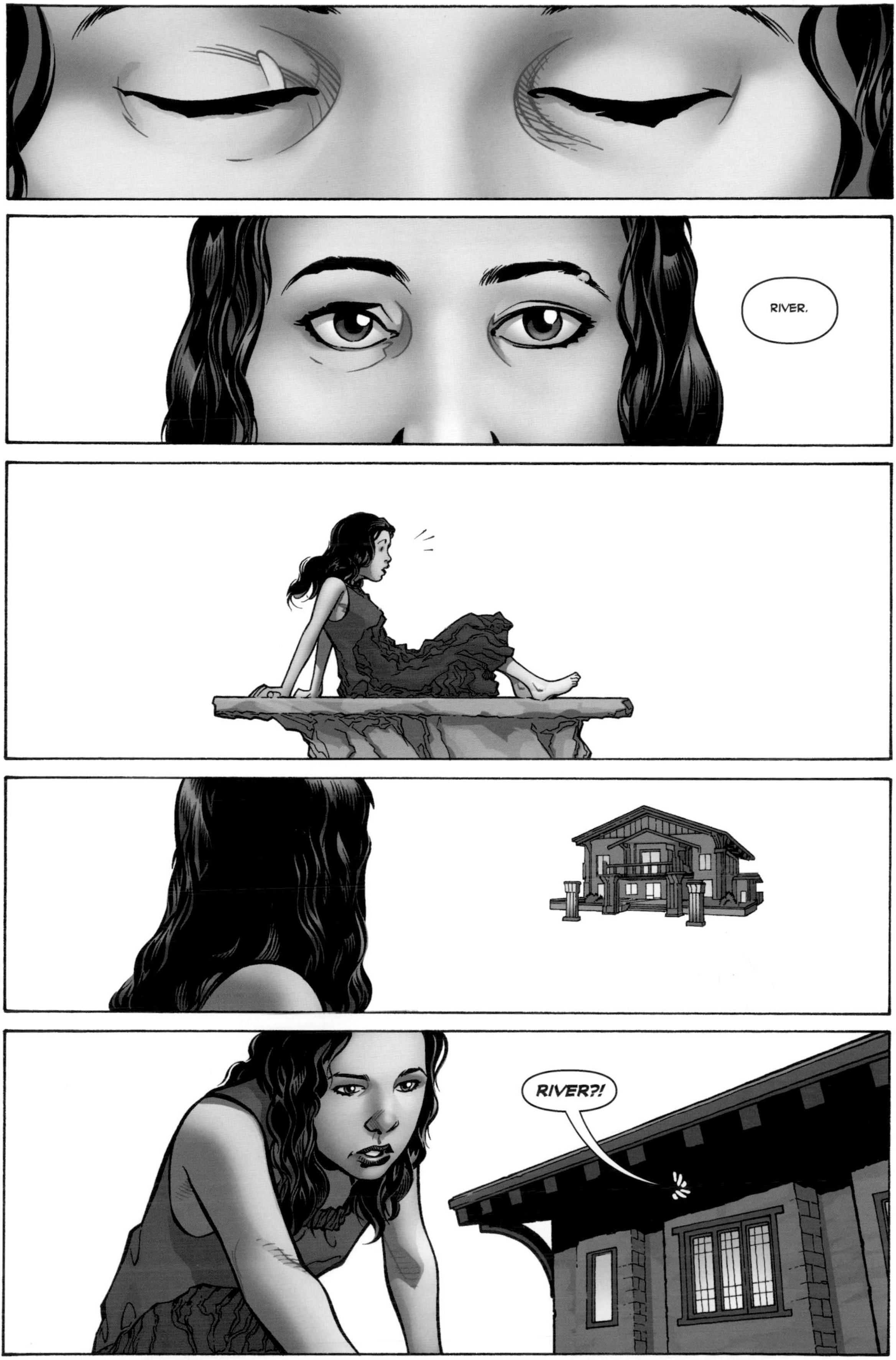
RIVER.
RIVER?!

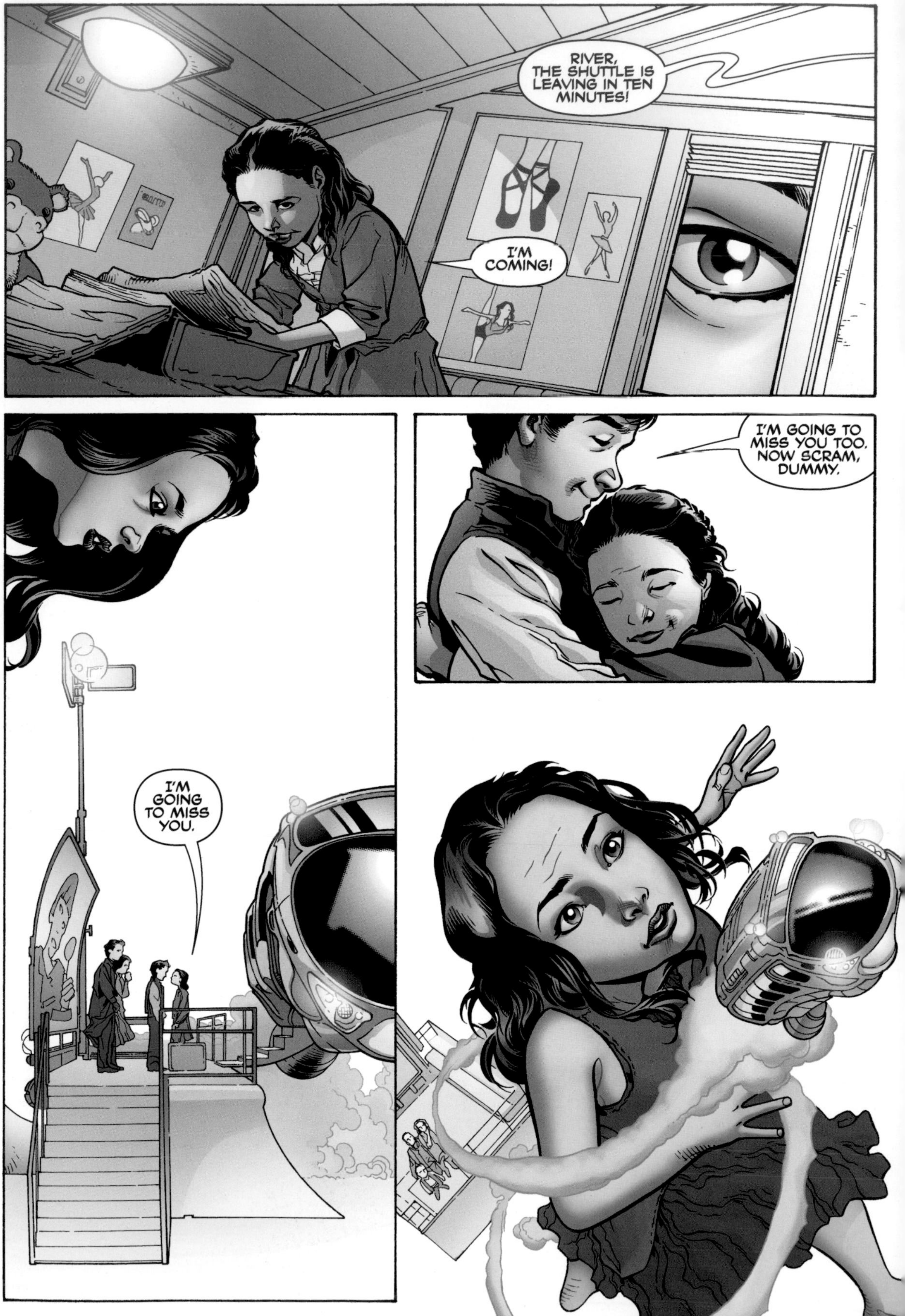

RIVER, THE SHUTTLE IS LEAVING IN TEN MINUTES!
I'M COMING!
I'M GOING TO MISS YOU.
I'M GOING TO MISS YOU TOO. NOW SCRAM, DUMMY.

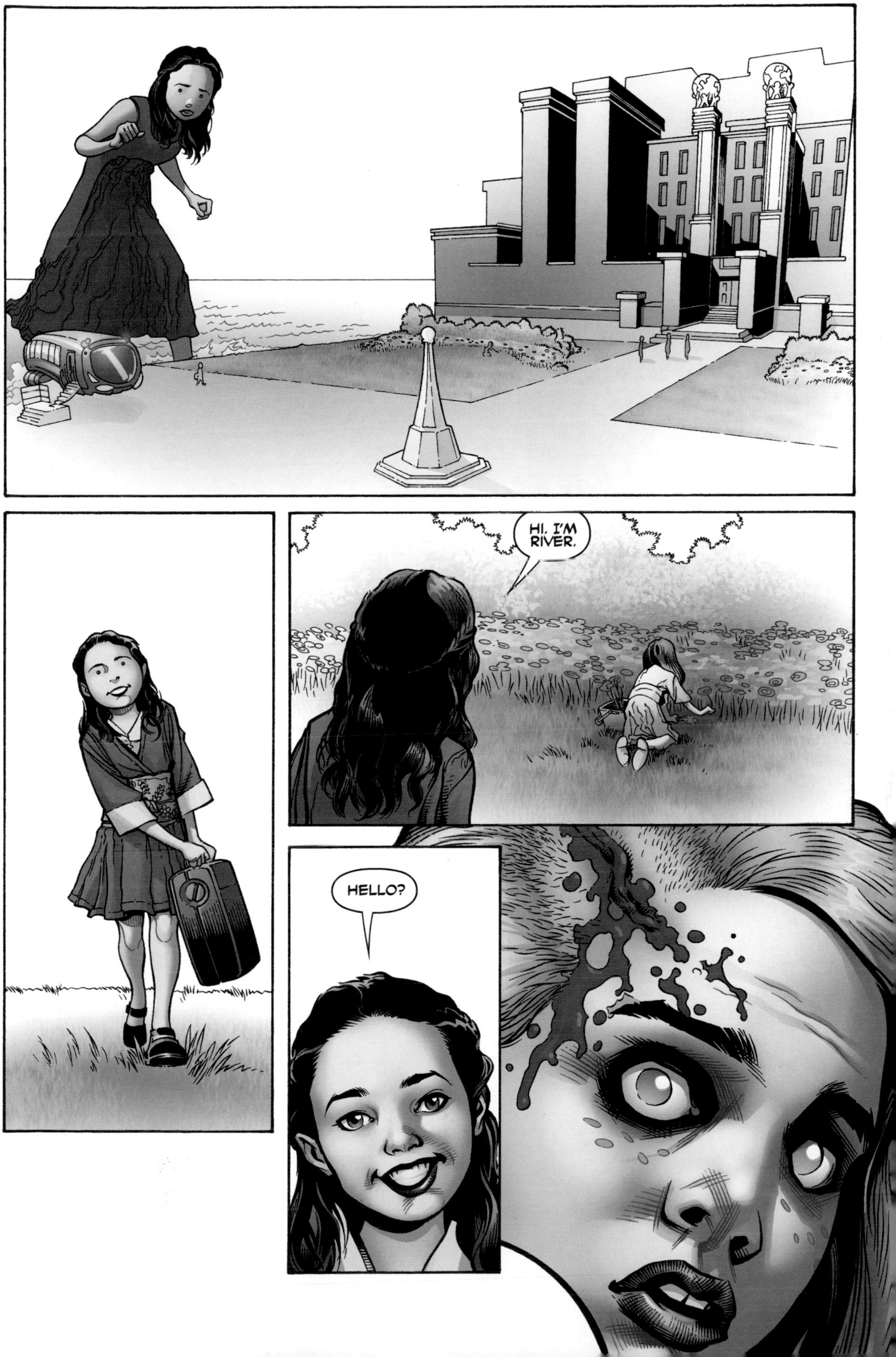
HI. I'M RIVER.
HELLO?

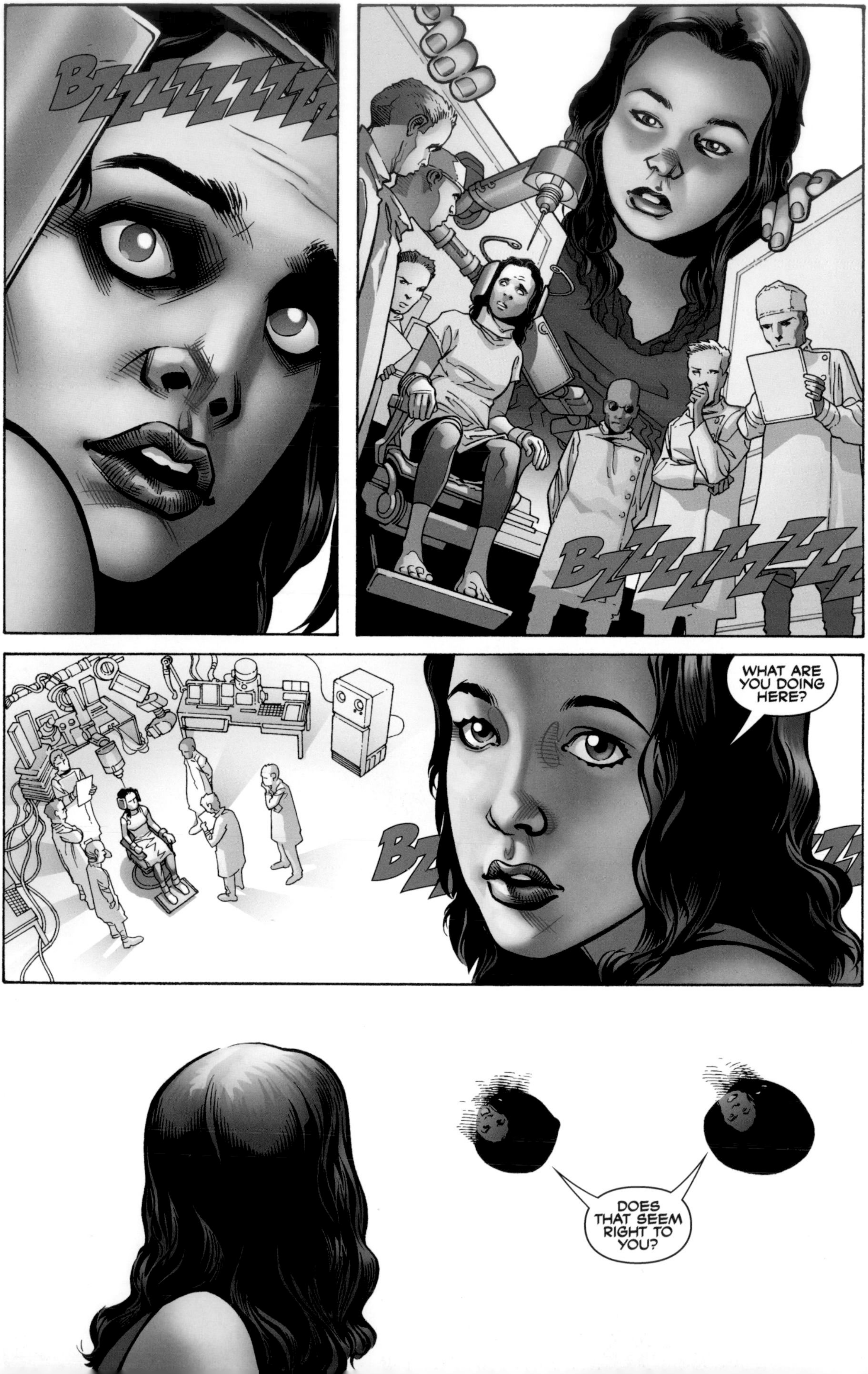
BZZZZZZZZZ
BZZZZZZZZ
WHAT ARE YOU DOING HERE?
BZZZZ
DOES THAT SEEM RIGHT TO YOU?

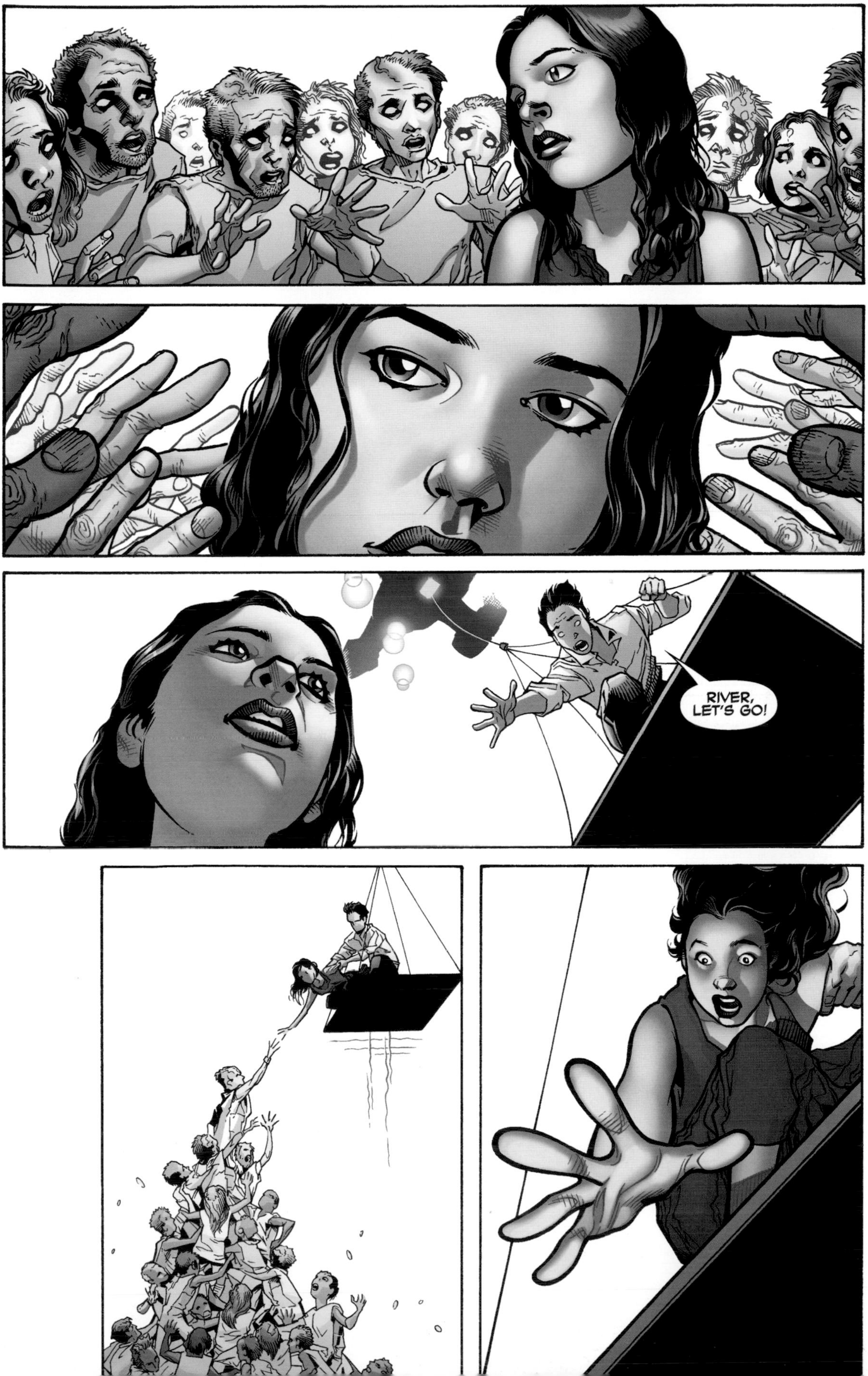
RIVER, LET'S GO!

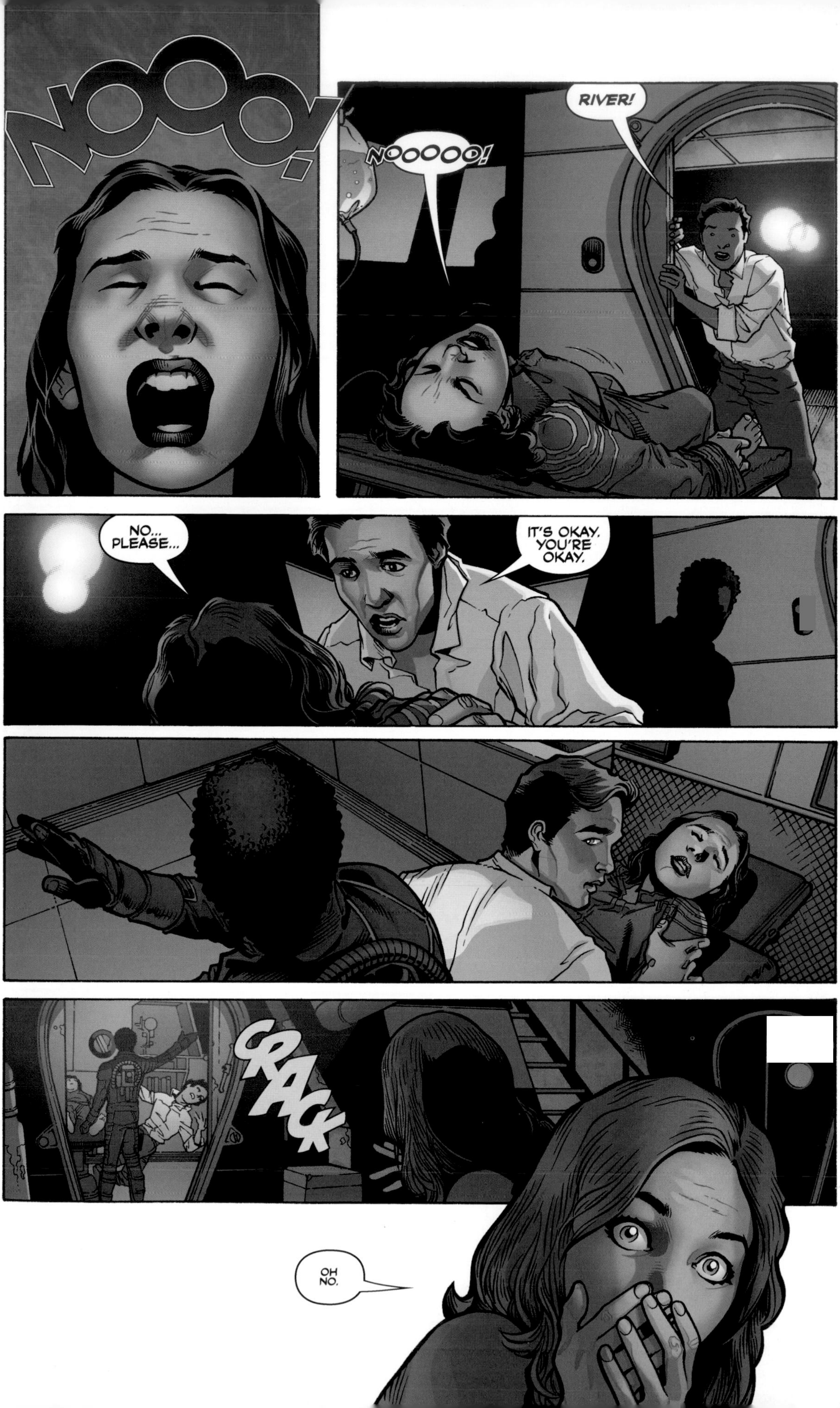
NOOO!
RIVER!
NOOOOO!
NO... PLEASE...
IT'S OKAY. YOU'RE OKAY.
CRACK
OH NO.

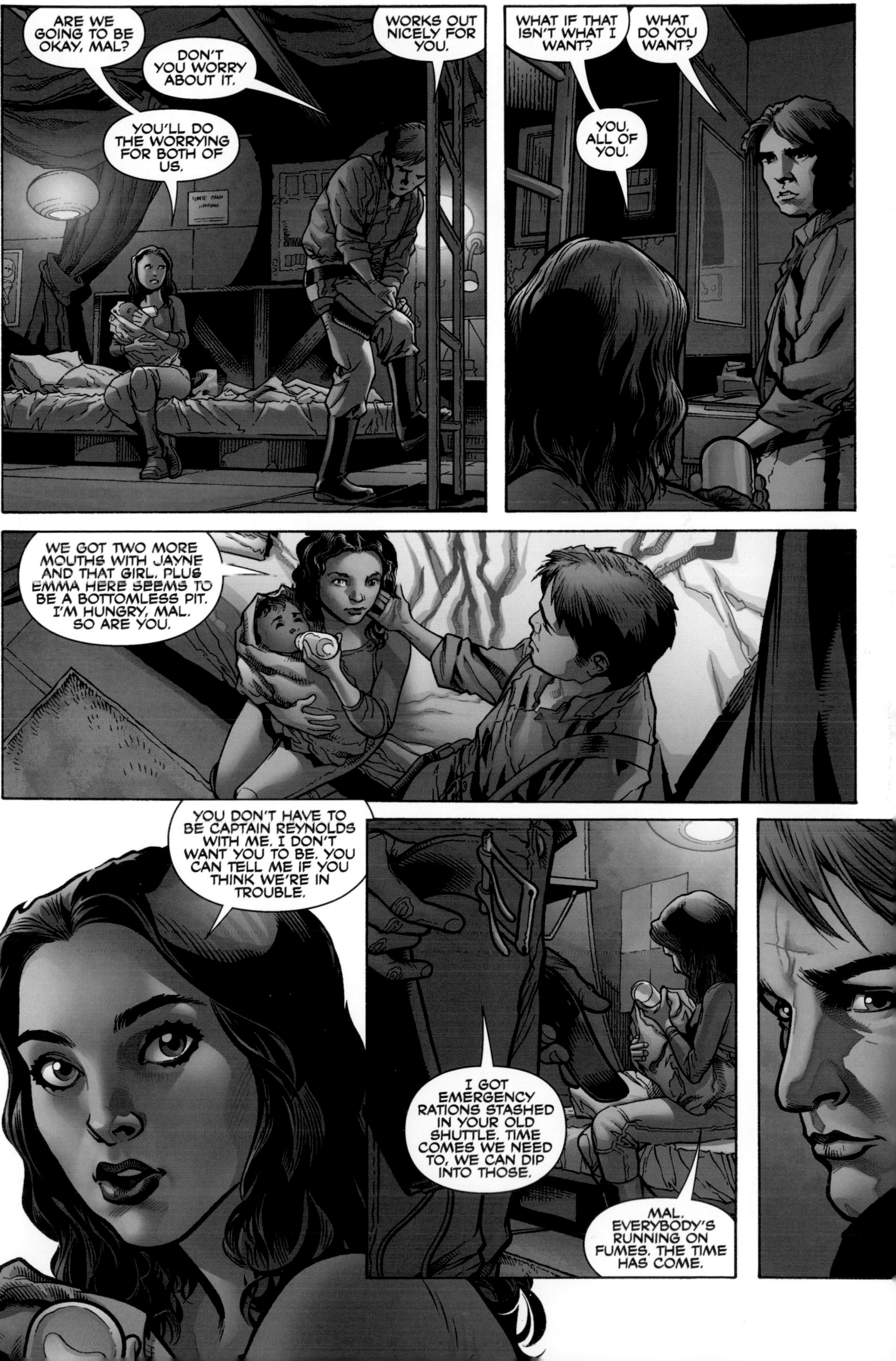
ARE WE GOING TO BE OKAY, MAL?
DON'T YOU WORRY ABOUT IT.
YOU'LL DO THE WORRYING FOR BOTH OF US.
WORKS OUT NICELY FOR YOU.
WHAT IF THAT ISN'T WHAT I WANT?
WHAT DO YOU WANT?
YOU. ALL OF YOU.
WE GOT TWO MORE MOUTHS WITH JAYNE AND THAT GIRL. PLUS EMMA HERE SEEMS TO BE A BOTTOMLESS PIT. I'M HUNGRY, MAL. SO ARE YOU.
YOU DON'T HAVE TO BE CAPTAIN REYNOLDS WITH ME. I DON'T WANT YOU TO BE. YOU CAN TELL ME IF YOU THINK WE'RE IN TROUBLE.
I GOT EMERGENCY RATIONS STASHED IN YOUR OLD SHUTTLE. TIME COMES WE NEED TO, WE CAN DIP INTO THOSE.
MAL. EVERYBODY'S RUNNING ON FUMES. THE TIME HAS COME.

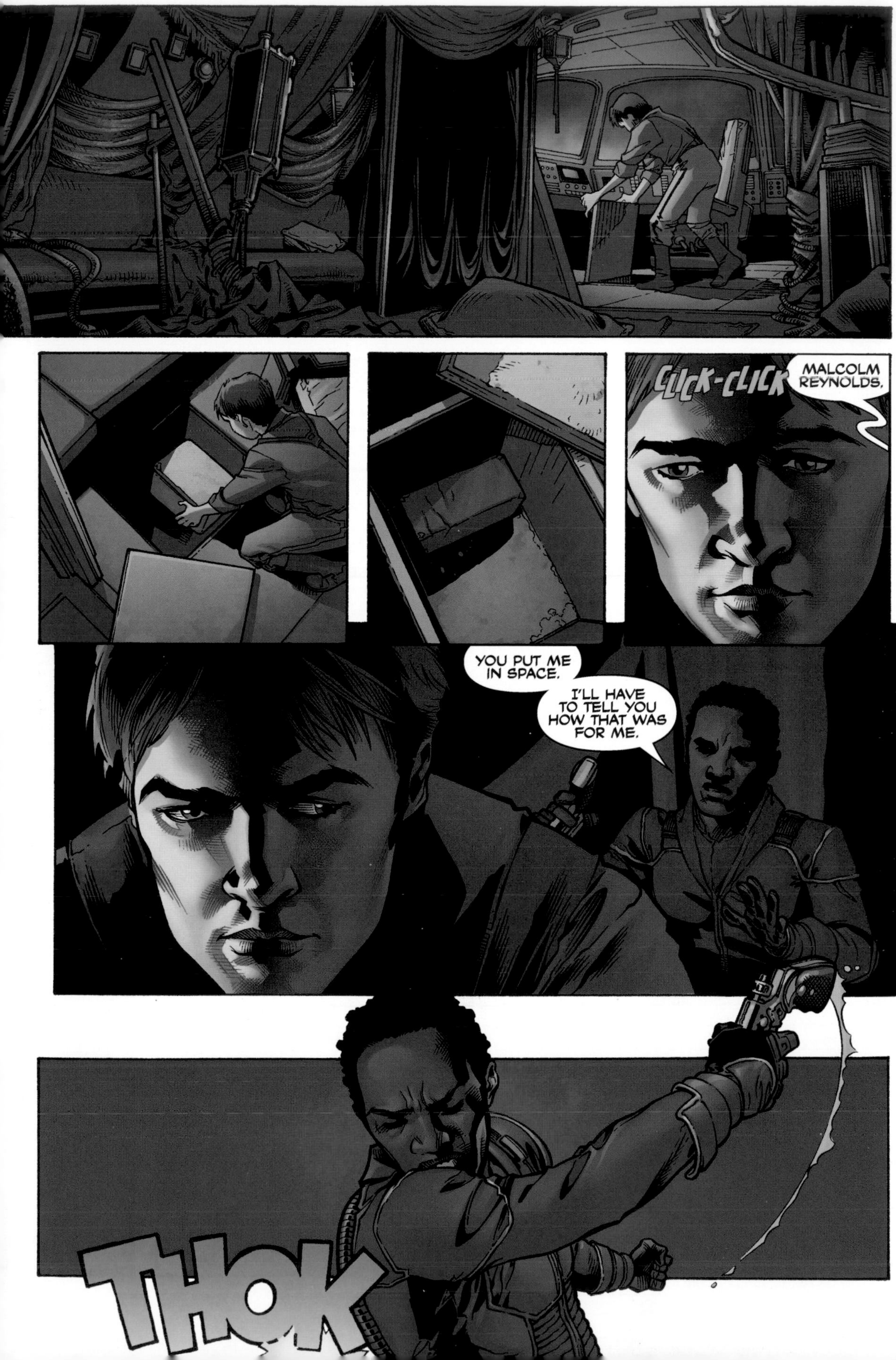
CLICK-CLICK
MALCOLM REYNOLDS.
YOU PUT ME IN SPACE.
I'LL HAVE TO TELL YOU HOW THAT WAS FOR ME.
THOK

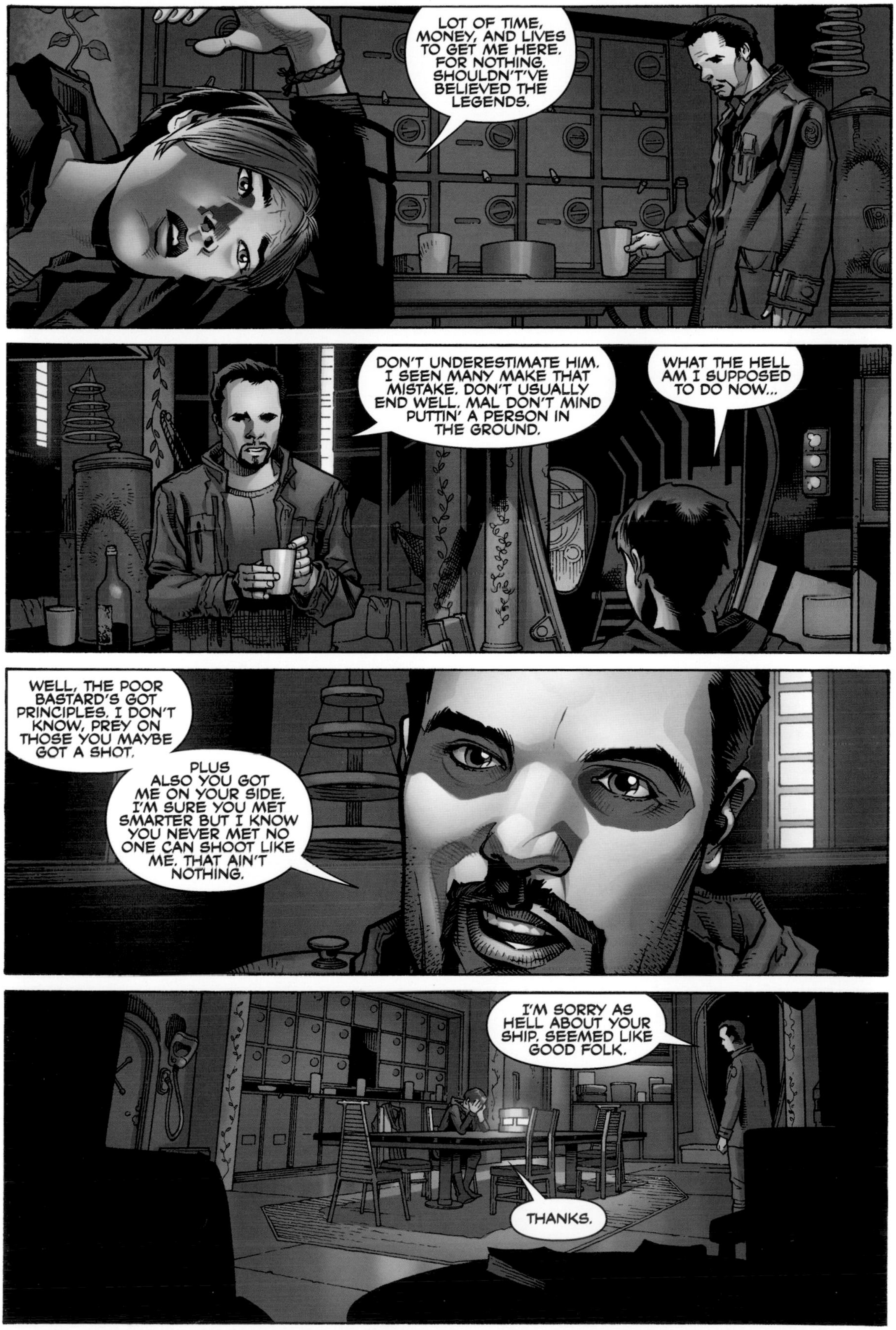
LOT OF TIME, MONEY, AND LIVES TO GET ME HERE. FOR NOTHING. SHOULDN'T'VE BELIEVED THE LEGENDS.
DON'T UNDERESTIMATE HIM. I SEEN MANY MAKE THAT MISTAKE. DON'T USUALLY END WELL. MAL DON'T MIND PUTTIN' A PERSON IN THE GROUND.
WHAT THE HELL AM I SUPPOSED TO DO NOW...
WELL, THE POOR BASTARD'S GOT PRINCIPLES. I DON'T KNOW, PREY ON THOSE YOU MAYBE GOT A SHOT.
PLUS ALSO YOU GOT ME ON YOUR SIDE. I'M SURE YOU MET SMARTER BUT I KNOW YOU NEVER MET NO ONE CAN SHOOT LIKE ME. THAT AIN'T NOTHING.
I'M SORRY AS HELL ABOUT YOUR SHIP. SEEMED LIKE GOOD FOLK.
THANKS.

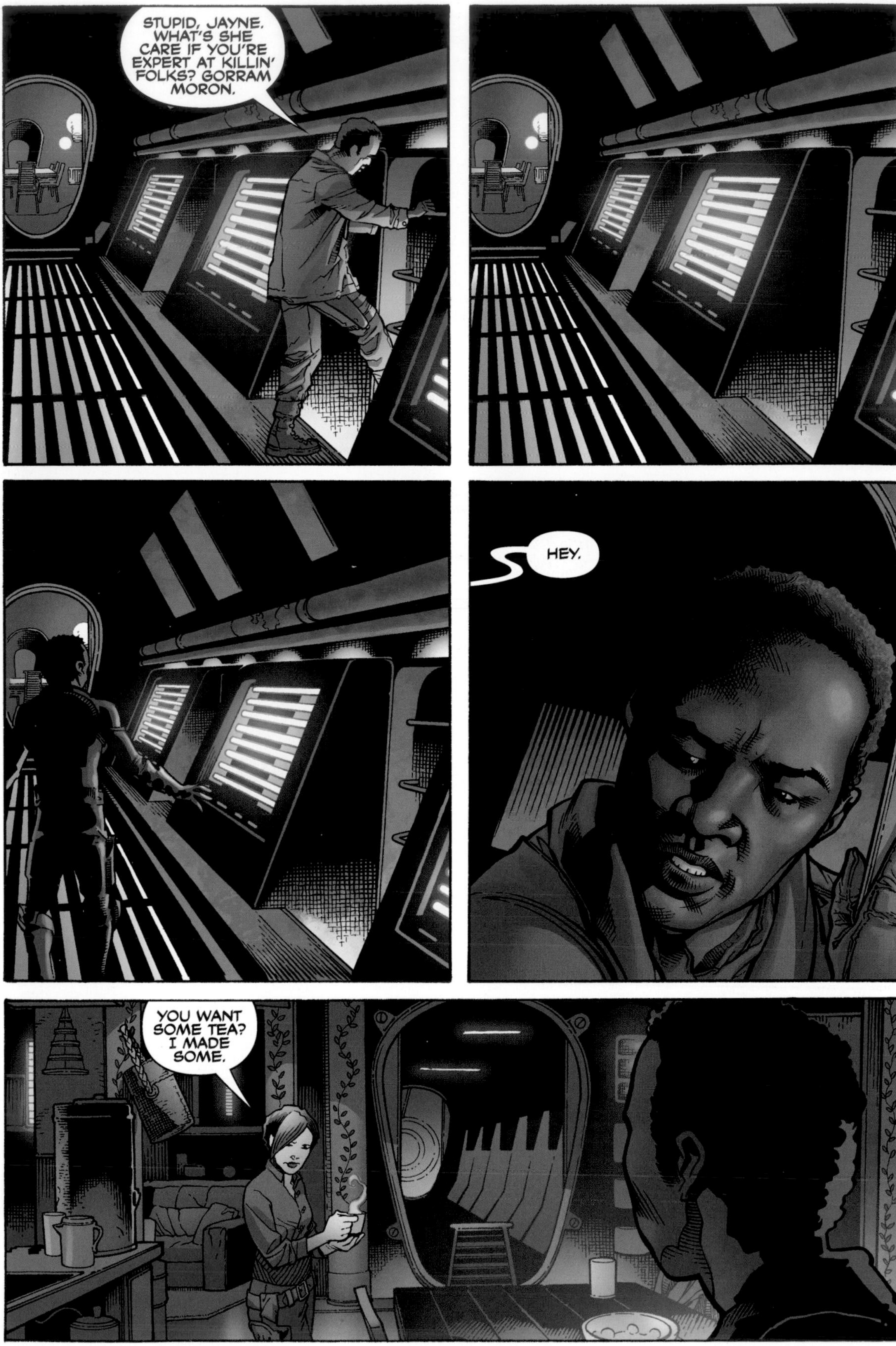
STUPID, JAYNE. WHAT'S SHE CARE IF YOU'RE EXPERT AT KILLIN' FOLKS? GORRAM MORON.
HEY.
YOU WANT SOME TEA? I MADE SOME.

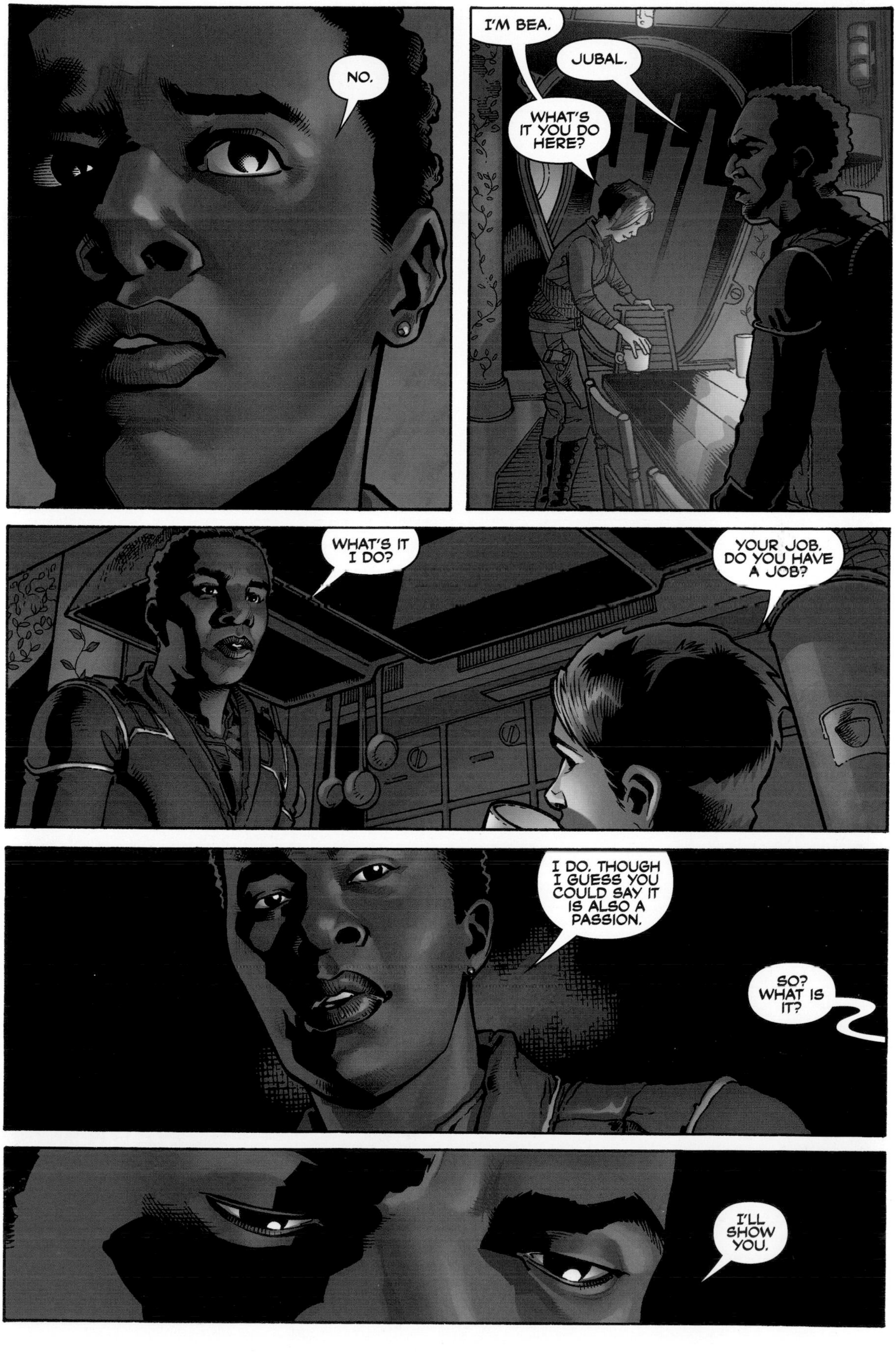
NO.
I'M BEA.
JUBAL.
WHAT'S IT YOU DO HERE?
WHAT'S IT I DO?
YOUR JOB. DO YOU HAVE A JOB?
I DO. THOUGH I GUESS YOU COULD SAY IT IS ALSO A PASSION.
SO? WHAT IS IT?
I'LL SHOW YOU.

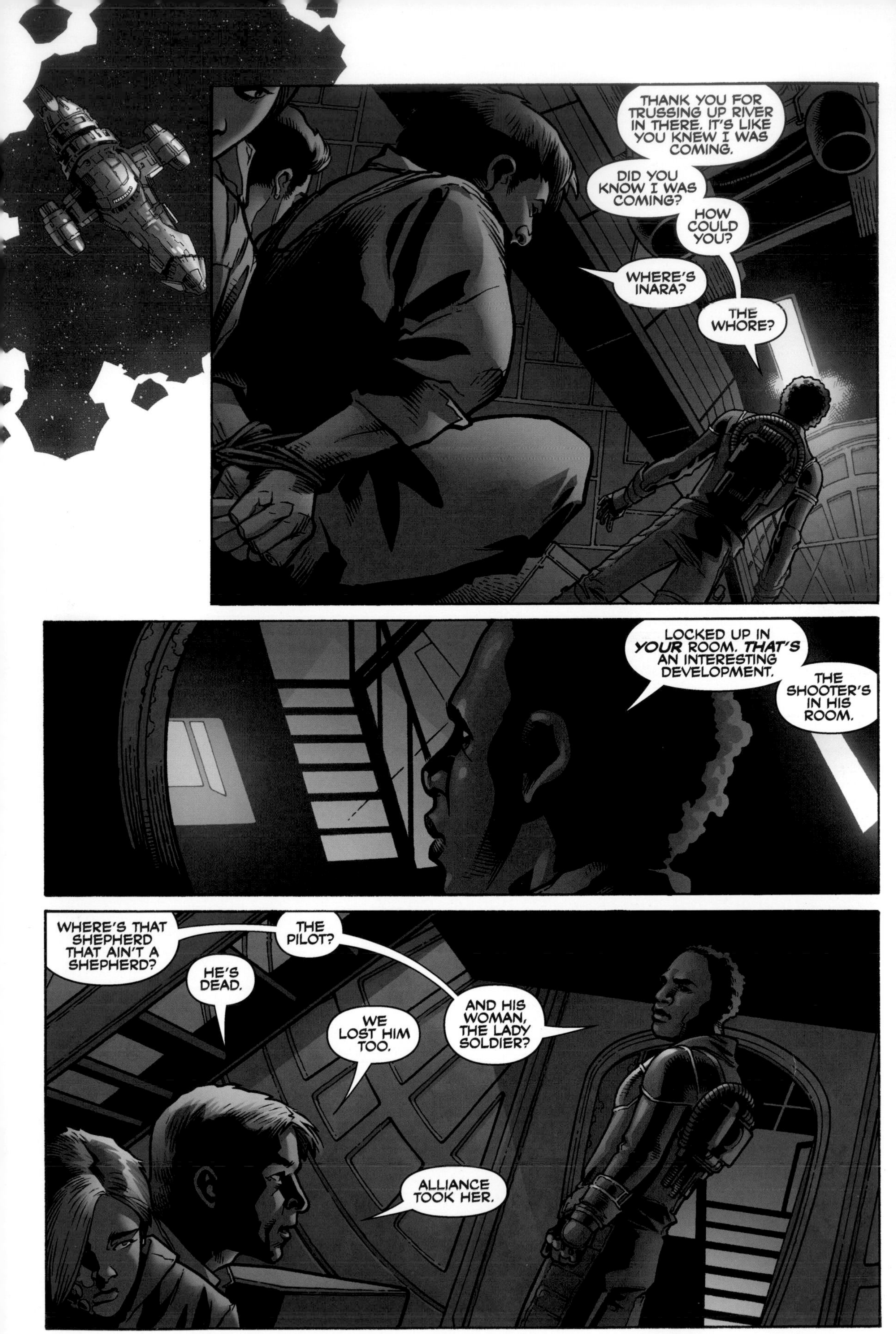
THANK YOU FOR TRUSSING UP RIVER IN THERE. IT'S LIKE YOU KNEW I WAS COMING.
DID YOU KNOW I WAS COMING?
HOW COULD YOU?
WHERE'S INARA?
THE WHORE?
LOCKED UP IN *YOUR* ROOM. *THAT'S* AN INTERESTING DEVELOPMENT.
THE SHOOTER'S IN HIS ROOM.
WHERE'S THAT SHEPHERD THAT AIN'T A SHEPHERD?
HE'S DEAD.
THE PILOT?
WE LOST HIM TOO.
AND HIS WOMAN, THE LADY SOLDIER?
ALLIANCE TOOK HER.

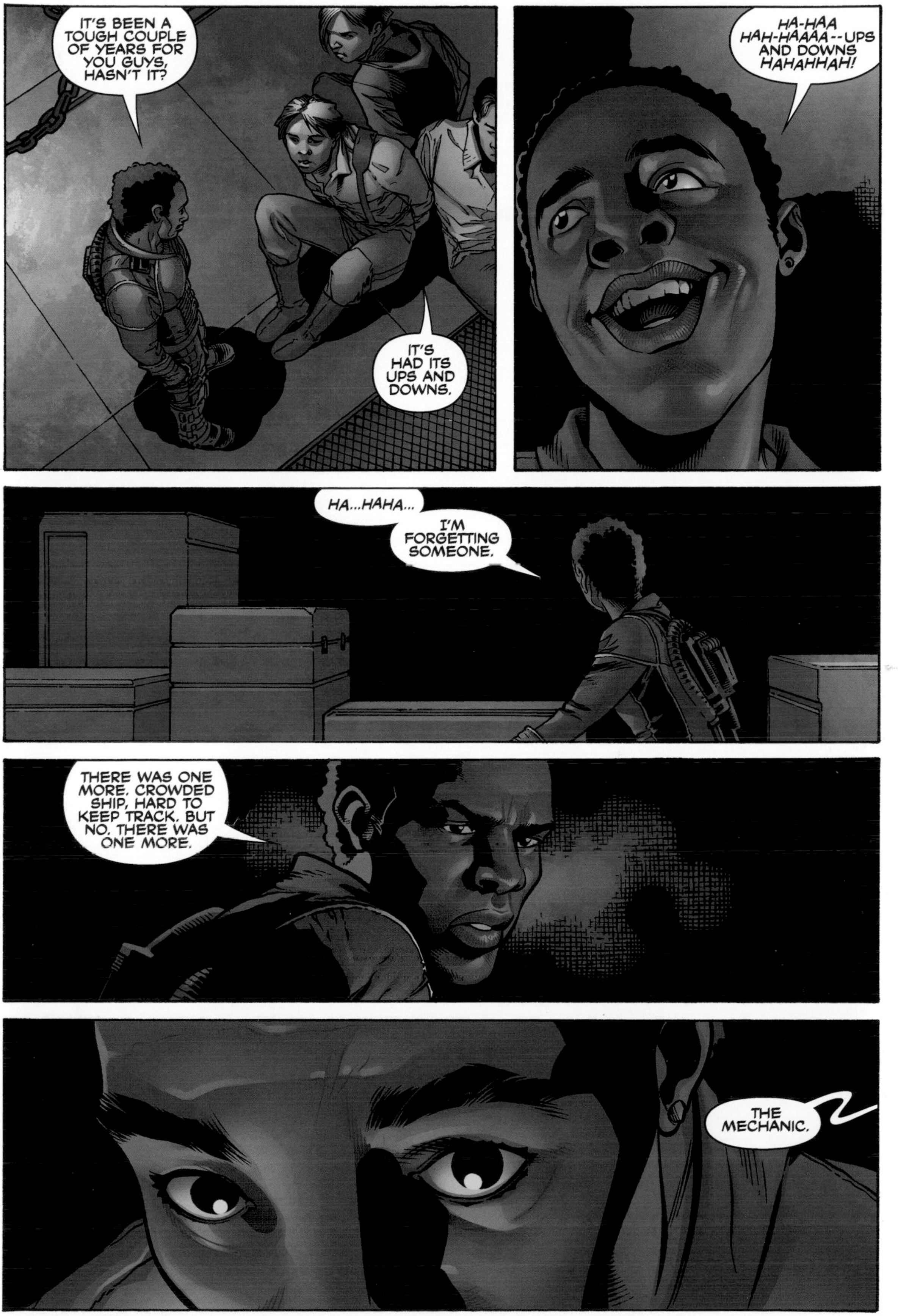
IT'S BEEN A TOUGH COUPLE OF YEARS FOR YOU GUYS, HASN'T IT?
IT'S HAD ITS UPS AND DOWNS.
HA-HAA HAH-HAAAA--UPS AND DOWNS HAHAHHAH!
HA...HAHA...
I'M FORGETTING SOMEONE.
THERE WAS ONE MORE. CROWDED SHIP, HARD TO KEEP TRACK. BUT NO. THERE WAS ONE MORE.
THE MECHANIC.

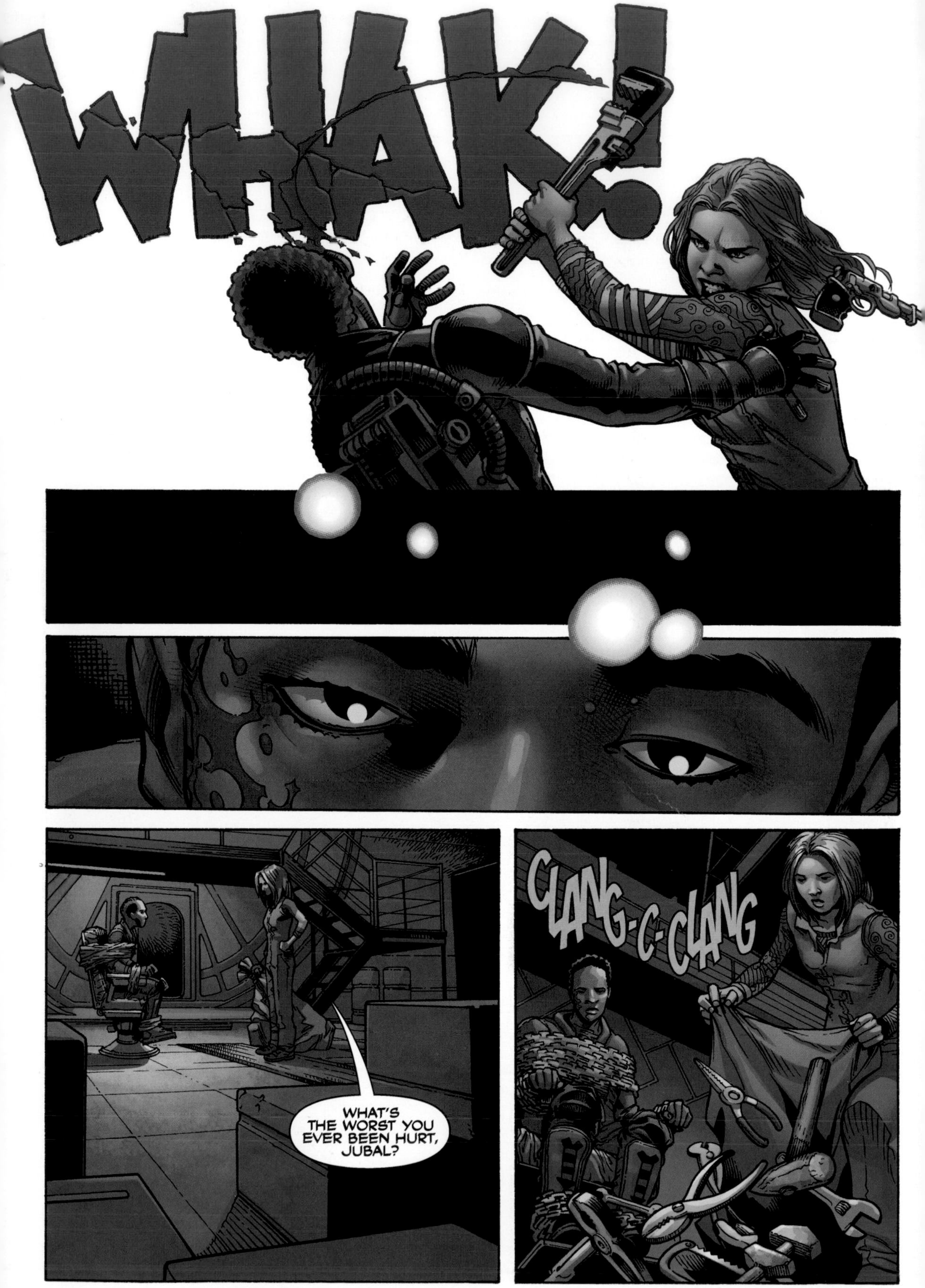
WHAK!
WHAT'S THE WORST YOU EVER BEEN HURT, JUBAL?
CLANG-C-CLANG

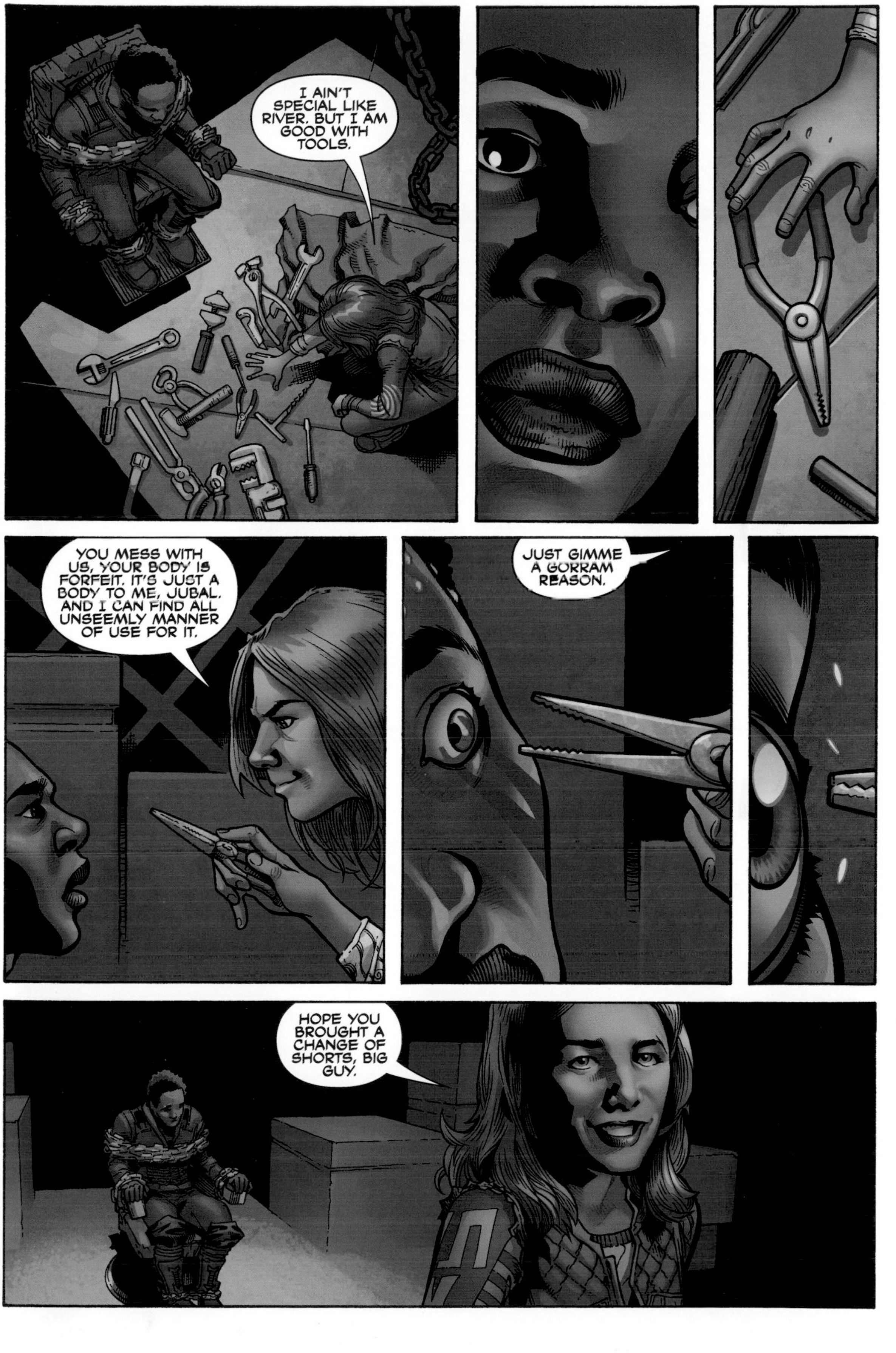
I AIN'T SPECIAL LIKE RIVER. BUT I AM GOOD WITH TOOLS.
YOU MESS WITH US, YOUR BODY IS FORFEIT. IT'S JUST A BODY TO ME, JUBAL. AND I CAN FIND ALL UNSEEMLY MANNER OF USE FOR IT.
JUST GIMME A GORRAM REASON.
HOPE YOU BROUGHT A CHANGE OF SHORTS, BIG GUY.

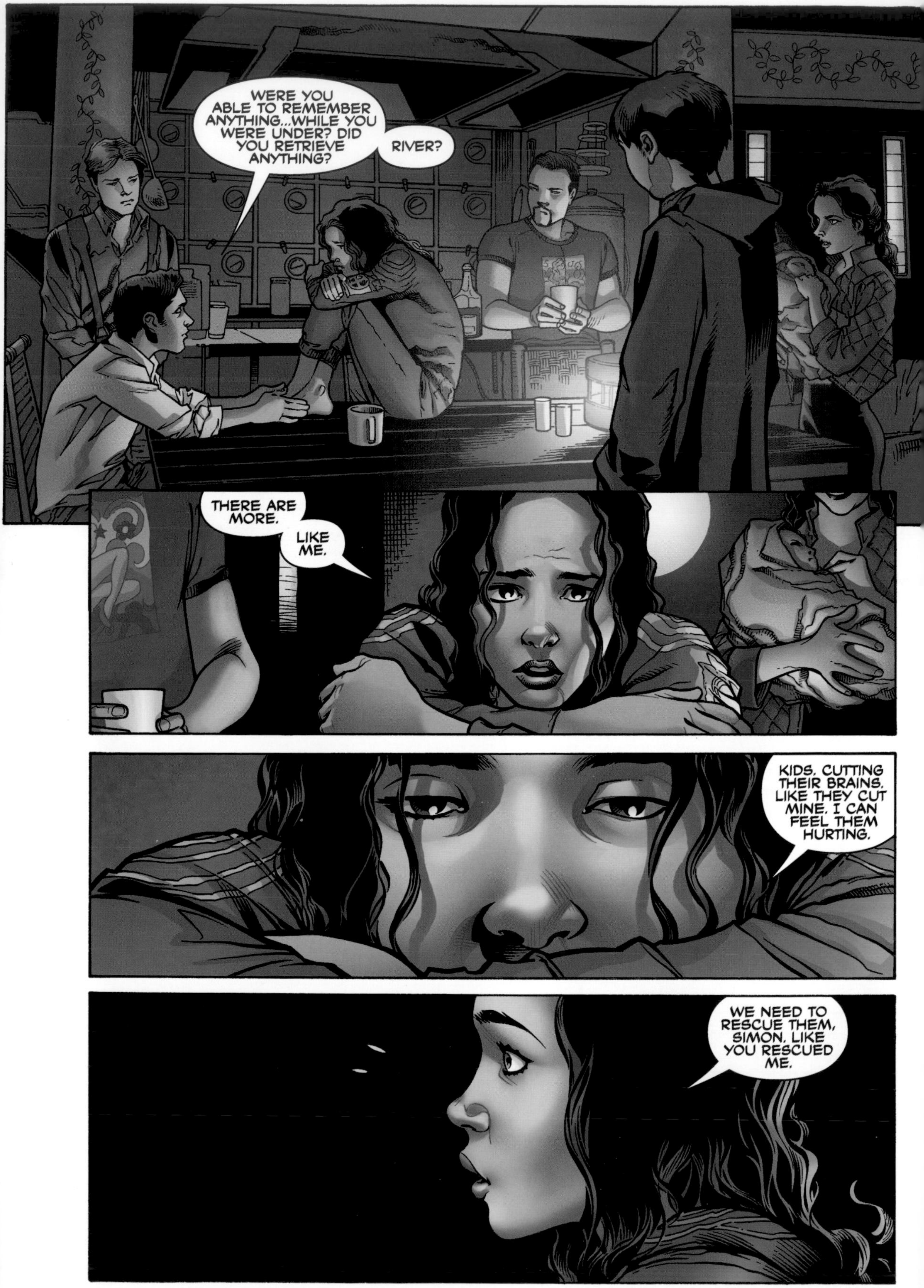
WERE YOU ABLE TO REMEMBER ANYTHING...WHILE YOU WERE UNDER? DID YOU RETRIEVE ANYTHING?
RIVER?
THERE ARE MORE.
LIKE ME.
KIDS. CUTTING THEIR BRAINS. LIKE THEY CUT MINE. I CAN FEEL THEM HURTING.
WE NEED TO RESCUE THEM, SIMON. LIKE YOU RESCUED ME.

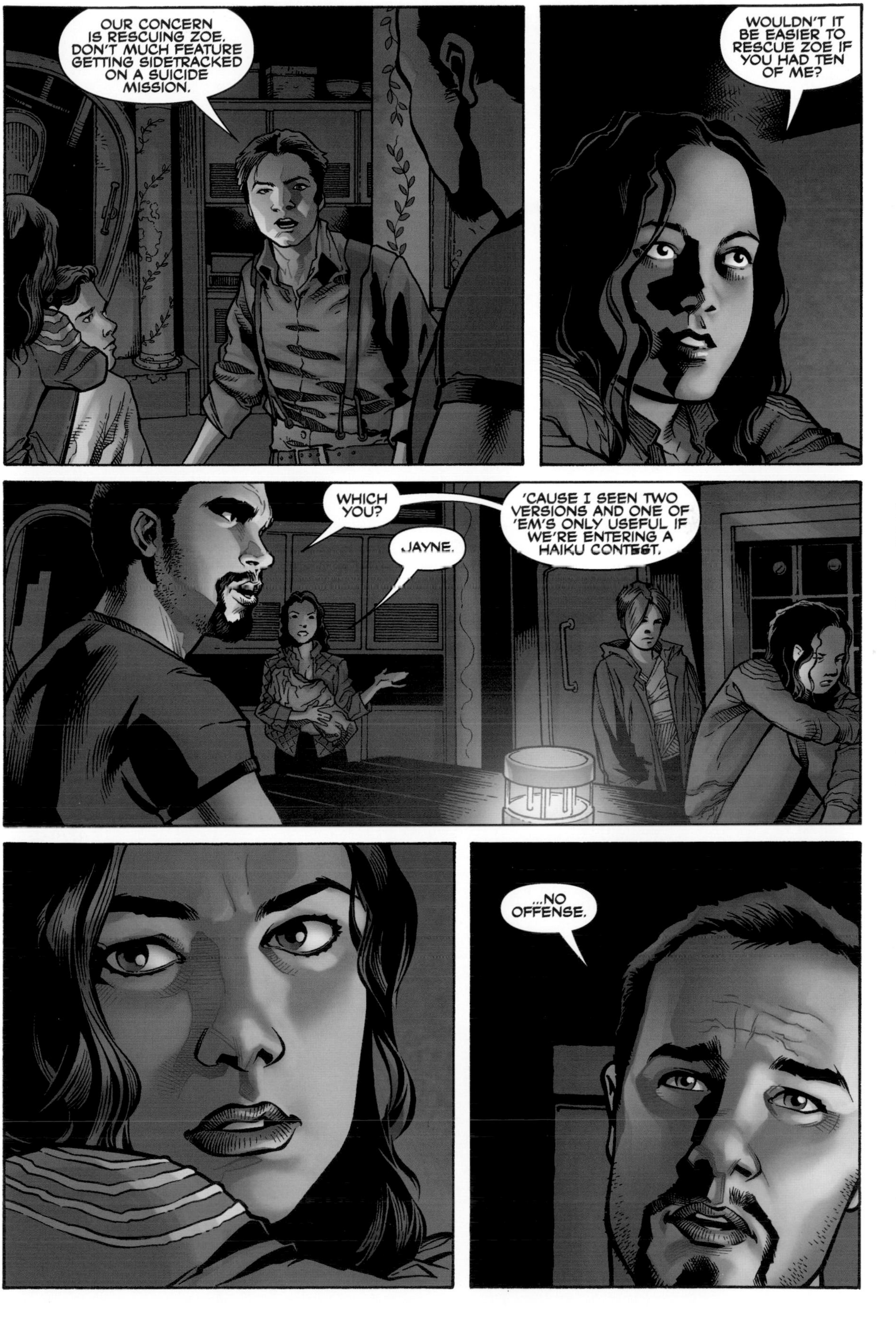
OUR CONCERN IS RESCUING ZOE. DON'T MUCH FEATURE GETTING SIDETRACKED ON A SUICIDE MISSION.
WOULDN'T IT BE EASIER TO RESCUE ZOE IF YOU HAD TEN OF ME?
WHICH YOU?
JAYNE.
'CAUSE I SEEN TWO VERSIONS AND ONE OF 'EM'S ONLY USEFUL IF WE'RE ENTERING A HAIKU CONTEST.
...NO OFFENSE.

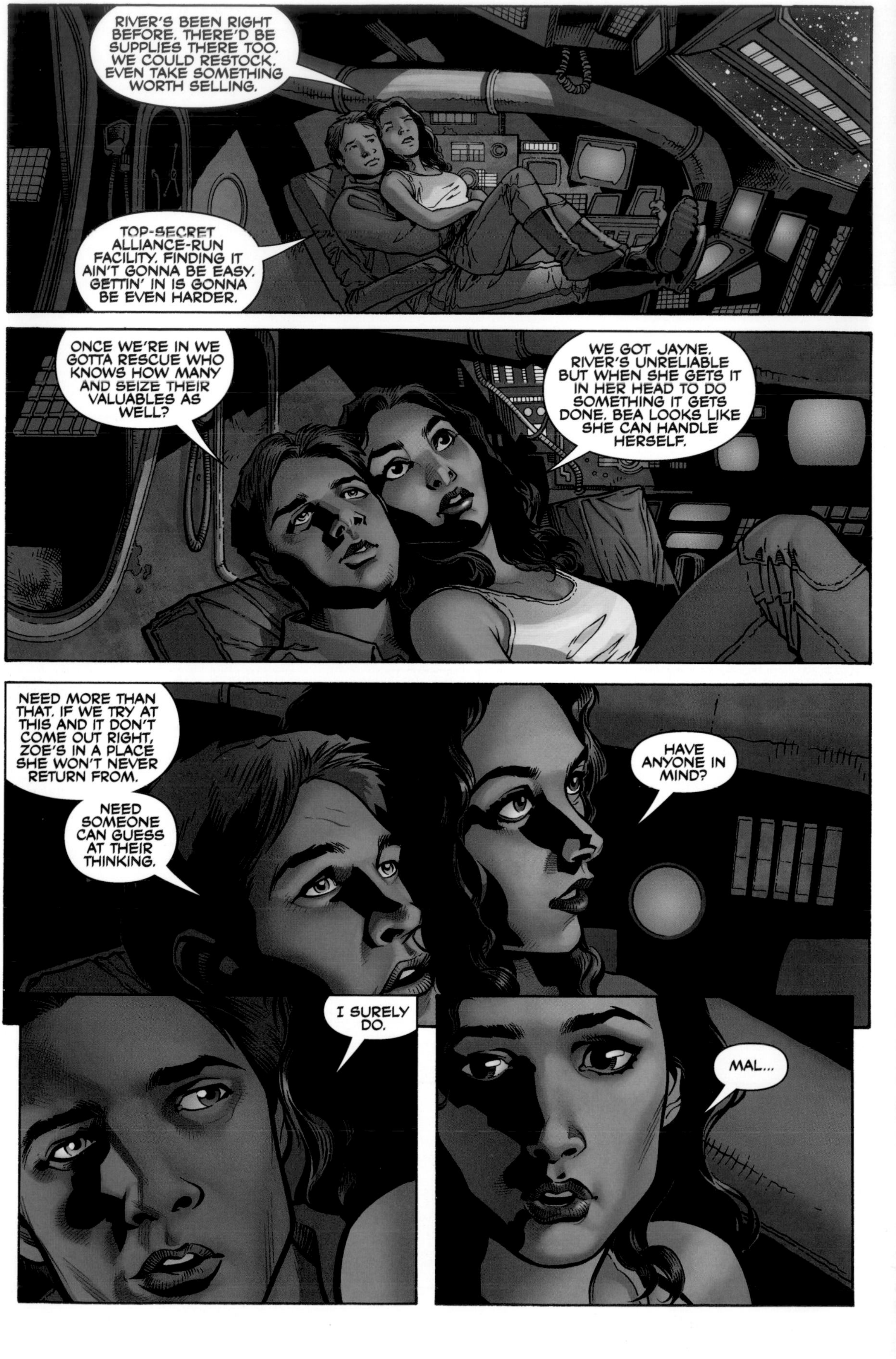
RIVER'S BEEN RIGHT BEFORE. THERE'D BE SUPPLIES THERE TOO. WE COULD RESTOCK. EVEN TAKE SOMETHING WORTH SELLING.
TOP-SECRET ALLIANCE-RUN FACILITY. FINDING IT AIN'T GONNA BE EASY. GETTIN' IN IS GONNA BE EVEN HARDER.
ONCE WE'RE IN WE GOTTA RESCUE WHO KNOWS HOW MANY AND SEIZE THEIR VALUABLES AS WELL?
WE GOT JAYNE. RIVER'S UNRELIABLE BUT WHEN SHE GETS IT IN HER HEAD TO DO SOMETHING IT GETS DONE. BEA LOOKS LIKE SHE CAN HANDLE HERSELF.
NEED MORE THAN THAT. IF WE TRY AT THIS AND IT DON'T COME OUT RIGHT, ZOE'S IN A PLACE SHE WON'T NEVER RETURN FROM.
NEED SOMEONE CAN GUESS AT THEIR THINKING.
HAVE ANYONE IN MIND?
I SURELY DO.
MAL...

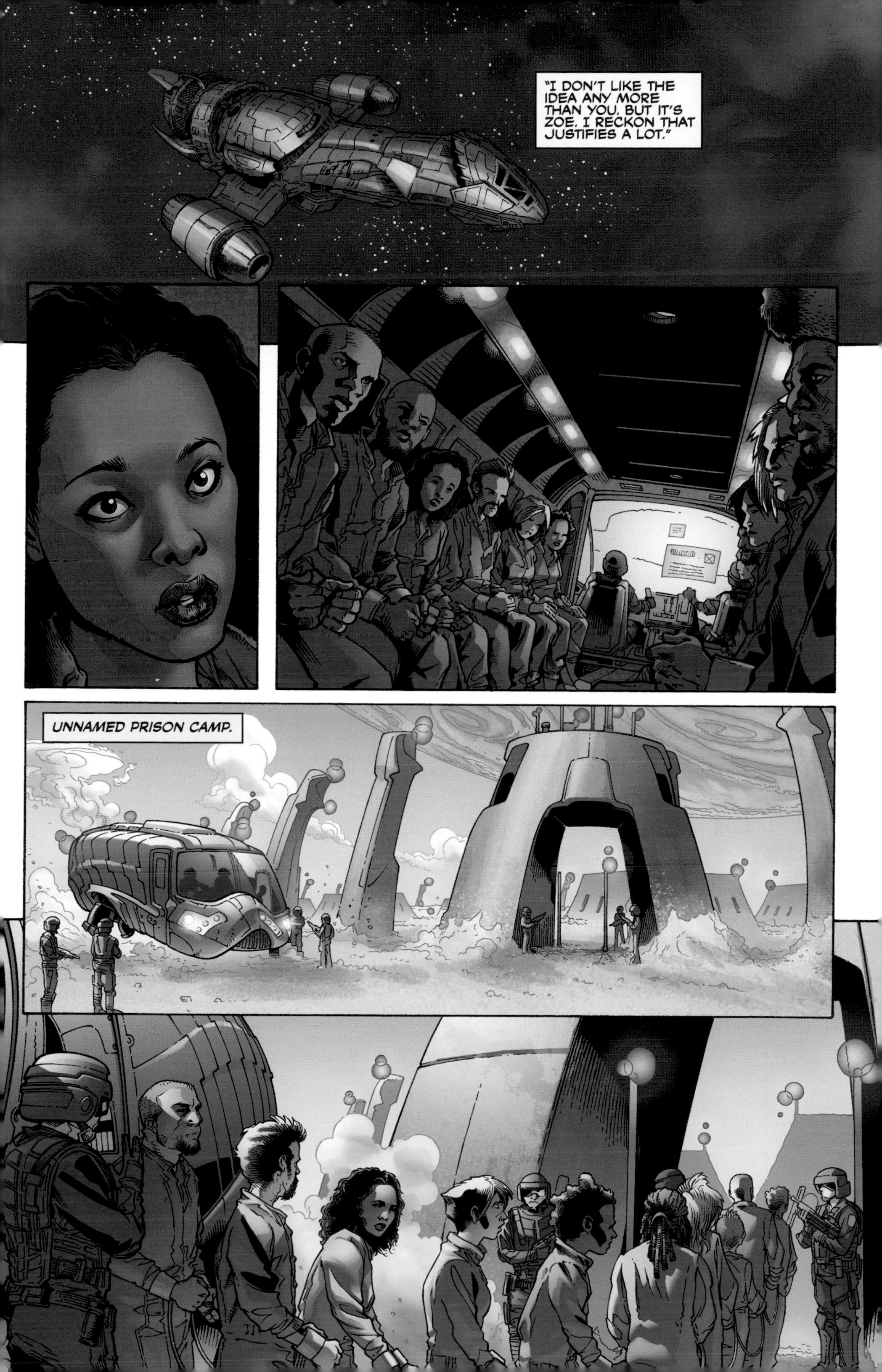
"I DON'T LIKE THE IDEA ANY MORE THAN YOU. BUT IT'S ZOE. I RECKON THAT JUSTIFIES A LOT."
UNNAMED PRISON CAMP.

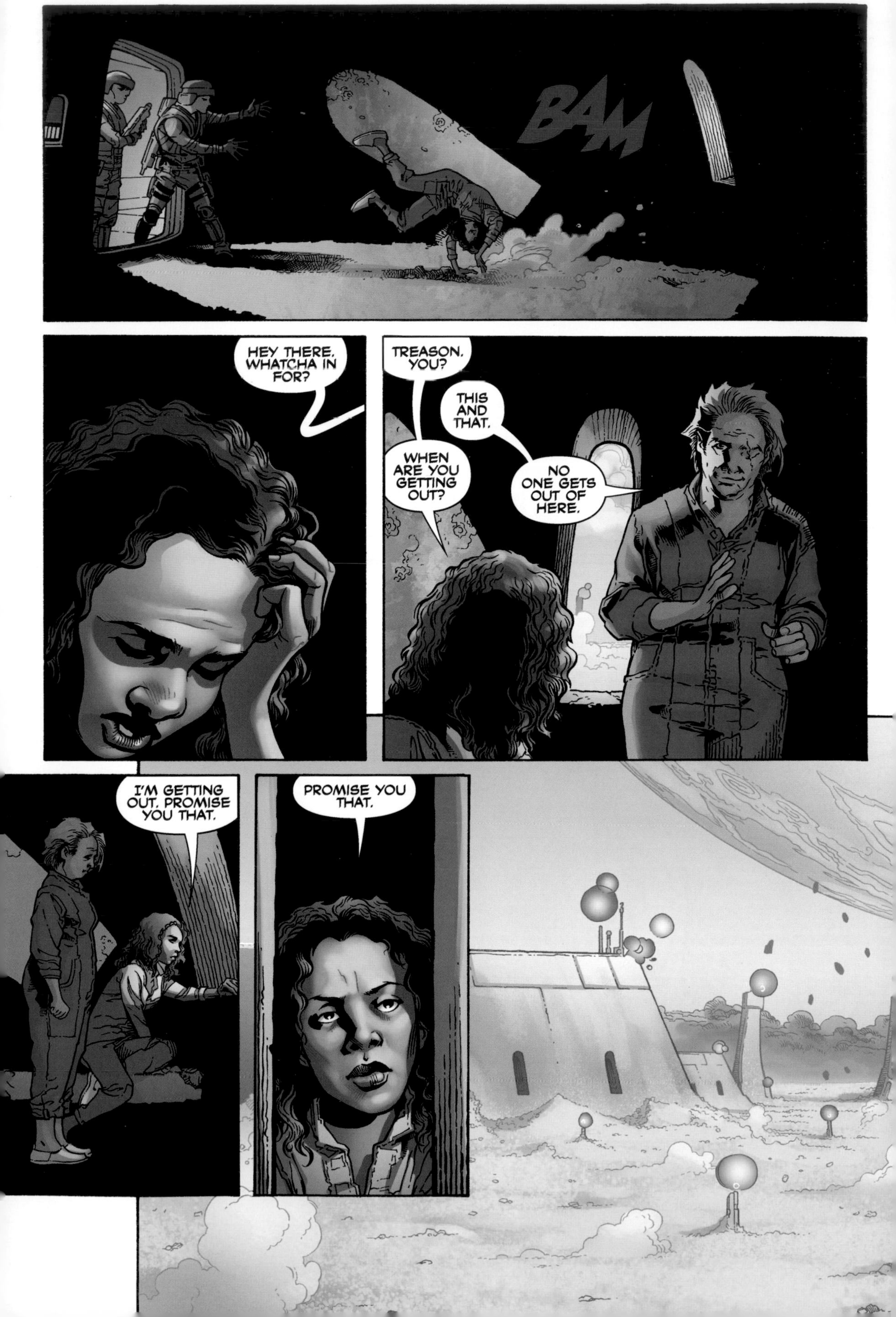
BAM
HEY THERE. WHATCHA IN FOR?
TREASON. YOU?
THIS AND THAT.
WHEN ARE YOU GETTING OUT?
NO ONE GETS OUT OF HERE.
I'M GETTING OUT. PROMISE YOU THAT.
PROMISE YOU THAT.

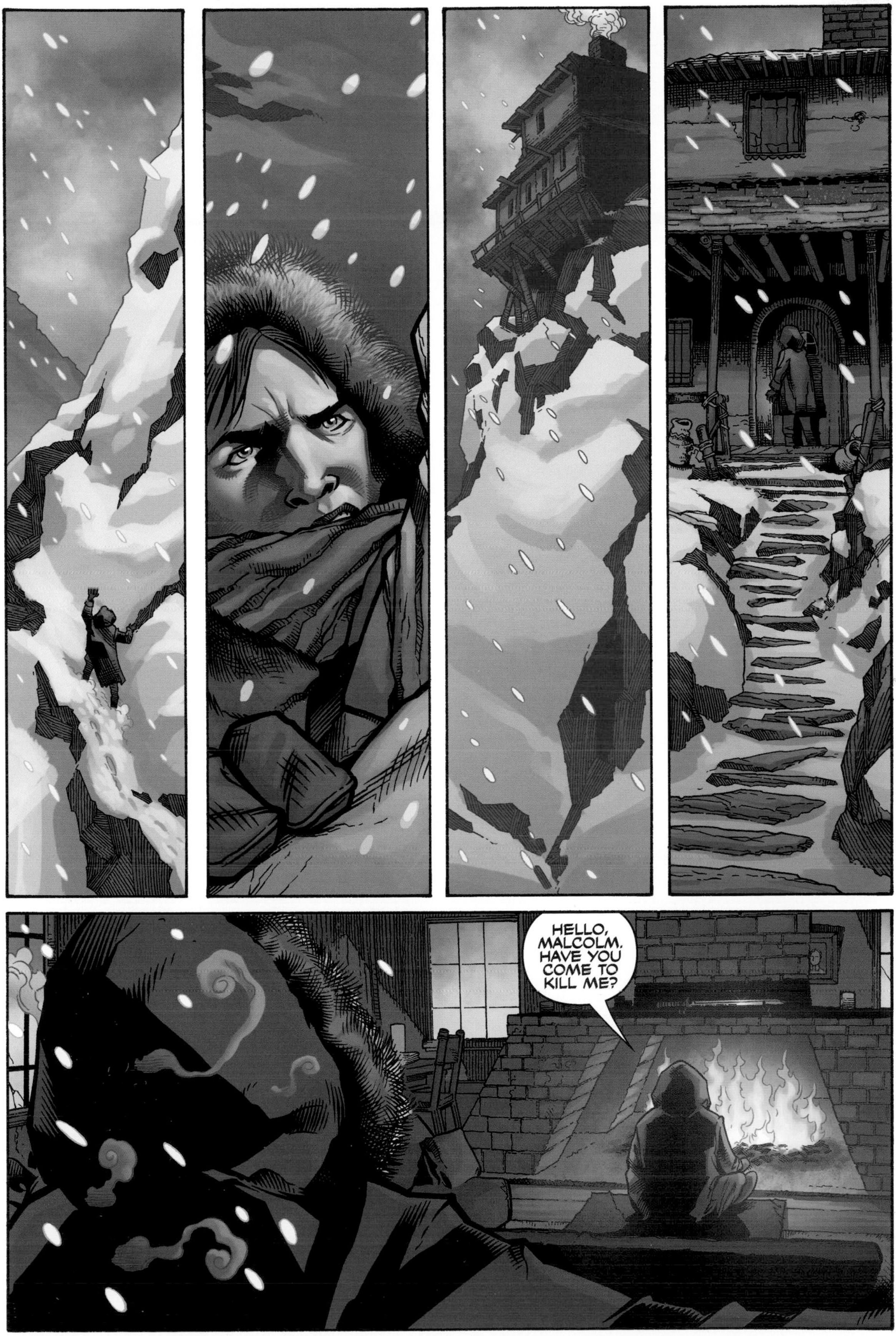
HELLO, MALCOLM. HAVE YOU COME TO KILL ME?

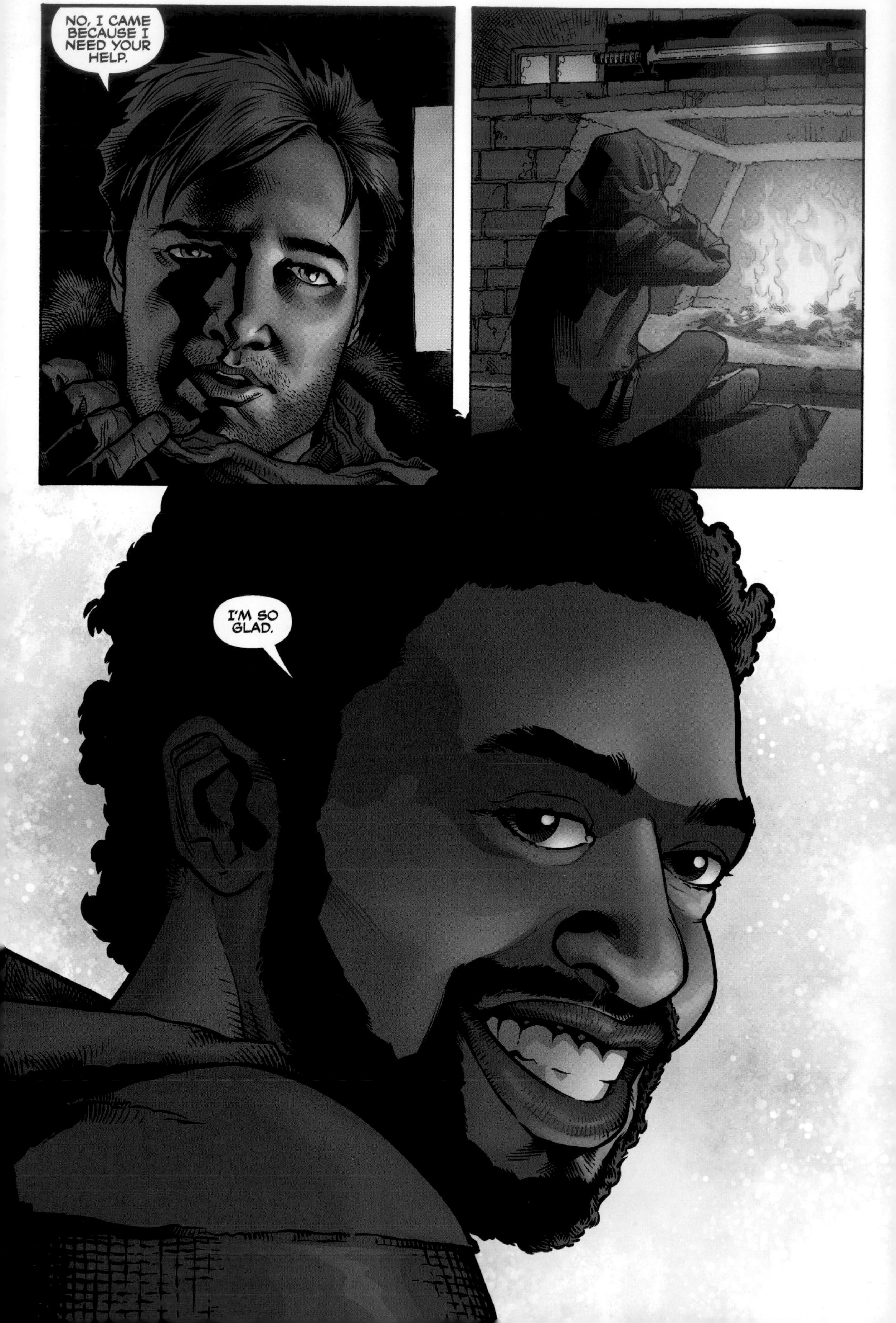
NO, I CAME BECAUSE I NEED YOUR HELP.
I'M SO GLAD.

CHAPTER FOUR

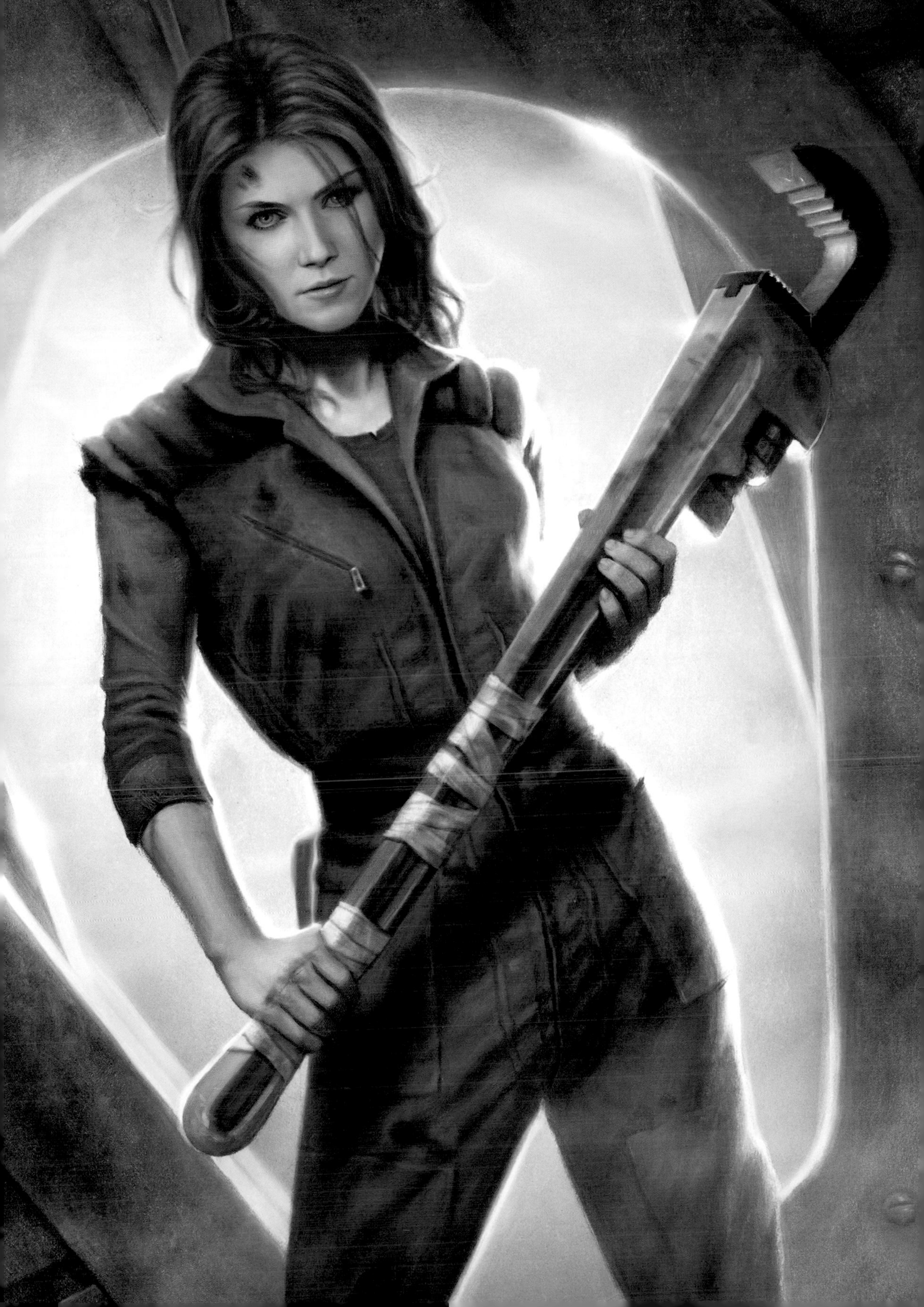

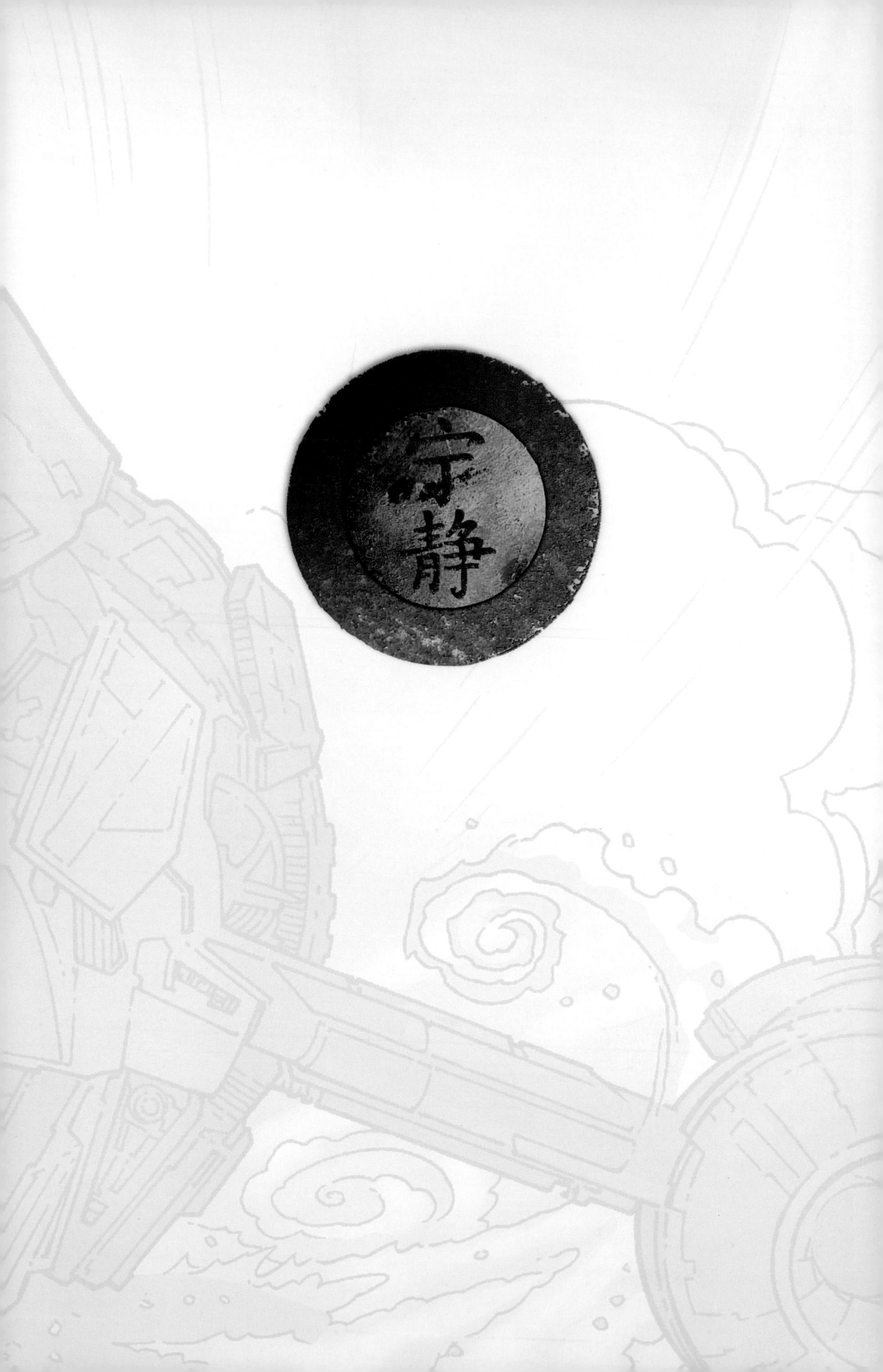
守静

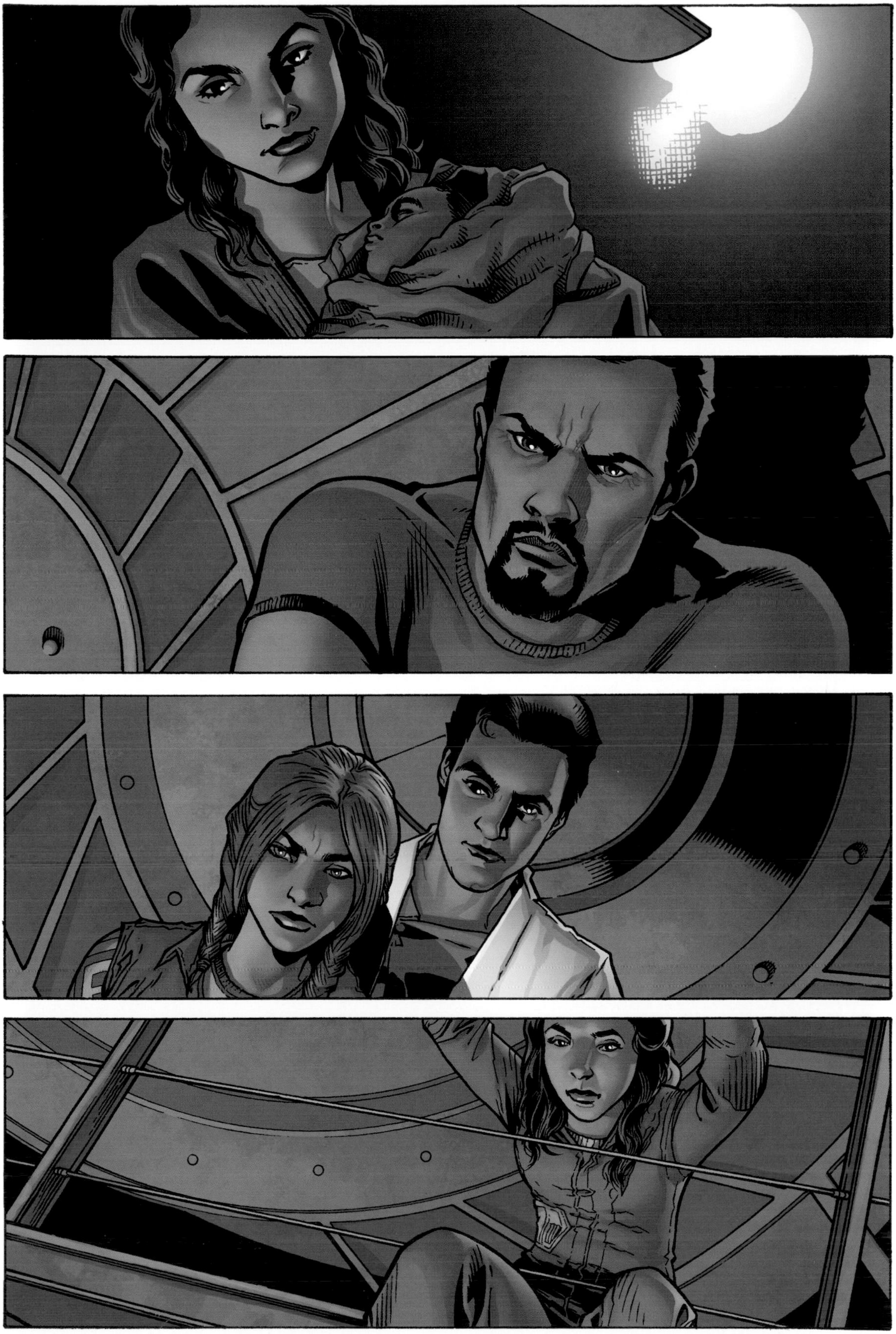

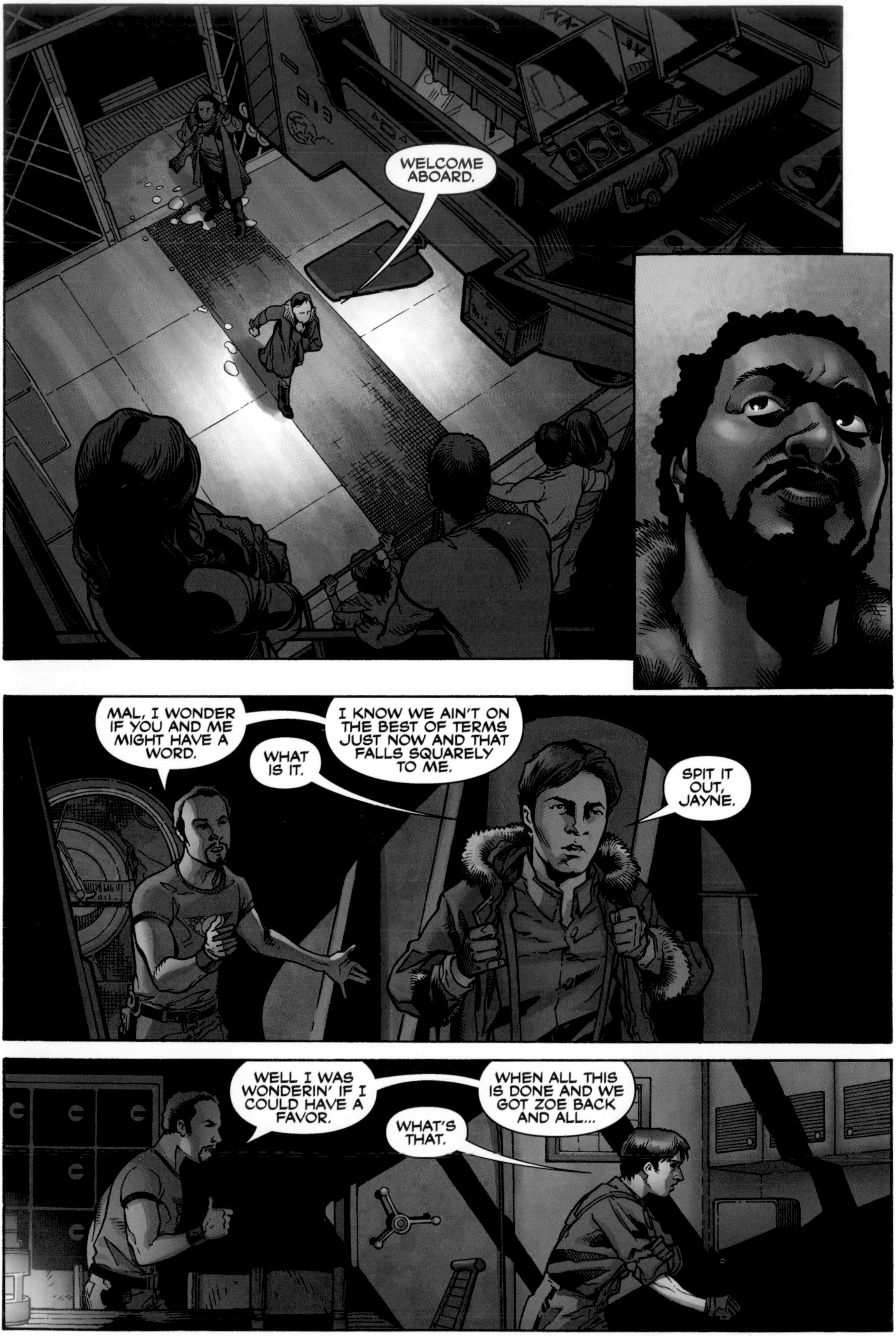
WELCOME ABOARD.
MAL, I WONDER IF YOU AND ME MIGHT HAVE A WORD.
WHAT IS IT.
I KNOW WE AIN'T ON THE BEST OF TERMS JUST NOW AND THAT FALLS SQUARELY TO ME.
SPIT IT OUT, JAYNE.
WELL I WAS WONDERIN' IF I COULD HAVE A FAVOR.
WHAT'S THAT.
WHEN ALL THIS IS DONE AND WE GOT ZOE BACK AND ALL...

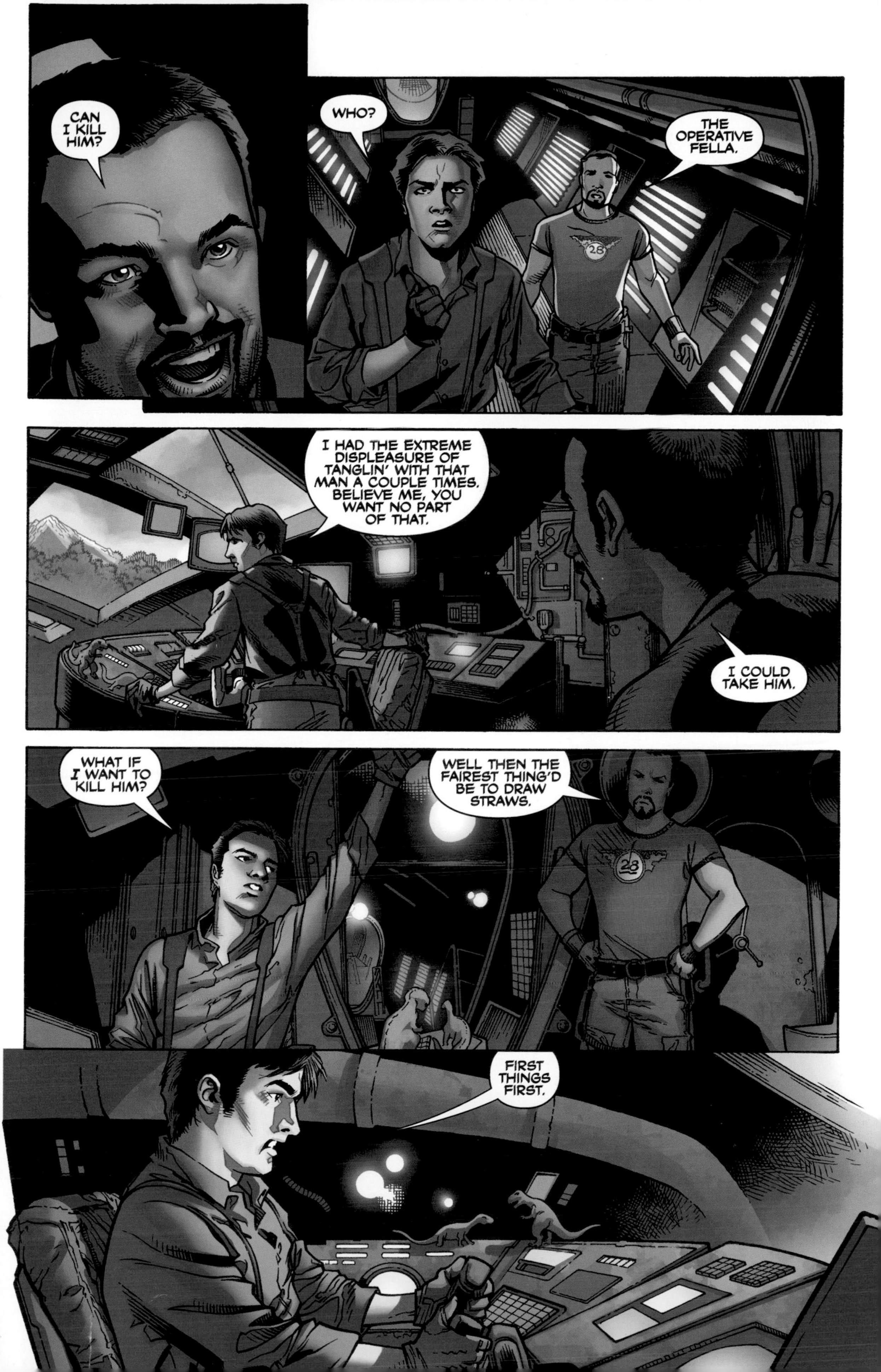
CAN I KILL HIM?
WHO?
THE OPERATIVE FELLA.
I HAD THE EXTREME DISPLEASURE OF TANGLIN' WITH THAT MAN A COUPLE TIMES. BELIEVE ME, YOU WANT NO PART OF THAT.
I COULD TAKE HIM.
WHAT IF I WANT TO KILL HIM?
WELL THEN THE FAIREST THING'D BE TO DRAW STRAWS.
FIRST THINGS FIRST.

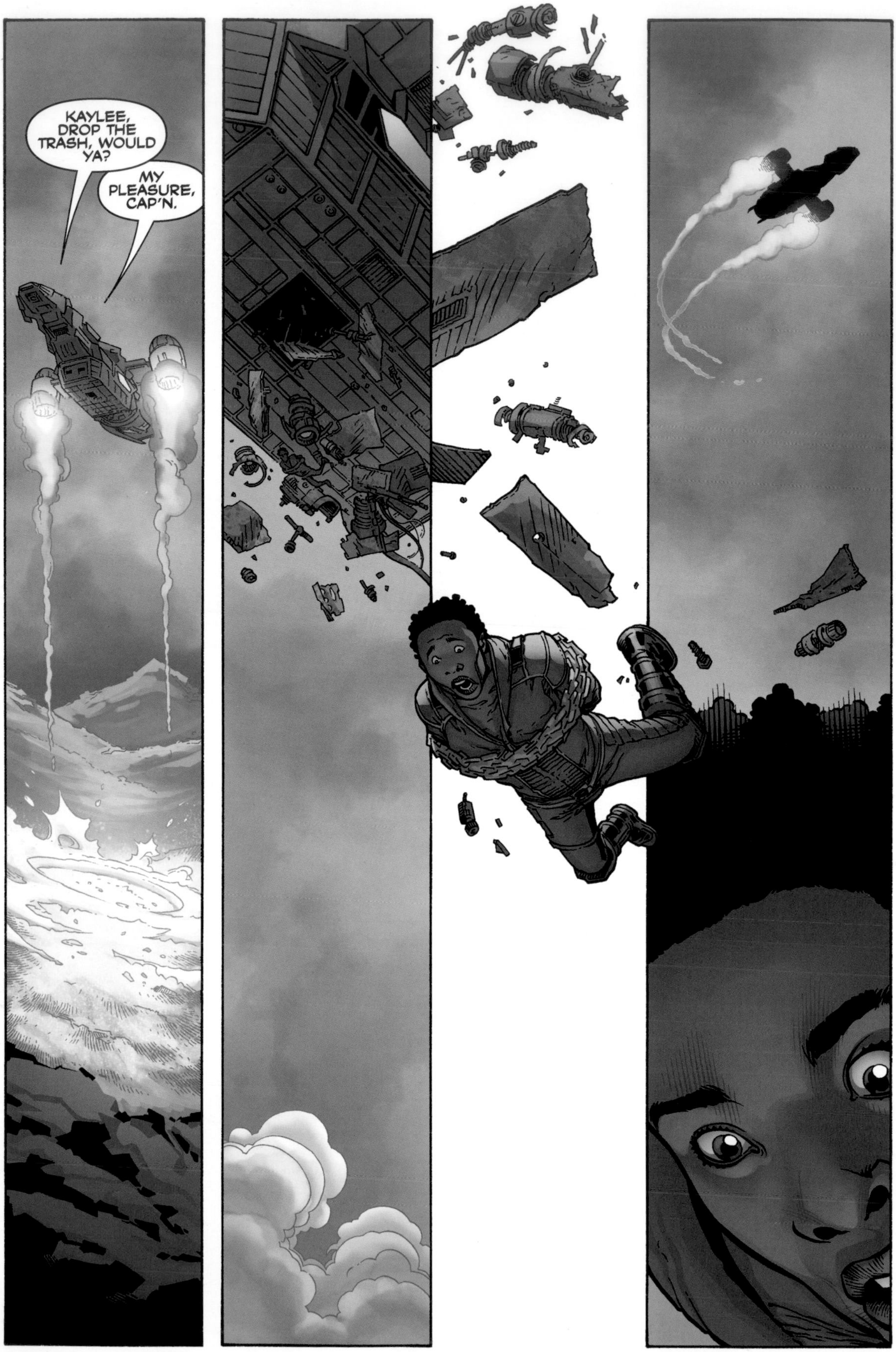
KAYLEE, DROP THE TRASH, WOULD YA?
MY PLEASURE, CAP'N.

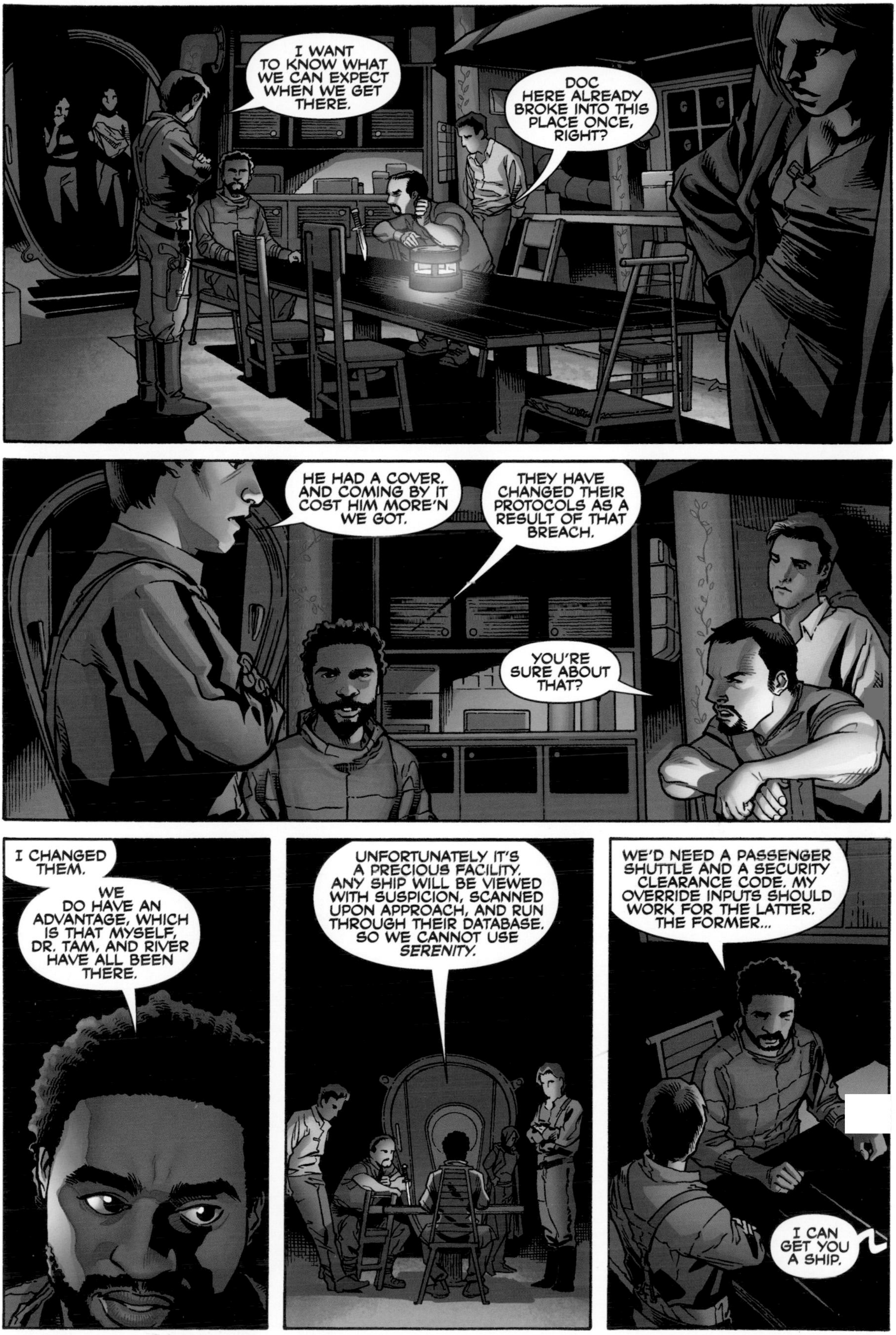
I WANT TO KNOW WHAT WE CAN EXPECT WHEN WE GET THERE.
DOC HERE ALREADY BROKE INTO THIS PLACE ONCE, RIGHT?
HE HAD A COVER. AND COMING BY IT COST HIM MORE'N WE GOT.
THEY HAVE CHANGED THEIR PROTOCOLS AS A RESULT OF THAT BREACH.
YOU'RE SURE ABOUT THAT?
I CHANGED THEM.
WE DO HAVE AN ADVANTAGE, WHICH IS THAT MYSELF, DR. TAM, AND RIVER HAVE ALL BEEN THERE.
UNFORTUNATELY IT'S A PRECIOUS FACILITY. ANY SHIP WILL BE VIEWED WITH SUSPICION, SCANNED UPON APPROACH, AND RUN THROUGH THEIR DATABASE. SO WE CANNOT USE *SERENITY*.
WE'D NEED A PASSENGER SHUTTLE AND A SECURITY CLEARANCE CODE. MY OVERRIDE INPUTS SHOULD WORK FOR THE LATTER. THE FORMER...
I CAN GET YOU A SHIP.

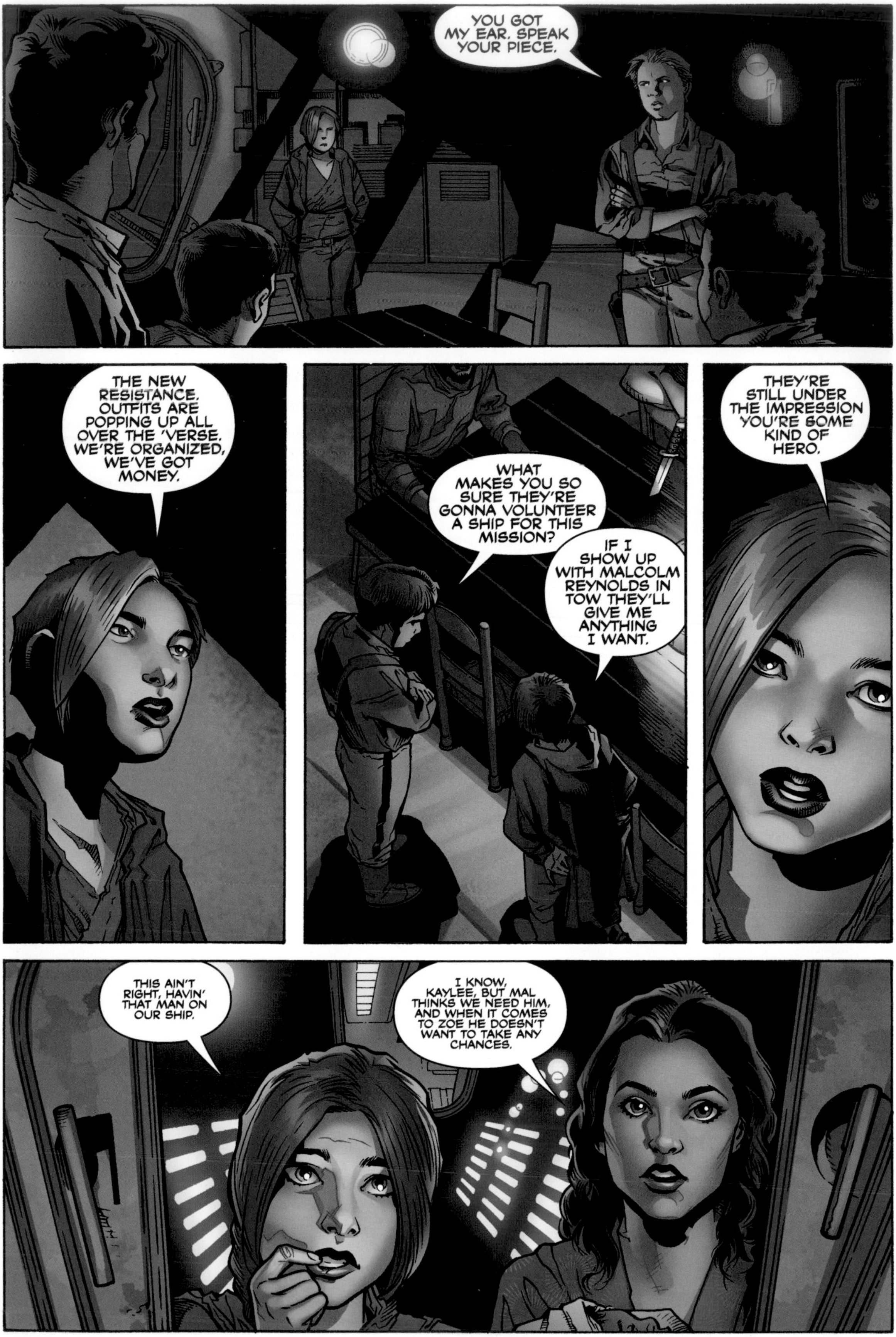
YOU GOT MY EAR. SPEAK YOUR PIECE.
THE NEW RESISTANCE. OUTFITS ARE POPPING UP ALL OVER THE 'VERSE. WE'RE ORGANIZED, WE'VE GOT MONEY.
WHAT MAKES YOU SO SURE THEY'RE GONNA VOLUNTEER A SHIP FOR THIS MISSION?
IF I SHOW UP WITH MALCOLM REYNOLDS IN TOW THEY'LL GIVE ME ANYTHING I WANT.
THEY'RE STILL UNDER THE IMPRESSION YOU'RE SOME KIND OF HERO.
THIS AIN'T RIGHT, HAVIN' THAT MAN ON OUR SHIP.
I KNOW, KAYLEE, BUT MAL THINKS WE NEED HIM, AND WHEN IT COMES TO ZOE HE DOESN'T WANT TO TAKE ANY CHANCES.

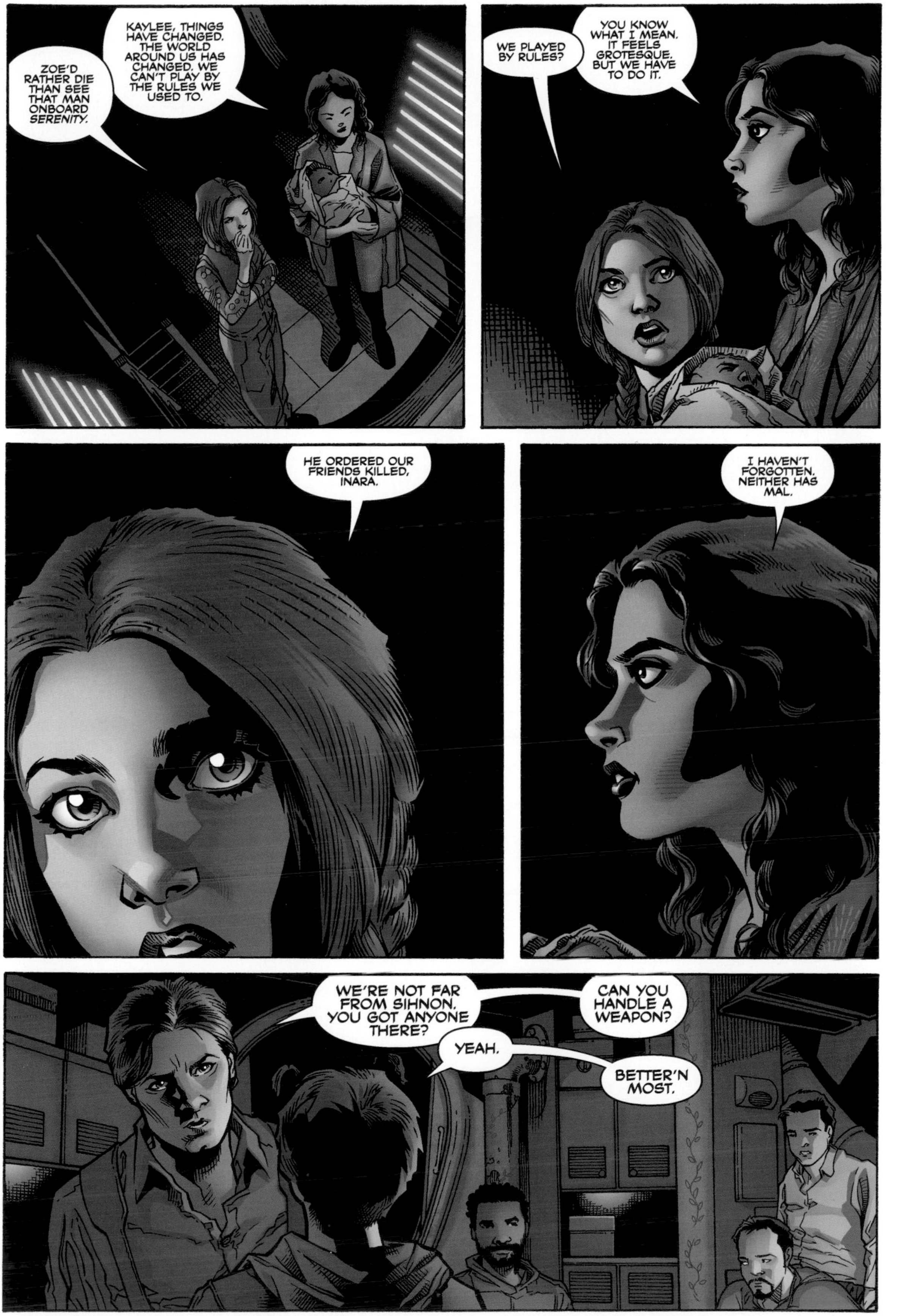

KAYLEE, THINGS HAVE CHANGED. THE WORLD AROUND US HAS CHANGED. WE CAN'T PLAY BY THE RULES WE USED TO.
ZOE'D RATHER DIE THAN SEE THAT MAN ONBOARD *SERENITY*.
WE PLAYED BY RULES?
YOU KNOW WHAT I MEAN. IT FEELS GROTESQUE. BUT WE HAVE TO DO IT.
HE ORDERED OUR FRIENDS KILLED, INARA.
I HAVEN'T FORGOTTEN. NEITHER HAS MAL.
WE'RE NOT FAR FROM SIHNON. YOU GOT ANYONE THERE?
YEAH.
CAN YOU HANDLE A WEAPON?
BETTER'N MOST.

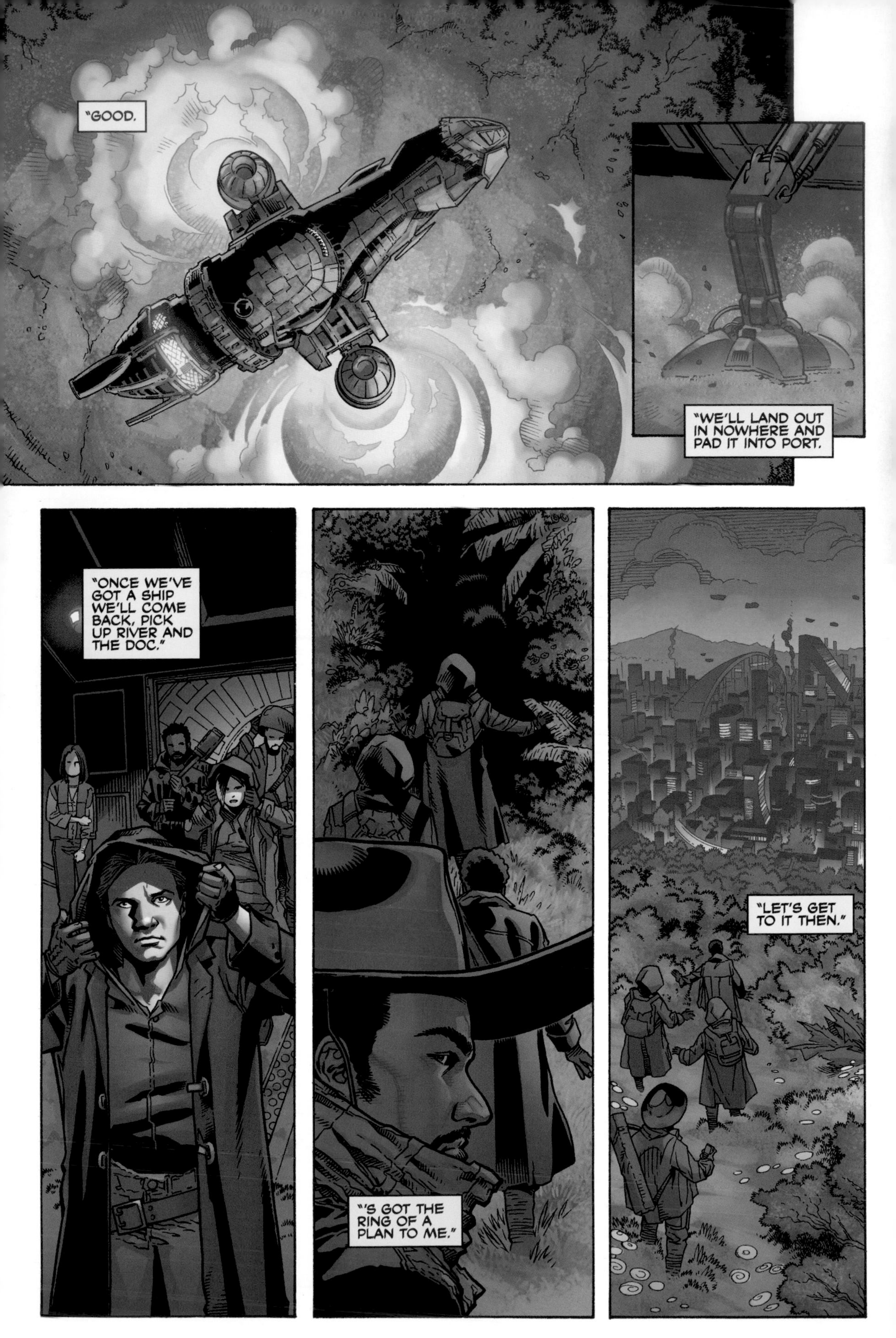
"GOOD.
"WE'LL LAND OUT IN NOWHERE AND PAD IT INTO PORT.
"ONCE WE'VE GOT A SHIP WE'LL COME BACK, PICK UP RIVER AND THE DOC."
"'S GOT THE RING OF A PLAN TO ME."
"LET'S GET TO IT THEN."

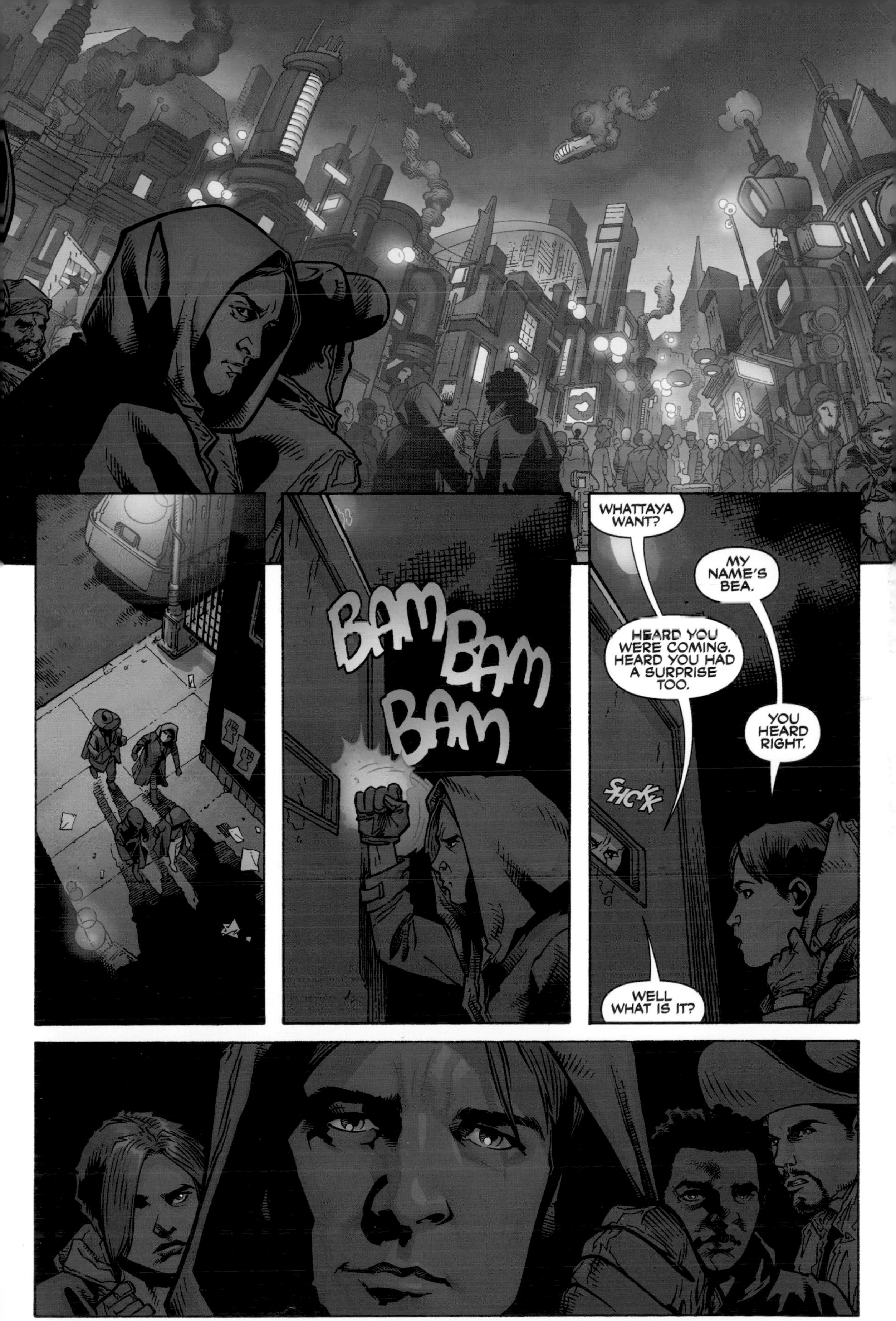
BAM BAM BAM
WHATTAYA WANT?
MY NAME'S BEA.
HEARD YOU WERE COMING. HEARD YOU HAD A SURPRISE TOO.
YOU HEARD RIGHT.
SHCKK
WELL WHAT IS IT?

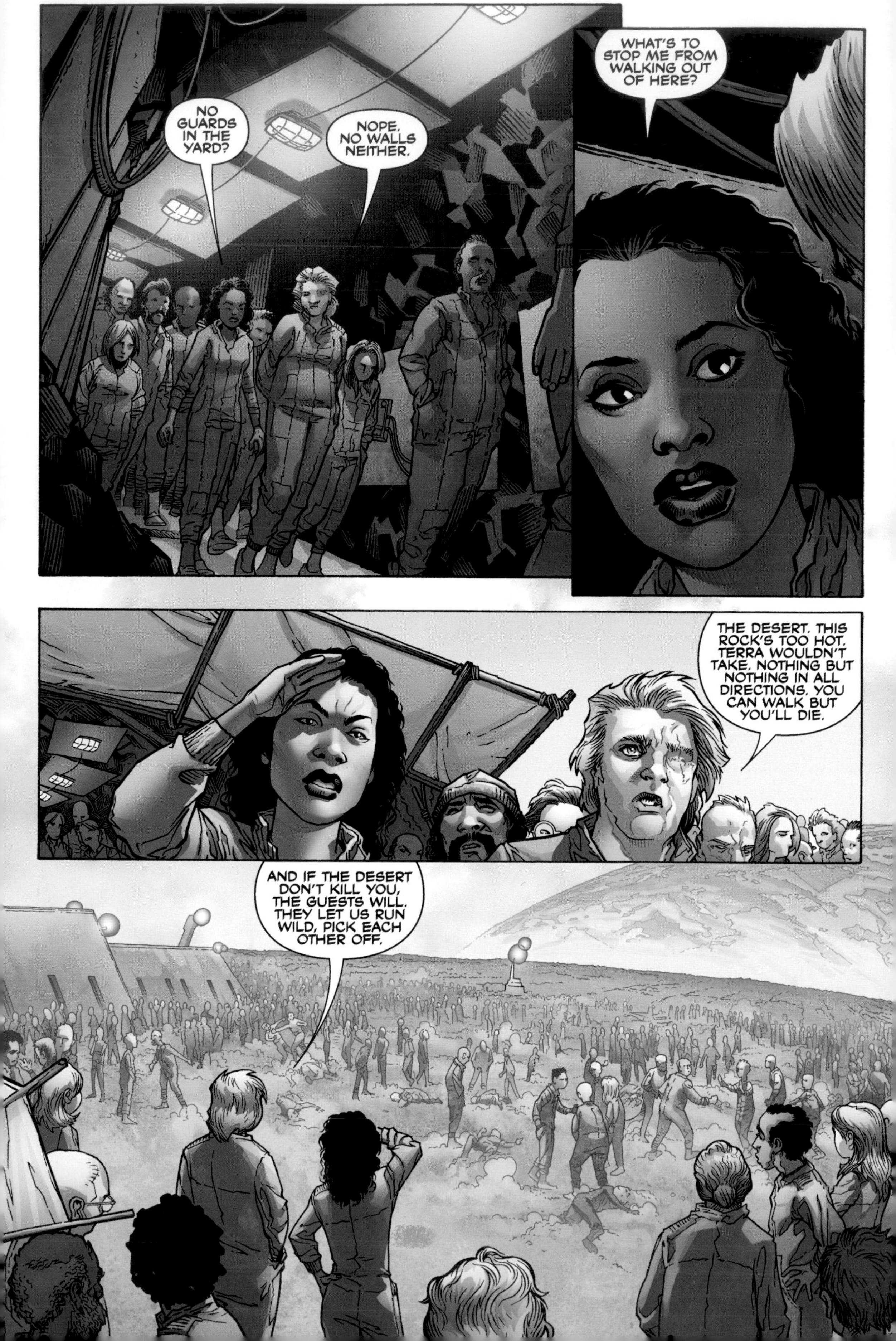
NO GUARDS IN THE YARD?
NOPE. NO WALLS NEITHER.
WHAT'S TO STOP ME FROM WALKING OUT OF HERE?
THE DESERT. THIS ROCK'S TOO HOT. TERRA WOULDN'T TAKE. NOTHING BUT NOTHING IN ALL DIRECTIONS. YOU CAN WALK BUT YOU'LL DIE.
AND IF THE DESERT DON'T KILL YOU, THE GUESTS WILL. THEY LET US RUN WILD, PICK EACH OTHER OFF.

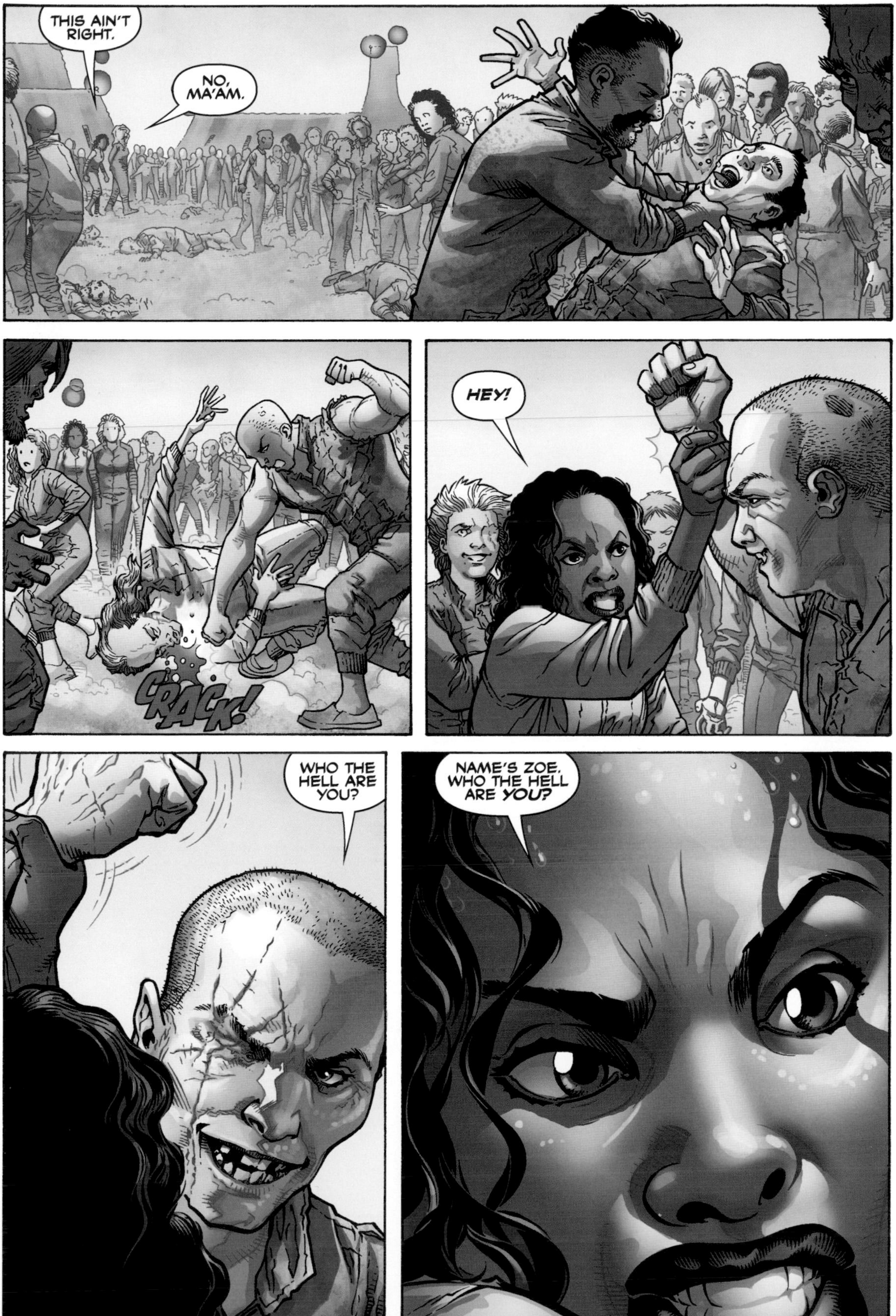

THIS AIN'T RIGHT.
NO, MA'AM.
CRACK!
HEY!
WHO THE HELL ARE YOU?
NAME'S ZOE. WHO THE HELL ARE *YOU?*

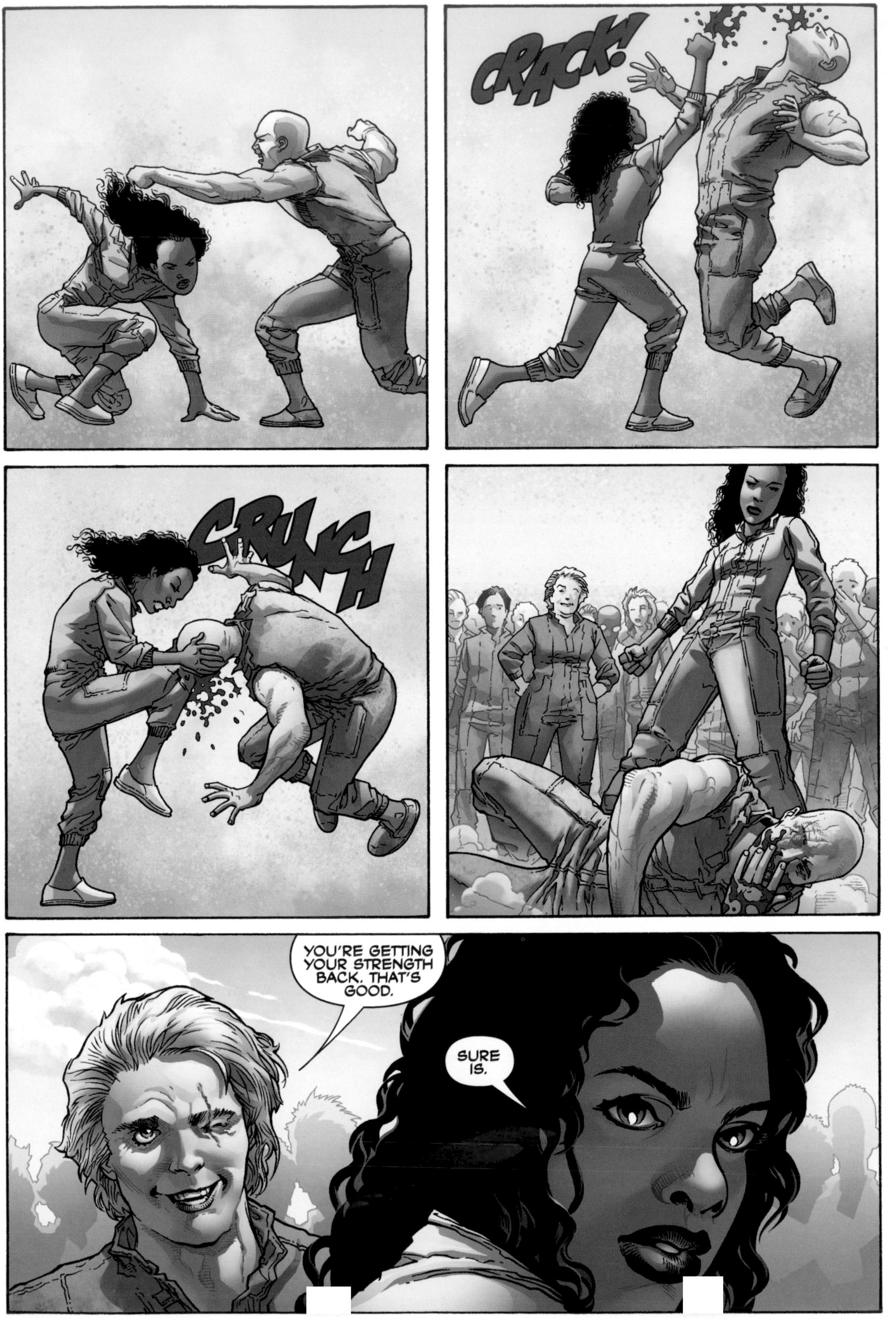
CRACK!
CRUNCH
YOU'RE GETTING YOUR STRENGTH BACK. THAT'S GOOD.
SURE IS.

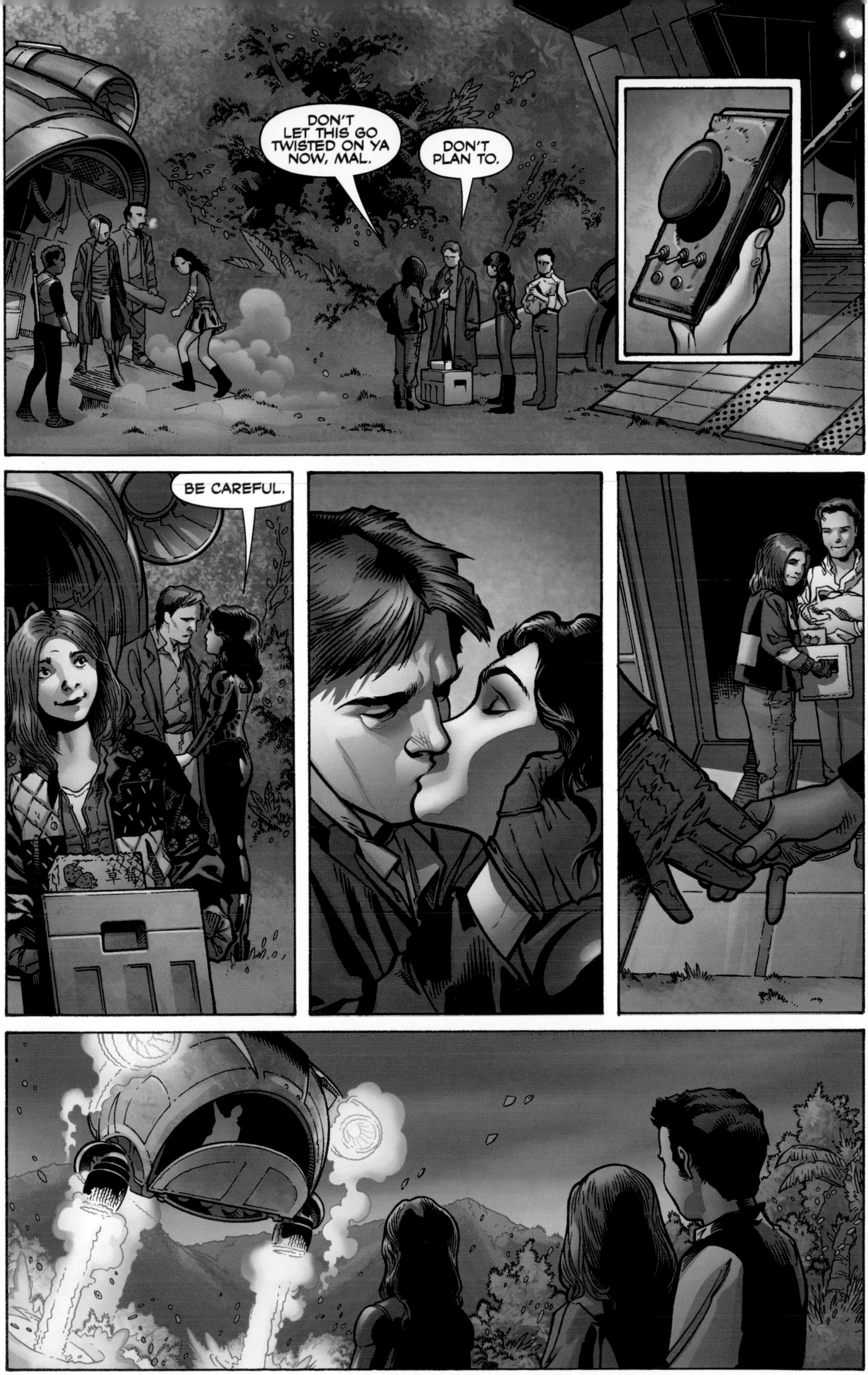
DON'T LET THIS GO TWISTED ON YA NOW, MAL.
DON'T PLAN TO.
BE CAREFUL.
草莓

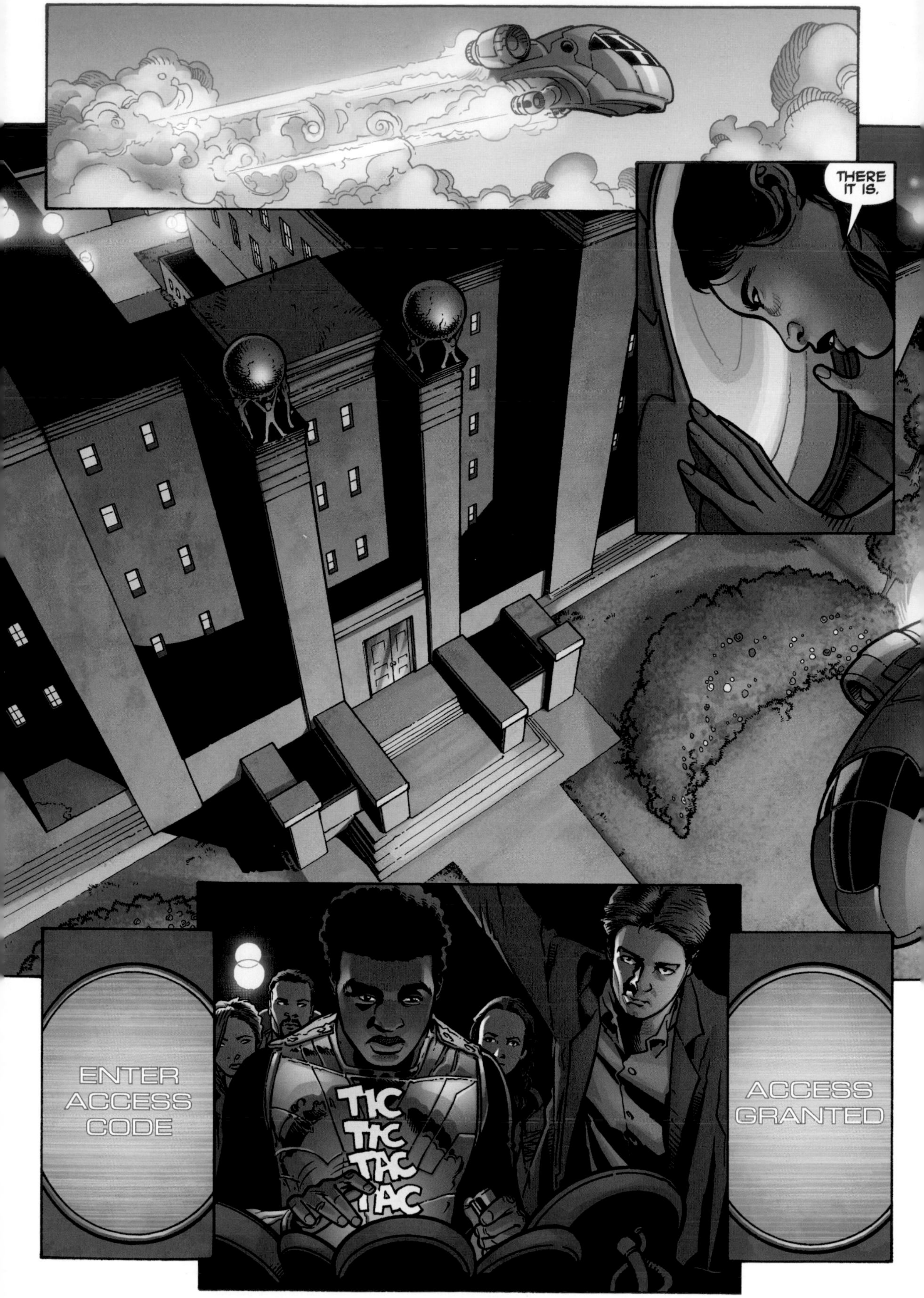
THERE IT IS.
ENTER ACCESS CODE
TIC TIC TAC TAC
ACCESS GRANTED

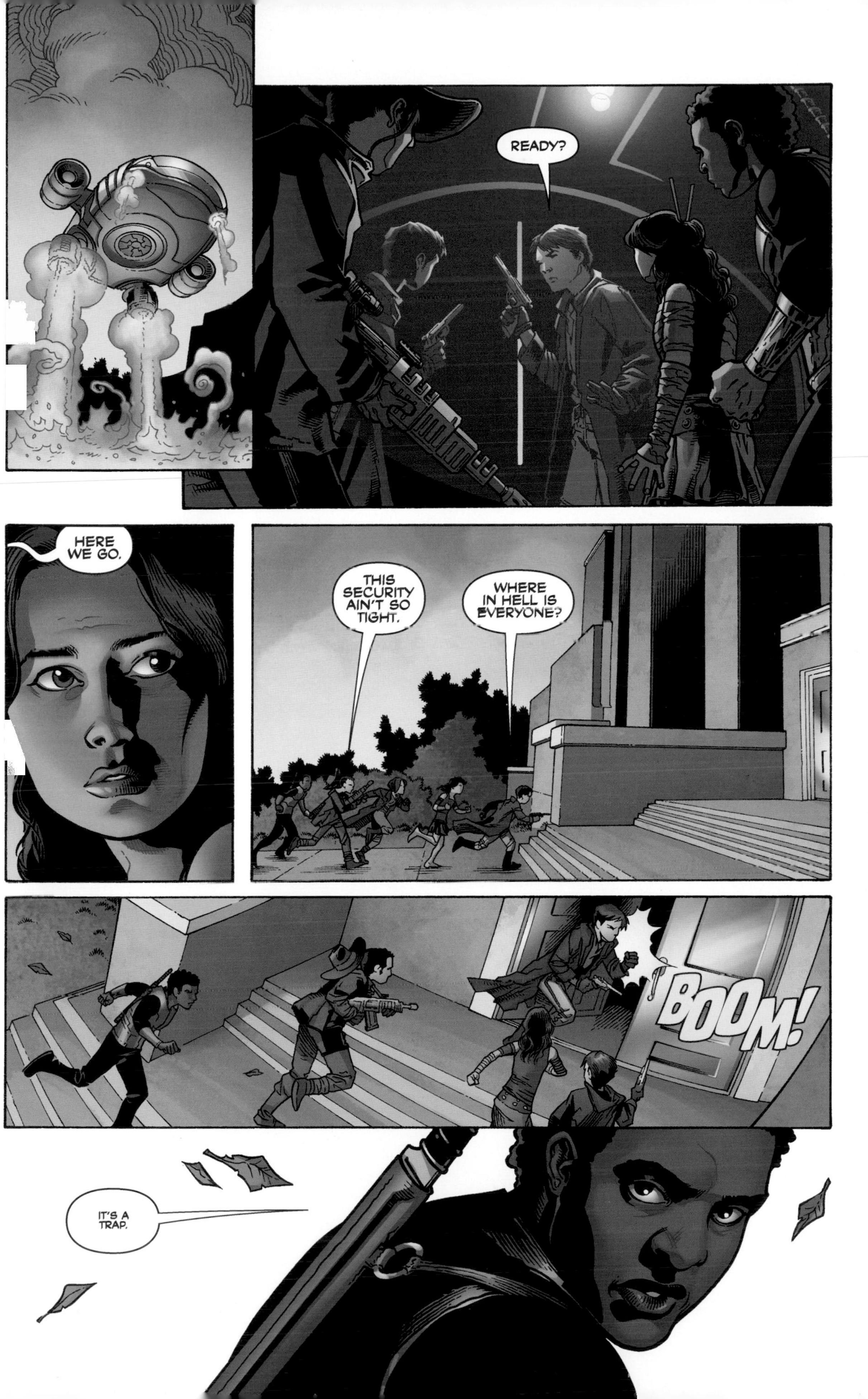
READY?
HERE WE GO.
THIS SECURITY AIN'T SO TIGHT.
WHERE IN HELL IS EVERYONE?
BOOM!
IT'S A TRAP.

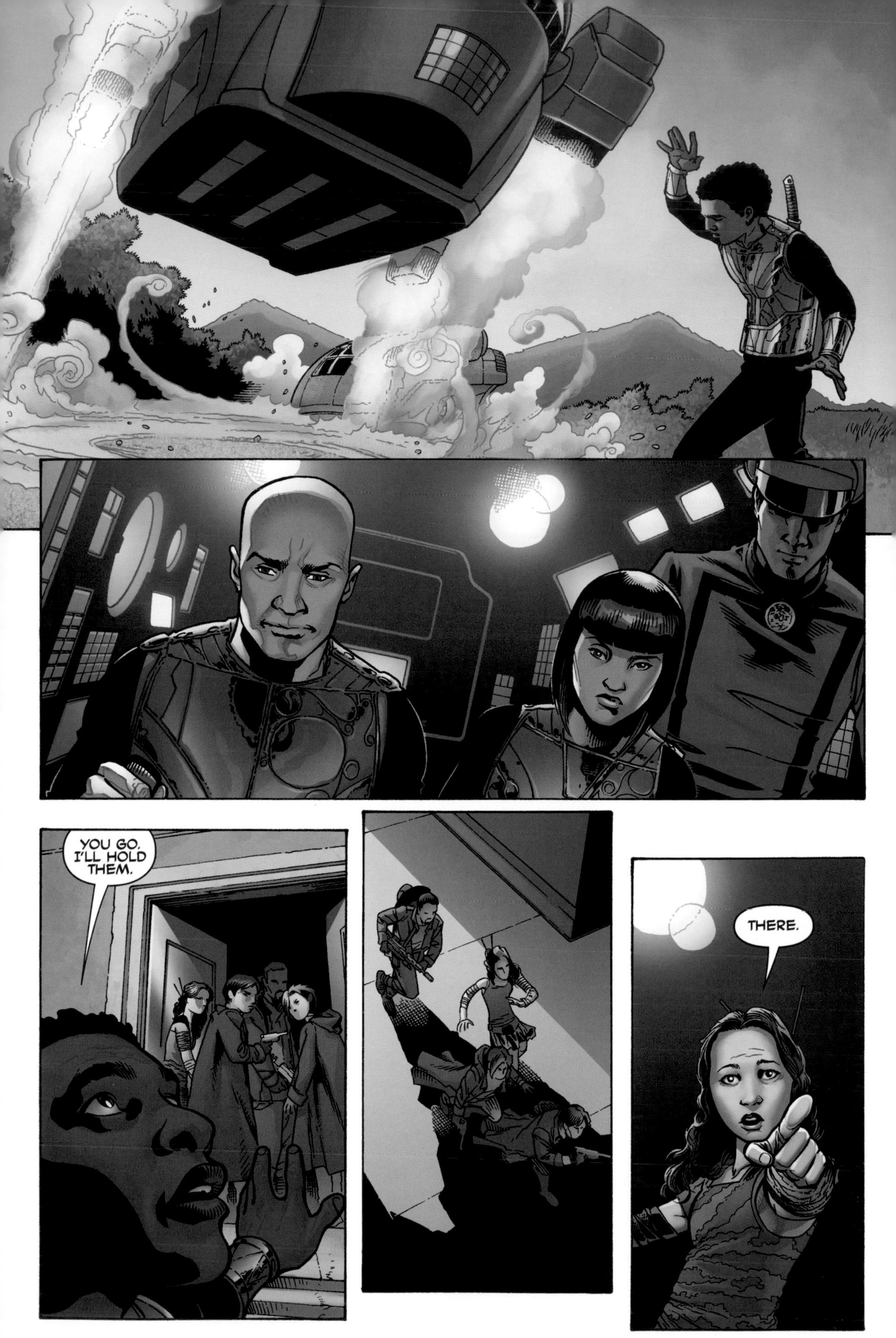
YOU GO, I'LL HOLD THEM.
THERE.

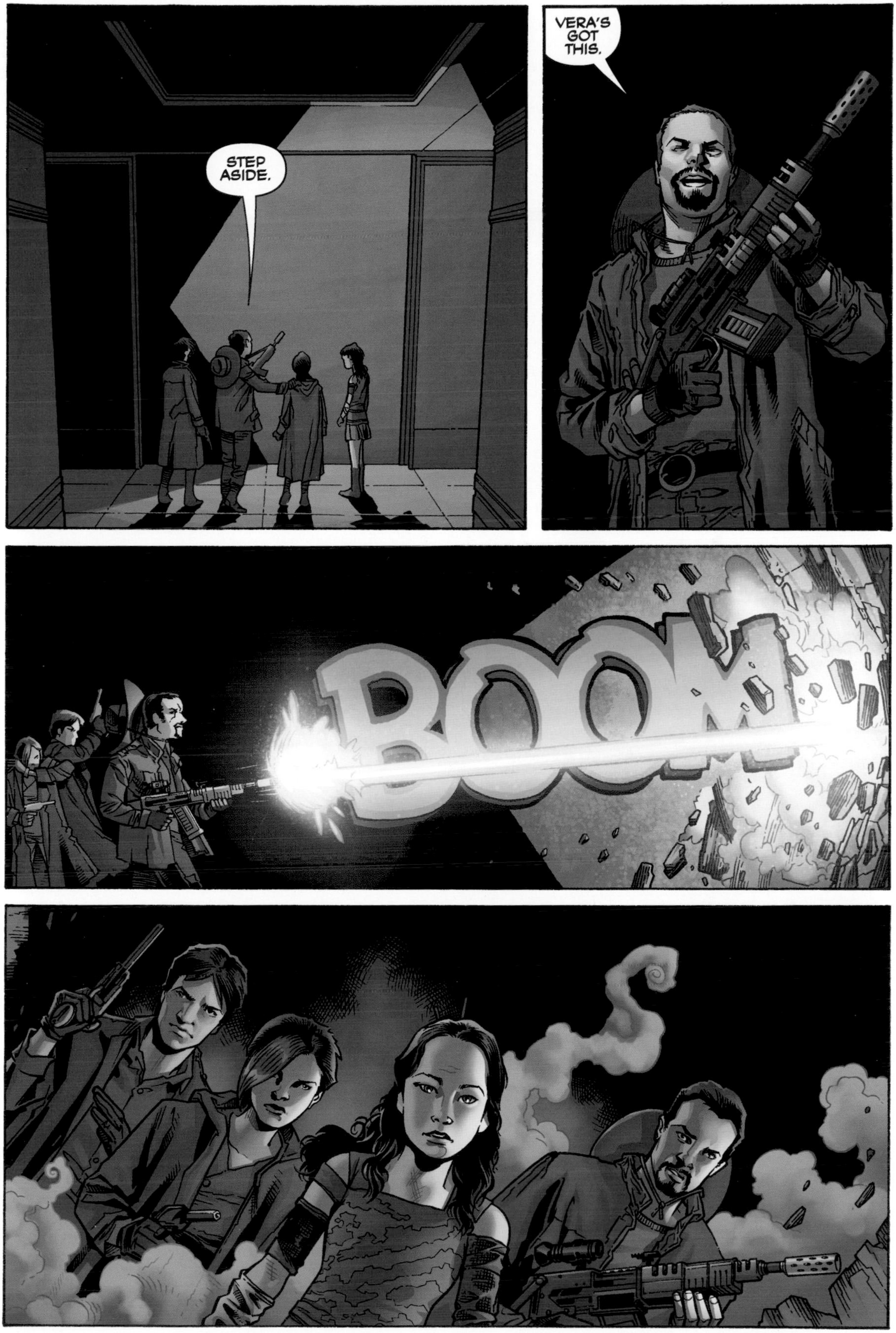
STEP ASIDE.
VERA'S GOT THIS.
BOOM

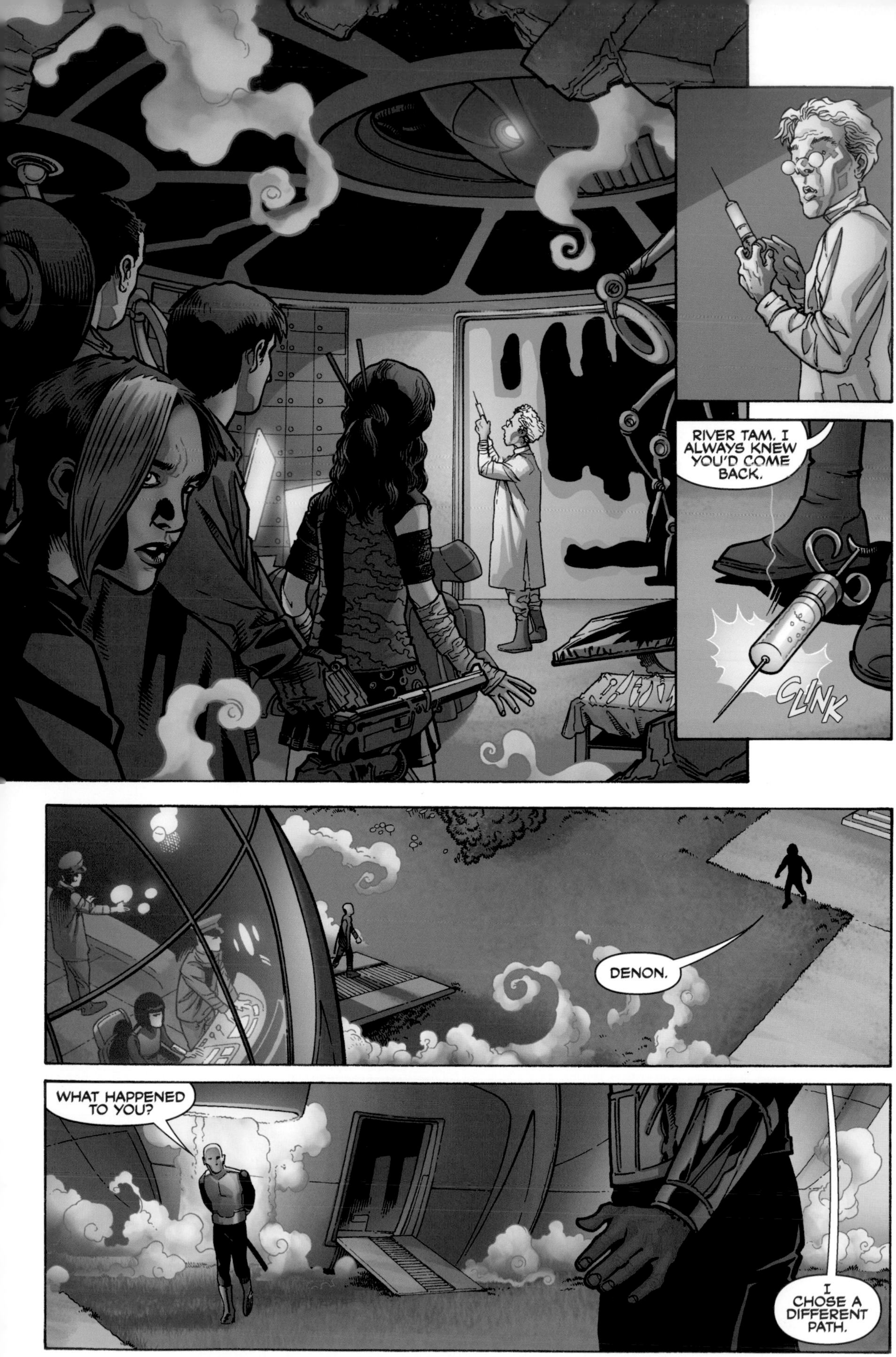
RIVER TAM. I ALWAYS KNEW YOU'D COME BACK.
CLINK
DENON.
WHAT HAPPENED TO YOU?
I CHOSE A DIFFERENT PATH.

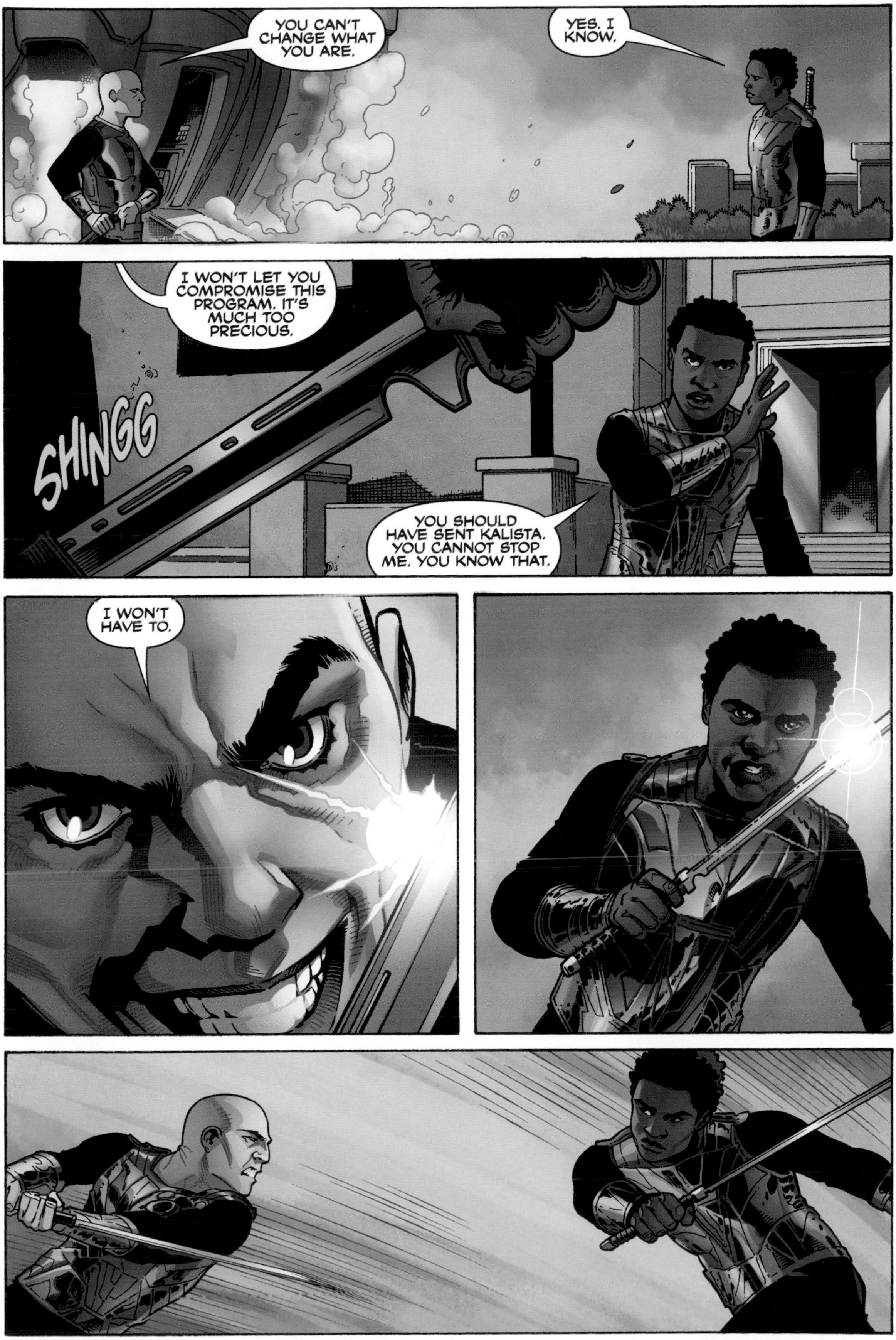
YOU CAN'T CHANGE WHAT YOU ARE.
YES. I KNOW.
I WON'T LET YOU COMPROMISE THIS PROGRAM. IT'S MUCH TOO PRECIOUS.
SHINGG
YOU SHOULD HAVE SENT KALISTA. YOU CANNOT STOP ME. YOU KNOW THAT.
I WON'T HAVE TO.

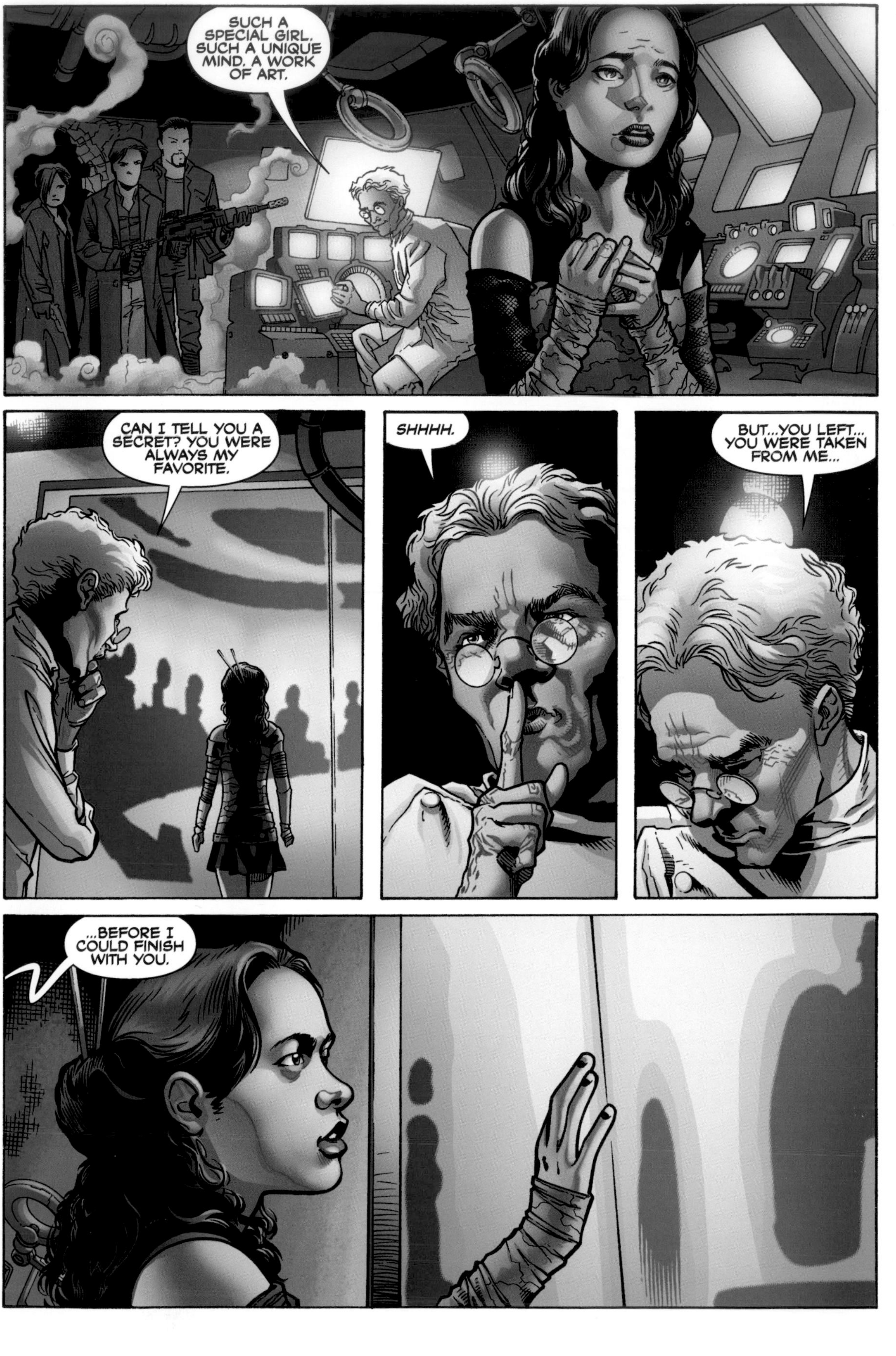
SUCH A SPECIAL GIRL. SUCH A UNIQUE MIND. A WORK OF ART.
CAN I TELL YOU A SECRET? YOU WERE ALWAYS MY FAVORITE.
SHHHH.
BUT...YOU LEFT... YOU WERE TAKEN FROM ME...
...BEFORE I COULD FINISH WITH YOU.

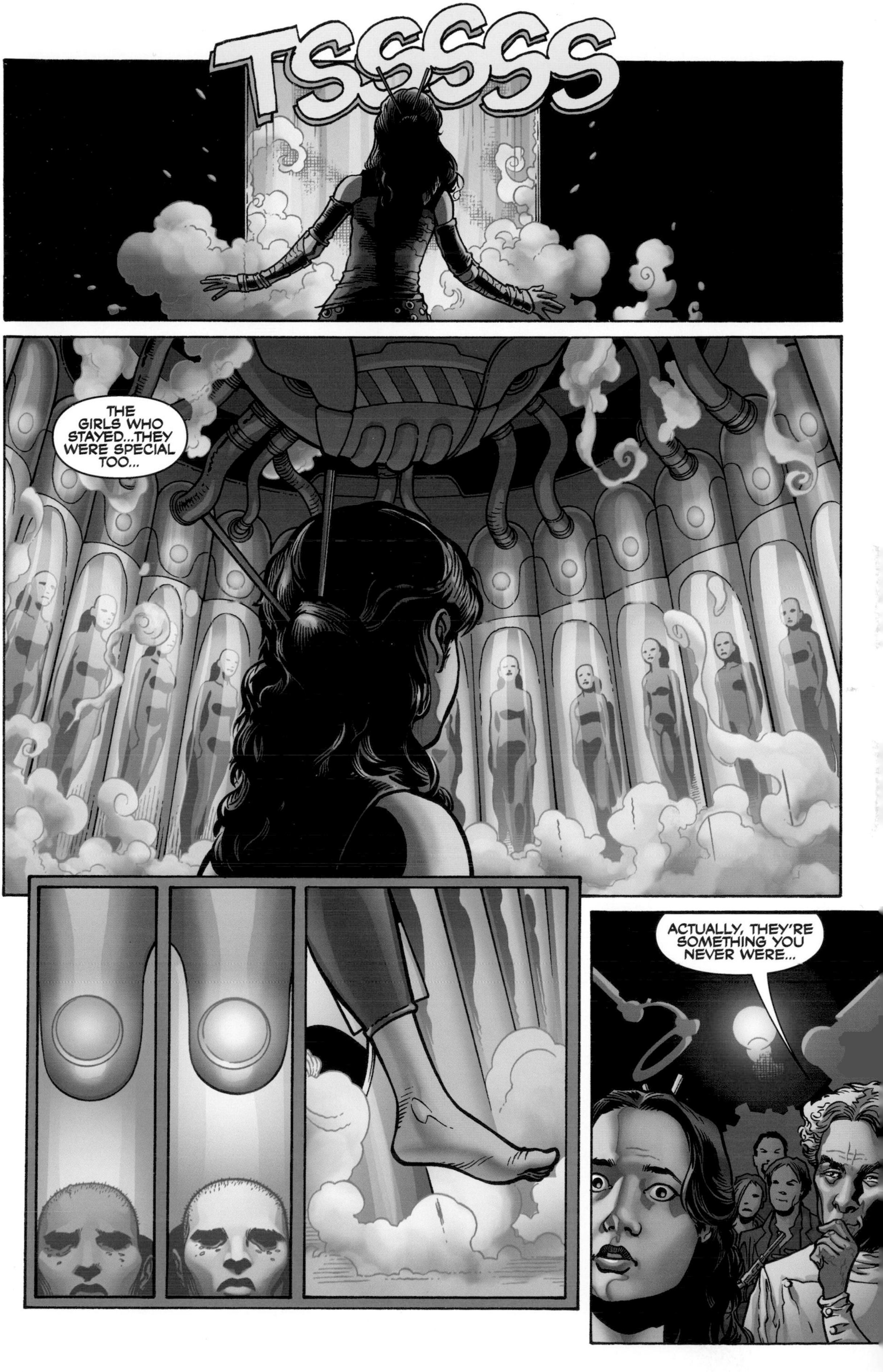
TSSSSS
THE GIRLS WHO STAYED...THEY WERE SPECIAL TOO...
ACTUALLY, THEY'RE SOMETHING YOU NEVER WERE...

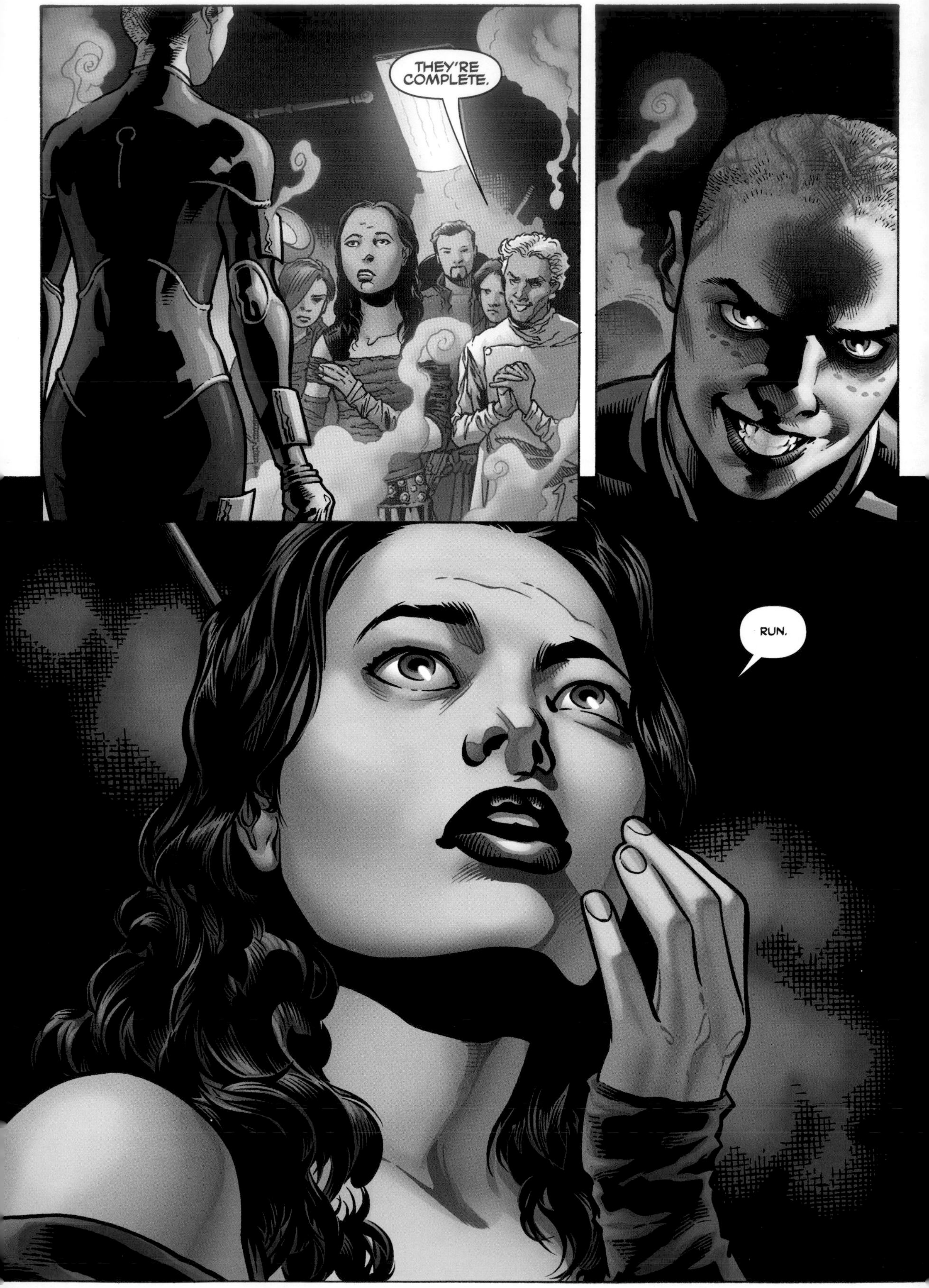
THEY'RE COMPLETE.
RUN.

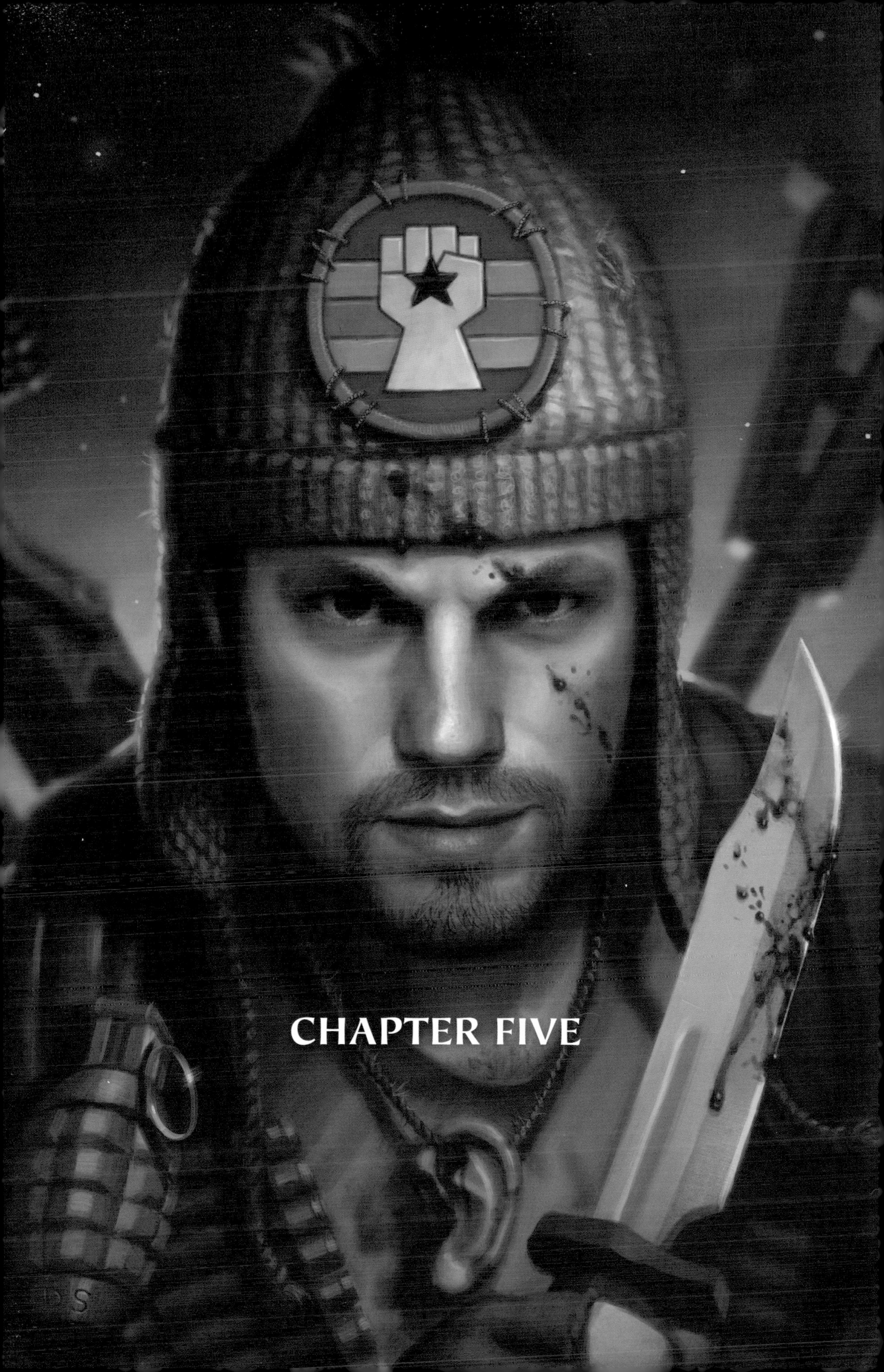

CHAPTER FIVE

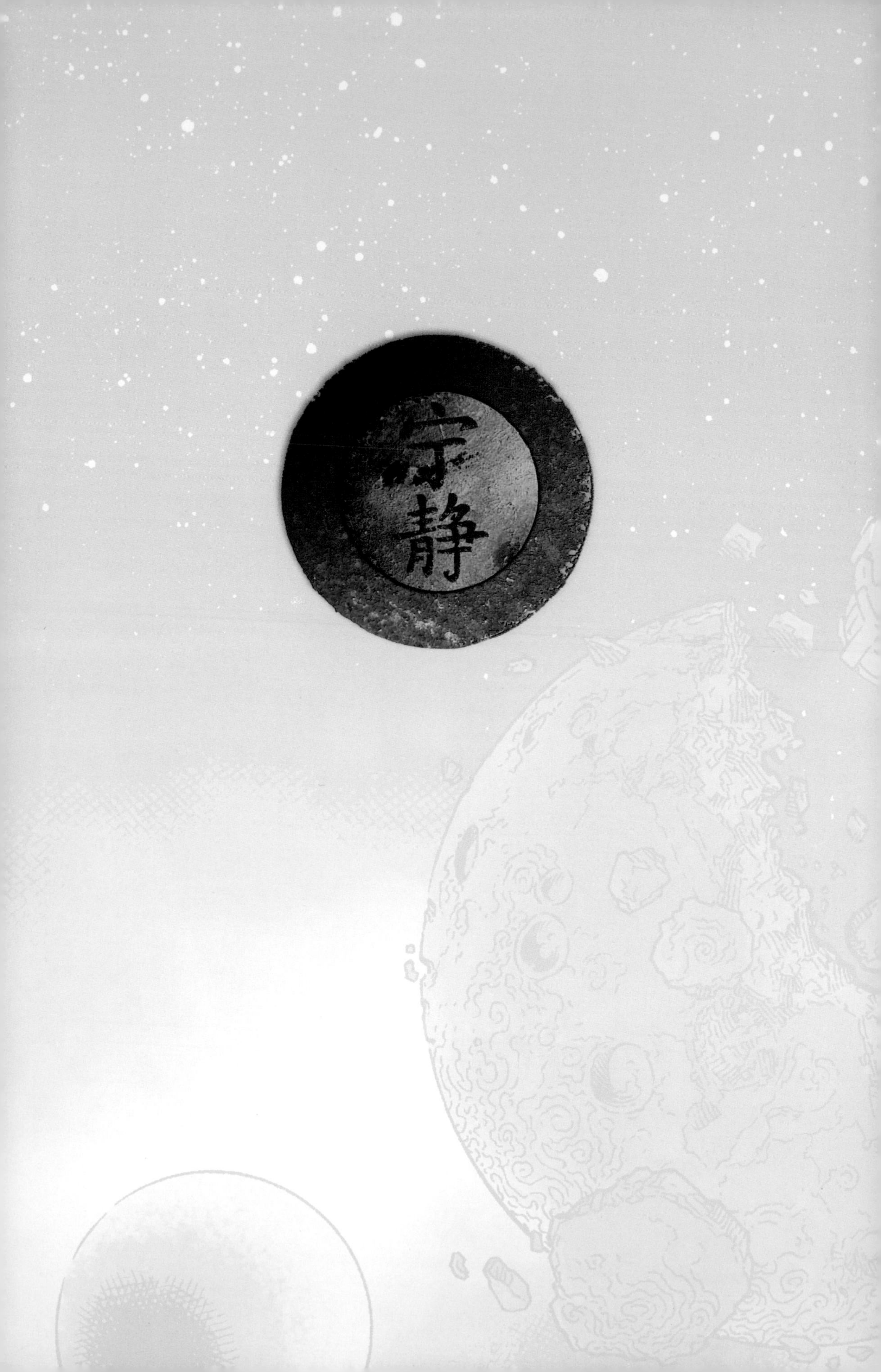
守静

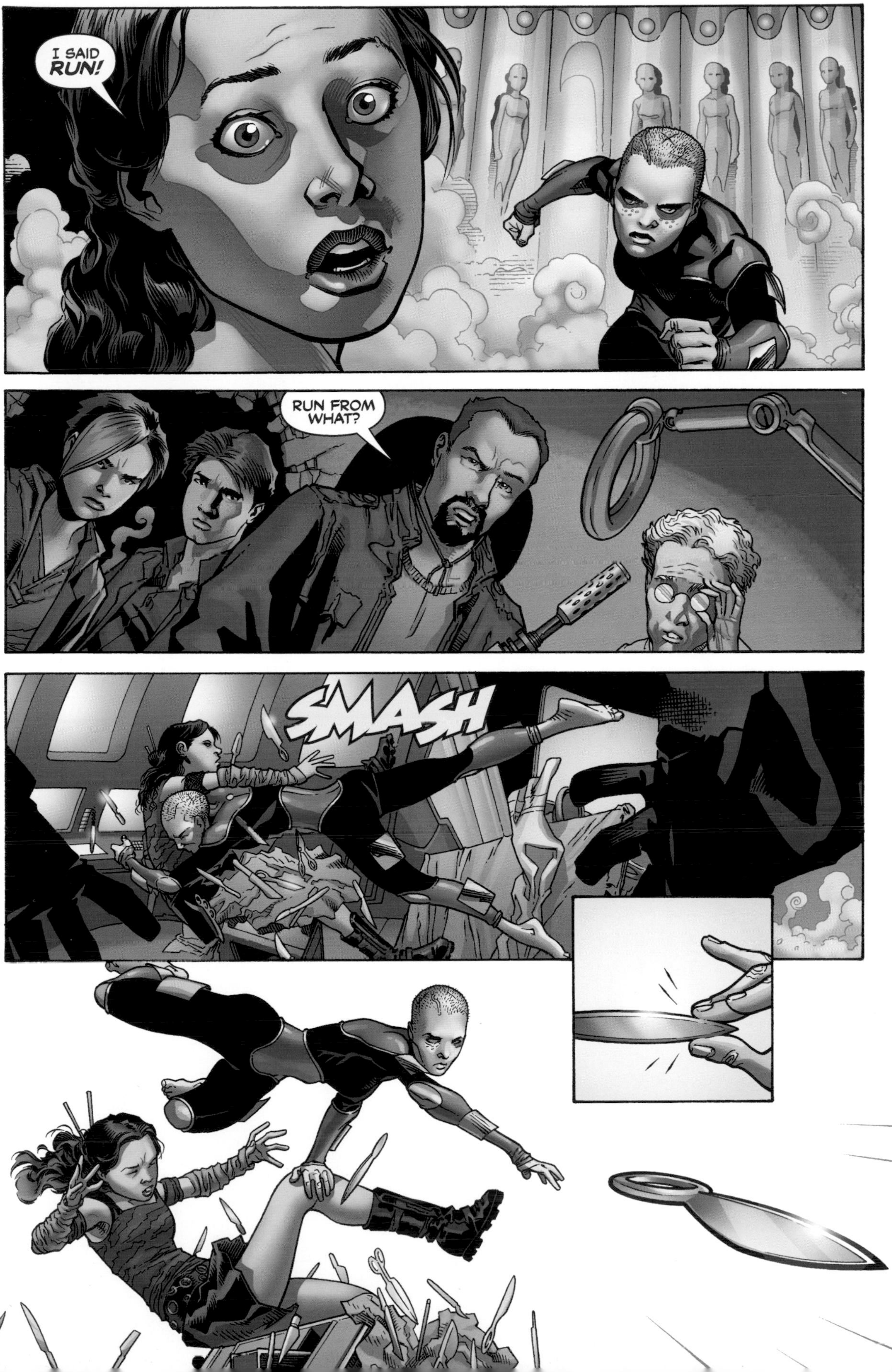

I SAID RUN!
RUN FROM WHAT?
SMASH

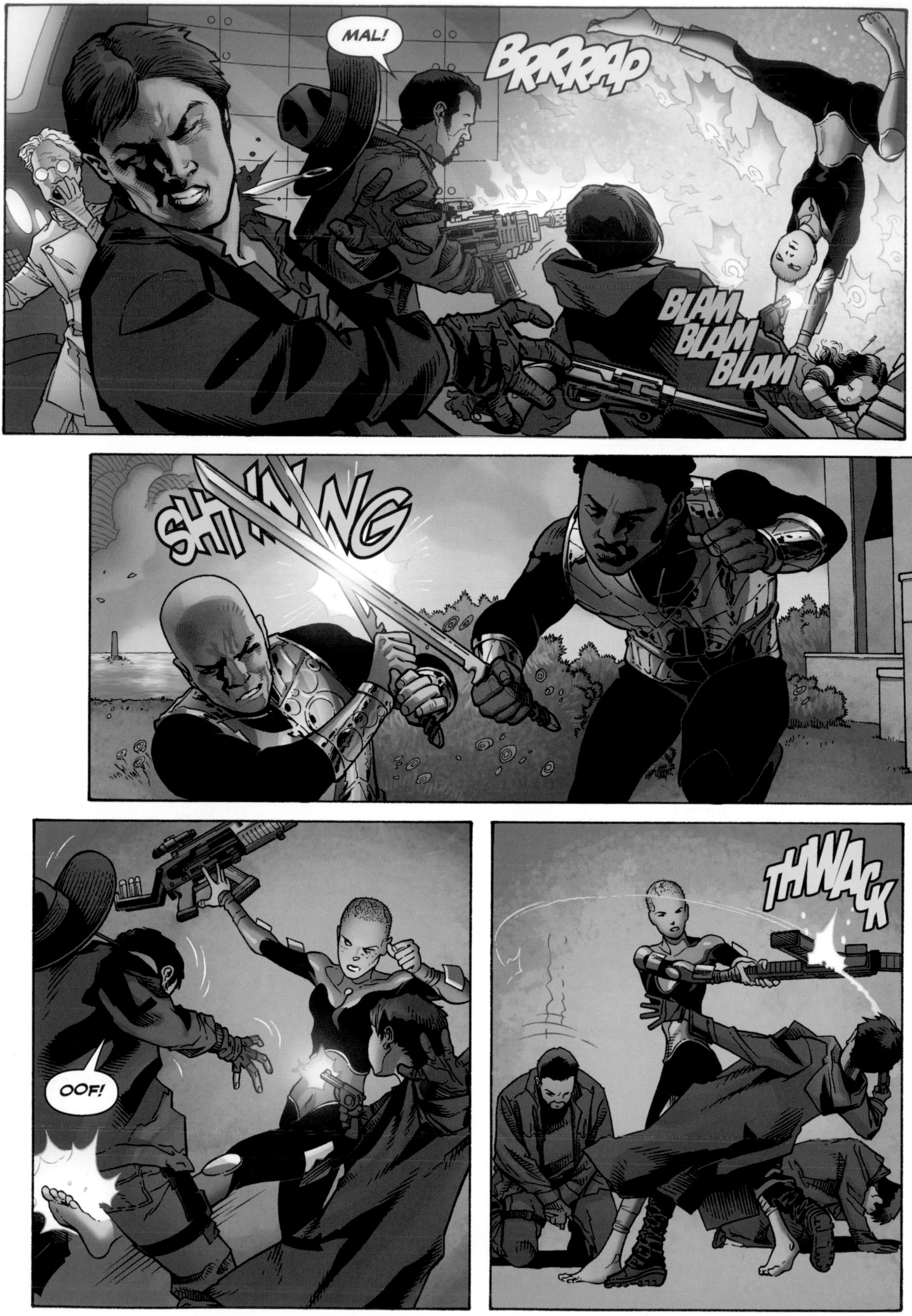
MAL!
BRRRAP
BLAM
BLAM
BLAM
SHNNNG
OOF!
THWACK

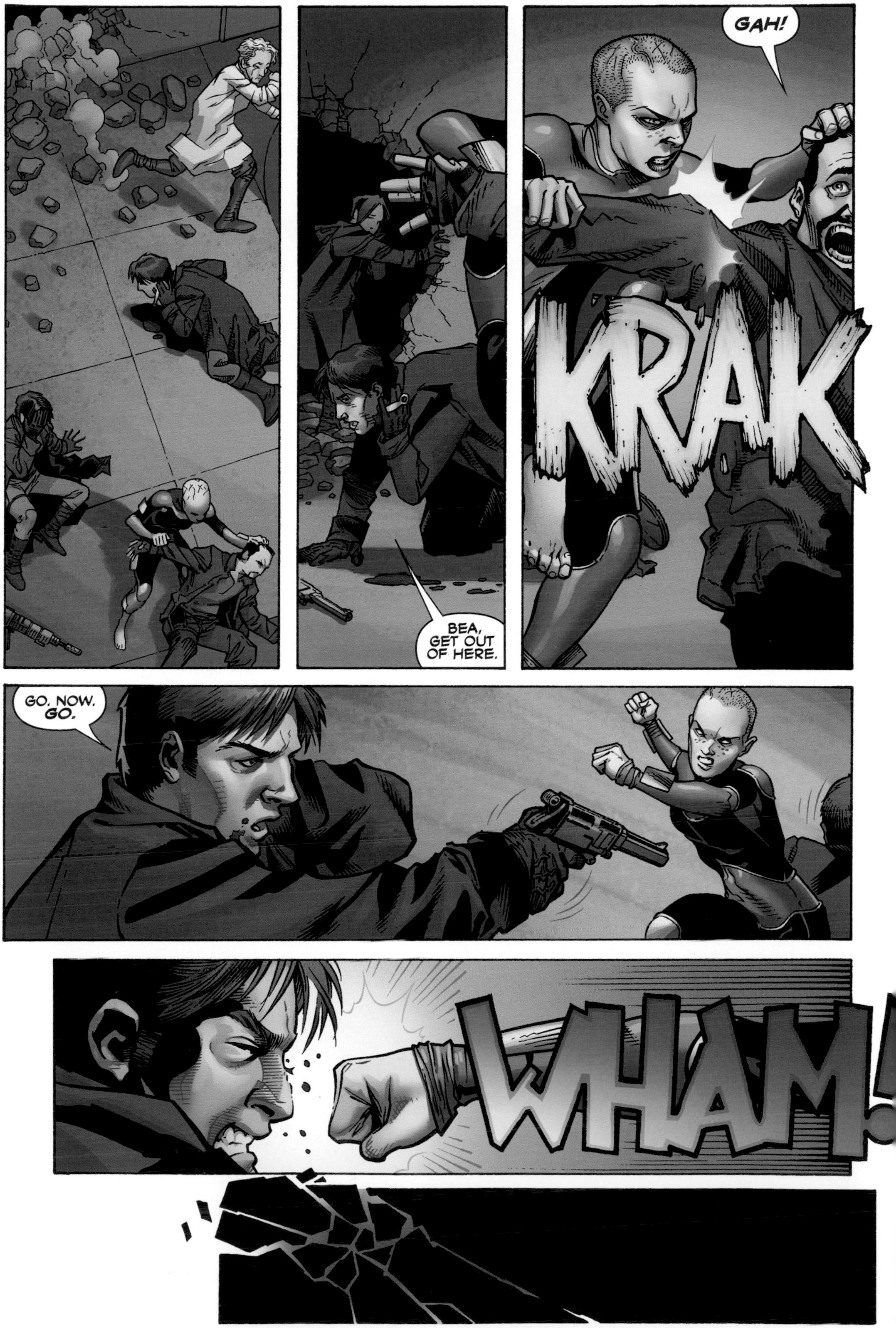
BEA, GET OUT OF HERE.
GAH!
KRAK
GO. NOW. GO.
WHAM!

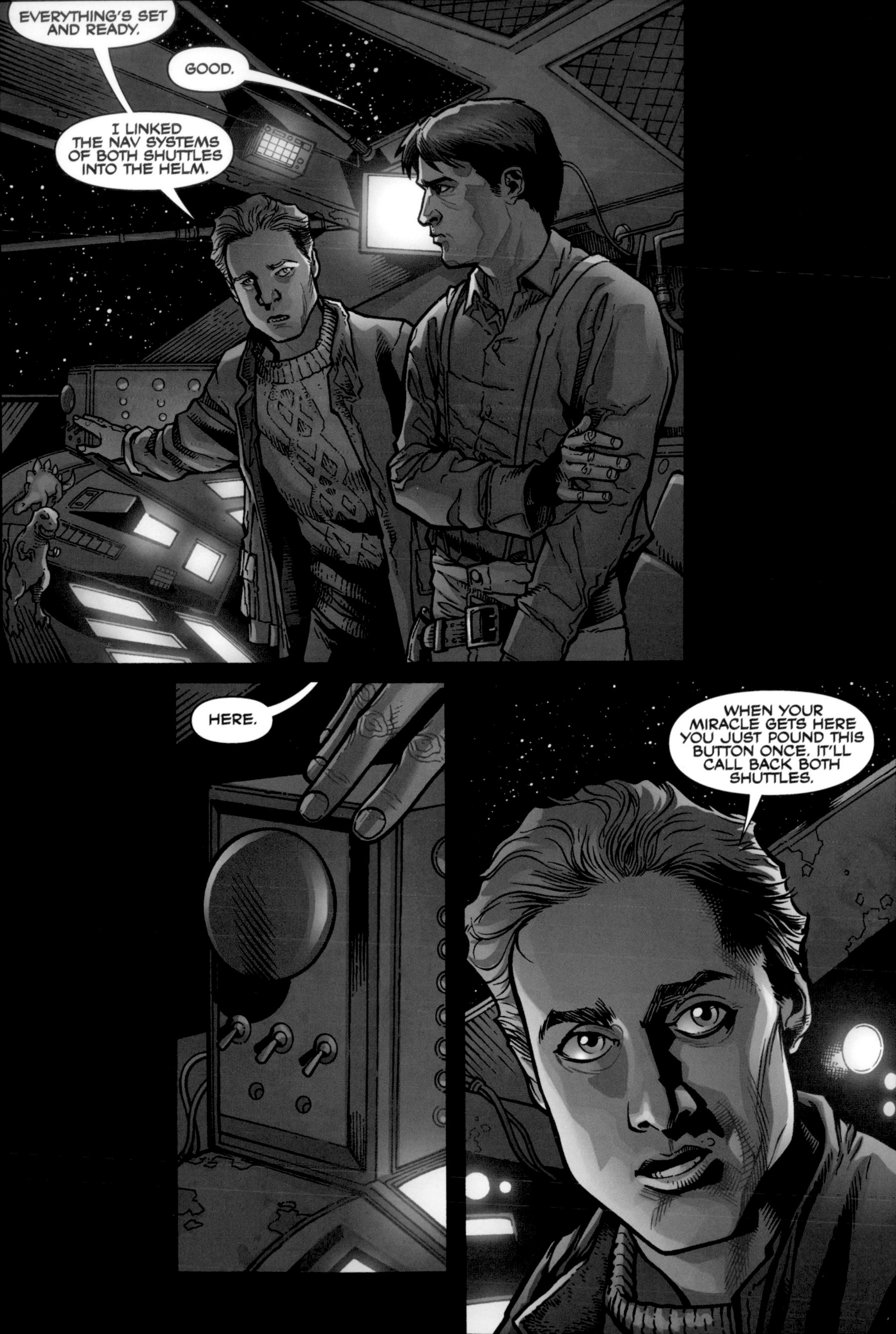
EVERYTHING'S SET AND READY.
GOOD.
I LINKED THE NAV SYSTEMS OF BOTH SHUTTLES INTO THE HELM.
HERE.
WHEN YOUR MIRACLE GETS HERE YOU JUST POUND THIS BUTTON ONCE. IT'LL CALL BACK BOTH SHUTTLES.

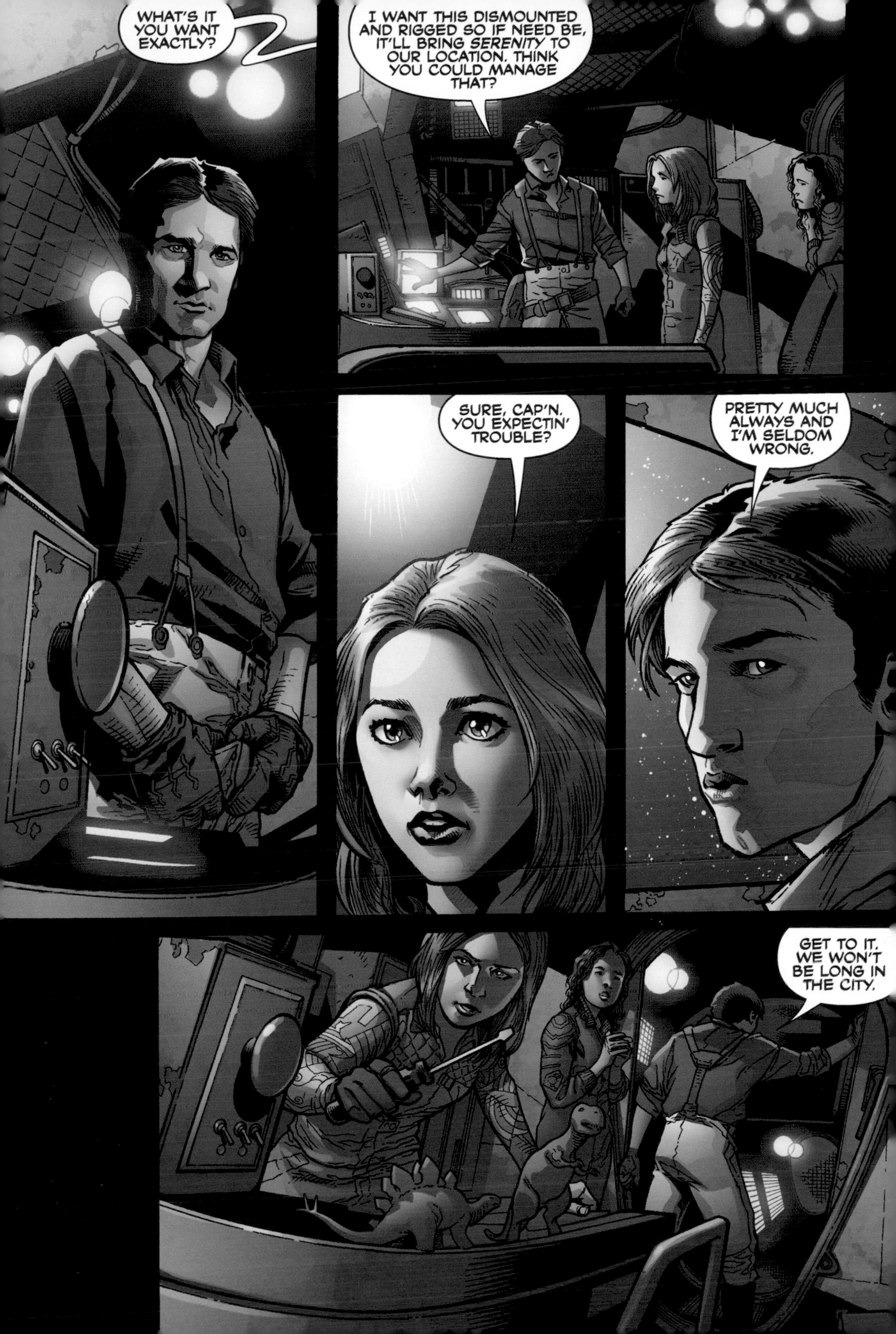
WHAT'S IT YOU WANT EXACTLY?
I WANT THIS DISMOUNTED AND RIGGED SO IF NEED BE, IT'LL BRING *SERENITY* TO OUR LOCATION. THINK YOU COULD MANAGE THAT?
SURE, CAP'N. YOU EXPECTIN' TROUBLE?
PRETTY MUCH ALWAYS AND I'M SELDOM WRONG.
GET TO IT. WE WON'T BE LONG IN THE CITY.

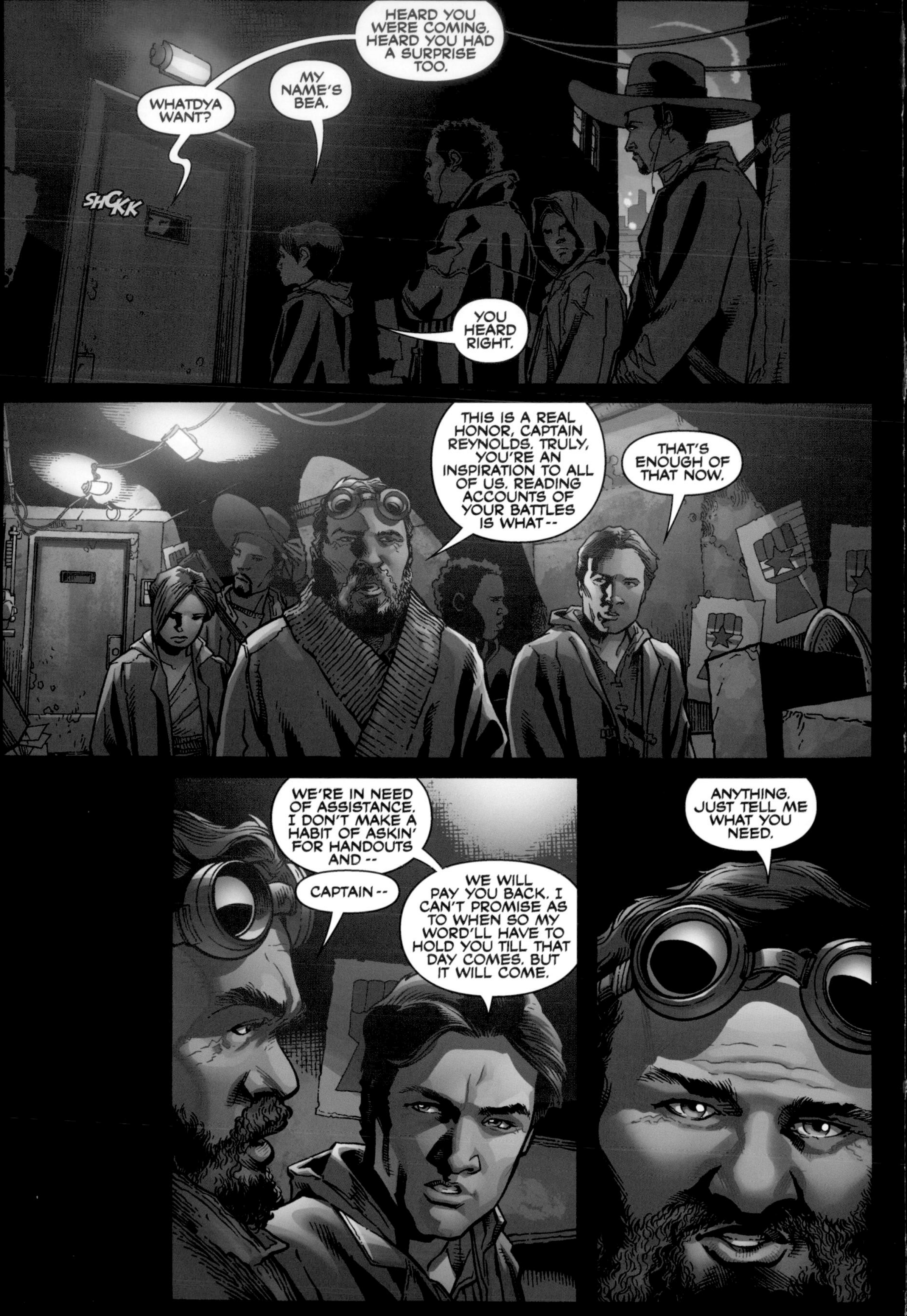

SHCKK
WHATDYA WANT?
HEARD YOU WERE COMING. HEARD YOU HAD A SURPRISE TOO.
MY NAME'S BEA.
YOU HEARD RIGHT.
THIS IS A REAL HONOR, CAPTAIN REYNOLDS. TRULY, YOU'RE AN INSPIRATION TO ALL OF US. READING ACCOUNTS OF YOUR BATTLES IS WHAT --
THAT'S ENOUGH OF THAT NOW.
WE'RE IN NEED OF ASSISTANCE. I DON'T MAKE A HABIT OF ASKIN' FOR HANDOUTS AND --
CAPTAIN --
WE WILL PAY YOU BACK. I CAN'T PROMISE AS TO WHEN SO MY WORD'LL HAVE TO HOLD YOU TILL THAT DAY COMES, BUT IT WILL COME.
ANYTHING. JUST TELL ME WHAT YOU NEED.

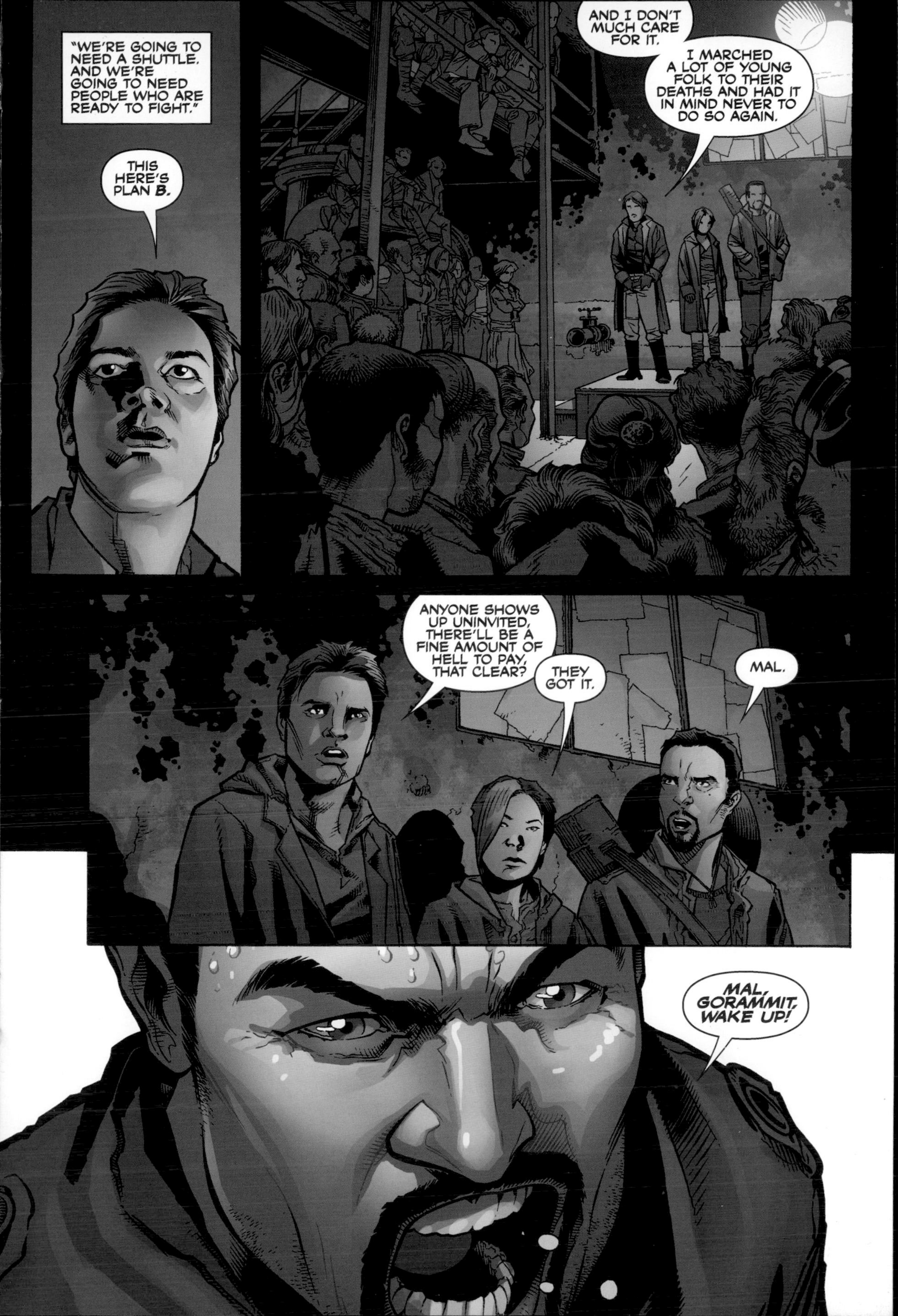
"WE'RE GOING TO NEED A SHUTTLE. AND WE'RE GOING TO NEED PEOPLE WHO ARE READY TO FIGHT."
THIS HERE'S PLAN B.
AND I DON'T MUCH CARE FOR IT.
I MARCHED A LOT OF YOUNG FOLK TO THEIR DEATHS AND HAD IT IN MIND NEVER TO DO SO AGAIN.
ANYONE SHOWS UP UNINVITED, THERE'LL BE A FINE AMOUNT OF HELL TO PAY, THAT CLEAR?
THEY GOT IT.
MAL.
MAL, GORAMMIT, WAKE UP!

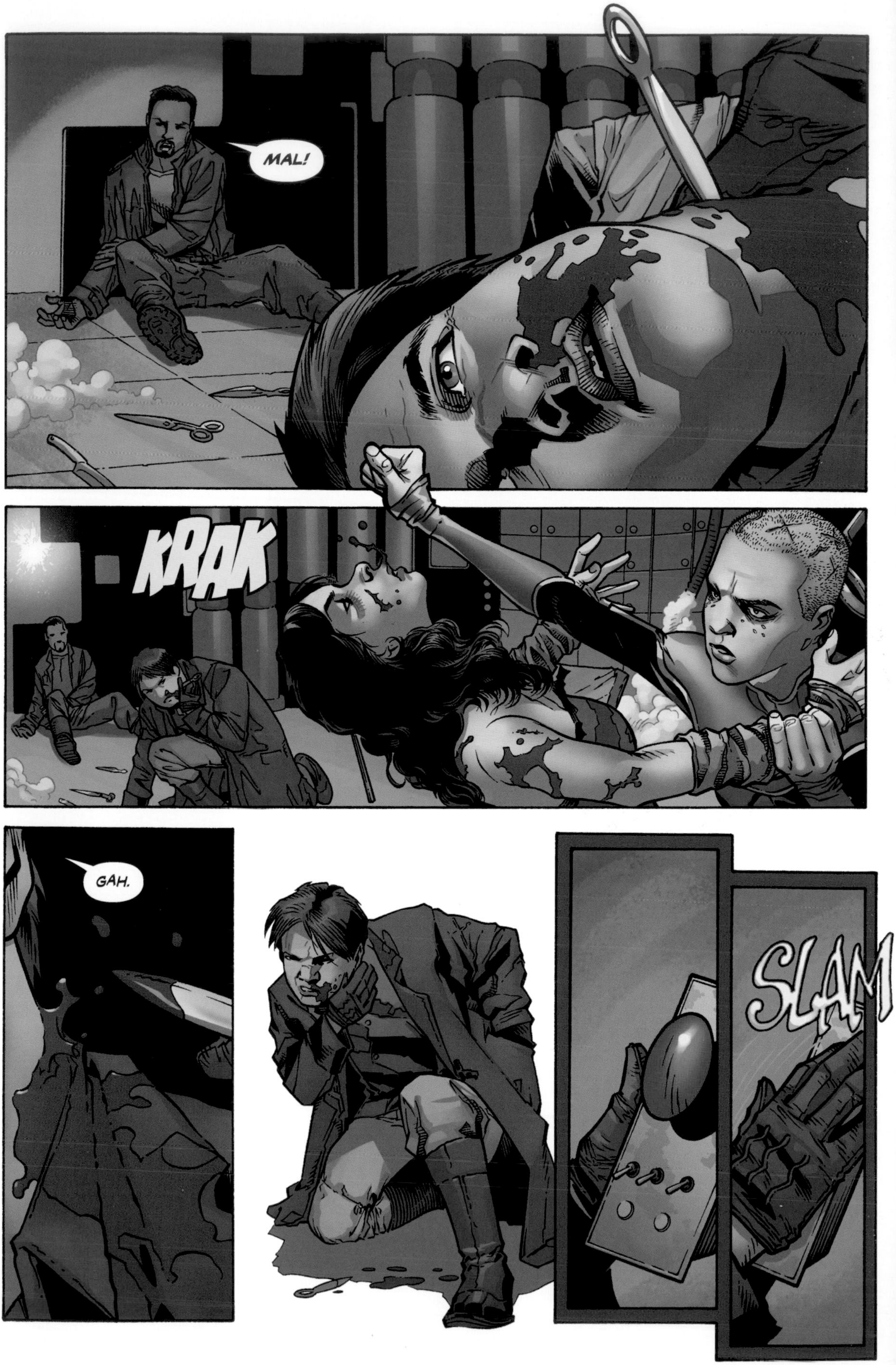
MAL!
KRAK
GAH.
SLAM

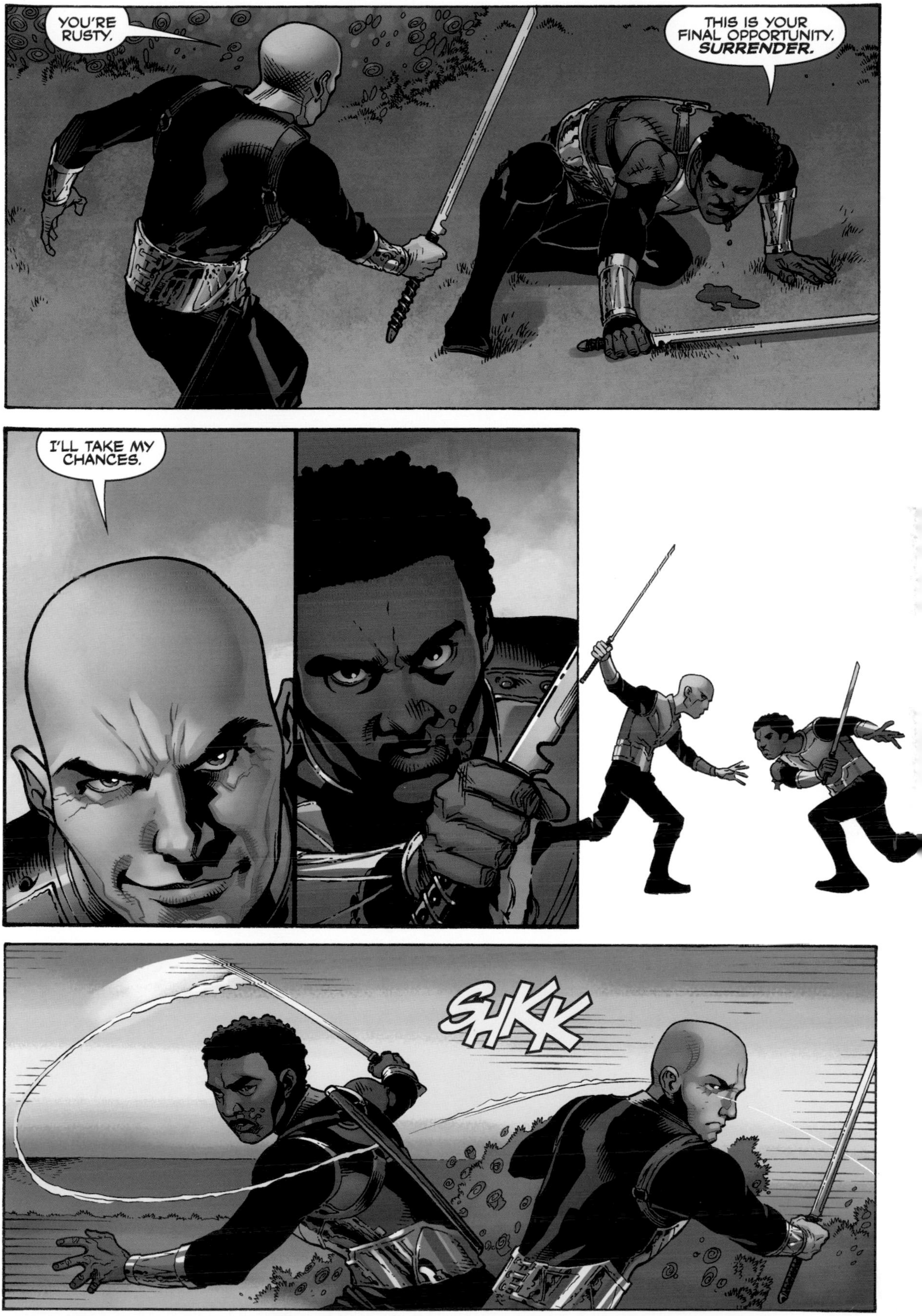
YOU'RE RUSTY.
THIS IS YOUR FINAL OPPORTUNITY. SURRENDER.
I'LL TAKE MY CHANCES.
SHKK

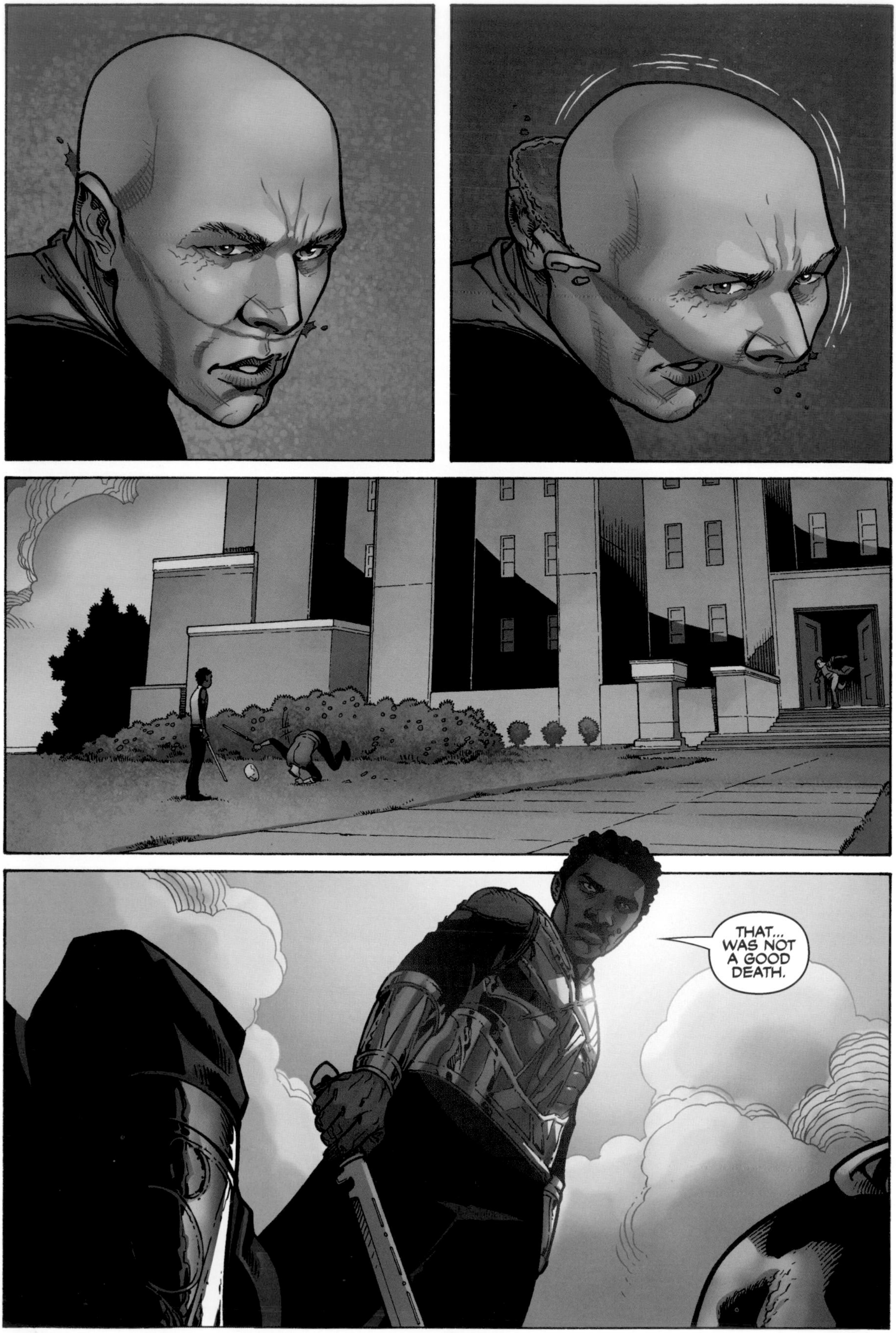
THAT... WAS NOT A GOOD DEATH.

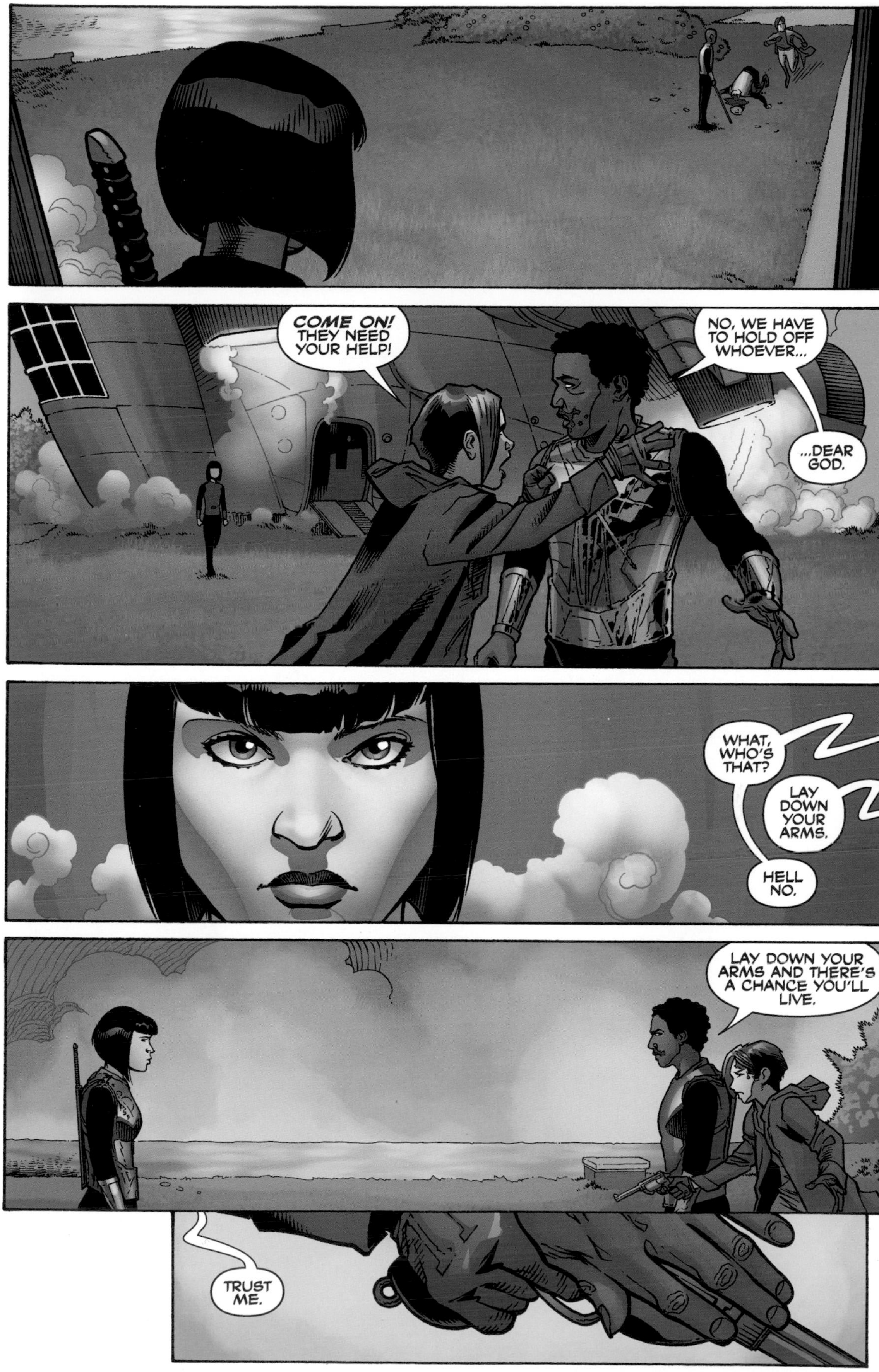
COME ON! THEY NEED YOUR HELP!
NO, WE HAVE TO HOLD OFF WHOEVER...
...DEAR GOD.
WHAT, WHO'S THAT?
LAY DOWN YOUR ARMS.
HELL NO.
LAY DOWN YOUR ARMS AND THERE'S A CHANCE YOU'LL LIVE.
TRUST ME.

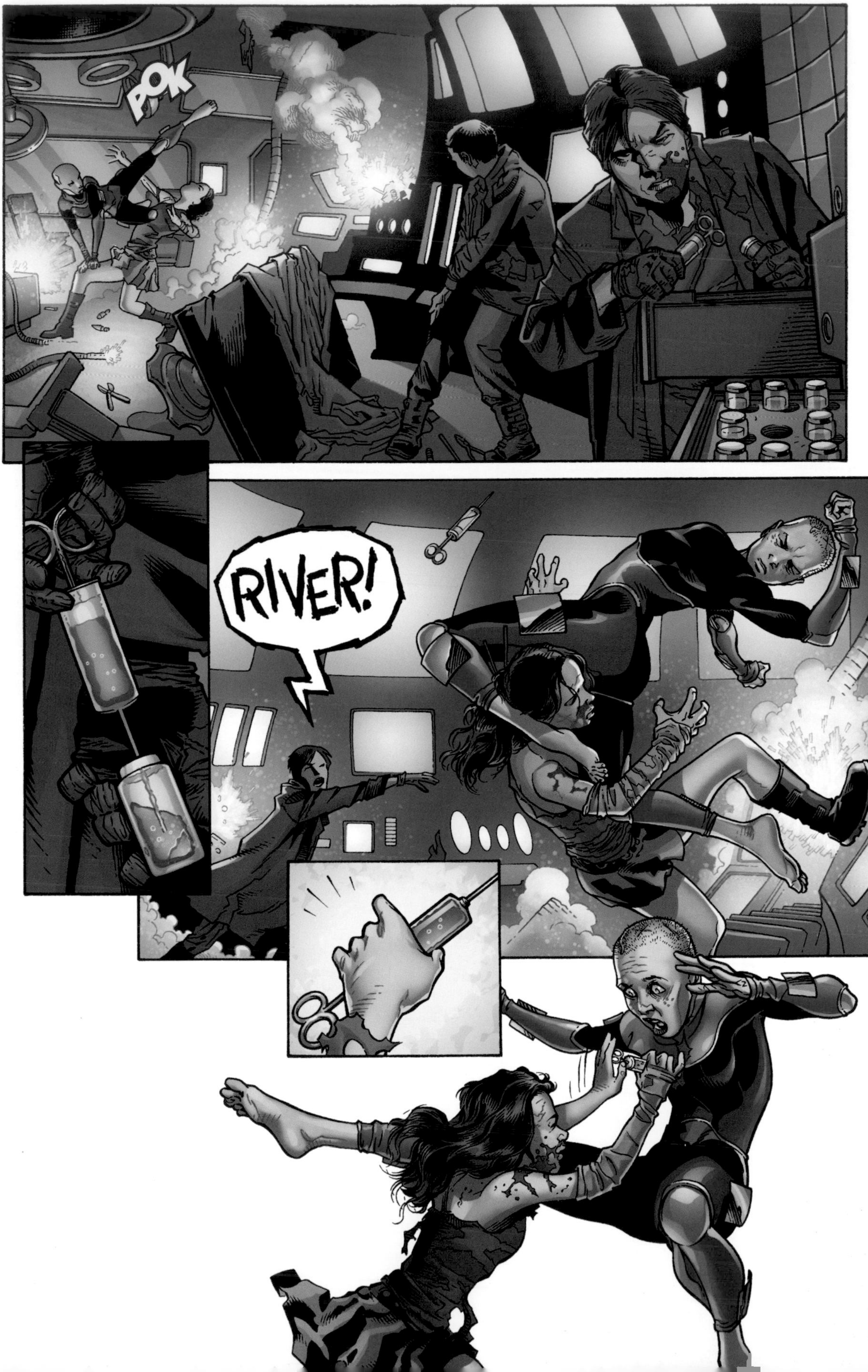
POK
RIVER!

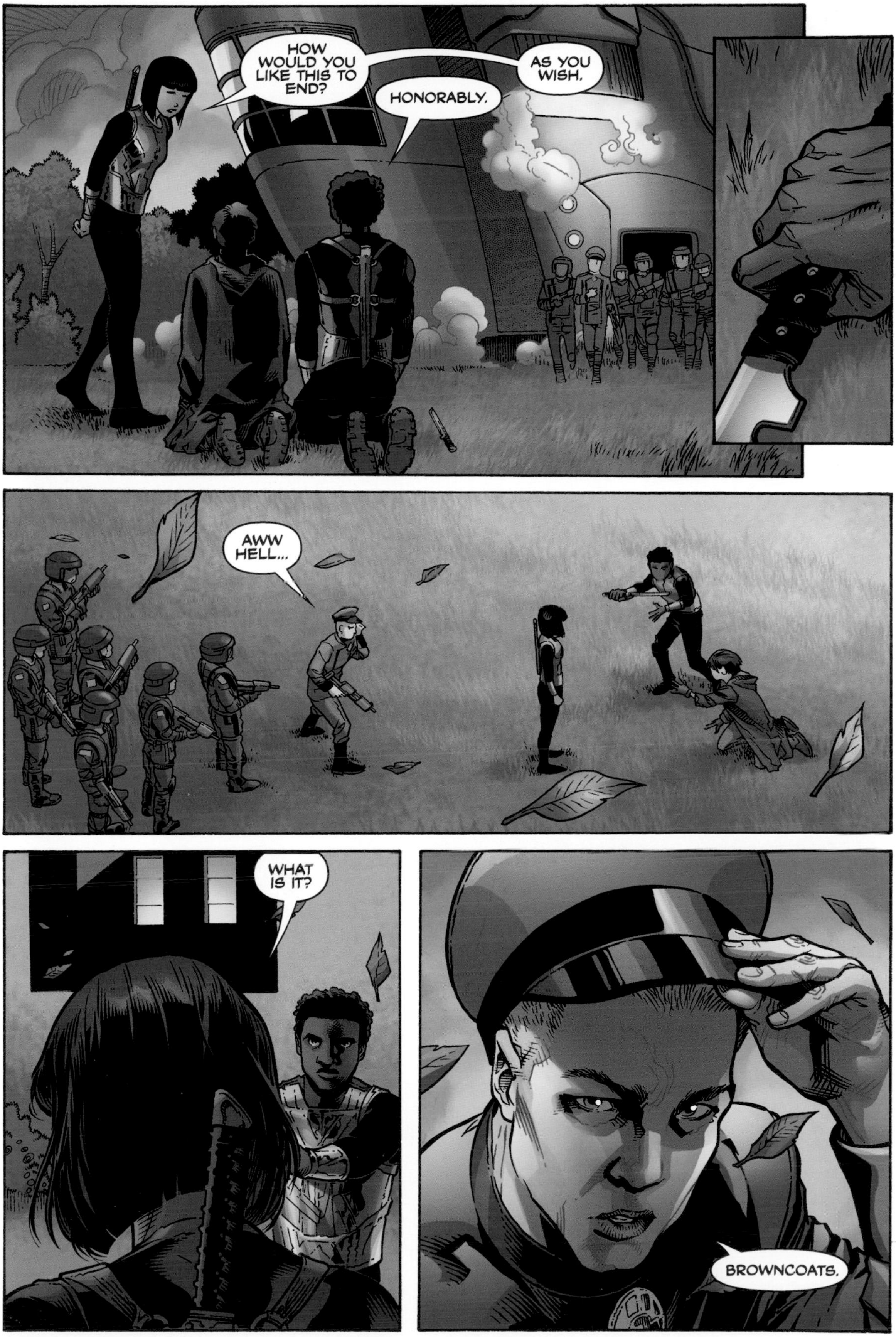
HOW WOULD YOU LIKE THIS TO END?
HONORABLY.
AS YOU WISH.
AWW HELL...
WHAT IS IT?
BROWNCOATS.

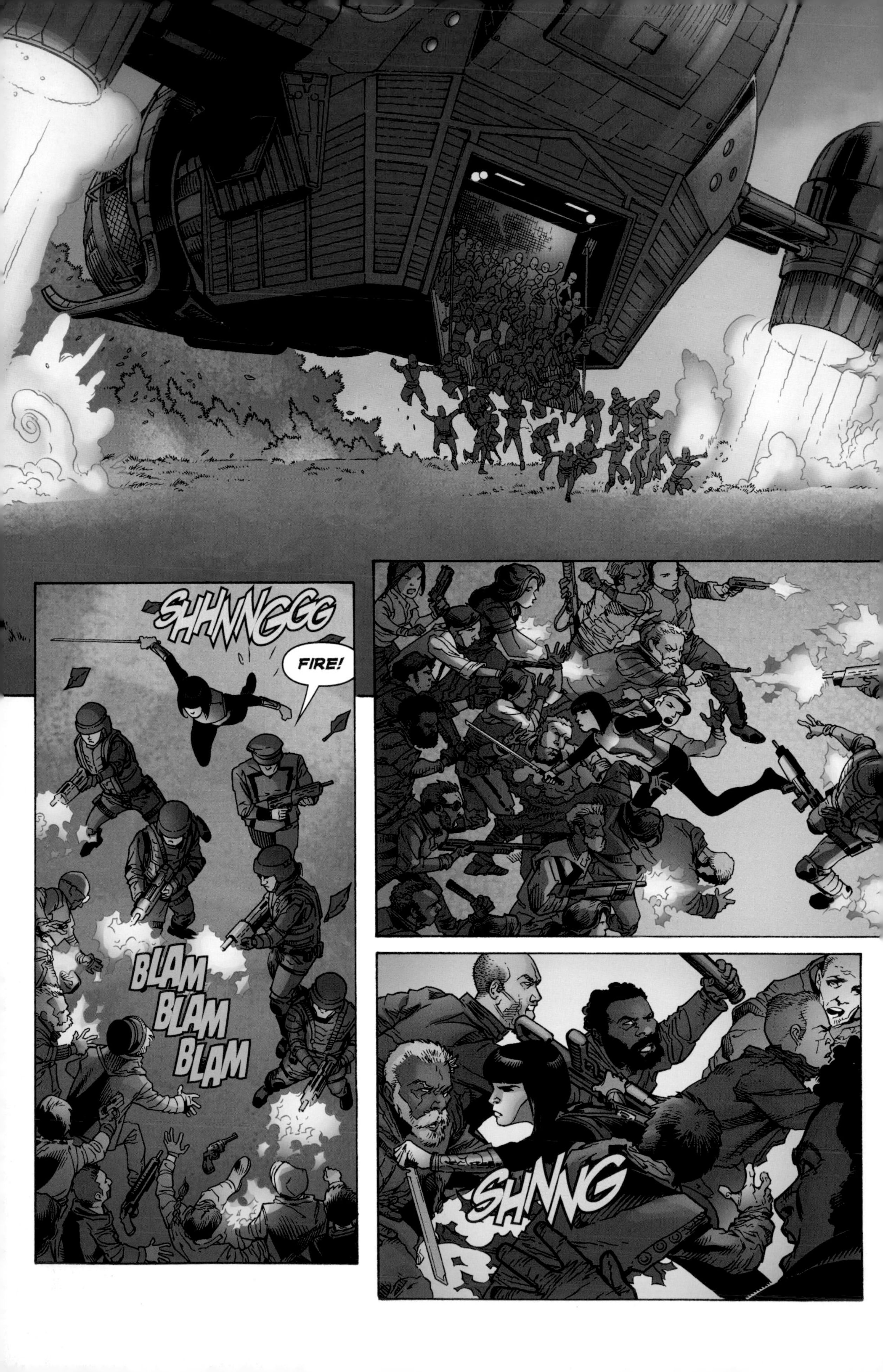
SHHNNGGG
FIRE!
BLAM
BLAM
BLAM
SHNNG

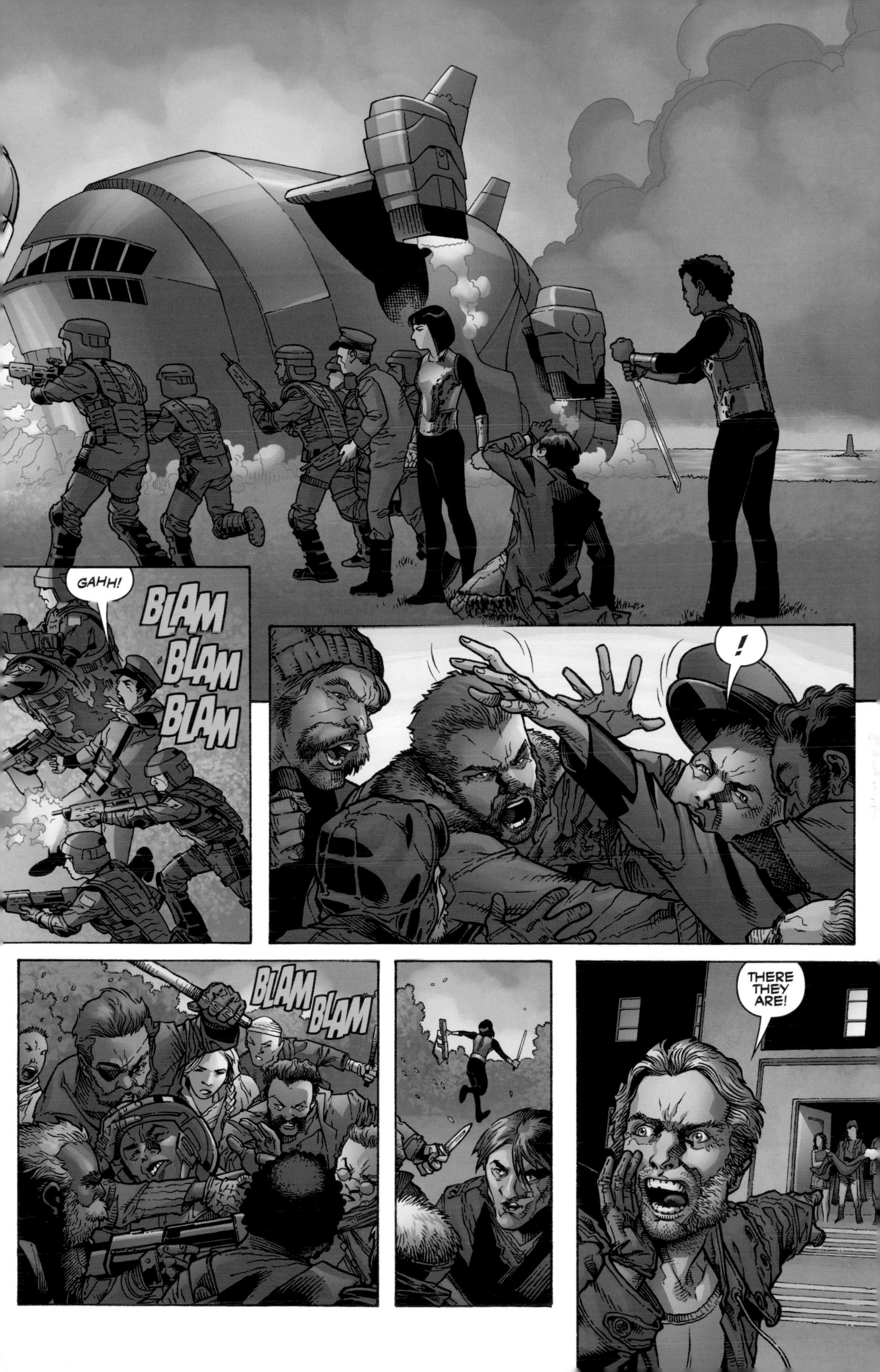
GAHH!
BLAM BLAM BLAM
!
BLAM BLAM
THERE THEY ARE!

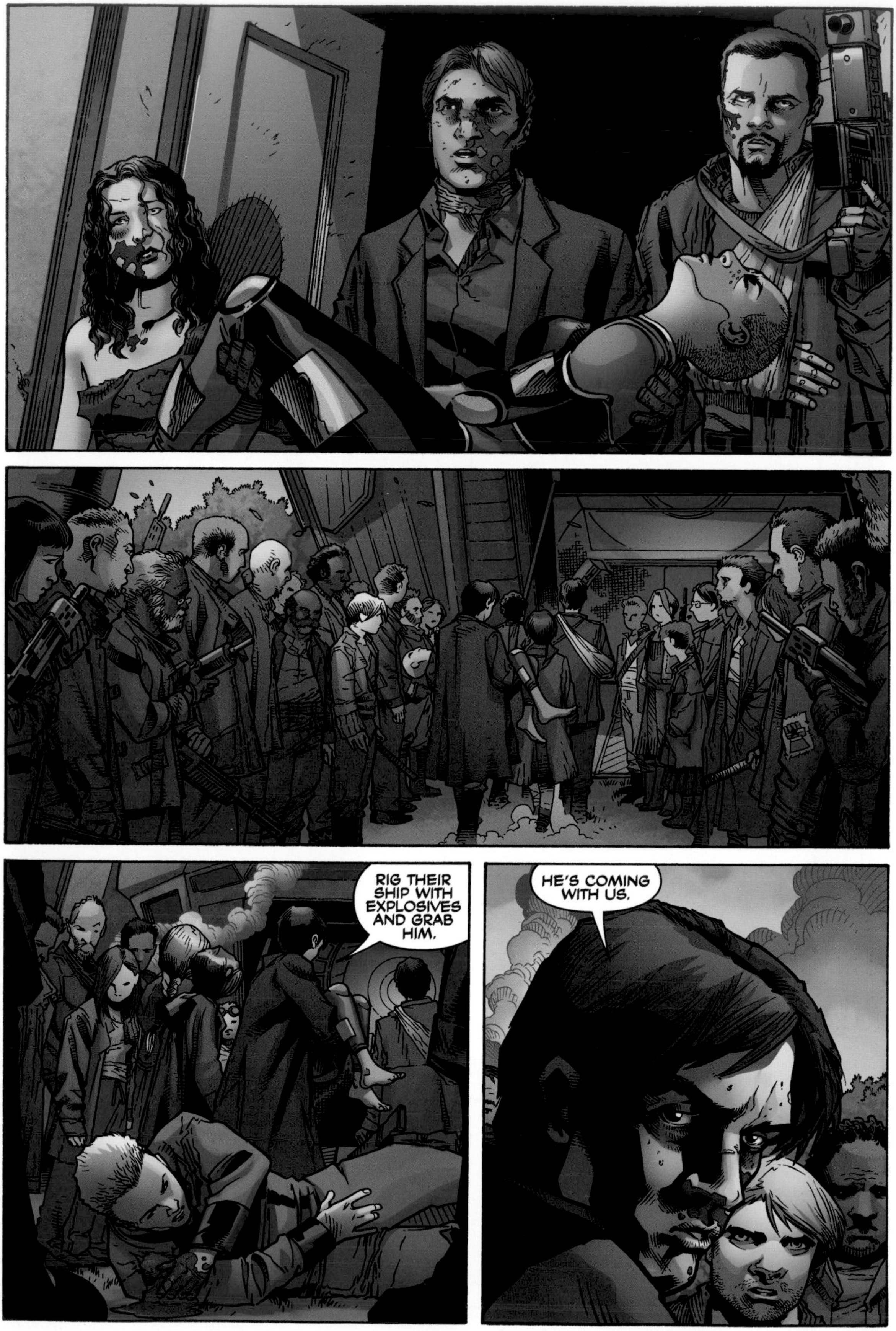
RIG THEIR SHIP WITH EXPLOSIVES AND GRAB HIM.
HE'S COMING WITH US.

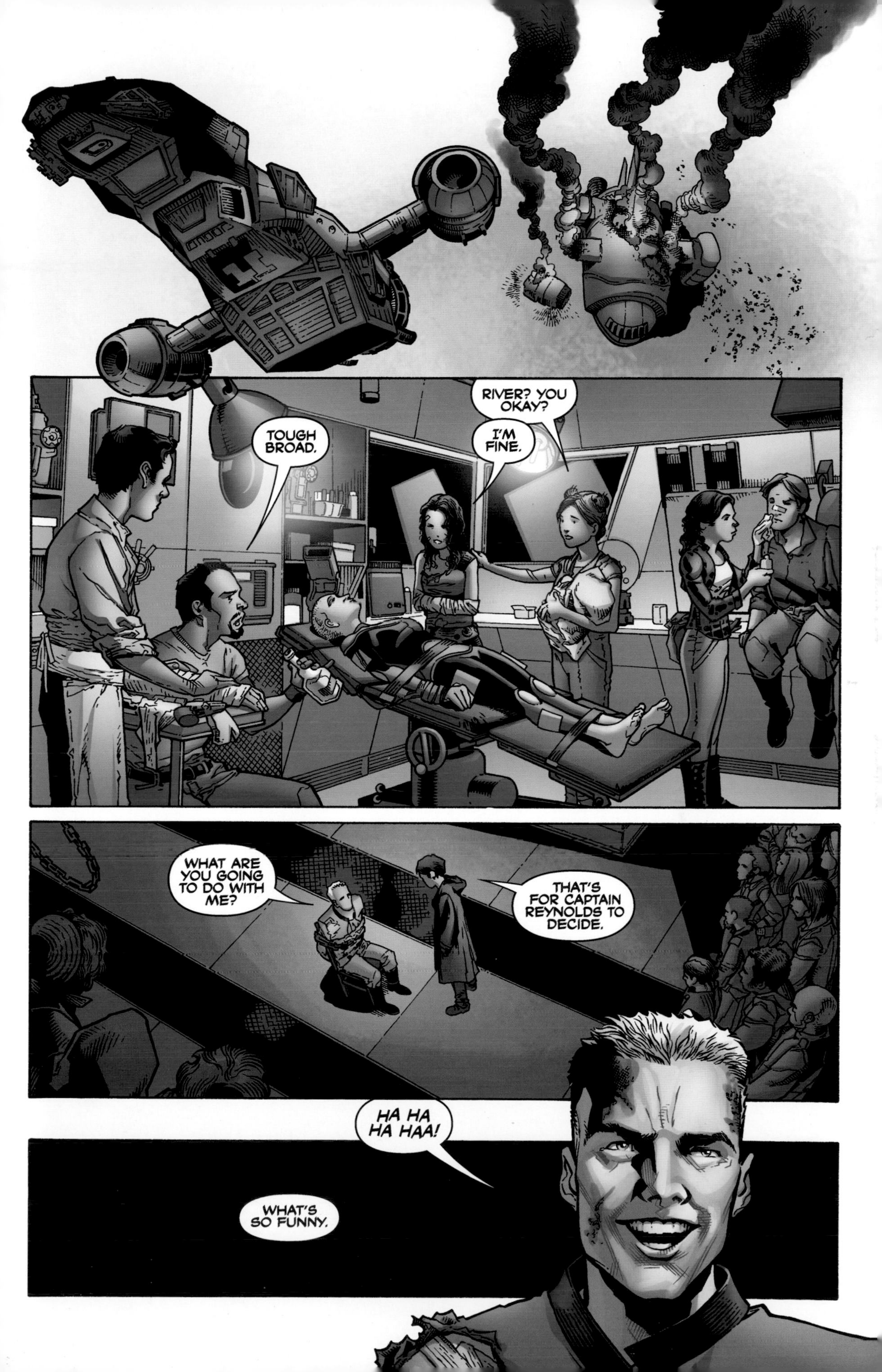
TOUGH BROAD.
RIVER? YOU OKAY?
I'M FINE.
WHAT ARE YOU GOING TO DO WITH ME?
THAT'S FOR CAPTAIN REYNOLDS TO DECIDE.
HA HA HA HAA!
WHAT'S SO FUNNY.

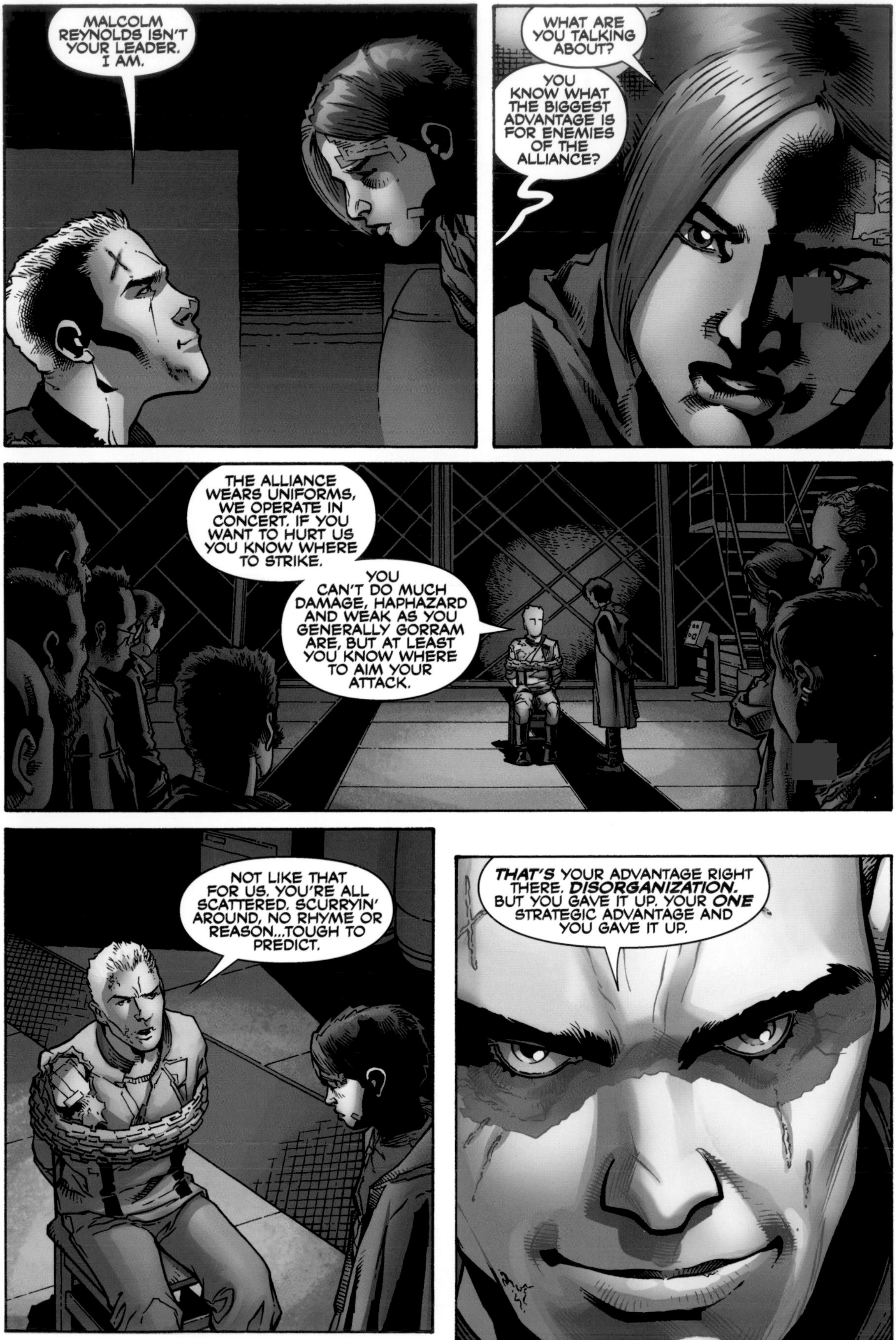
MALCOLM REYNOLDS ISN'T YOUR LEADER. I AM.
WHAT ARE YOU TALKING ABOUT?
YOU KNOW WHAT THE BIGGEST ADVANTAGE IS FOR ENEMIES OF THE ALLIANCE?
THE ALLIANCE WEARS UNIFORMS, WE OPERATE IN CONCERT. IF YOU WANT TO HURT US YOU KNOW WHERE TO STRIKE.
YOU CAN'T DO MUCH DAMAGE, HAPHAZARD AND WEAK AS YOU GENERALLY GORRAM ARE, BUT AT LEAST YOU KNOW WHERE TO AIM YOUR ATTACK.
NOT LIKE THAT FOR US. YOU'RE ALL SCATTERED, SCURRYIN' AROUND, NO RHYME OR REASON...TOUGH TO PREDICT.
THAT'S YOUR ADVANTAGE RIGHT THERE. *DISORGANIZATION.* BUT YOU GAVE IT UP. YOUR *ONE* STRATEGIC ADVANTAGE AND YOU GAVE IT UP.

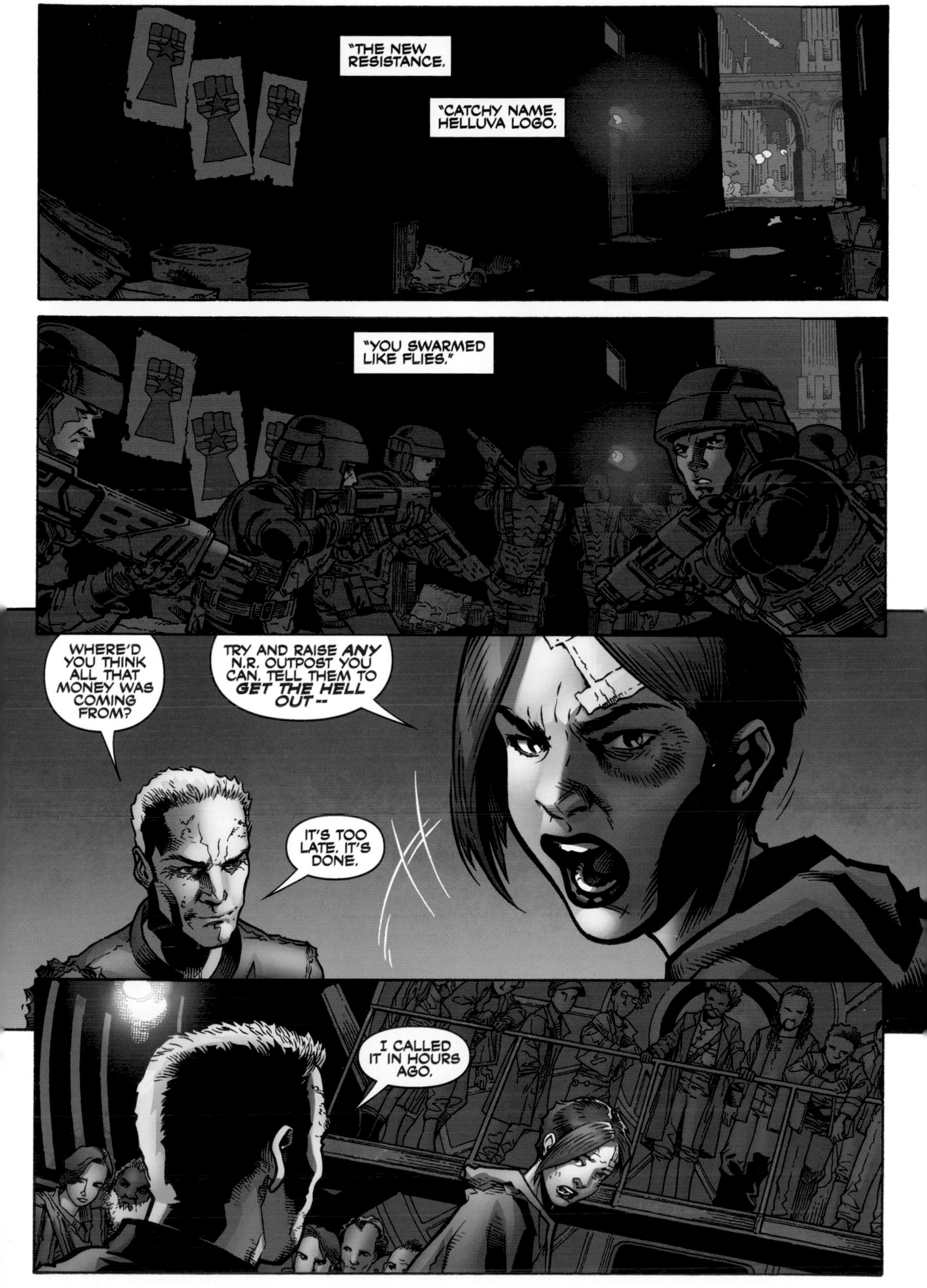
"THE NEW RESISTANCE.
"CATCHY NAME. HELLUVA LOGO.
"YOU SWARMED LIKE FLIES."
WHERE'D YOU THINK ALL THAT MONEY WAS COMING FROM?
TRY AND RAISE ANY N.R. OUTPOST YOU CAN. TELL THEM TO GET THE HELL OUT --
IT'S TOO LATE. IT'S DONE.
I CALLED IT IN HOURS AGO.

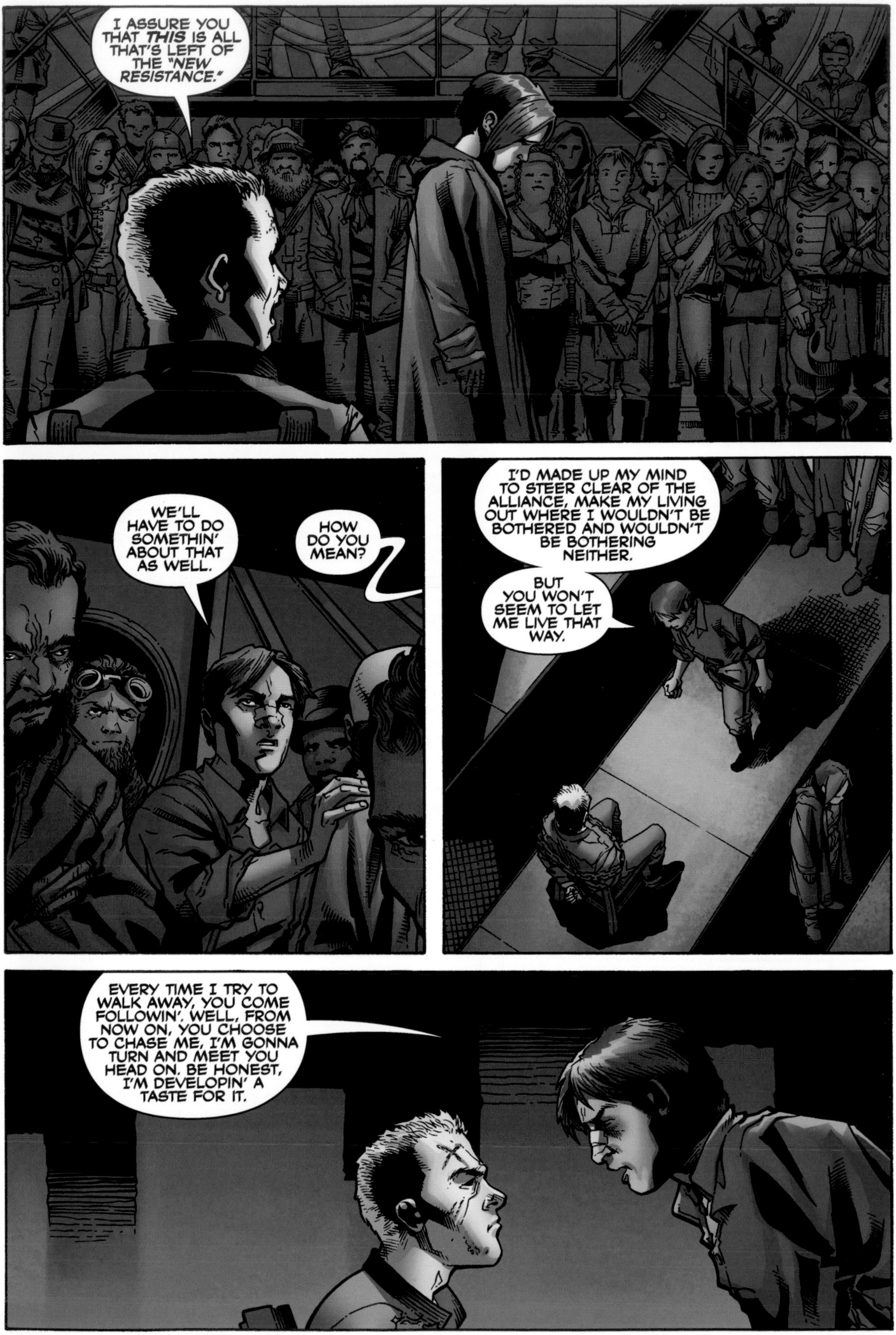
I ASSURE YOU THAT THIS IS ALL THAT'S LEFT OF THE "NEW RESISTANCE."
WE'LL HAVE TO DO SOMETHIN' ABOUT THAT AS WELL.
HOW DO YOU MEAN?
I'D MADE UP MY MIND TO STEER CLEAR OF THE ALLIANCE, MAKE MY LIVING OUT WHERE I WOULDN'T BE BOTHERED AND WOULDN'T BE BOTHERING NEITHER.
BUT YOU WON'T SEEM TO LET ME LIVE THAT WAY.
EVERY TIME I TRY TO WALK AWAY, YOU COME FOLLOWIN'. WELL, FROM NOW ON, YOU CHOOSE TO CHASE ME, I'M GONNA TURN AND MEET YOU HEAD ON. BE HONEST, I'M DEVELOPIN' A TASTE FOR IT.

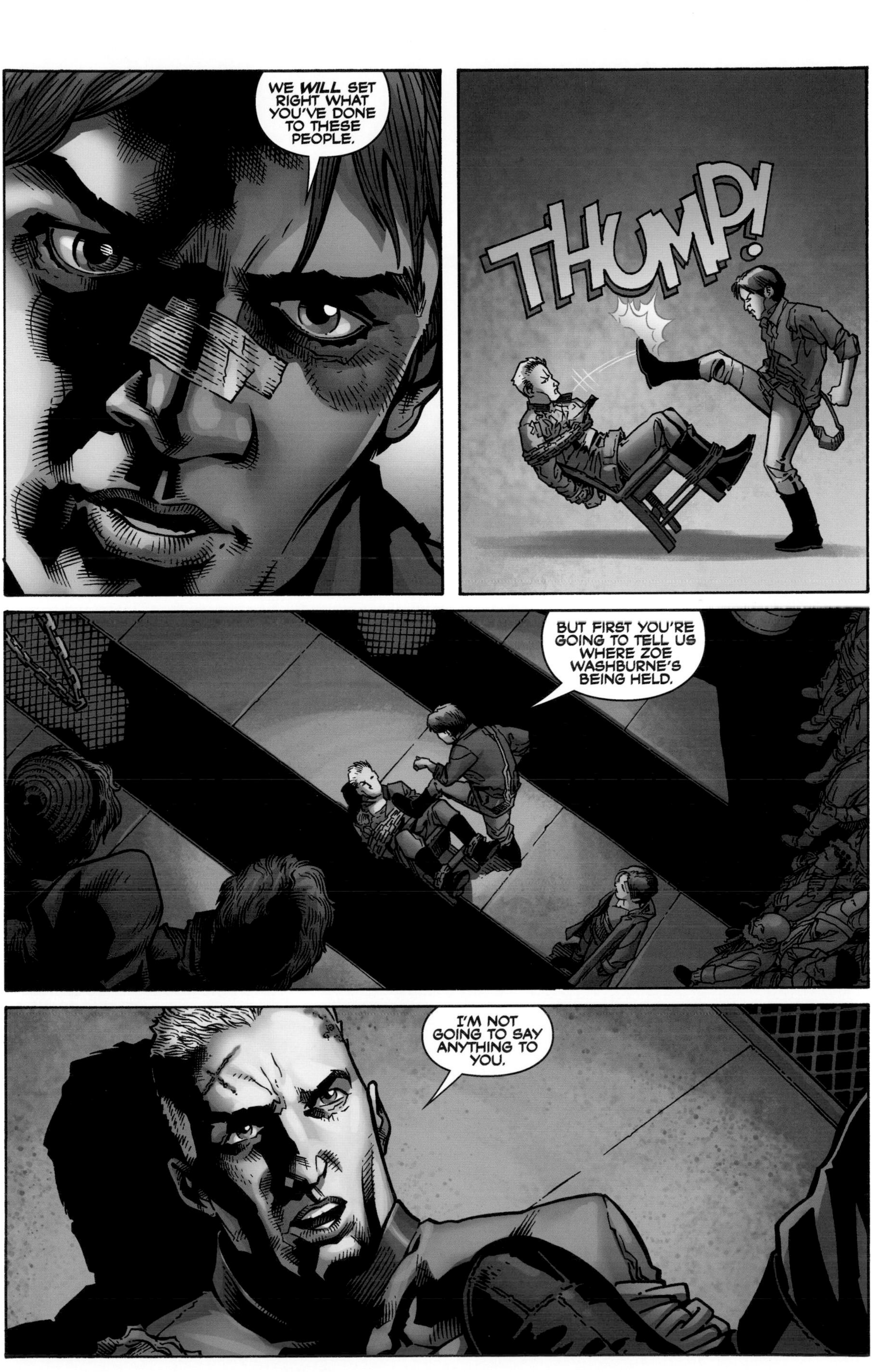
WE WILL SET RIGHT WHAT YOU'VE DONE TO THESE PEOPLE.
THUMP!
BUT FIRST YOU'RE GOING TO TELL US WHERE ZOE WASHBURNE'S BEING HELD.
I'M NOT GOING TO SAY ANYTHING TO YOU.

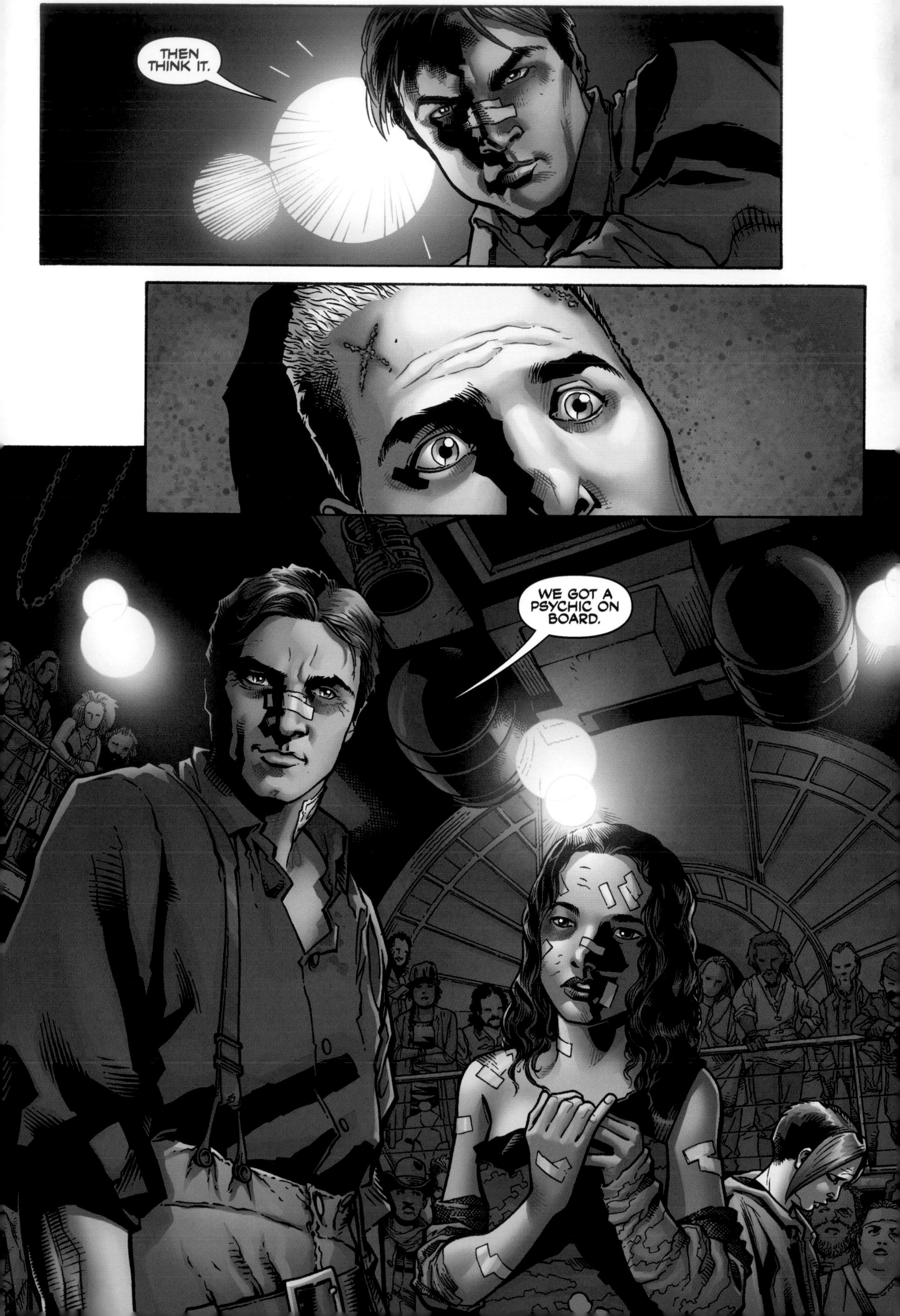
THEN THINK IT.
WE GOT A PSYCHIC ON BOARD.

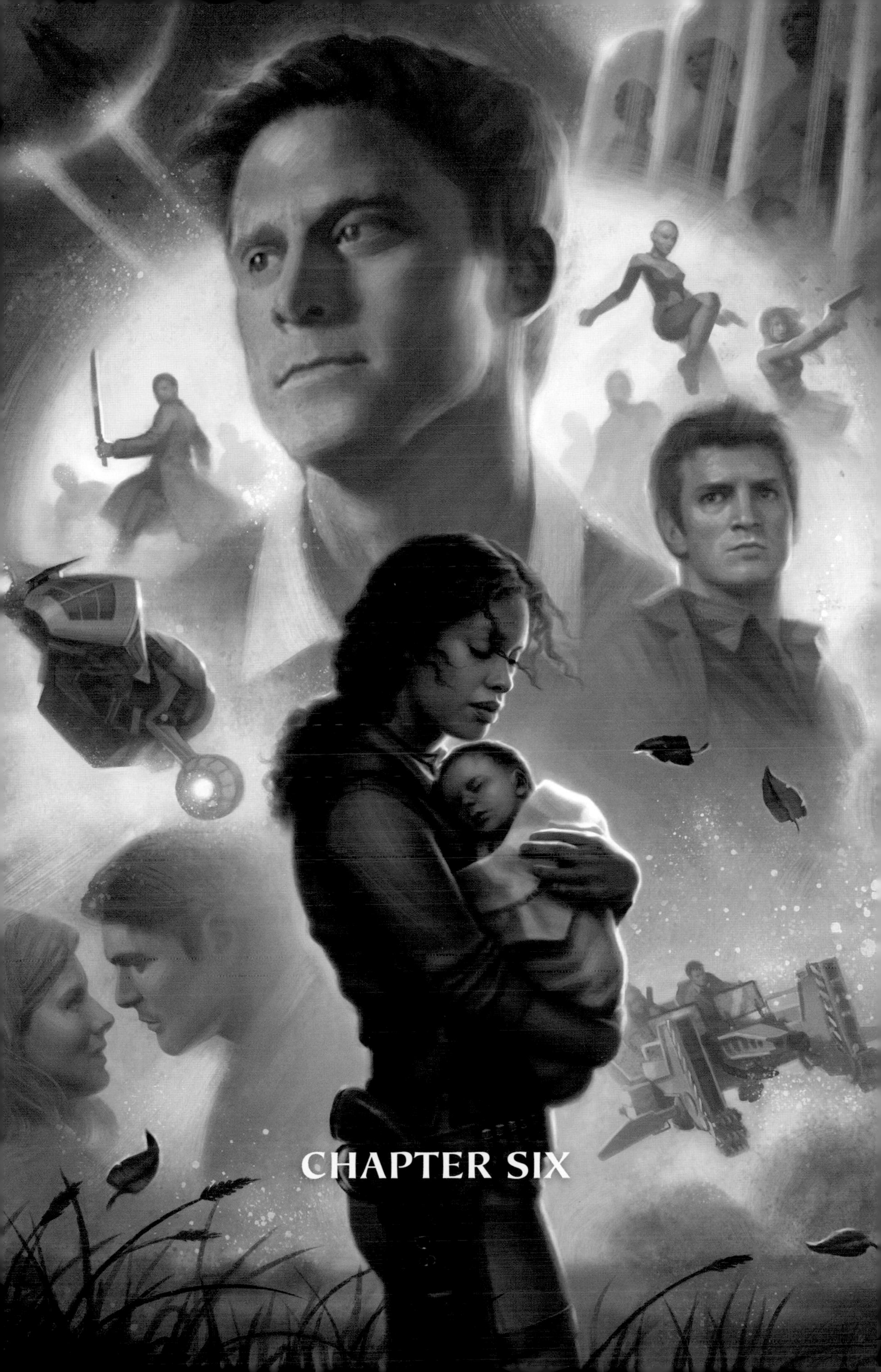

CHAPTER SIX

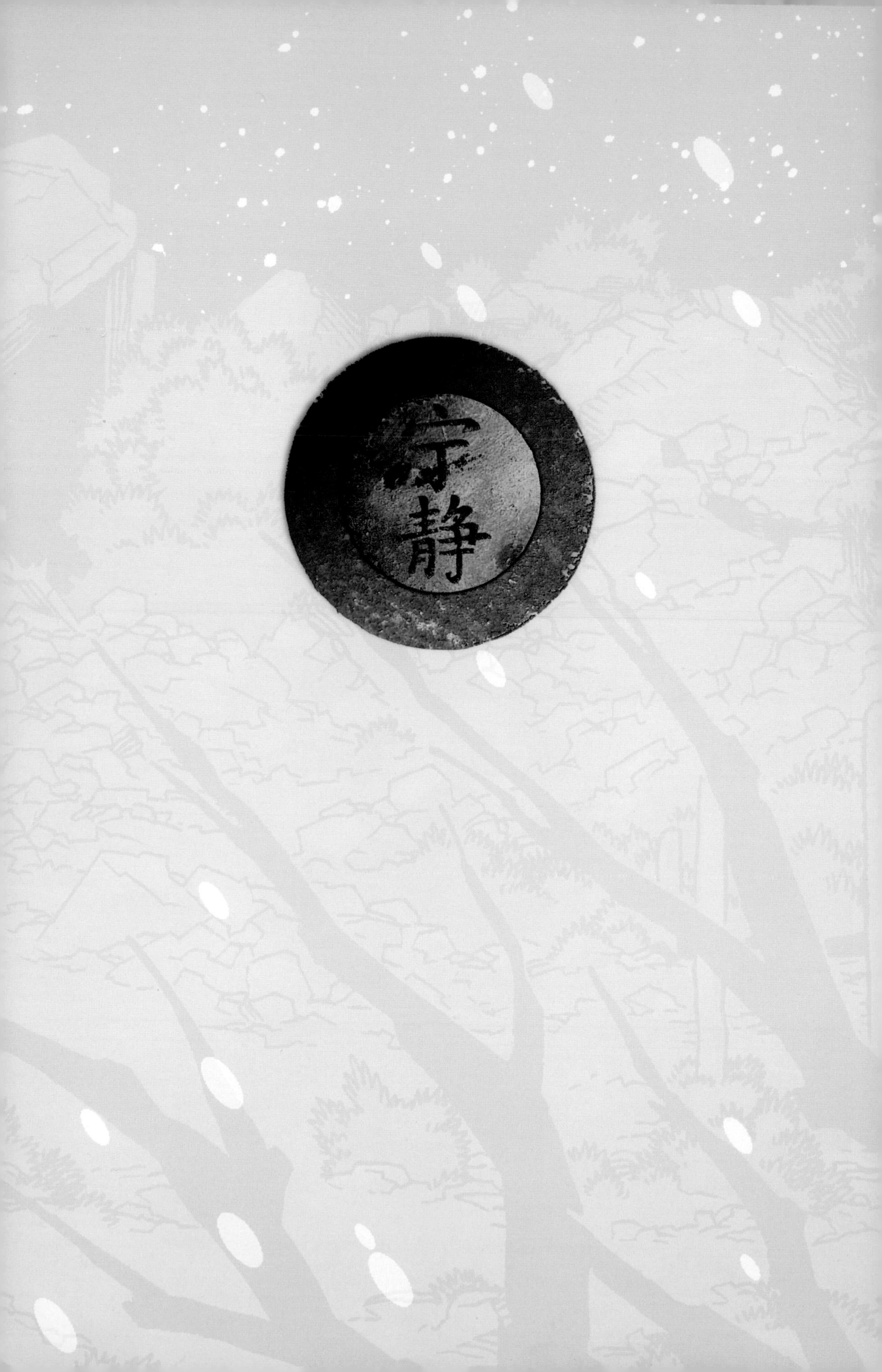
守静

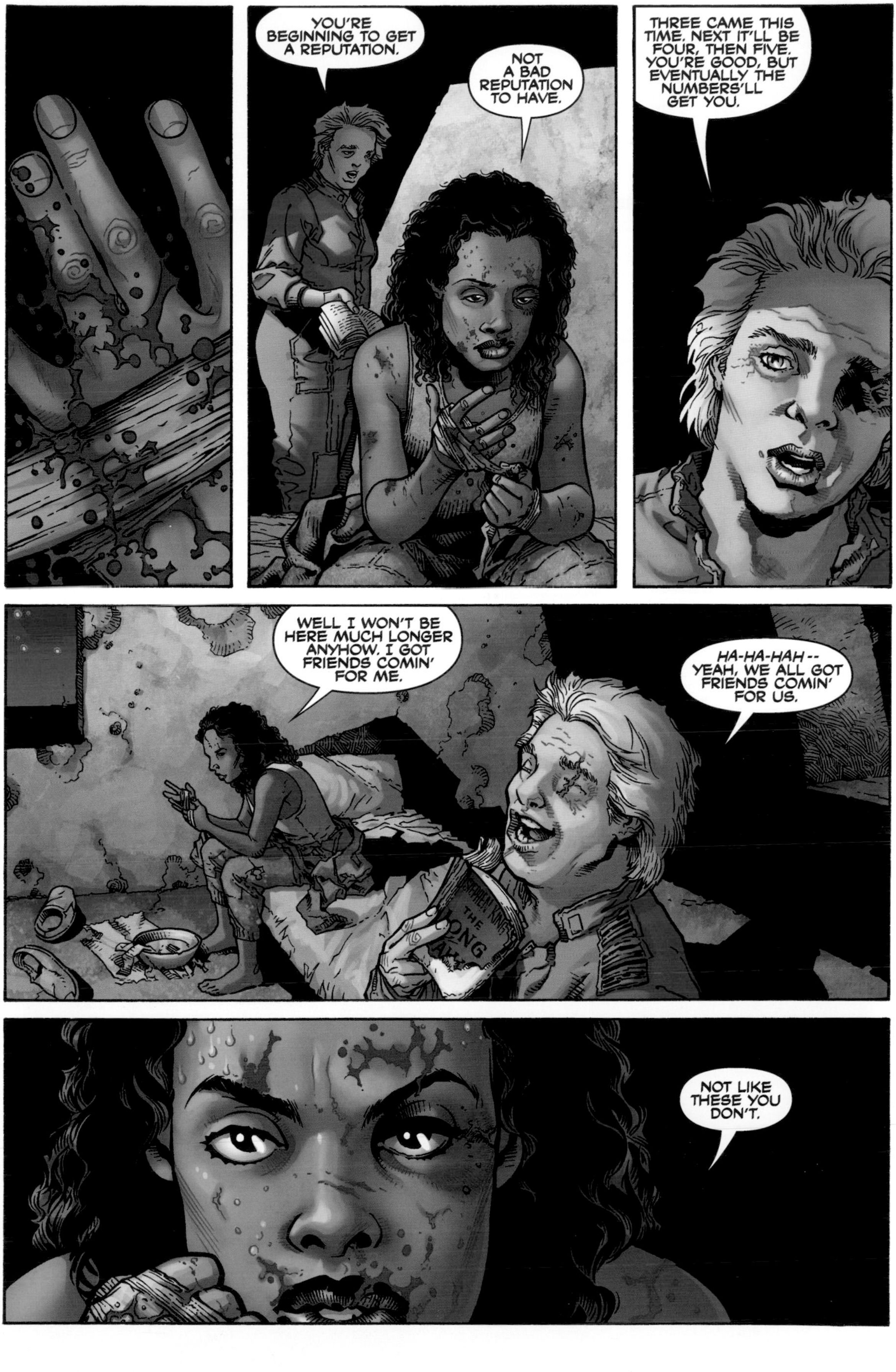
YOU'RE BEGINNING TO GET A REPUTATION.
NOT A BAD REPUTATION TO HAVE.
THREE CAME THIS TIME. NEXT IT'LL BE FOUR, THEN FIVE. YOU'RE GOOD, BUT EVENTUALLY THE NUMBERS'LL GET YOU.
WELL I WON'T BE HERE MUCH LONGER ANYHOW. I GOT FRIENDS COMIN' FOR ME.
HA-HA-HAH -- YEAH, WE ALL GOT FRIENDS COMIN' FOR US.
NOT LIKE THESE YOU DON'T.

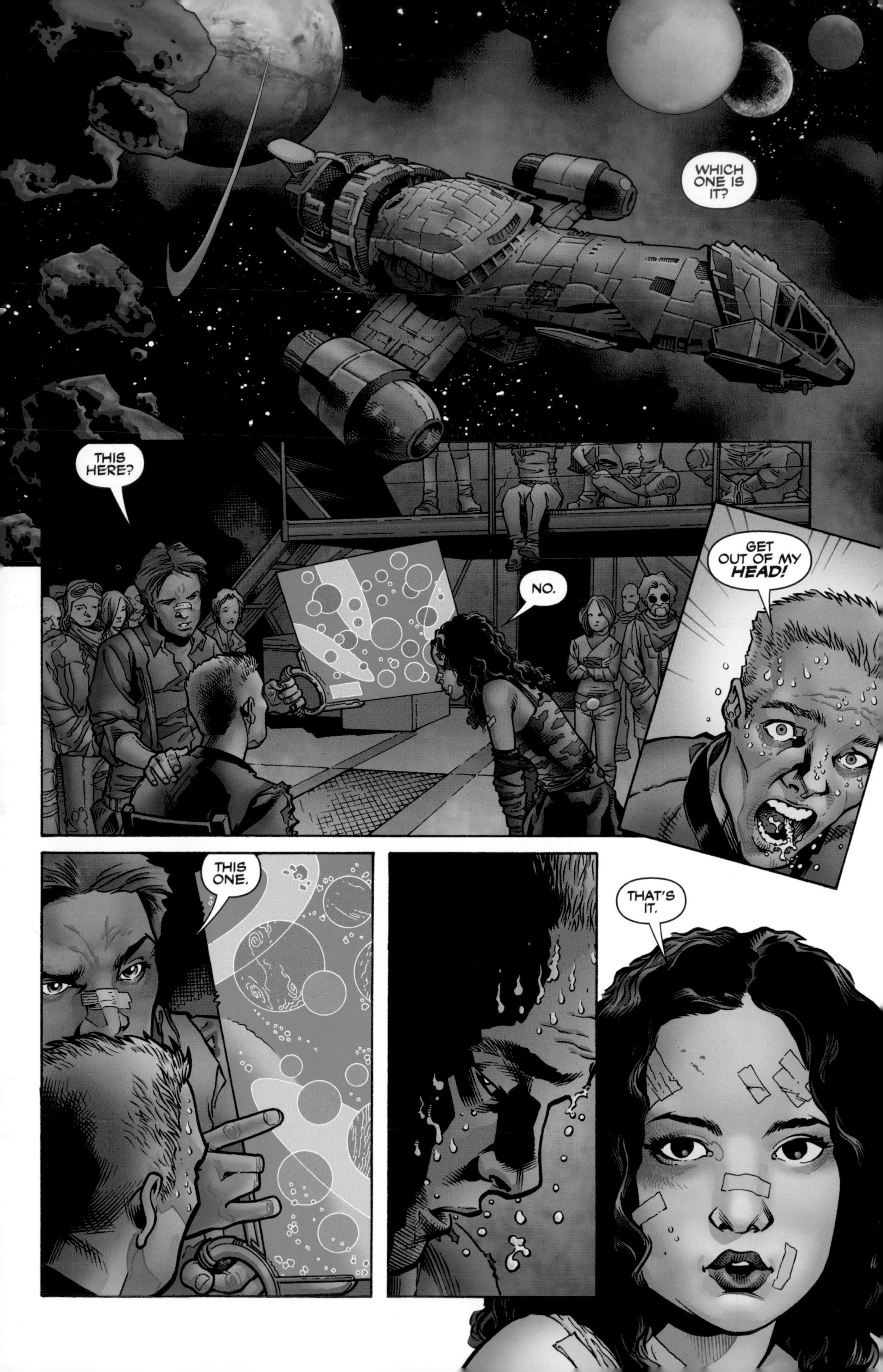
WHICH ONE IS IT?
THIS HERE?
NO.
GET OUT OF MY **HEAD!**
THIS ONE.
THAT'S IT.

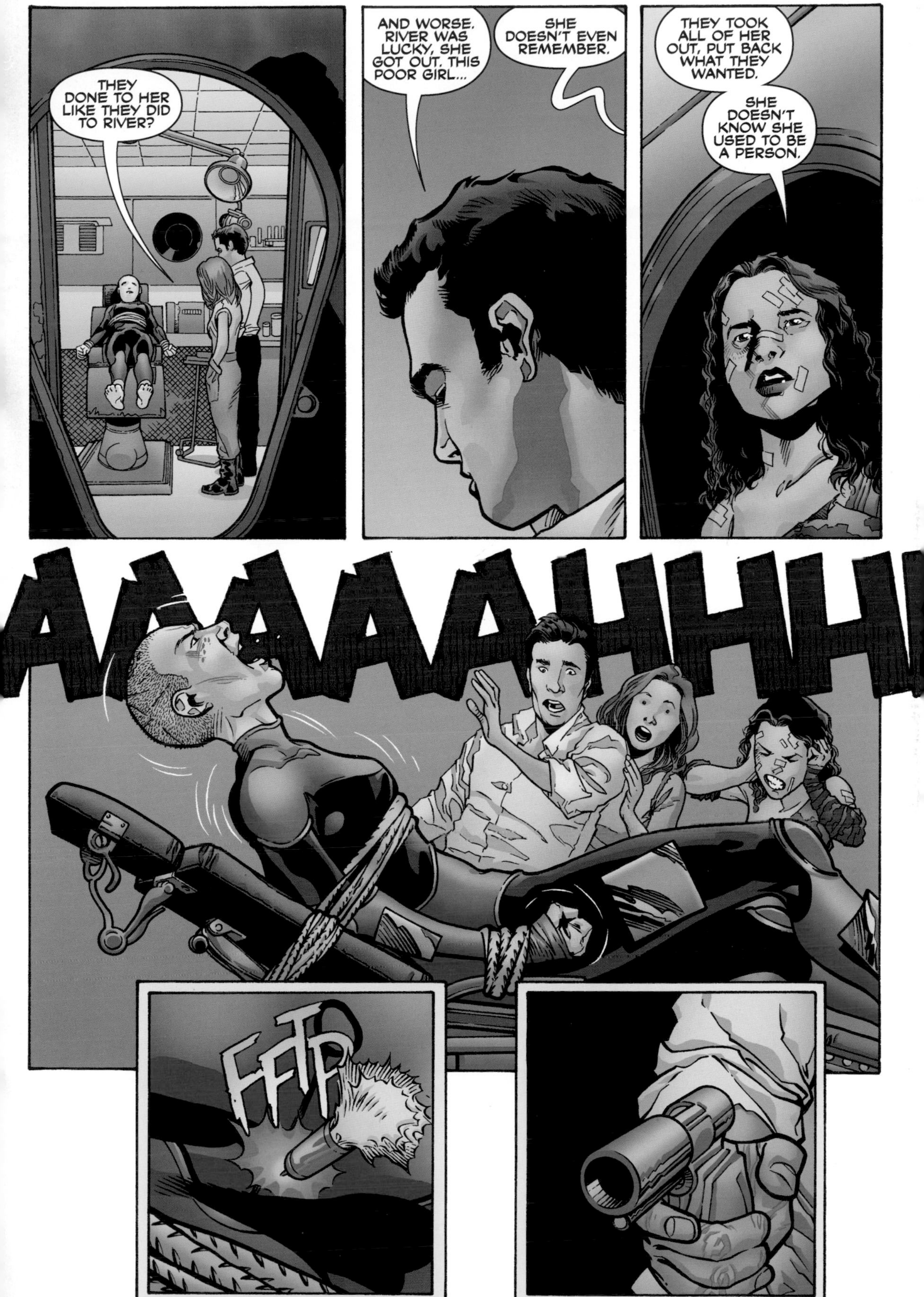
THEY DONE TO HER LIKE THEY DID TO RIVER?
AND WORSE. RIVER WAS LUCKY, SHE GOT OUT. THIS POOR GIRL...
SHE DOESN'T EVEN REMEMBER.
THEY TOOK ALL OF HER OUT, PUT BACK WHAT THEY WANTED.
SHE DOESN'T KNOW SHE USED TO BE A PERSON.
AAAAAHHHH
FFTP

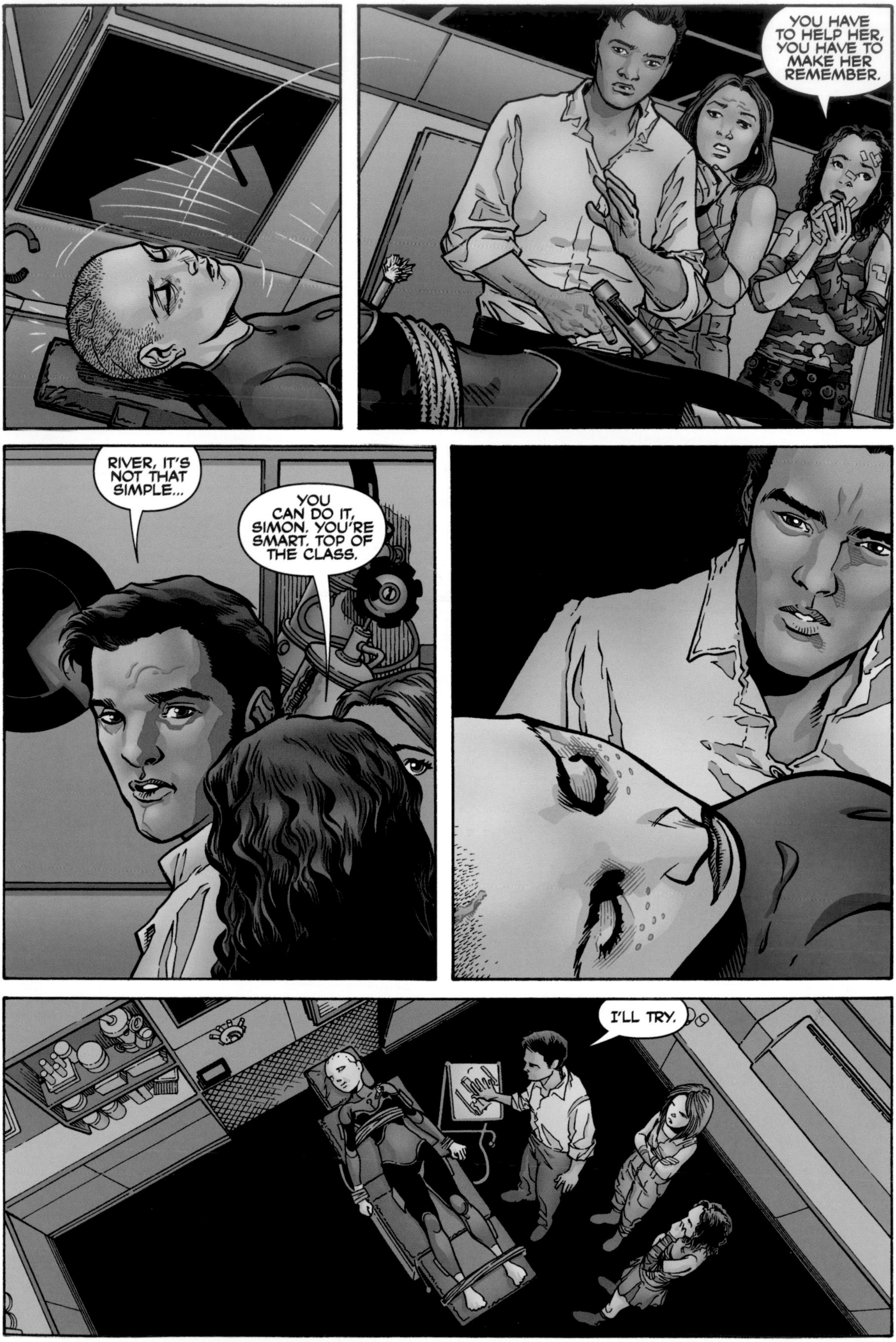
YOU HAVE TO HELP HER, YOU HAVE TO MAKE HER REMEMBER.
RIVER, IT'S NOT THAT SIMPLE...
YOU CAN DO IT, SIMON. YOU'RE SMART. TOP OF THE CLASS.
I'LL TRY.

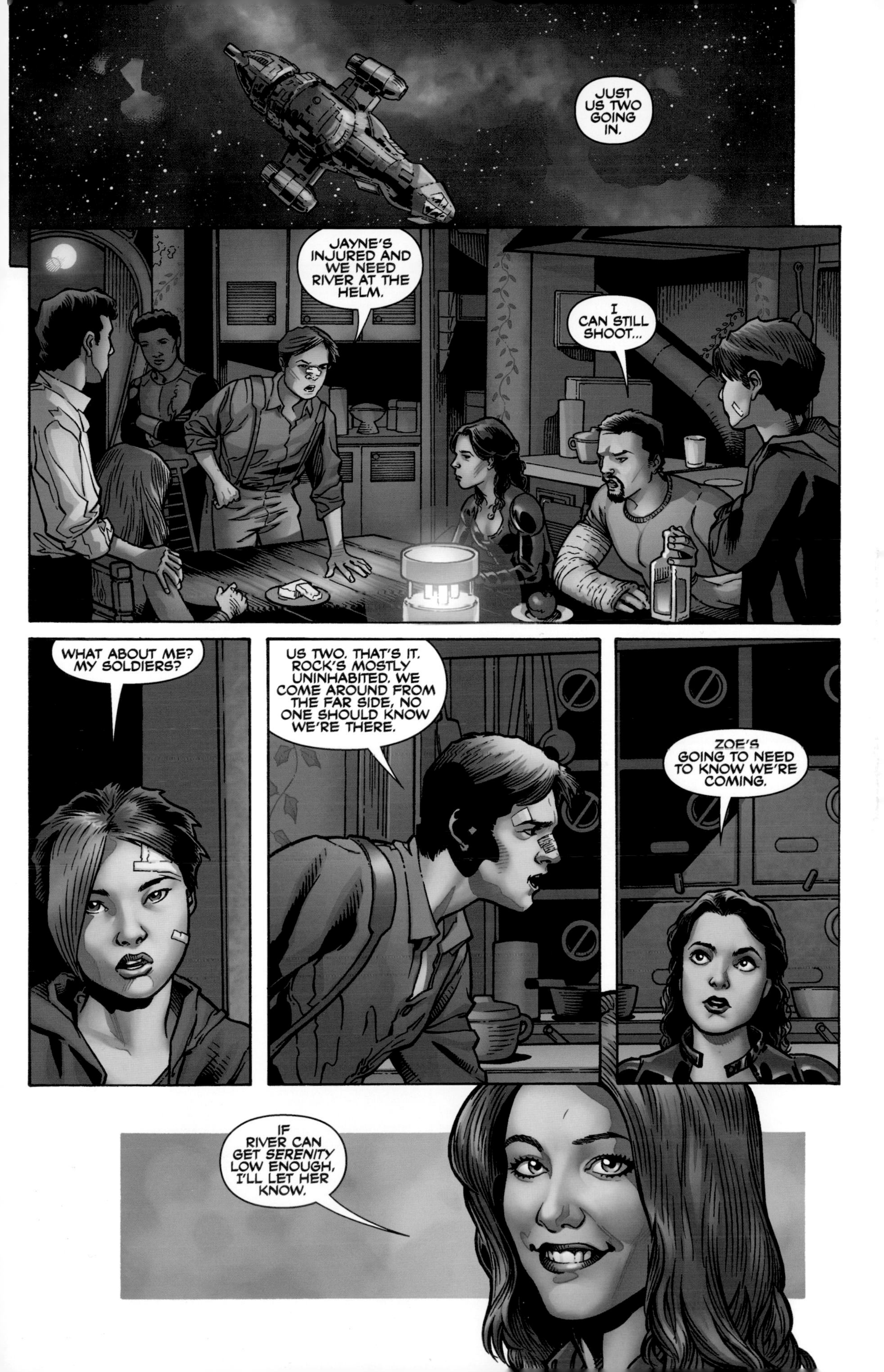
JUST US TWO GOING IN.
JAYNE'S INJURED AND WE NEED RIVER AT THE HELM.
I CAN STILL SHOOT...
WHAT ABOUT ME? MY SOLDIERS?
US TWO. THAT'S IT. ROCK'S MOSTLY UNINHABITED. WE COME AROUND FROM THE FAR SIDE, NO ONE SHOULD KNOW WE'RE THERE.
ZOE'S GOING TO NEED TO KNOW WE'RE COMING.
IF RIVER CAN GET *SERENITY* LOW ENOUGH, I'LL LET HER KNOW.

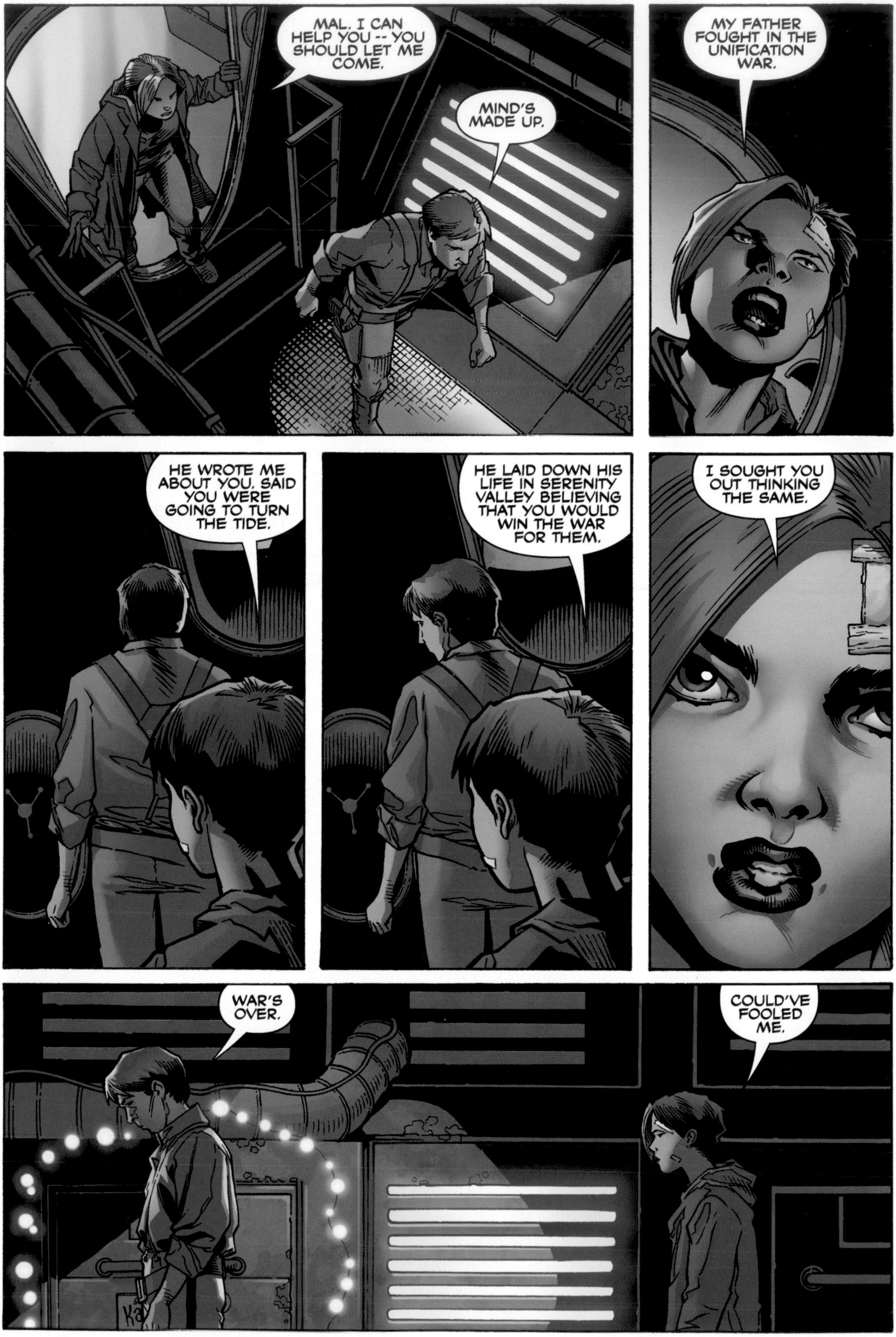
MAL, I CAN HELP YOU -- YOU SHOULD LET ME COME.
MIND'S MADE UP.
MY FATHER FOUGHT IN THE UNIFICATION WAR.
HE WROTE ME ABOUT YOU. SAID YOU WERE GOING TO TURN THE TIDE.
HE LAID DOWN HIS LIFE IN SERENITY VALLEY BELIEVING THAT YOU WOULD WIN THE WAR FOR THEM.
I SOUGHT YOU OUT THINKING THE SAME.
WAR'S OVER.
COULD'VE FOOLED ME.

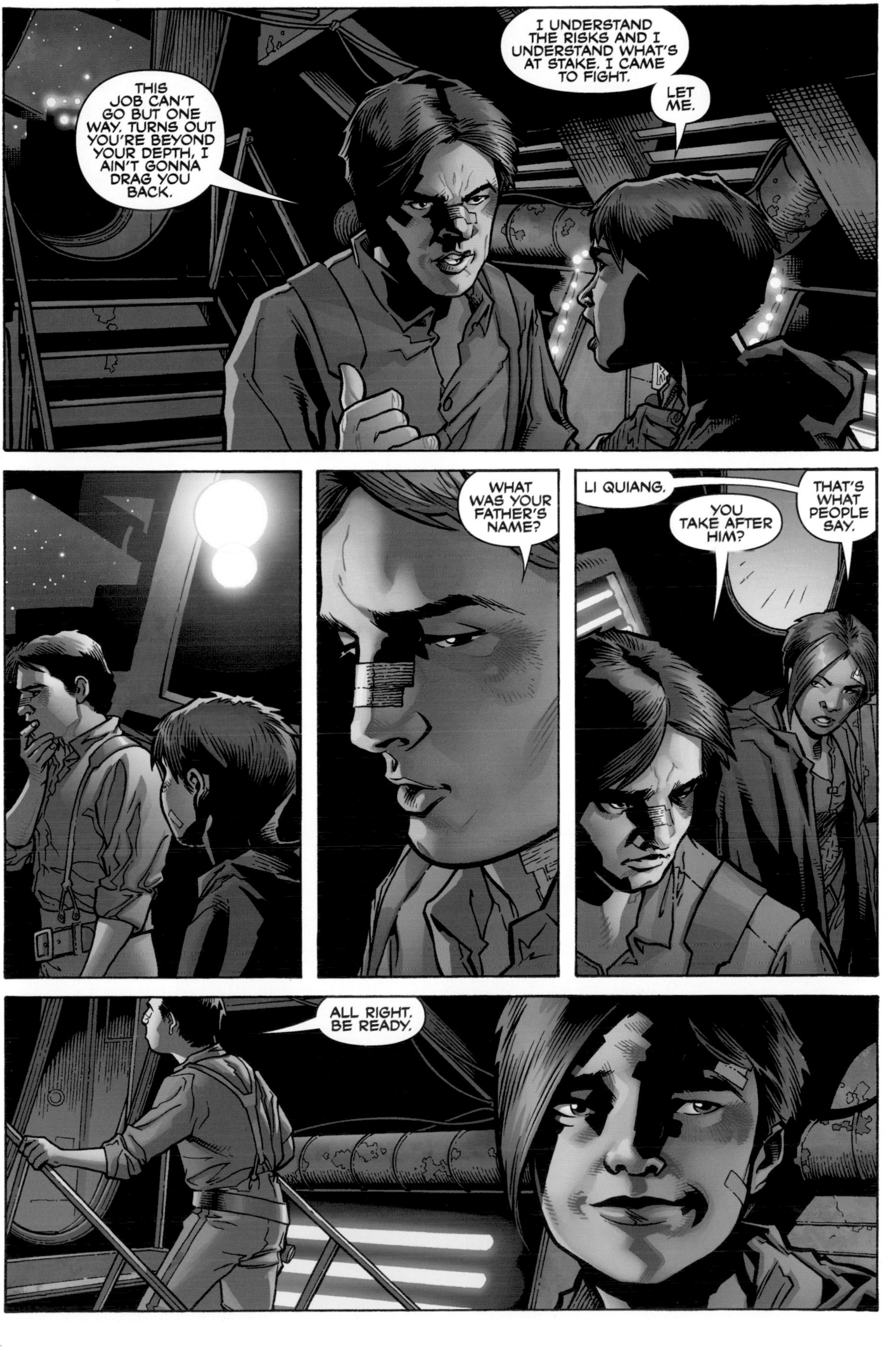
THIS JOB CAN'T GO BUT ONE WAY. TURNS OUT YOU'RE BEYOND YOUR DEPTH, I AIN'T GONNA DRAG YOU BACK.
I UNDERSTAND THE RISKS AND I UNDERSTAND WHAT'S AT STAKE. I CAME TO FIGHT.
LET ME.
WHAT WAS YOUR FATHER'S NAME?
LI QUIANG.
YOU TAKE AFTER HIM?
THAT'S WHAT PEOPLE SAY.
ALL RIGHT. BE READY.

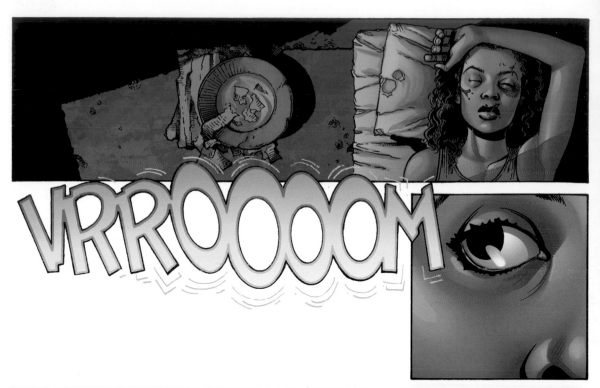

VRROOOOM

WHAT THE HELL WAS THAT?!

...A FIREFLY.

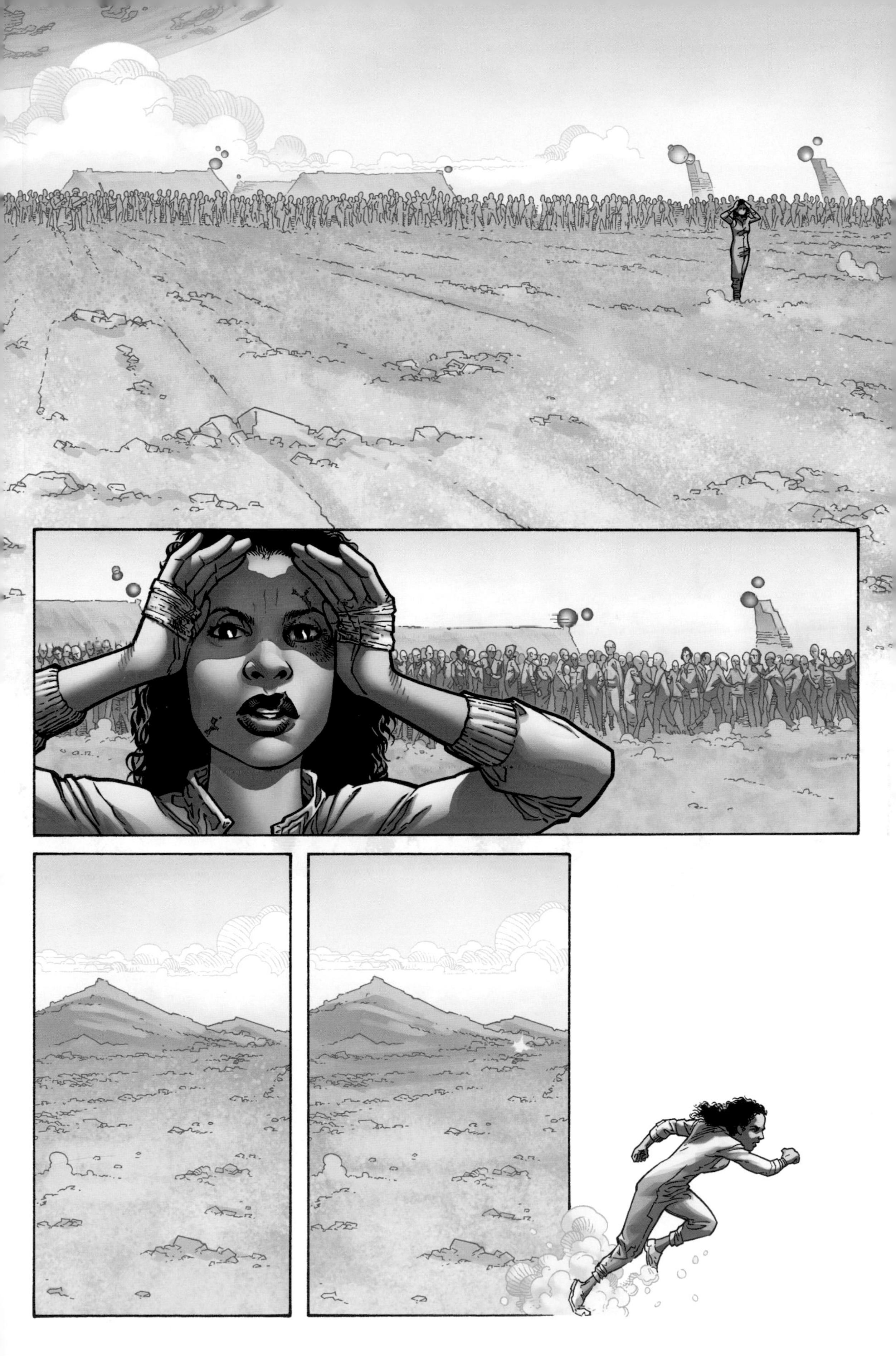

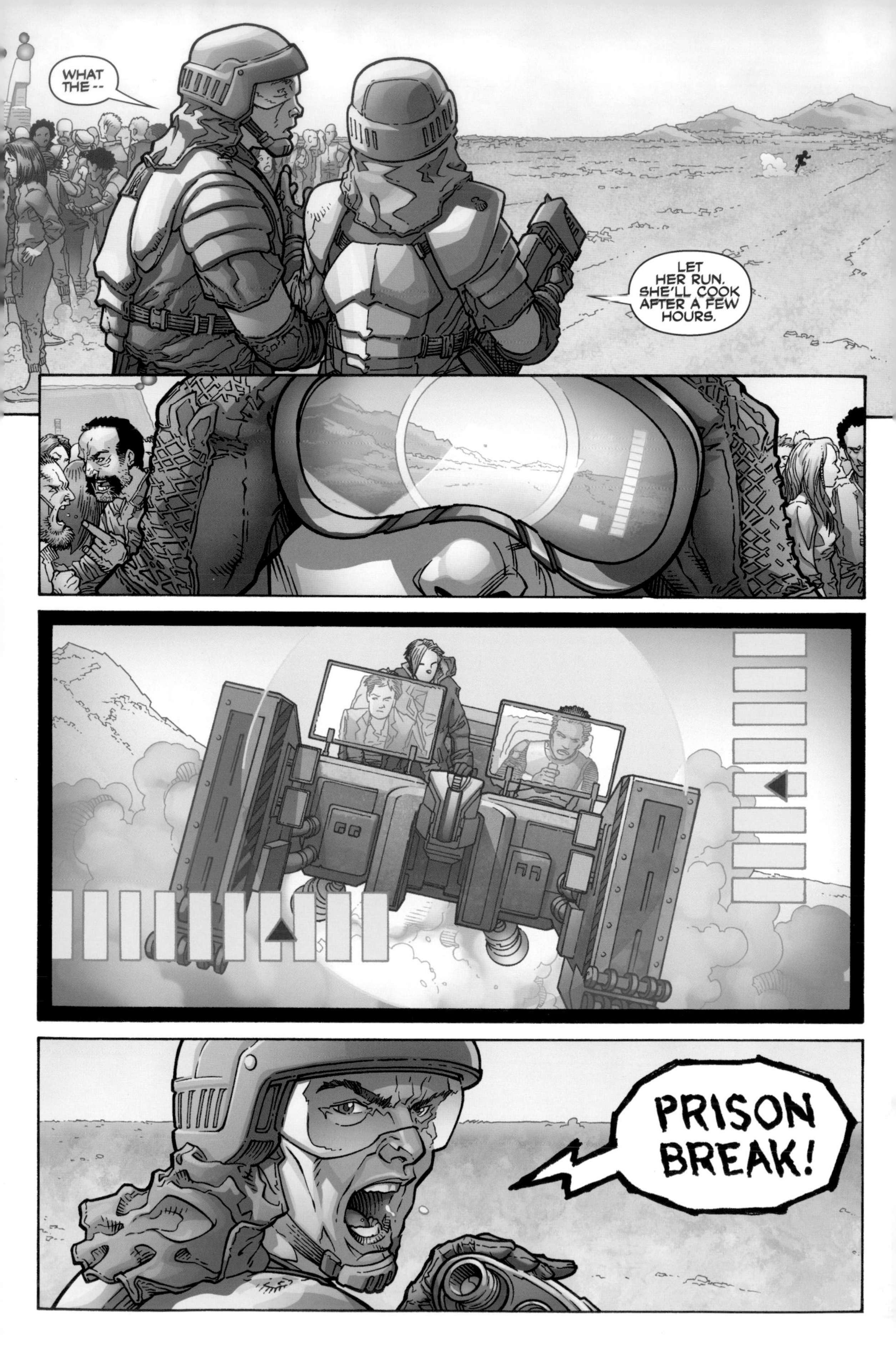
WHAT THE--
LET HER RUN. SHE'LL COOK AFTER A FEW HOURS.
PRISON BREAK!

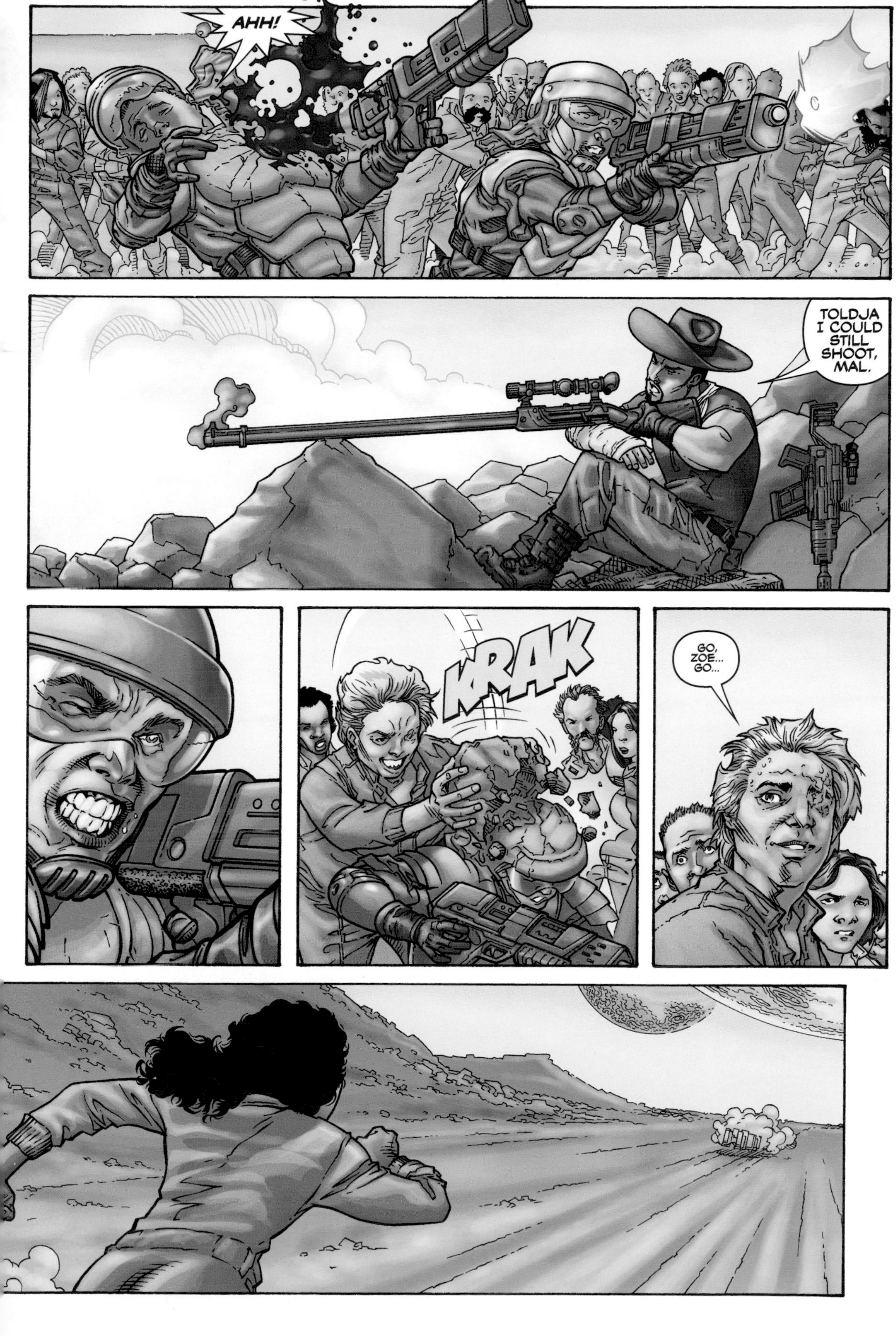
AHH!
TOLDJA I COULD STILL SHOOT, MAL.
KRAK
GO, ZOE... GO...

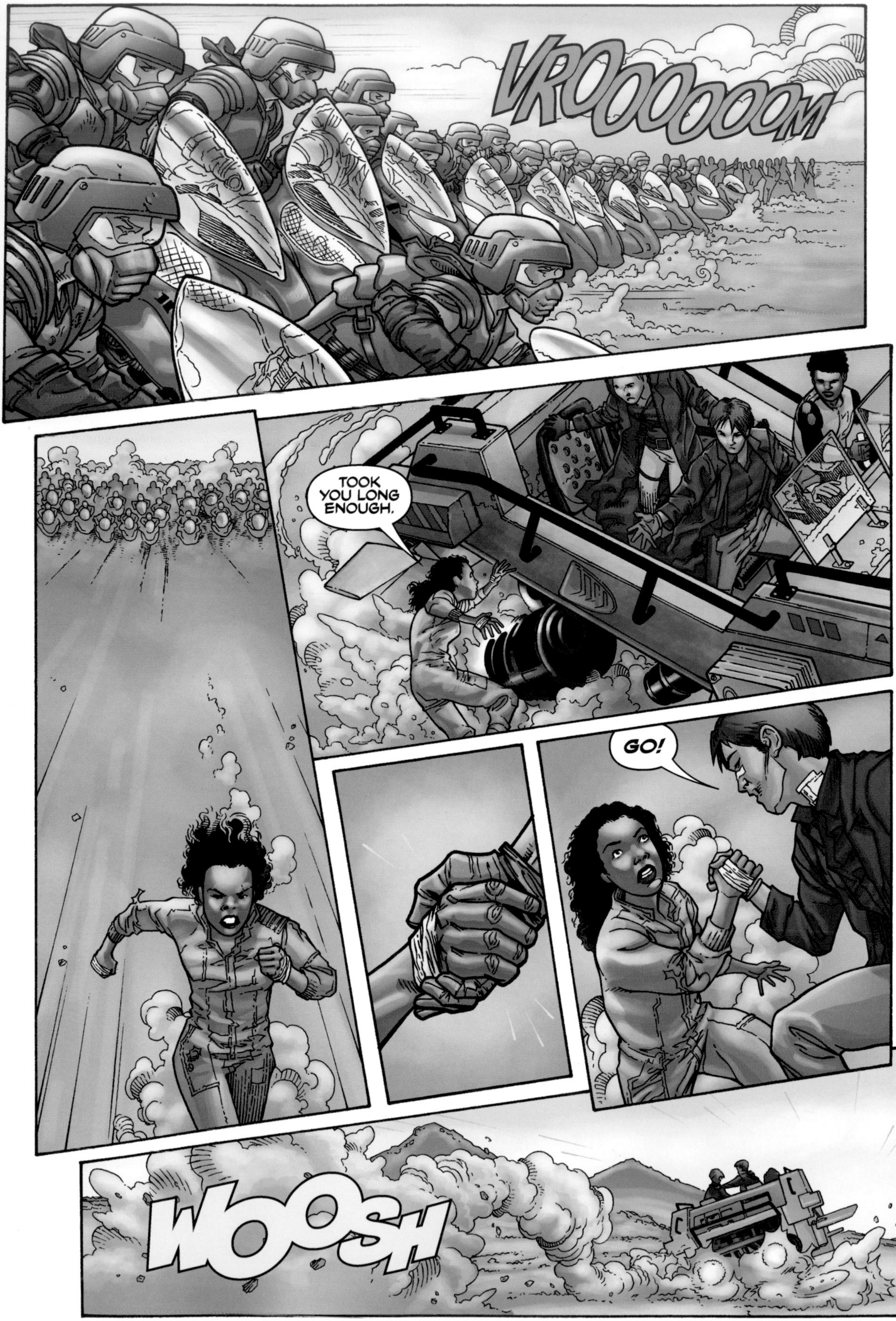
VROOOOOOOM
TOOK YOU LONG ENOUGH.
GO!
WOOSH

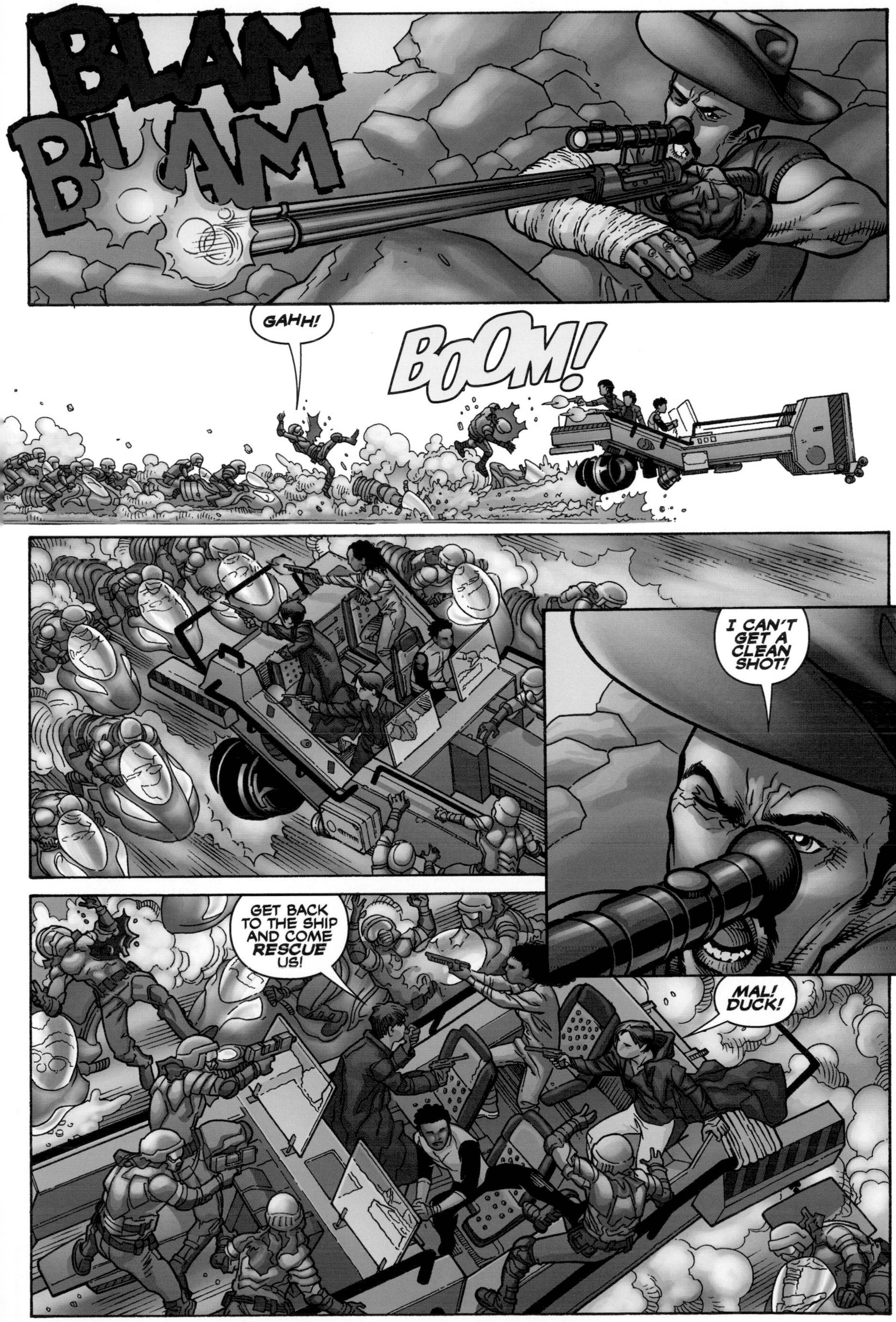
BLAM
BLAM
GAHH!
BOOM!
I CAN'T GET A CLEAN SHOT!
GET BACK TO THE SHIP AND COME RESCUE US!
MAL! DUCK!

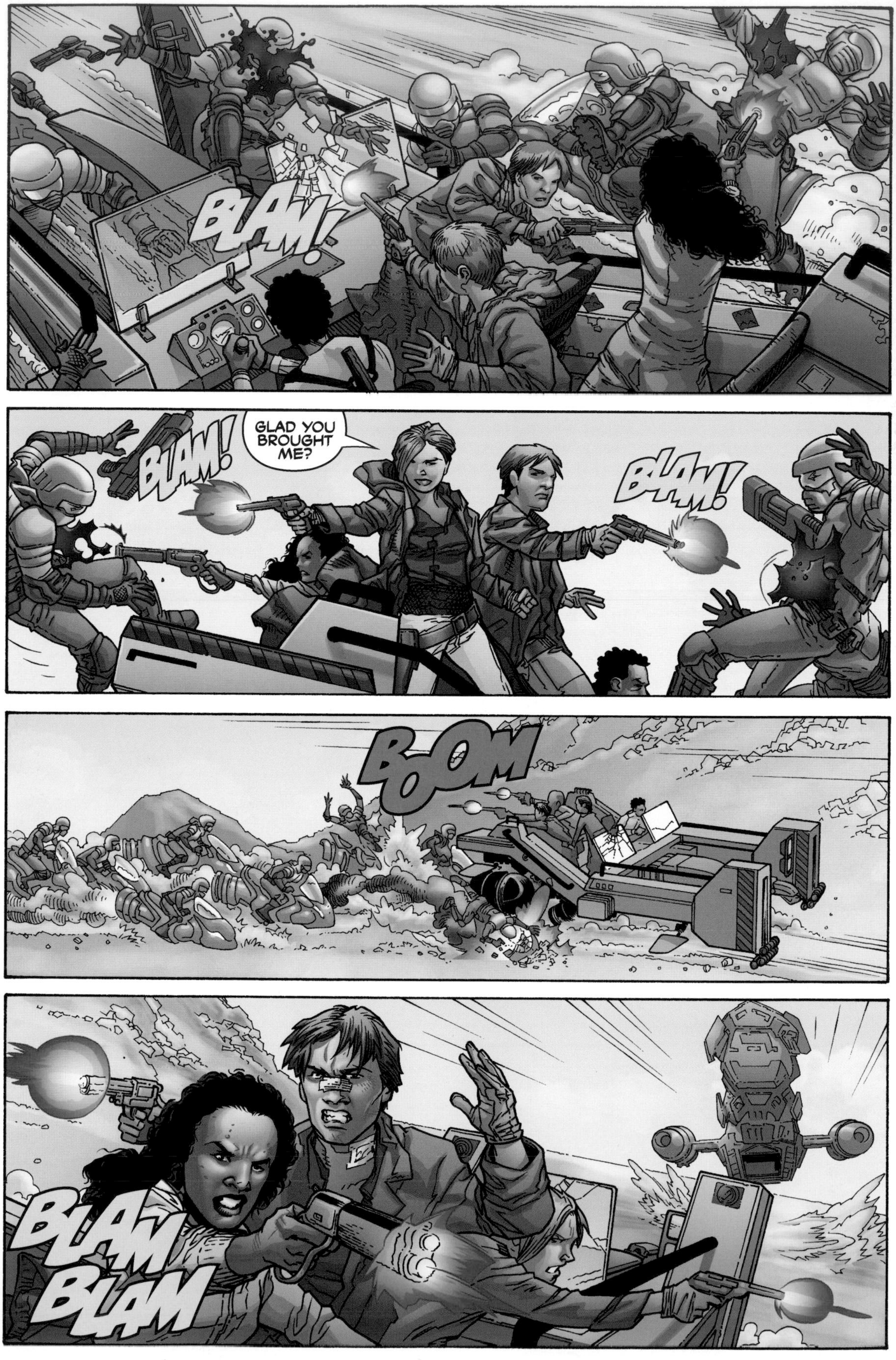
BLAM!
BLAM!
GLAD YOU BROUGHT ME?
BLAM!
BOOM
BLAM
BLAM

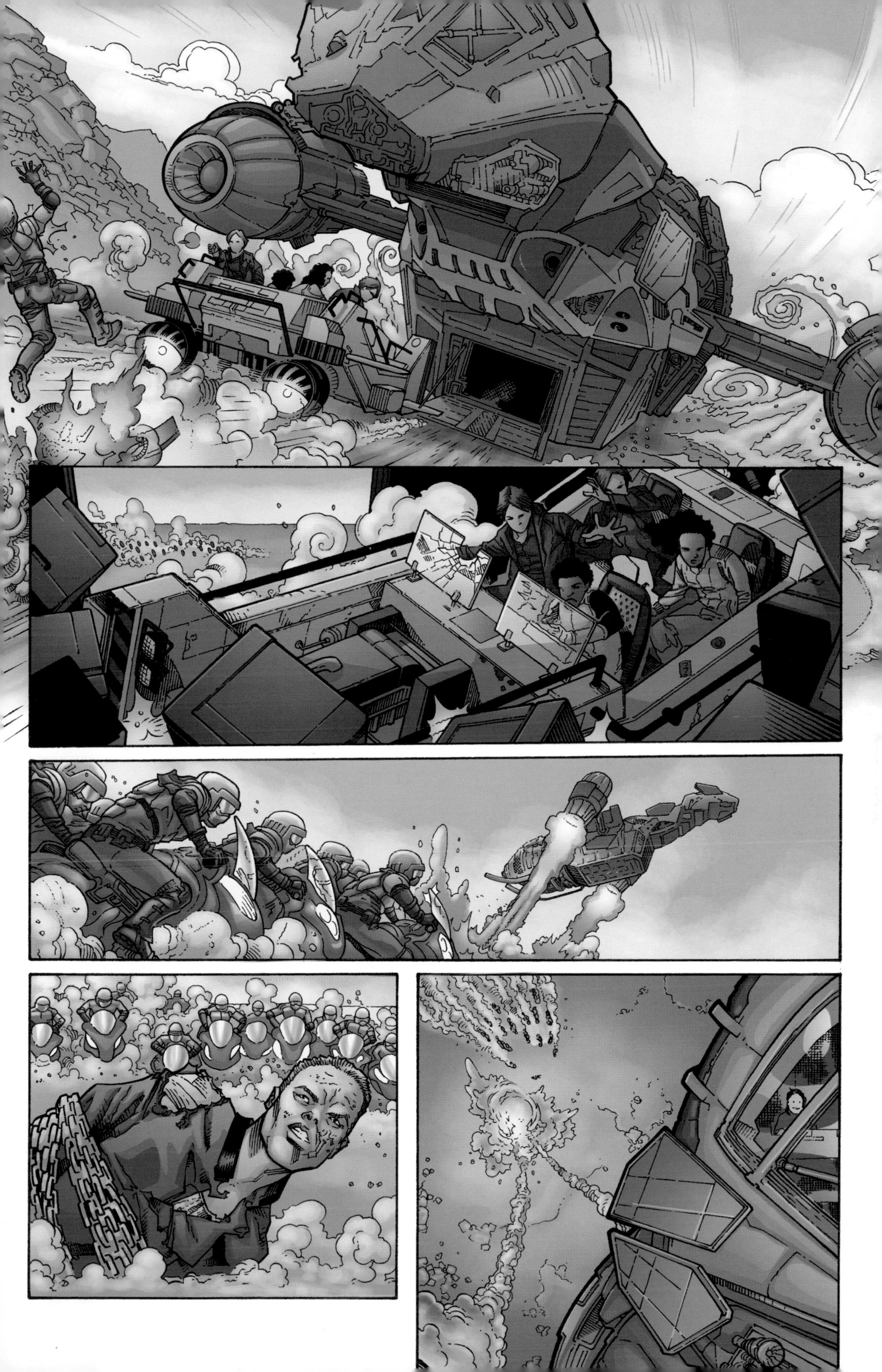

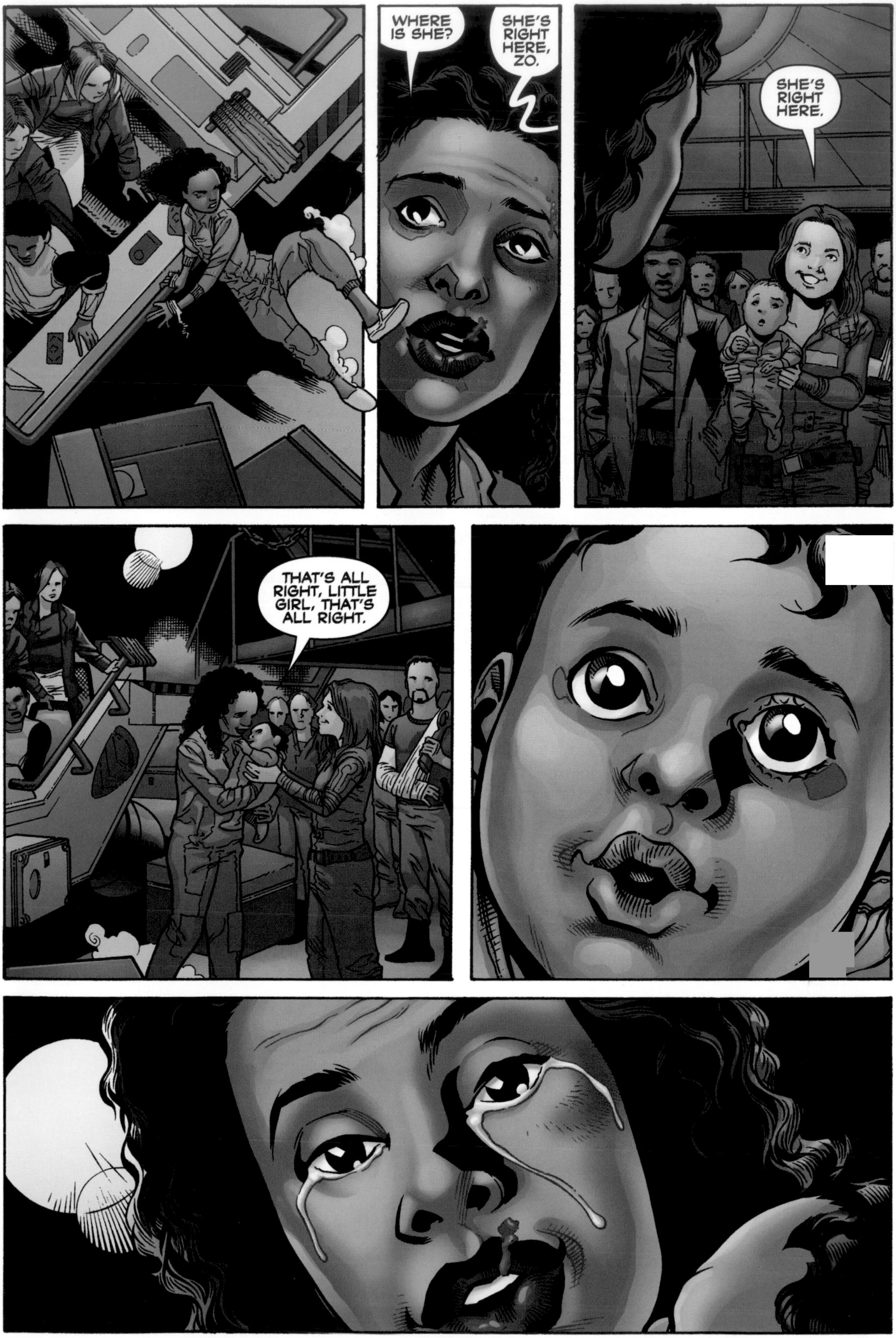
WHERE IS SHE?
SHE'S RIGHT HERE, ZO.
SHE'S RIGHT HERE.
THAT'S ALL RIGHT, LITTLE GIRL, THAT'S ALL RIGHT.

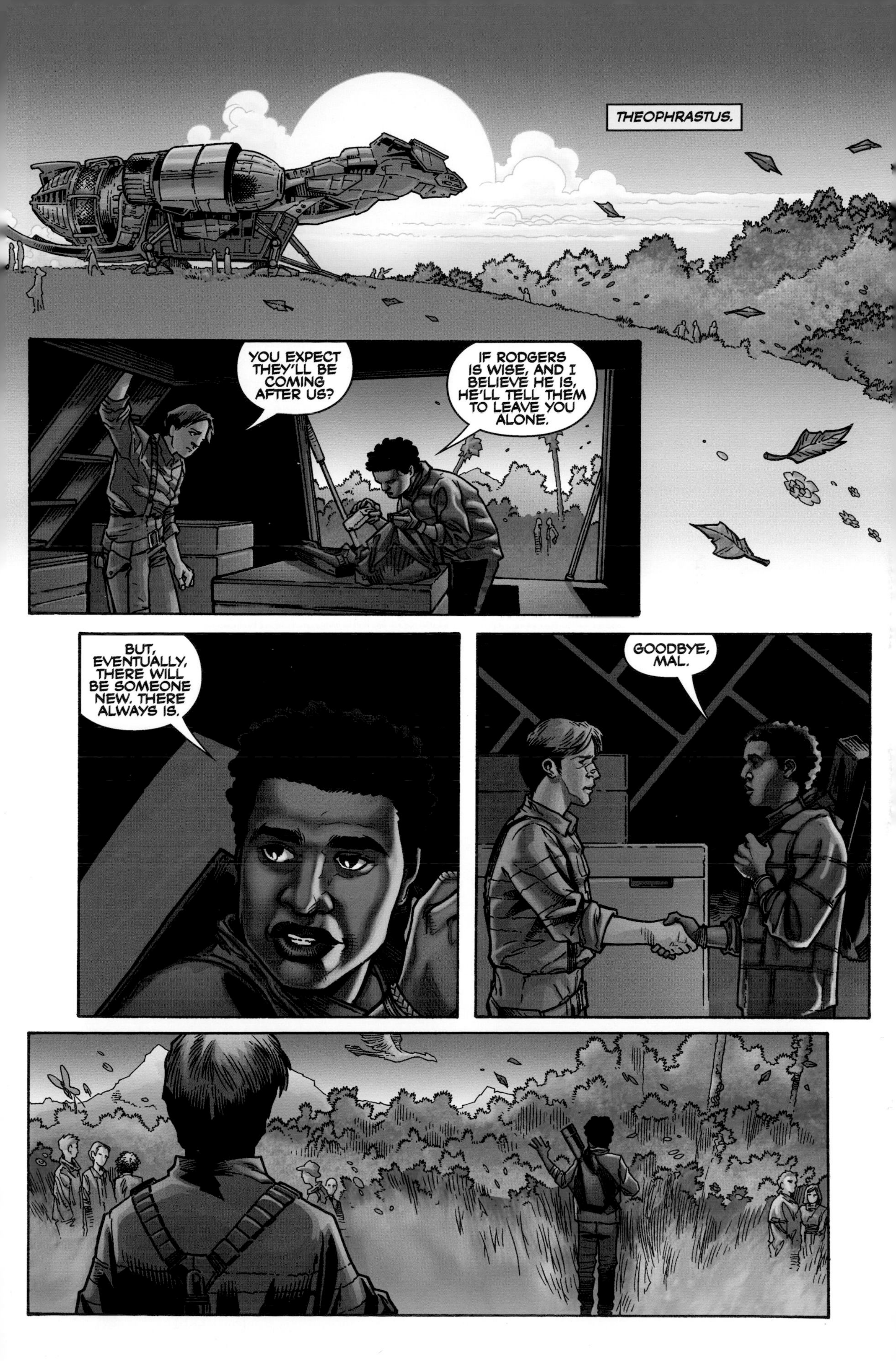
THEOPHRASTUS.
YOU EXPECT THEY'LL BE COMING AFTER US?
IF RODGERS IS WISE, AND I BELIEVE HE IS, HE'LL TELL THEM TO LEAVE YOU ALONE.
BUT, EVENTUALLY, THERE WILL BE SOMEONE NEW. THERE ALWAYS IS.
GOODBYE, MAL.

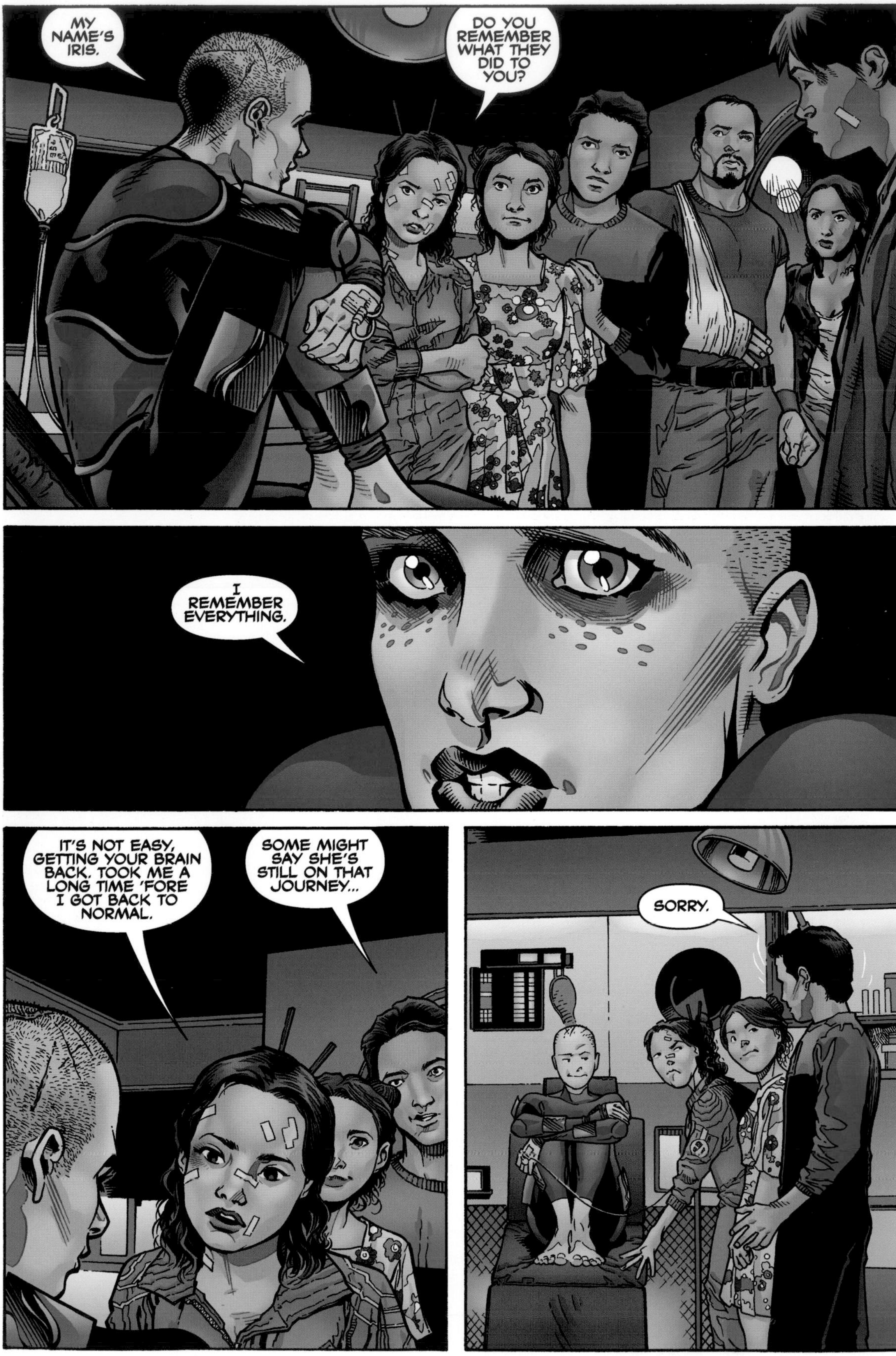
MY NAME'S IRIS.
DO YOU REMEMBER WHAT THEY DID TO YOU?
I REMEMBER EVERYTHING.
IT'S NOT EASY, GETTING YOUR BRAIN BACK. TOOK ME A LONG TIME 'FORE I GOT BACK TO NORMAL.
SOME MIGHT SAY SHE'S STILL ON THAT JOURNEY...
SORRY.

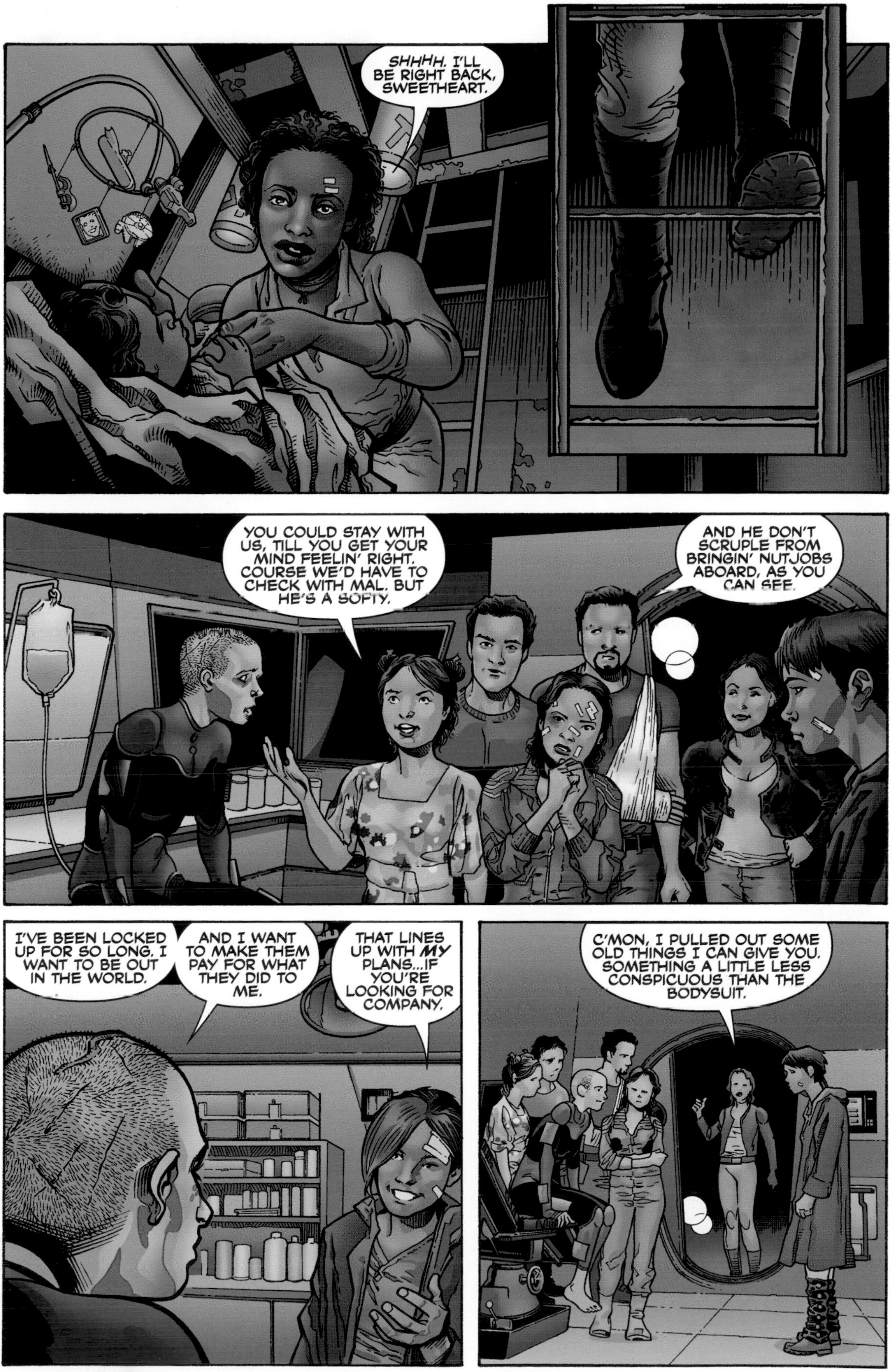
SHHHH. I'LL BE RIGHT BACK, SWEETHEART.
YOU COULD STAY WITH US, TILL YOU GET YOUR MIND FEELIN' RIGHT. COURSE WE'D HAVE TO CHECK WITH MAL. BUT HE'S A SOFTY.
AND HE DON'T SCRUPLE FROM BRINGIN' NUTJOBS ABOARD, AS YOU CAN SEE.
I'VE BEEN LOCKED UP FOR SO LONG. I WANT TO BE OUT IN THE WORLD.
AND I WANT TO MAKE THEM PAY FOR WHAT THEY DID TO ME.
THAT LINES UP WITH MY PLANS...IF YOU'RE LOOKING FOR COMPANY.
C'MON, I PULLED OUT SOME OLD THINGS I CAN GIVE YOU. SOMETHING A LITTLE LESS CONSPICUOUS THAN THE BODYSUIT.

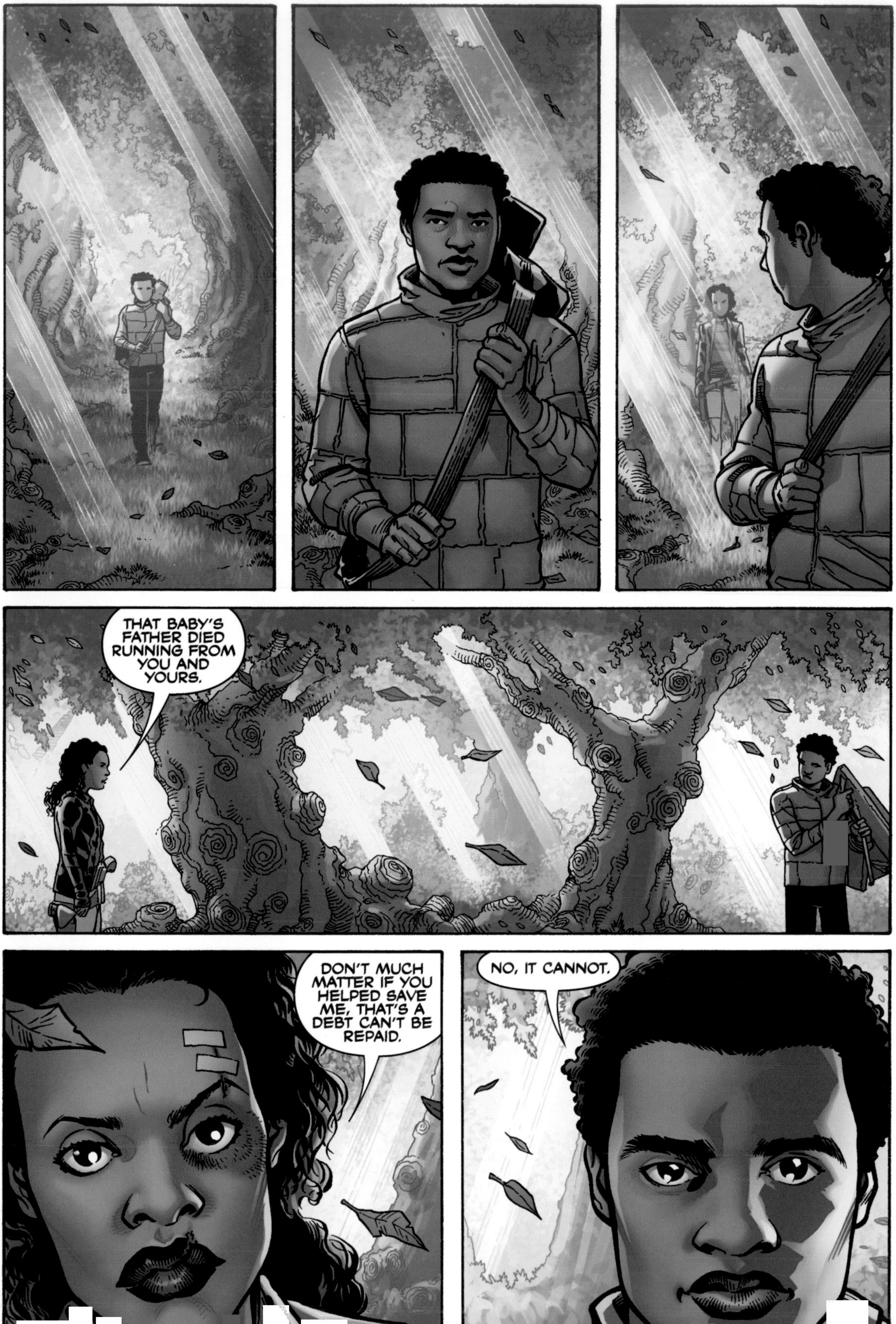
THAT BABY'S FATHER DIED RUNNING FROM YOU AND YOURS.
DON'T MUCH MATTER IF YOU HELPED SAVE ME, THAT'S A DEBT CAN'T BE REPAID.
NO, IT CANNOT.

I WILL DEFEND MYSELF.

I'M COUNTIN' ON IT.

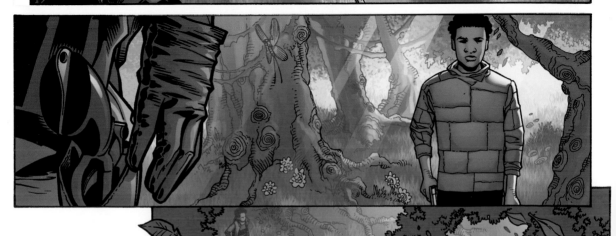

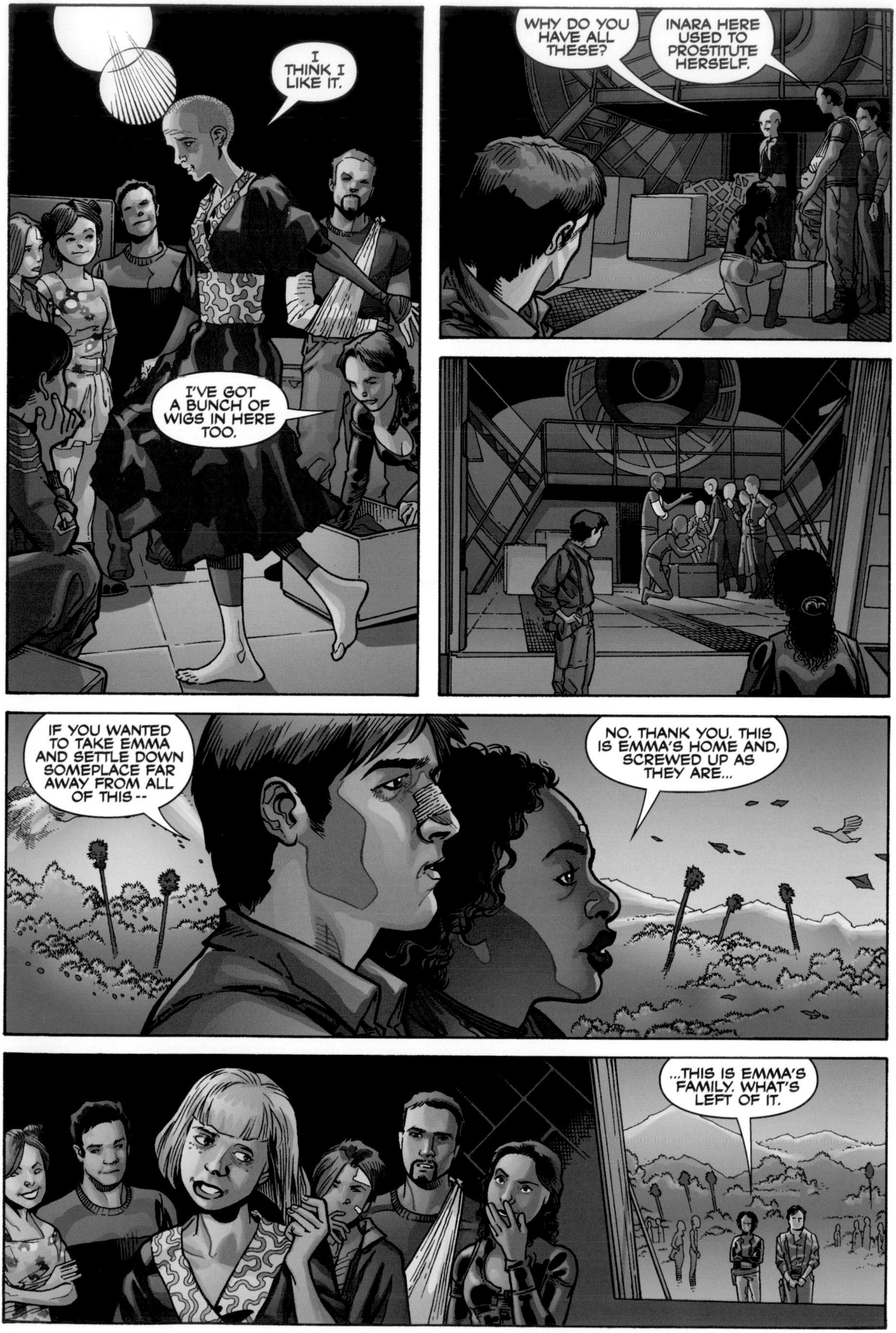
I THINK I LIKE IT.
I'VE GOT A BUNCH OF WIGS IN HERE TOO.
WHY DO YOU HAVE ALL THESE?
INARA HERE USED TO PROSTITUTE HERSELF.
IF YOU WANTED TO TAKE EMMA AND SETTLE DOWN SOMEPLACE FAR AWAY FROM ALL OF THIS --
NO. THANK YOU. THIS IS EMMA'S HOME AND, SCREWED UP AS THEY ARE...
...THIS IS EMMA'S FAMILY. WHAT'S LEFT OF IT.

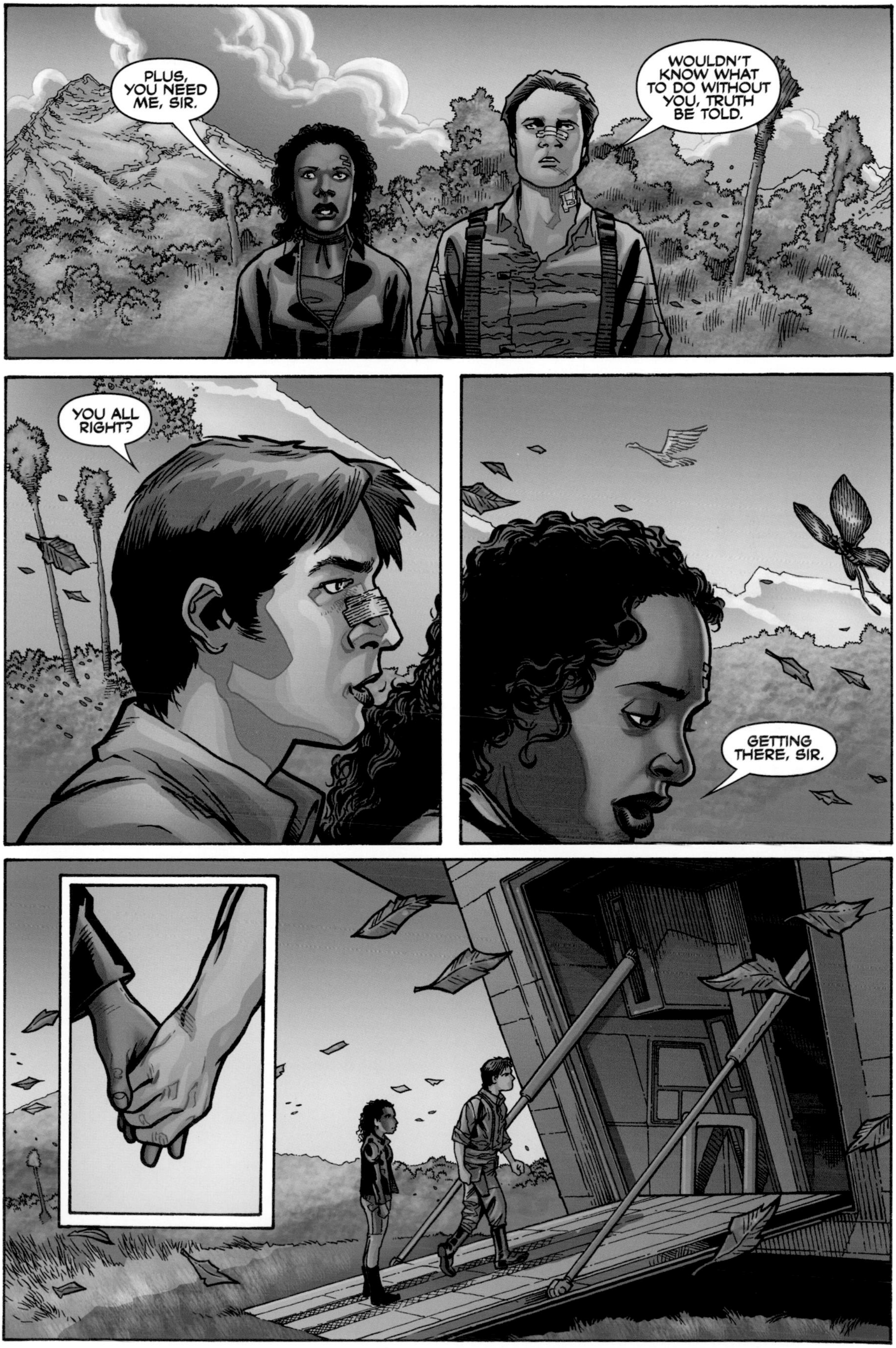
PLUS, YOU NEED ME, SIR.
WOULDN'T KNOW WHAT TO DO WITHOUT YOU, TRUTH BE TOLD.
YOU ALL RIGHT?
GETTING THERE, SIR.

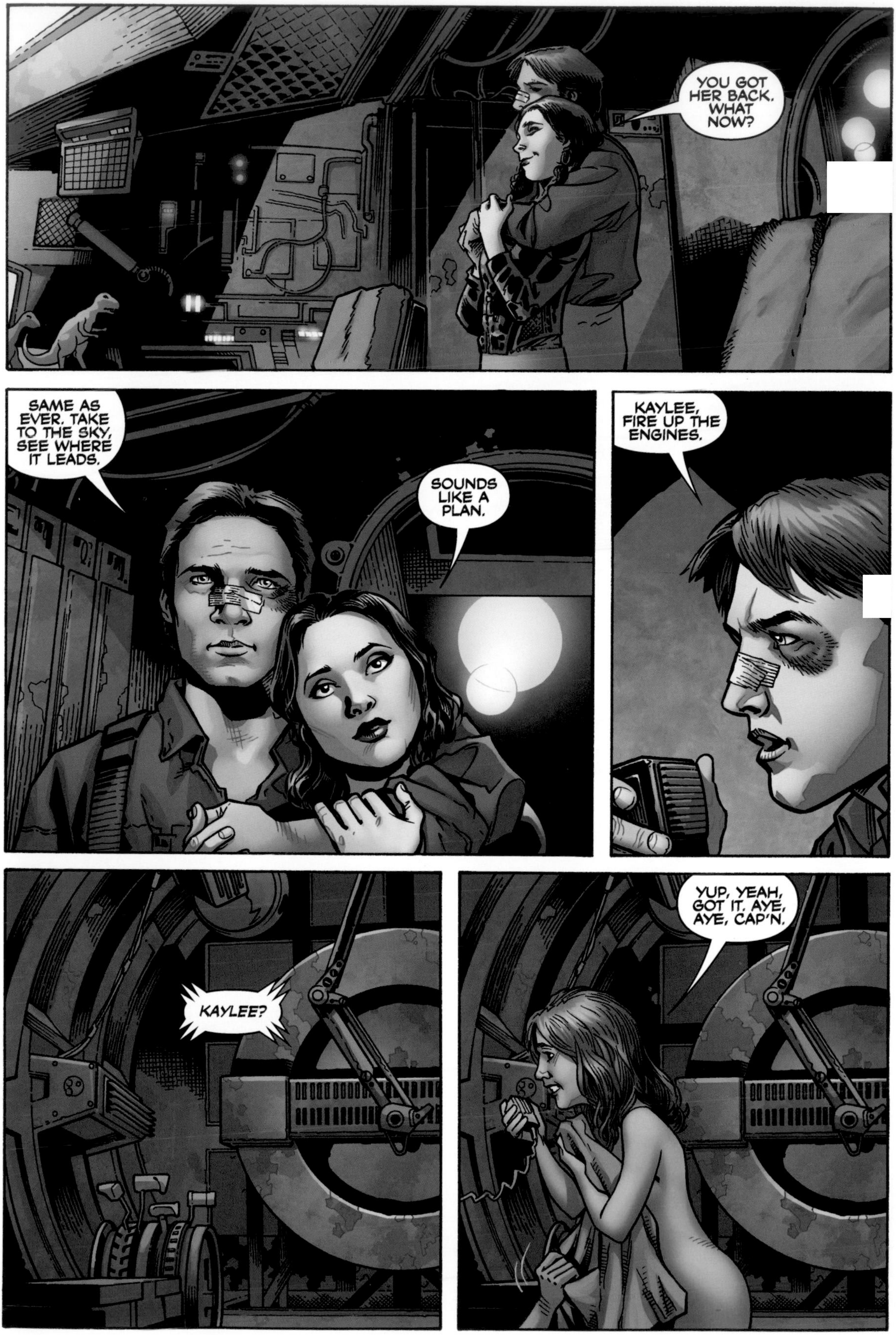
YOU GOT HER BACK. WHAT NOW?
SAME AS EVER. TAKE TO THE SKY, SEE WHERE IT LEADS.
SOUNDS LIKE A PLAN.
KAYLEE, FIRE UP THE ENGINES.
KAYLEE?
YUP, YEAH, GOT IT. AYE, AYE, CAP'N.

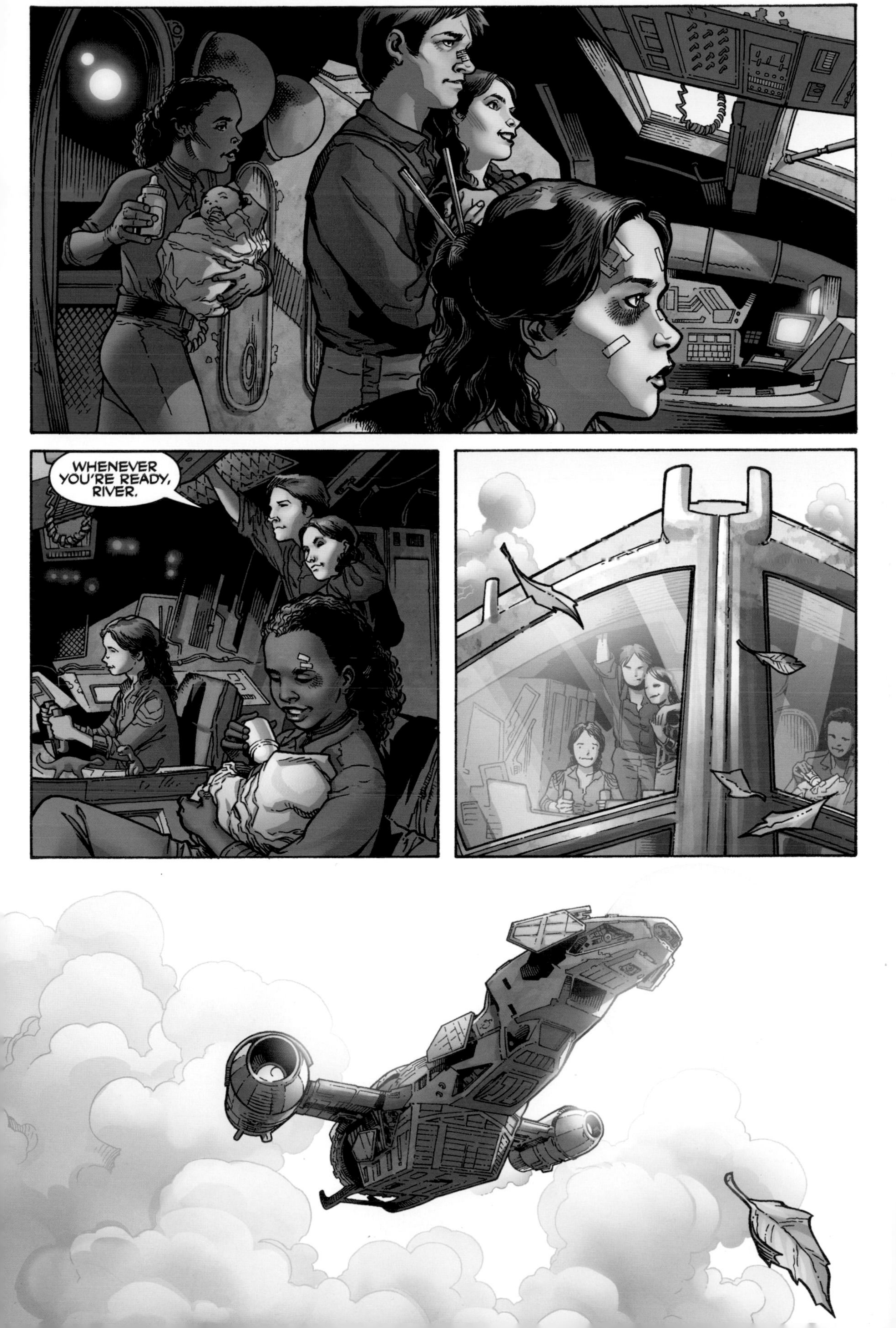
WHENEVER YOU'RE READY, RIVER.

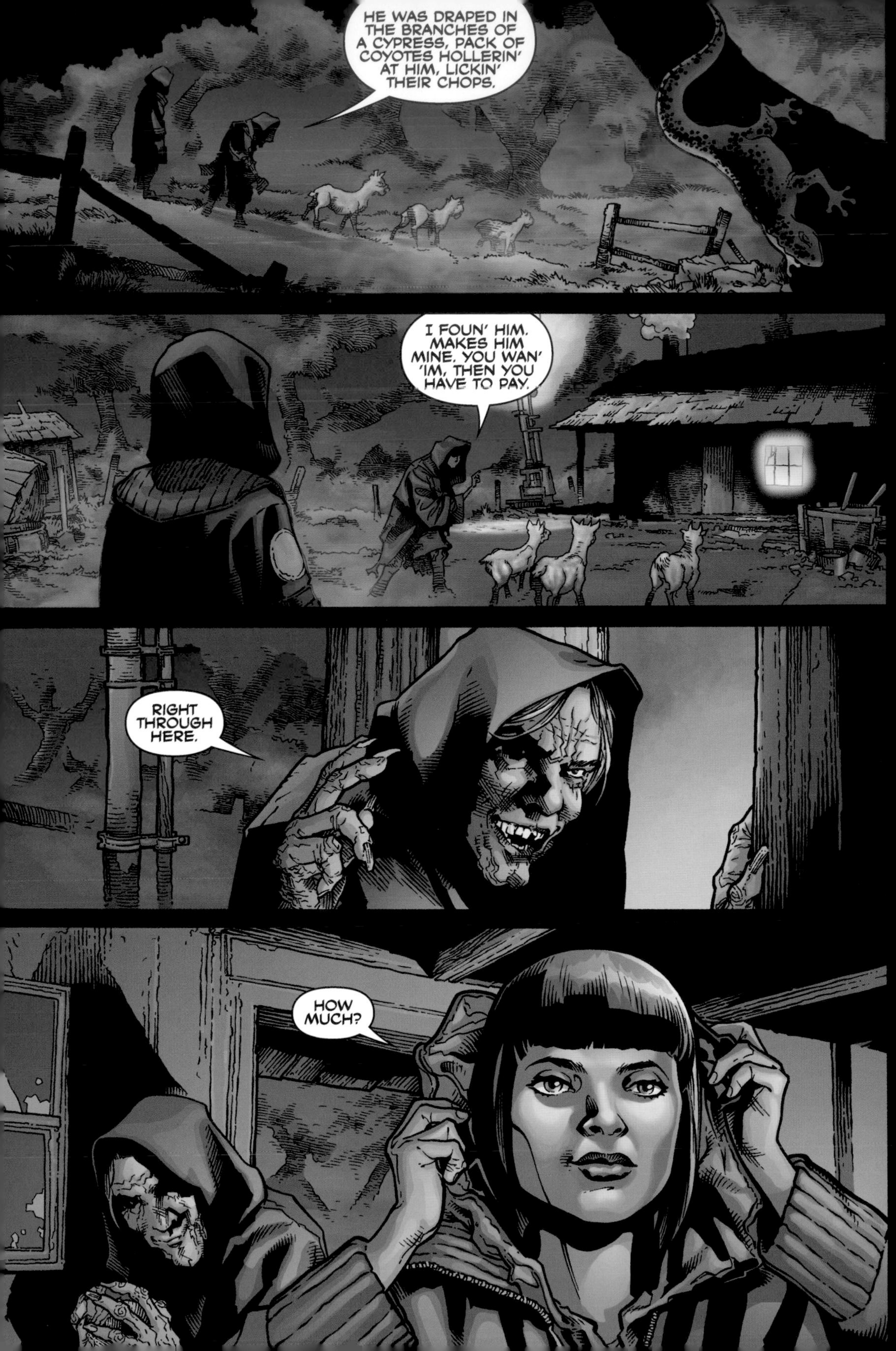
HE WAS DRAPED IN THE BRANCHES OF A CYPRESS, PACK OF COYOTES HOLLERIN' AT HIM, LICKIN' THEIR CHOPS.
I FOUN' HIM. MAKES HIM MINE. YOU WAN' 'IM, THEN YOU HAVE TO PAY.
RIGHT THROUGH HERE.
HOW MUCH?

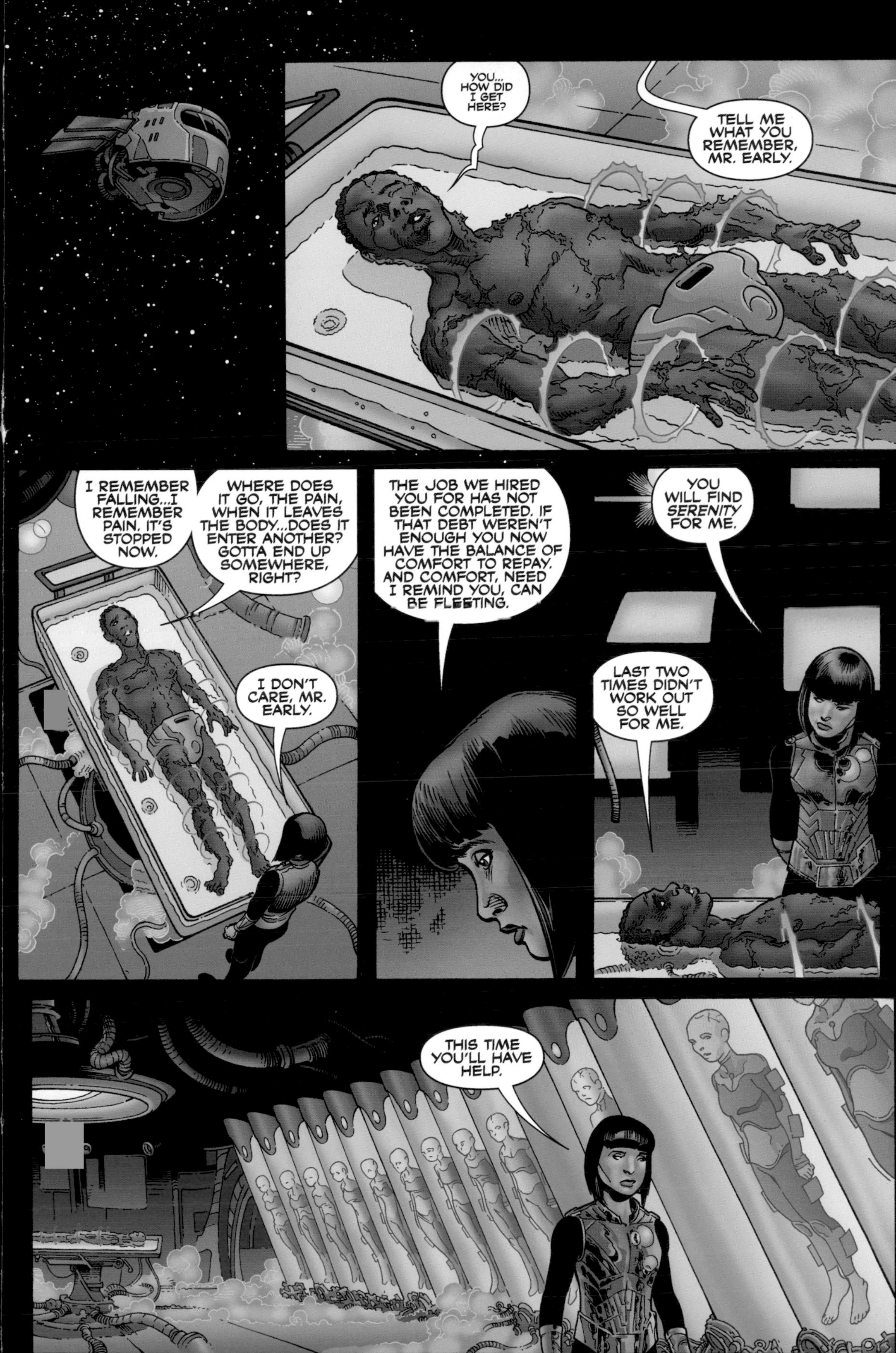

YOU... HOW DID I GET HERE?
TELL ME WHAT YOU REMEMBER, MR. EARLY.
I REMEMBER FALLING...I REMEMBER PAIN. IT'S STOPPED NOW.
WHERE DOES IT GO, THE PAIN, WHEN IT LEAVES THE BODY...DOES IT ENTER ANOTHER? GOTTA END UP SOMEWHERE, RIGHT?
I DON'T CARE, MR. EARLY.
THE JOB WE HIRED YOU FOR HAS NOT BEEN COMPLETED. IF THAT DEBT WEREN'T ENOUGH YOU NOW HAVE THE BALANCE OF COMFORT TO REPAY. AND COMFORT, NEED I REMIND YOU, CAN BE FLEETING.
YOU WILL FIND *SERENITY* FOR ME.
LAST TWO TIMES DIDN'T WORK OUT SO WELL FOR ME.
THIS TIME YOU'LL HAVE HELP.

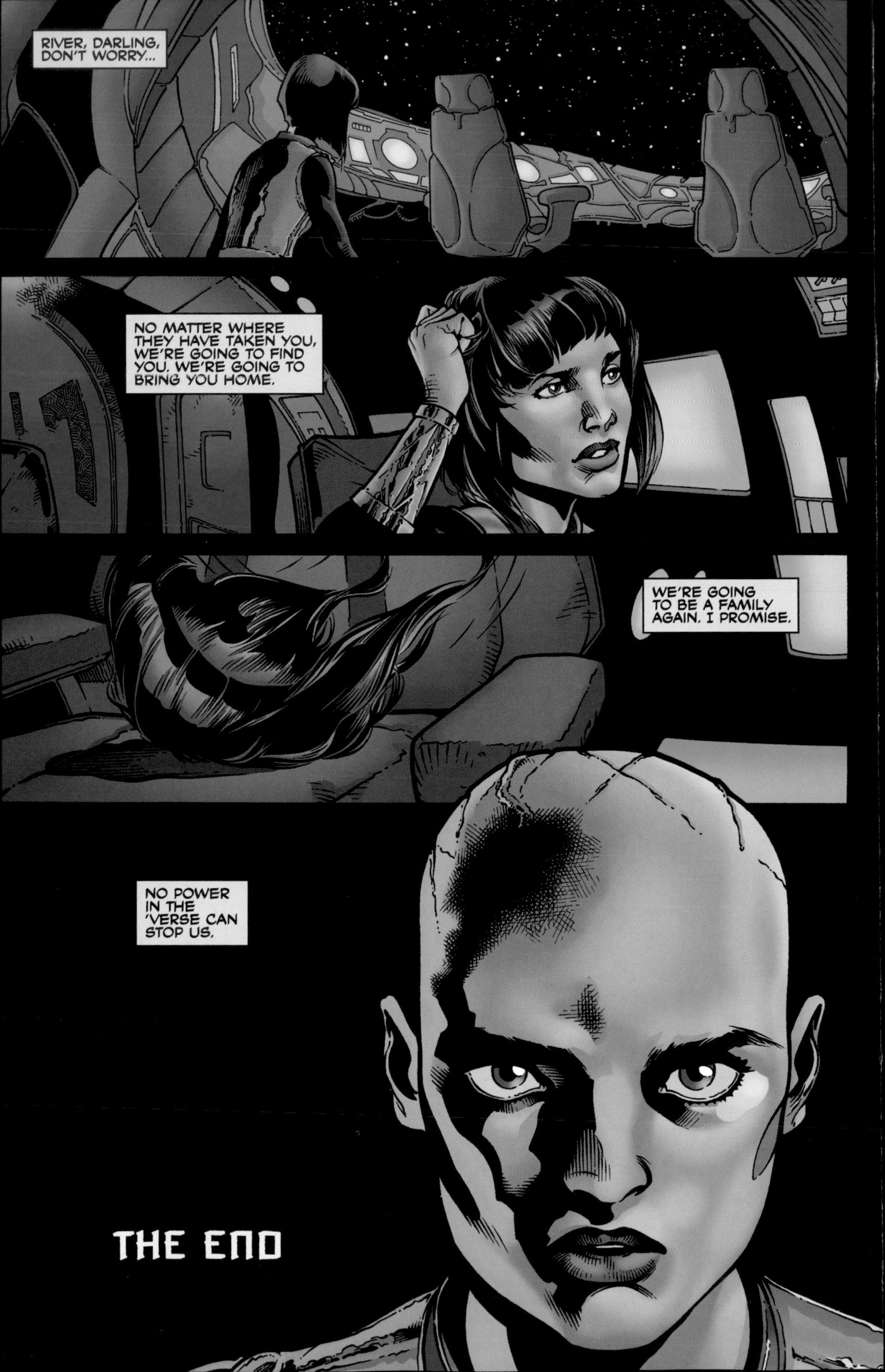
RIVER, DARLING, DON'T WORRY...
NO MATTER WHERE THEY HAVE TAKEN YOU, WE'RE GOING TO FIND YOU. WE'RE GOING TO BRING YOU HOME.
WE'RE GOING TO BE A FAMILY AGAIN. I PROMISE.
NO POWER IN THE 'VERSE CAN STOP US.
THE END

Serenity™

宁静 FIREFLY CLASS 03-K64

COVER GALLERY

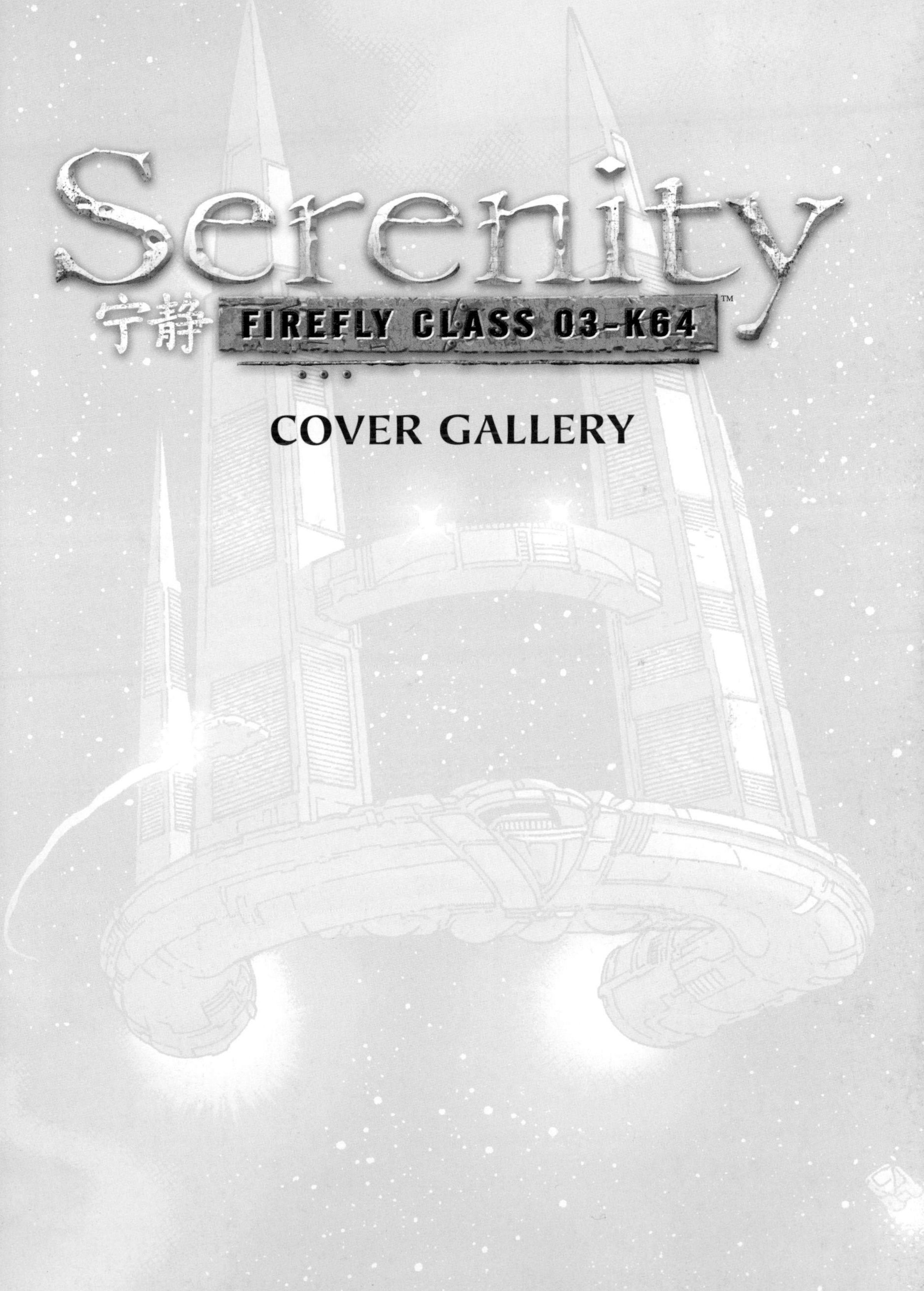

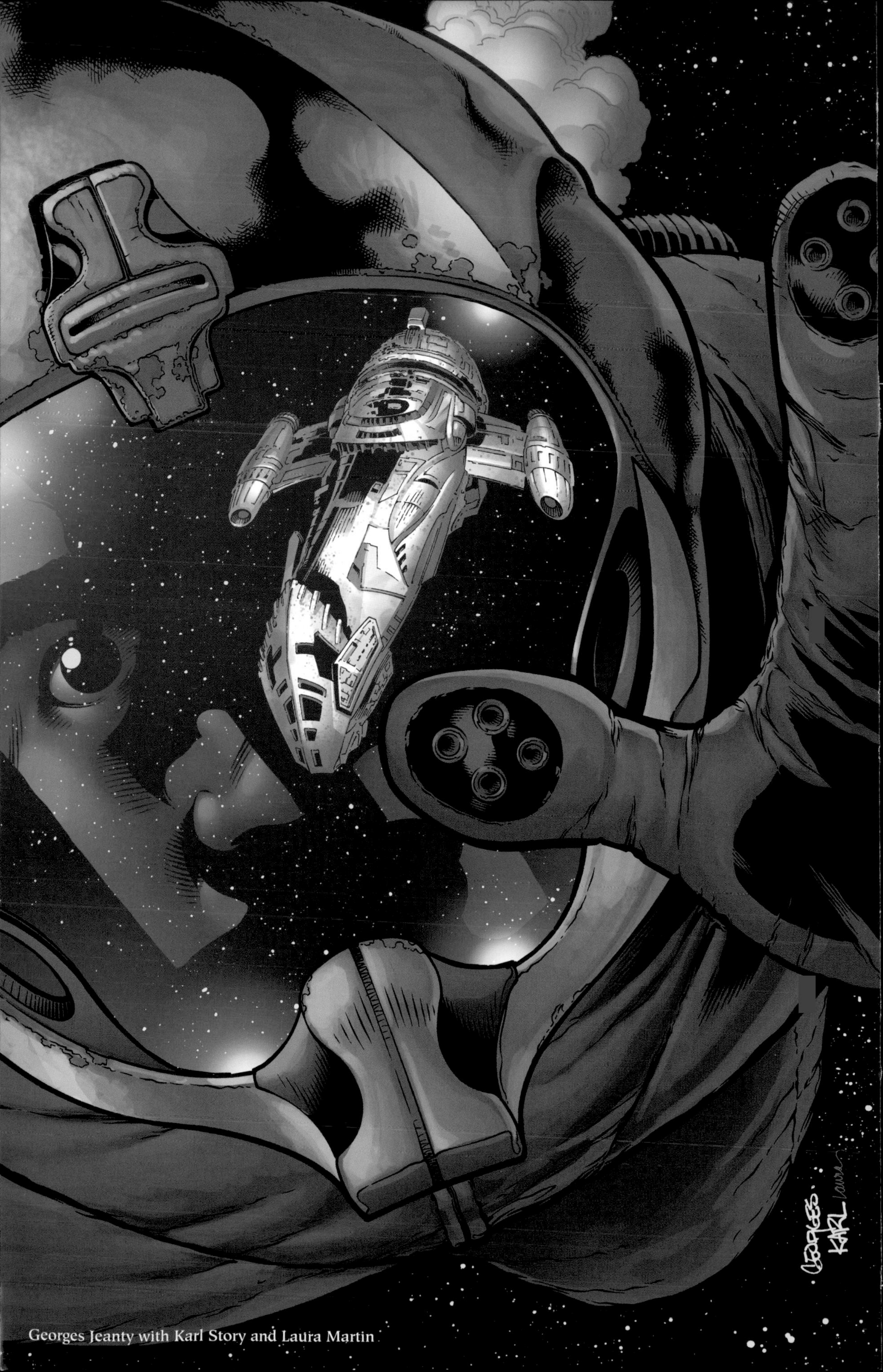
GEORGES
KARL
Laura
Georges Jeanty with Karl Story and Laura Martin

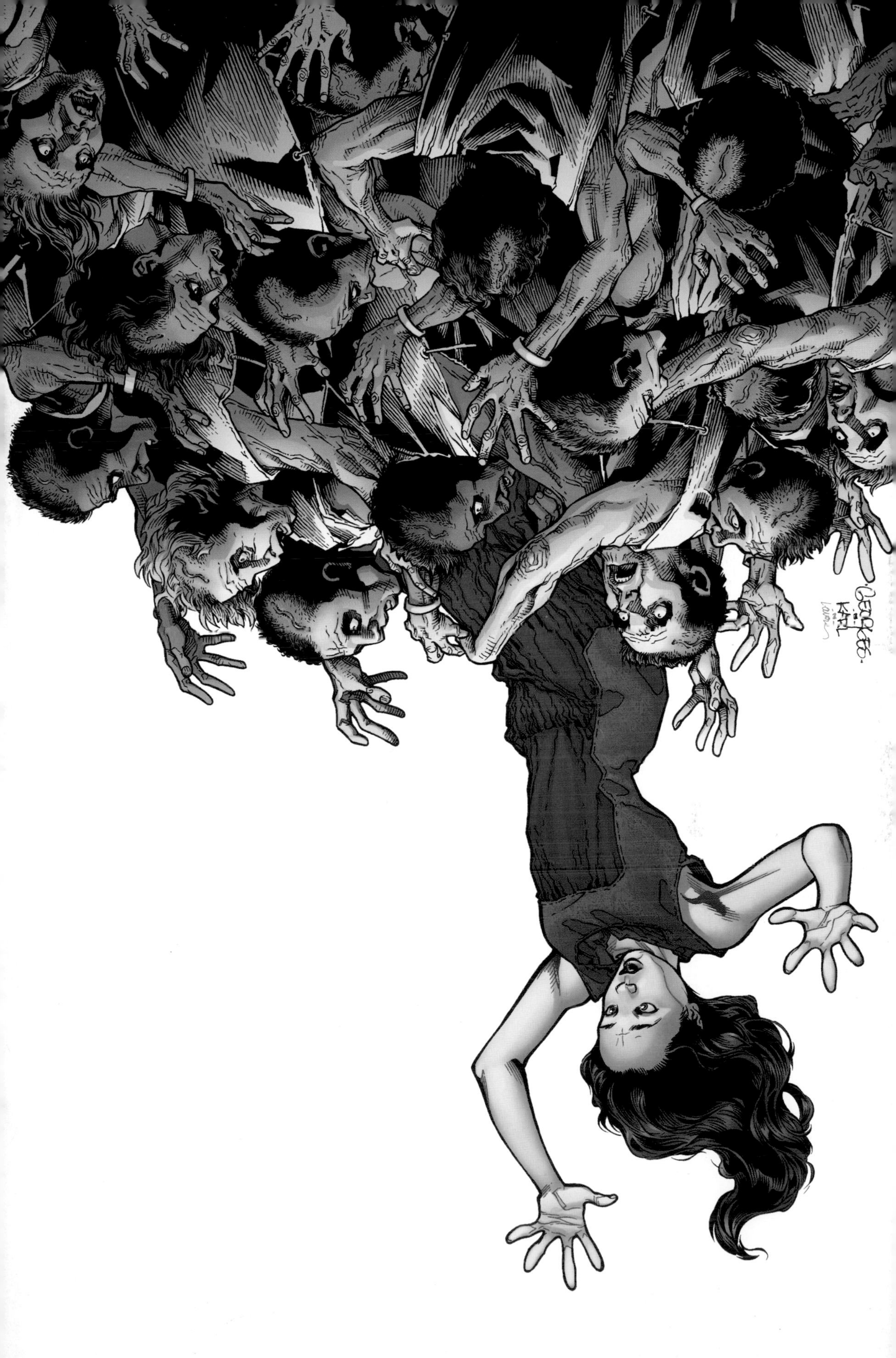

Georges Jeanty with Karl Story and Laura Martin

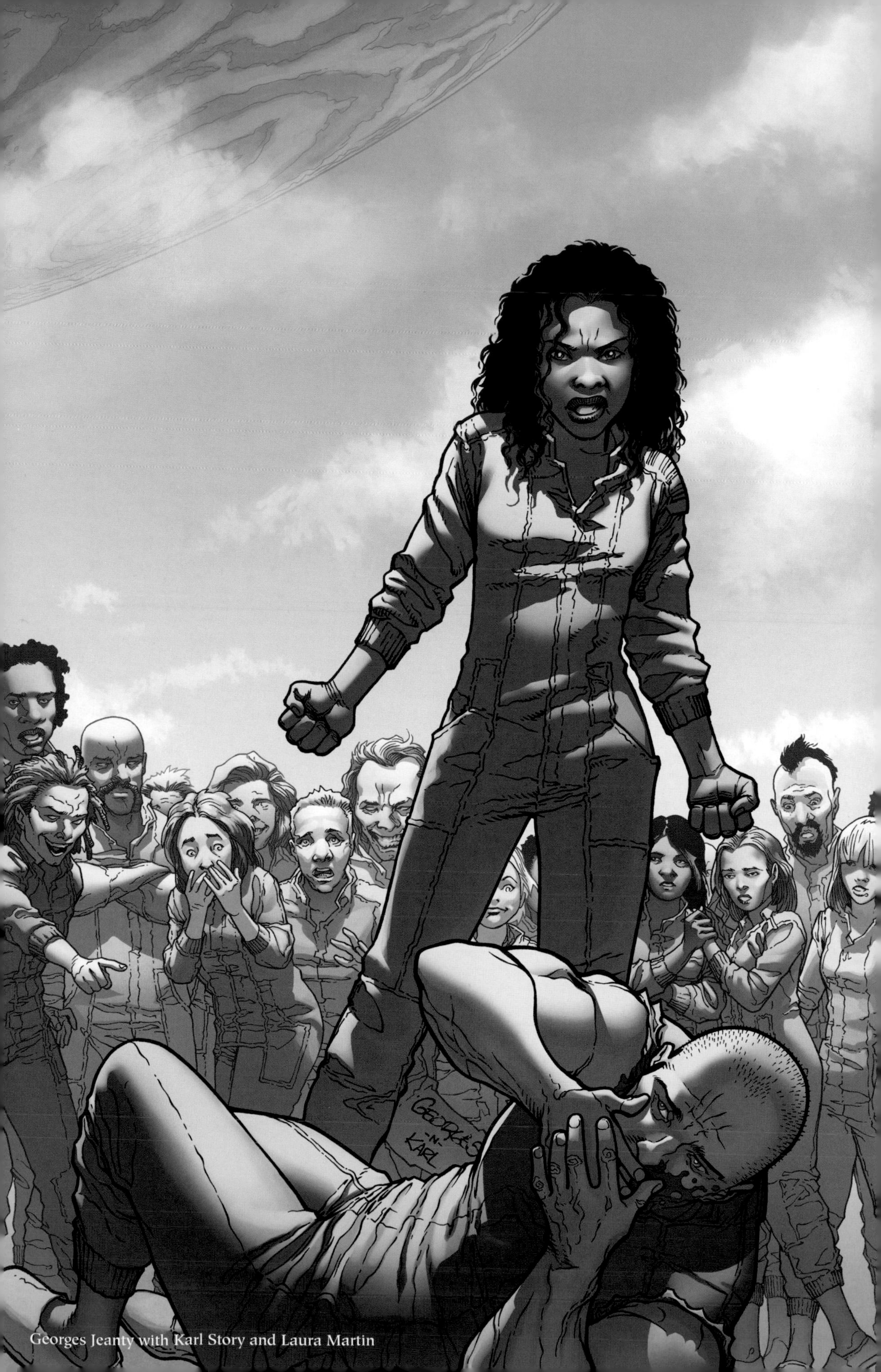
GEORGES
-N-
KARL

Georges Jeanty with Karl Story and Laura Martin

Georges Jeanty with Karl Story and Laura Martin

Georges Jeanty with Karl Story and Laura Martin

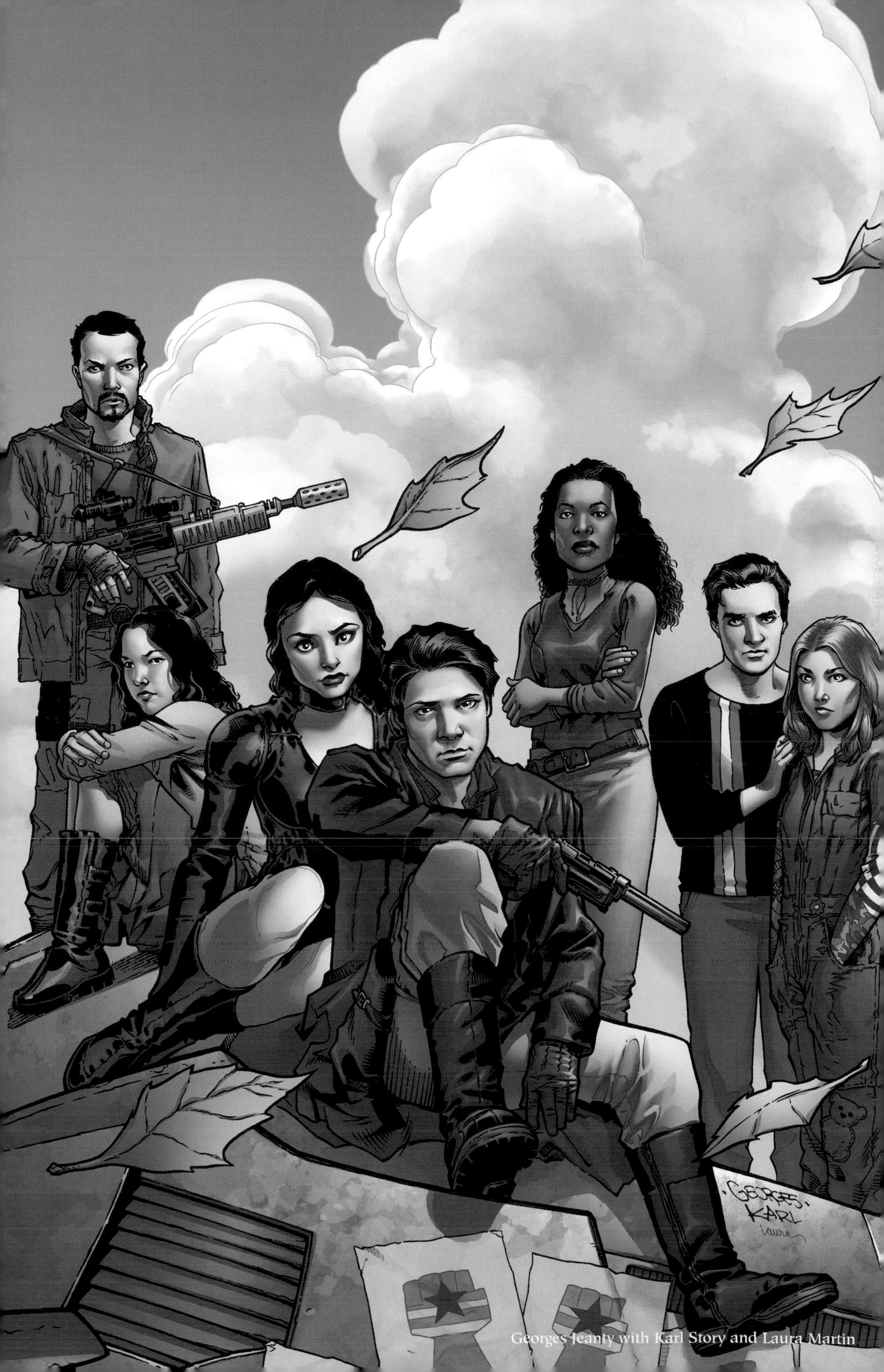
GEORGES
KARL

Georges Jeanty with Karl Story and Laura Martin

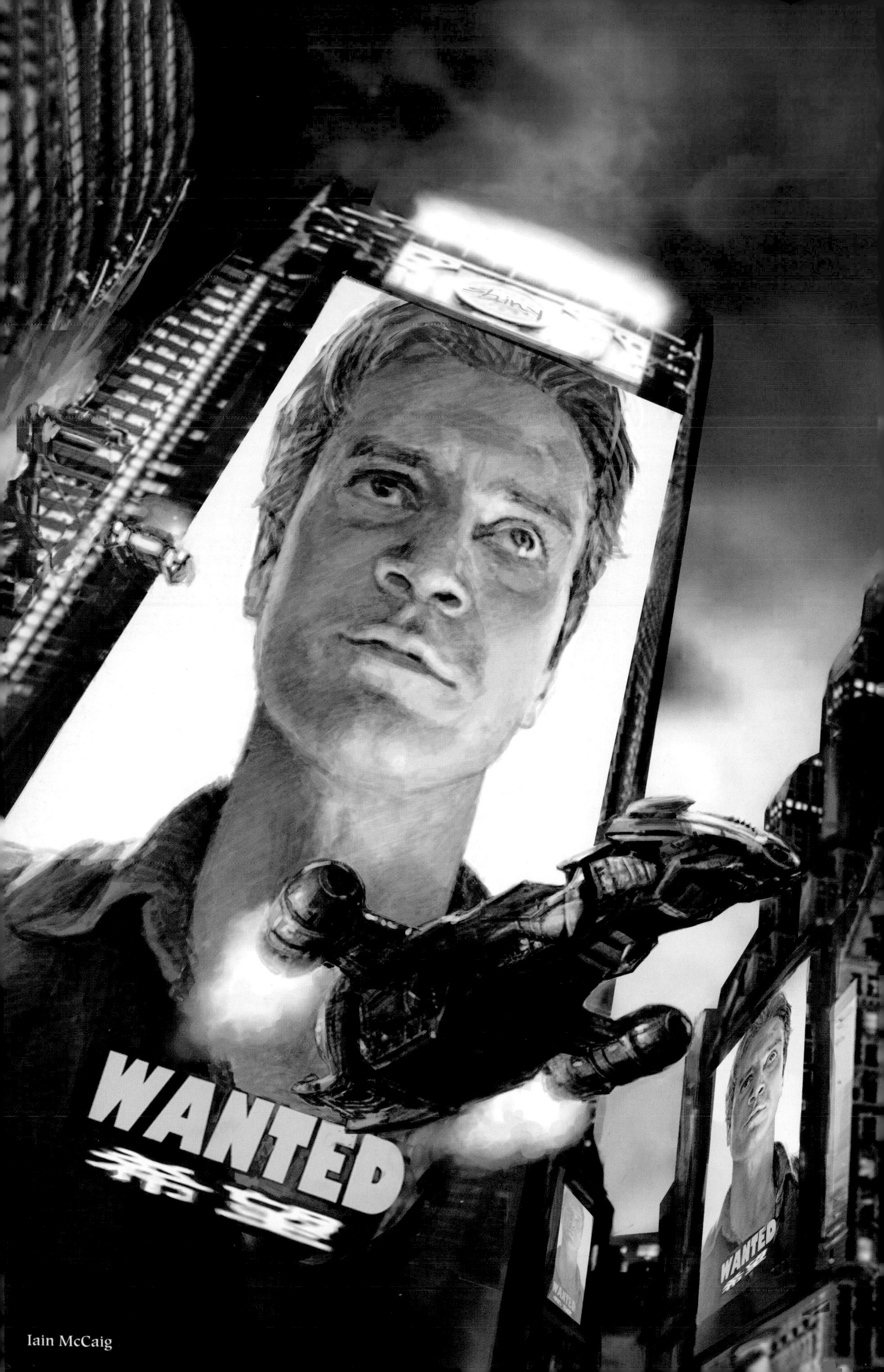
WANTED
WANTED
WANTED

Iain McCaig

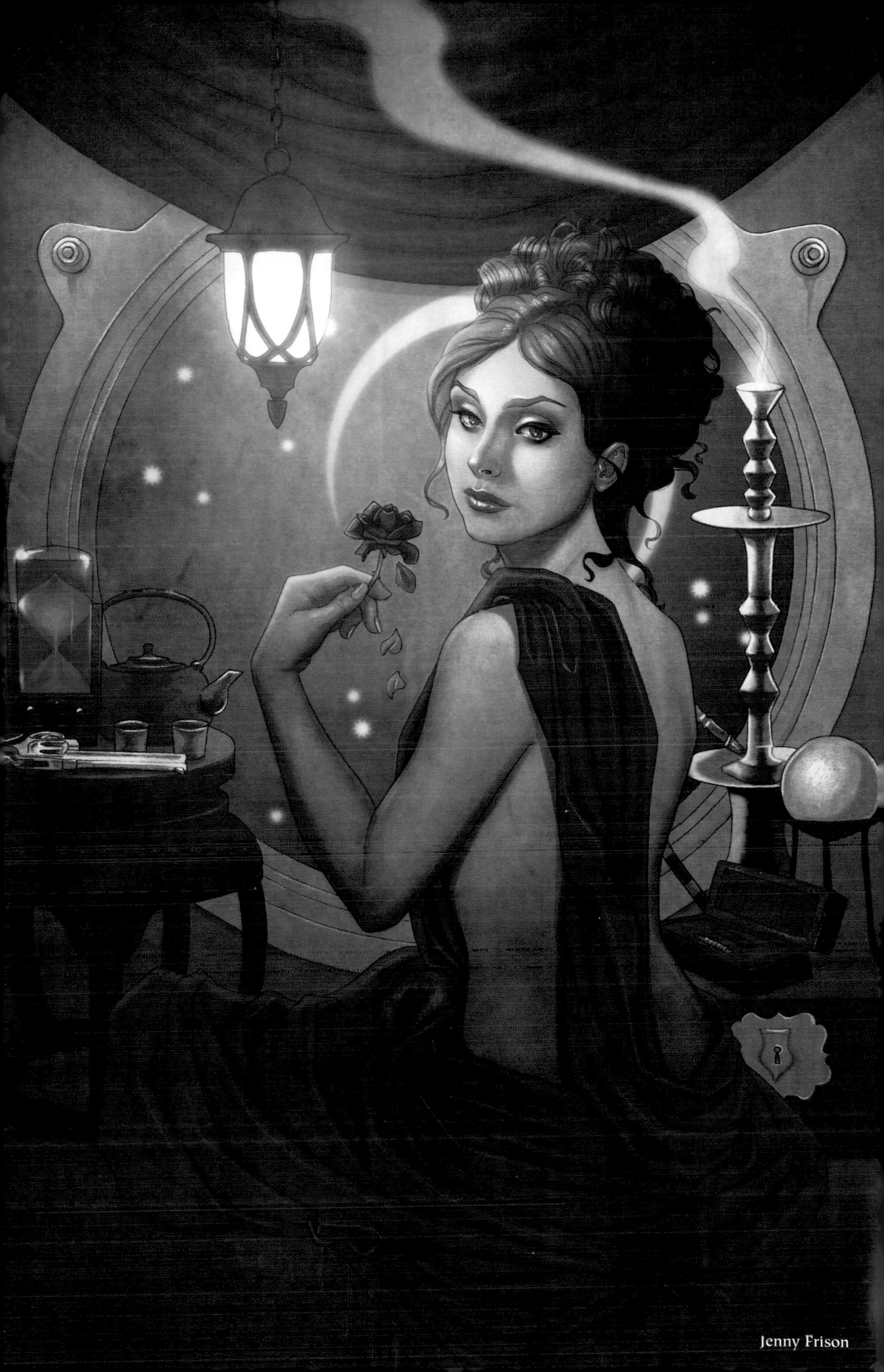

Jenny Frison

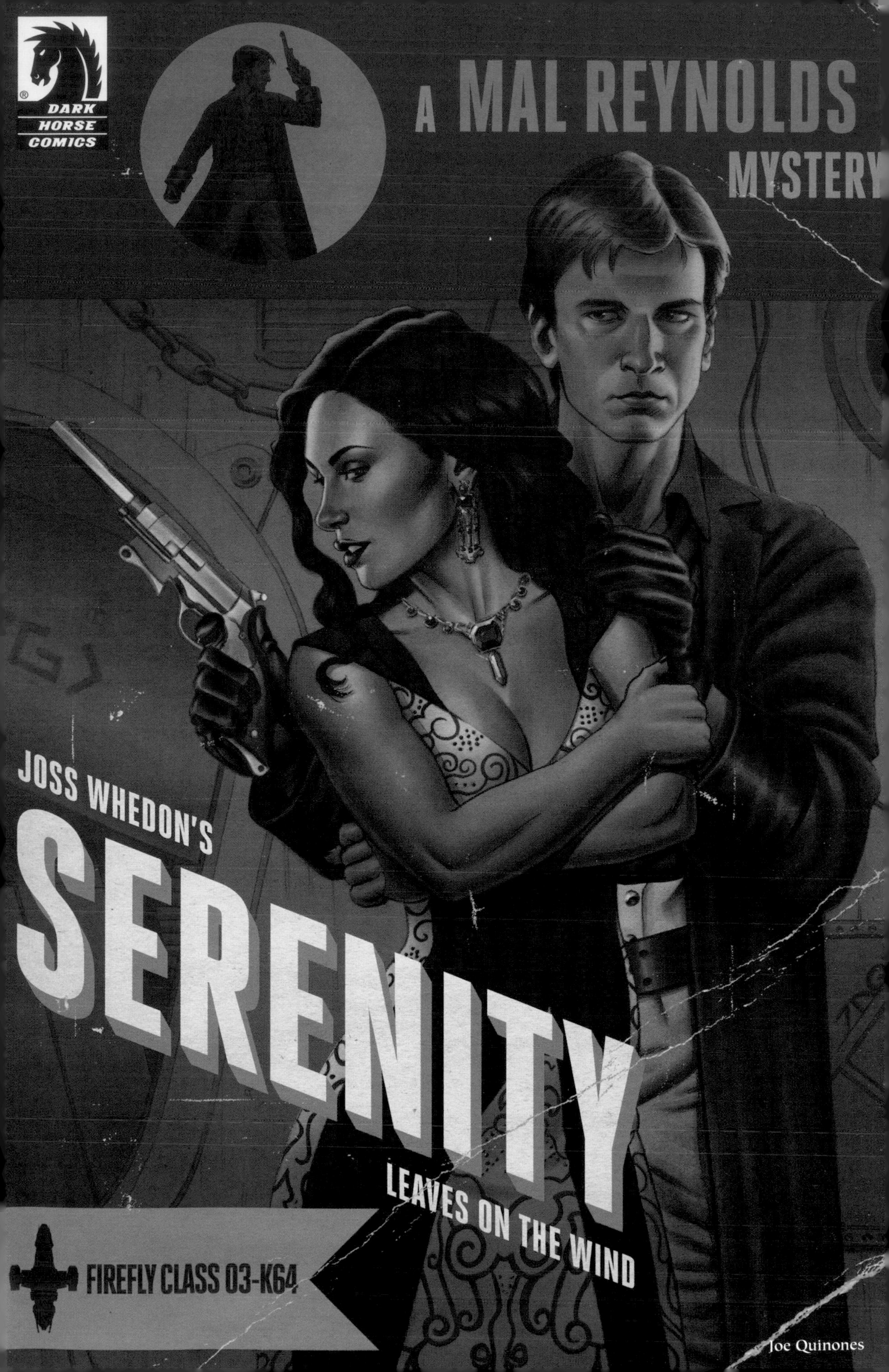

DARK HORSE COMICS

A MAL REYNOLDS
MYSTERY

JOSS WHEDON'S

SERENITY

LEAVES ON THE WIND

FIREFLY CLASS 03-K64

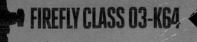

Joe Quinones

IT'S NEVER EASY

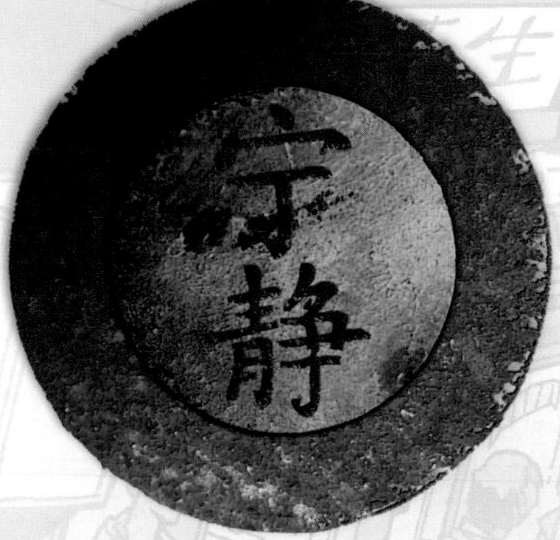
宁静

SCRIPT
ZACK WHEDON

ART
FÁBIO MOON

COLORS
CRIS PETER

LETTERS
MICHAEL HEISLER

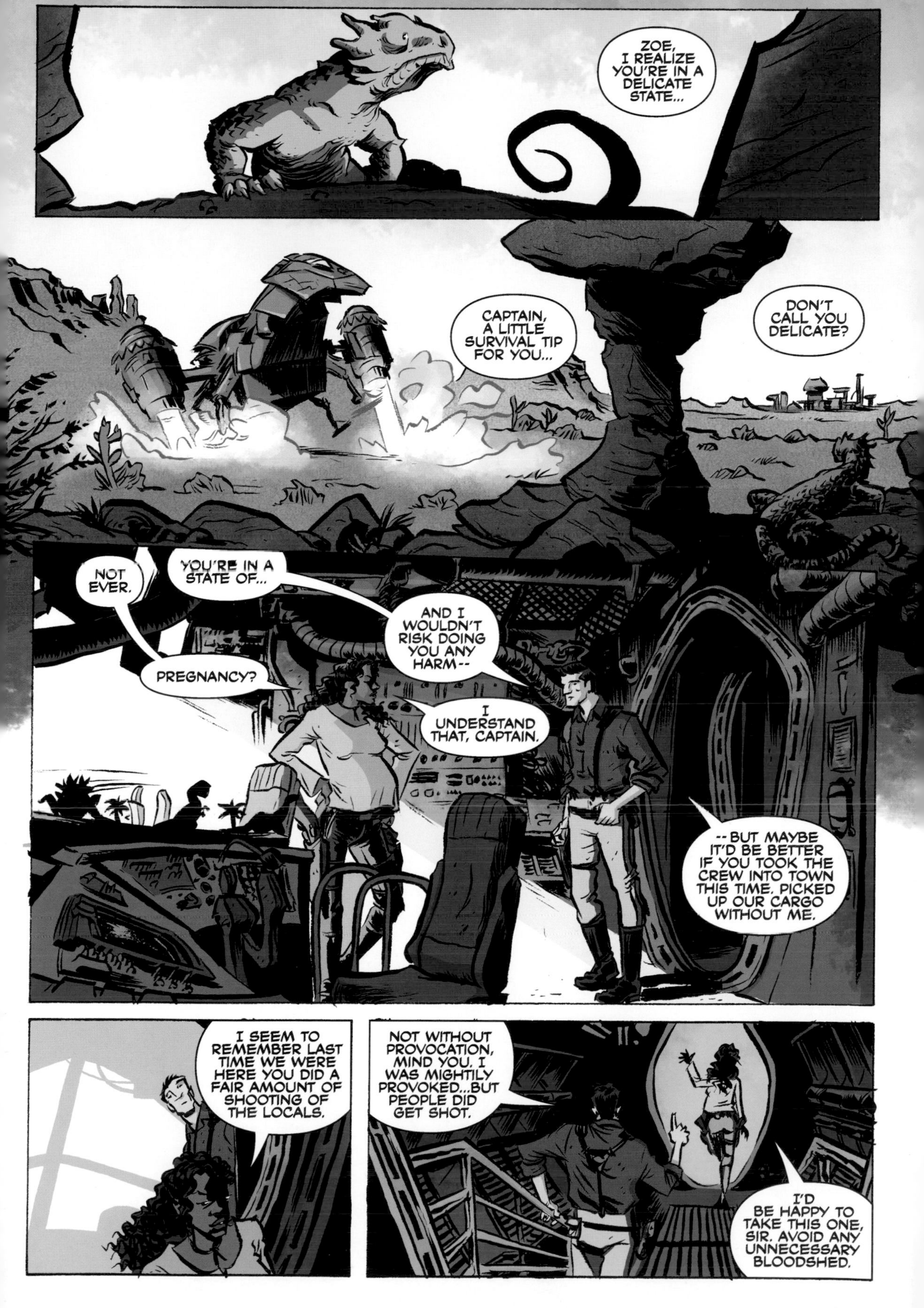
ZOE, I REALIZE YOU'RE IN A DELICATE STATE...
CAPTAIN, A LITTLE SURVIVAL TIP FOR YOU...
DON'T CALL YOU DELICATE?
NOT EVER.
YOU'RE IN A STATE OF...
PREGNANCY?
AND I WOULDN'T RISK DOING YOU ANY HARM--
I UNDERSTAND THAT, CAPTAIN.
--BUT MAYBE IT'D BE BETTER IF YOU TOOK THE CREW INTO TOWN THIS TIME. PICKED UP OUR CARGO WITHOUT ME.
I SEEM TO REMEMBER LAST TIME WE WERE HERE YOU DID A FAIR AMOUNT OF SHOOTING OF THE LOCALS.
NOT WITHOUT PROVOCATION, MIND YOU. I WAS MIGHTILY PROVOKED...BUT PEOPLE DID GET SHOT.
I'D BE HAPPY TO TAKE THIS ONE, SIR. AVOID ANY UNNECESSARY BLOODSHED.

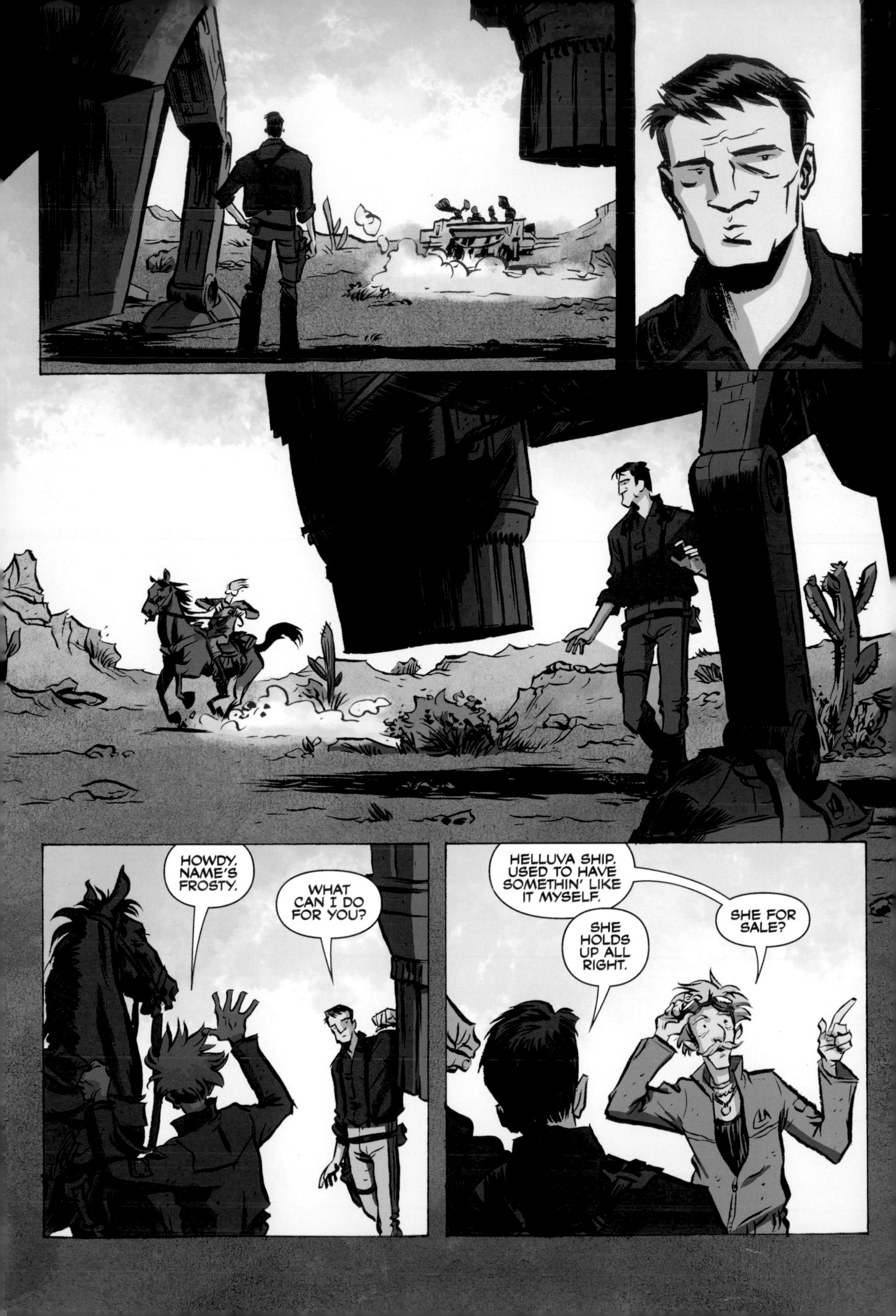
HOWDY. NAME'S FROSTY.
WHAT CAN I DO FOR YOU?
HELLUVA SHIP. USED TO HAVE SOMETHIN' LIKE IT MYSELF.
SHE HOLDS UP ALL RIGHT.
SHE FOR SALE?

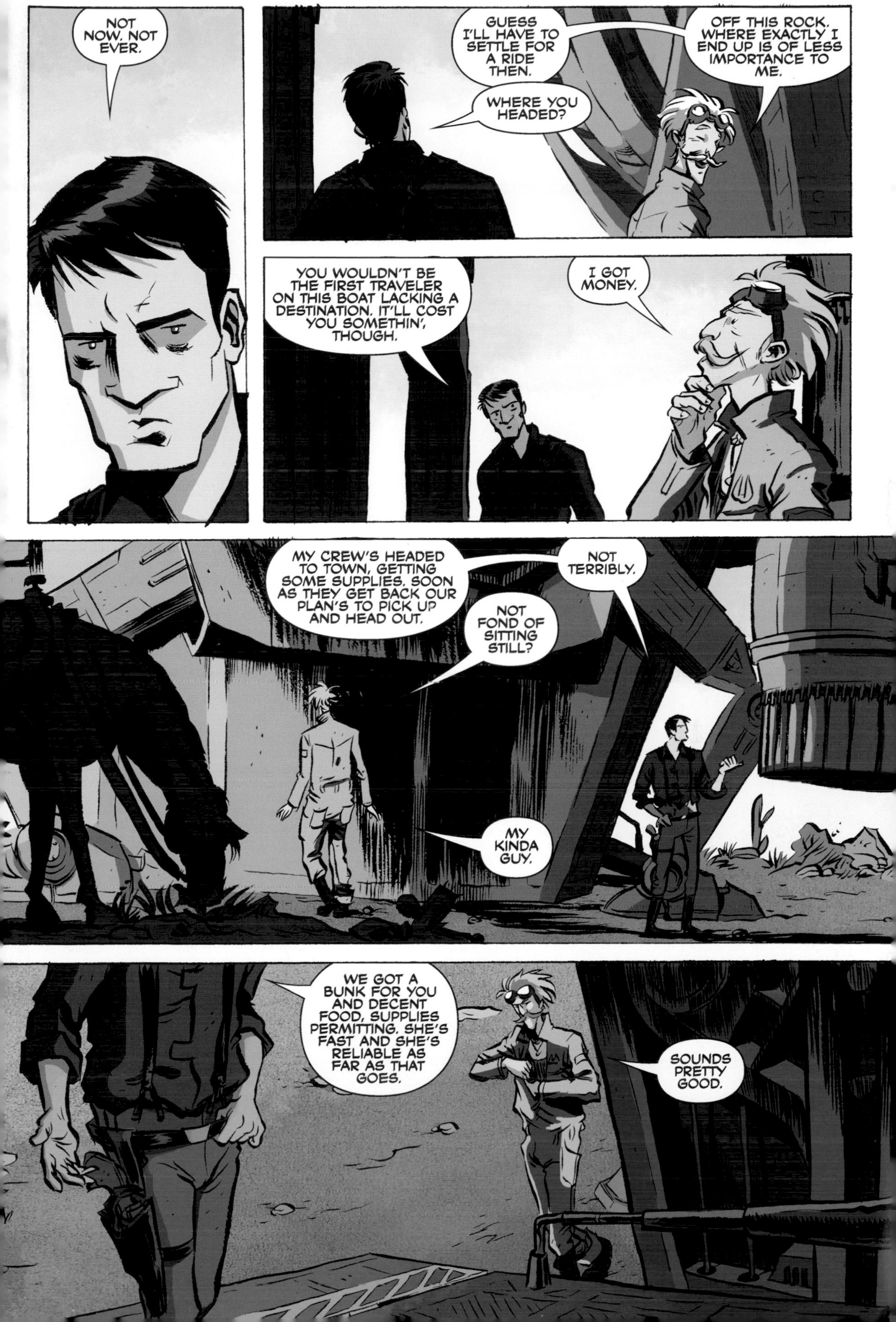
NOT NOW. NOT EVER.
GUESS I'LL HAVE TO SETTLE FOR A RIDE THEN.
OFF THIS ROCK. WHERE EXACTLY I END UP IS OF LESS IMPORTANCE TO ME.
WHERE YOU HEADED?
YOU WOULDN'T BE THE FIRST TRAVELER ON THIS BOAT LACKING A DESTINATION. IT'LL COST YOU SOMETHIN', THOUGH.
I GOT MONEY.
MY CREW'S HEADED TO TOWN, GETTING SOME SUPPLIES. SOON AS THEY GET BACK OUR PLAN'S TO PICK UP AND HEAD OUT.
NOT TERRIBLY.
NOT FOND OF SITTING STILL?
MY KINDA GUY.
WE GOT A BUNK FOR YOU AND DECENT FOOD, SUPPLIES PERMITTING. SHE'S FAST AND SHE'S RELIABLE AS FAR AS THAT GOES.
SOUNDS PRETTY GOOD.

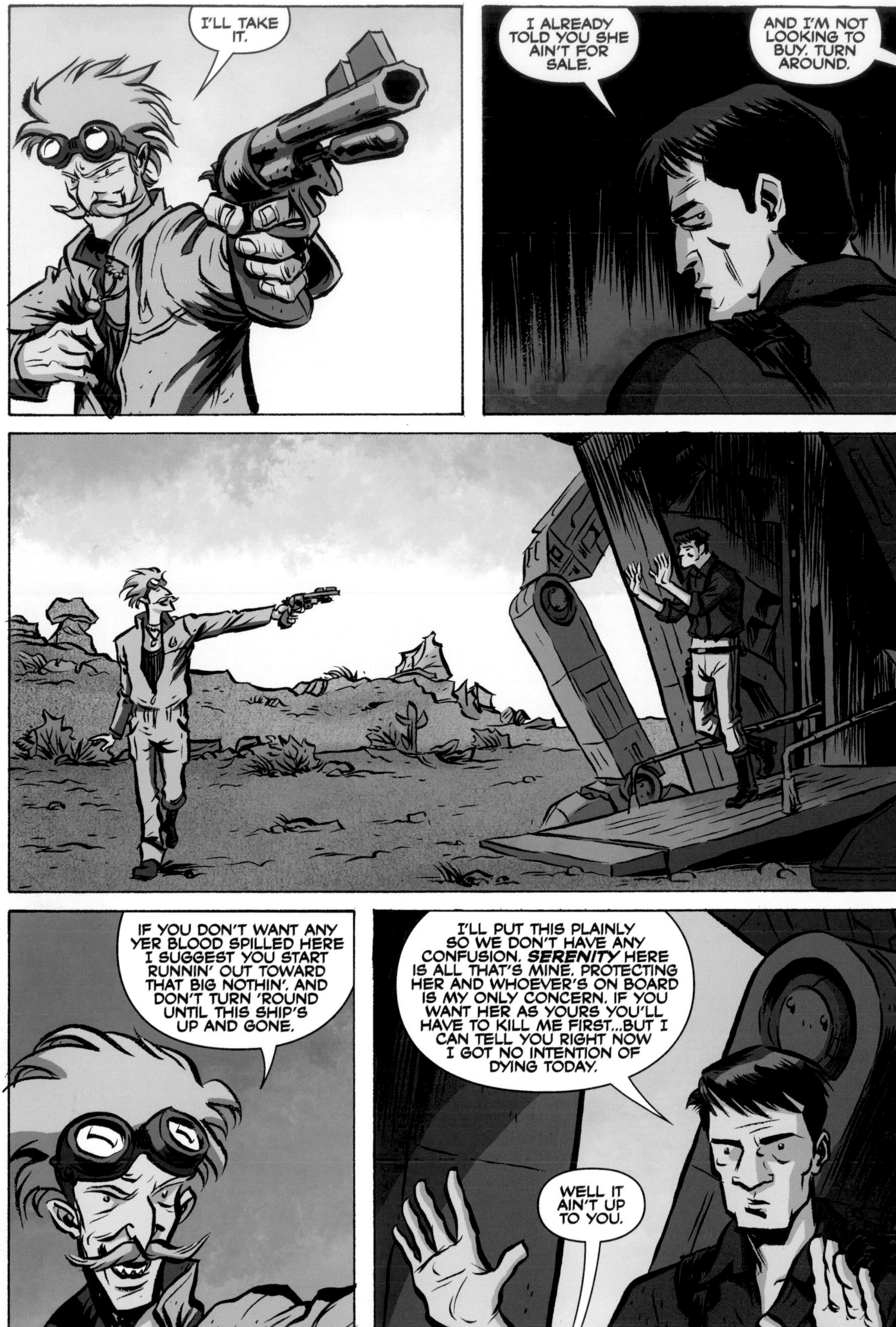
I'LL TAKE IT.
I ALREADY TOLD YOU SHE AIN'T FOR SALE.
AND I'M NOT LOOKING TO BUY. TURN AROUND.
IF YOU DON'T WANT ANY YER BLOOD SPILLED HERE I SUGGEST YOU START RUNNIN' OUT TOWARD THAT BIG NOTHIN', AND DON'T TURN 'ROUND UNTIL THIS SHIP'S UP AND GONE.
I'LL PUT THIS PLAINLY SO WE DON'T HAVE ANY CONFUSION. *SERENITY* HERE IS ALL THAT'S MINE. PROTECTING HER AND WHOEVER'S ON BOARD IS MY ONLY CONCERN. IF YOU WANT HER AS YOURS YOU'LL HAVE TO KILL ME FIRST...BUT I CAN TELL YOU RIGHT NOW I GOT NO INTENTION OF DYING TODAY.
WELL IT AIN'T UP TO YOU.

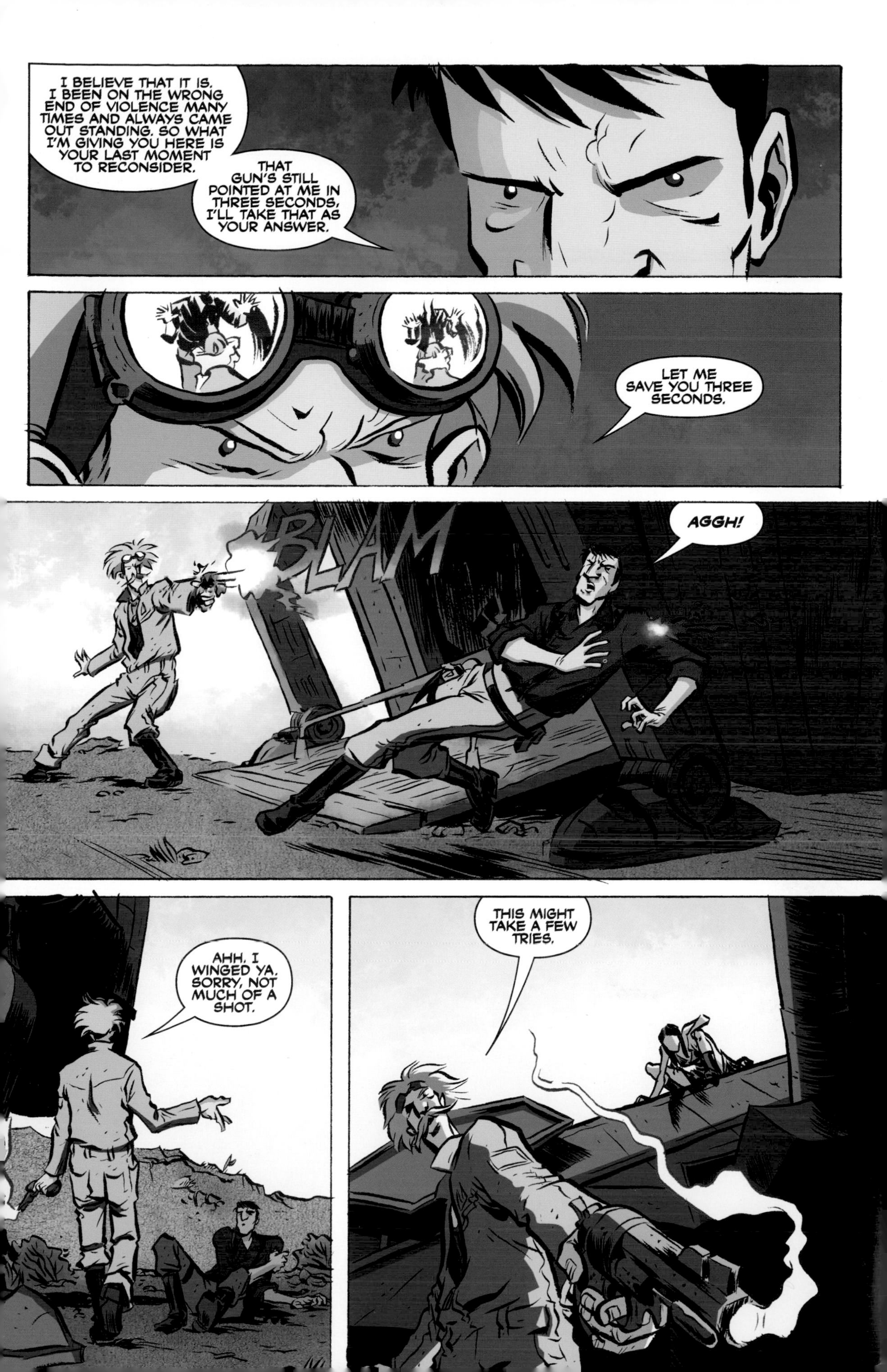
I BELIEVE THAT IT IS. I BEEN ON THE WRONG END OF VIOLENCE MANY TIMES AND ALWAYS CAME OUT STANDING. SO WHAT I'M GIVING YOU HERE IS YOUR LAST MOMENT TO RECONSIDER.
THAT GUN'S STILL POINTED AT ME IN THREE SECONDS, I'LL TAKE THAT AS YOUR ANSWER.
LET ME SAVE YOU THREE SECONDS.
BLAM
AGGH!
AHH, I WINGED YA. SORRY, NOT MUCH OF A SHOT.
THIS MIGHT TAKE A FEW TRIES.

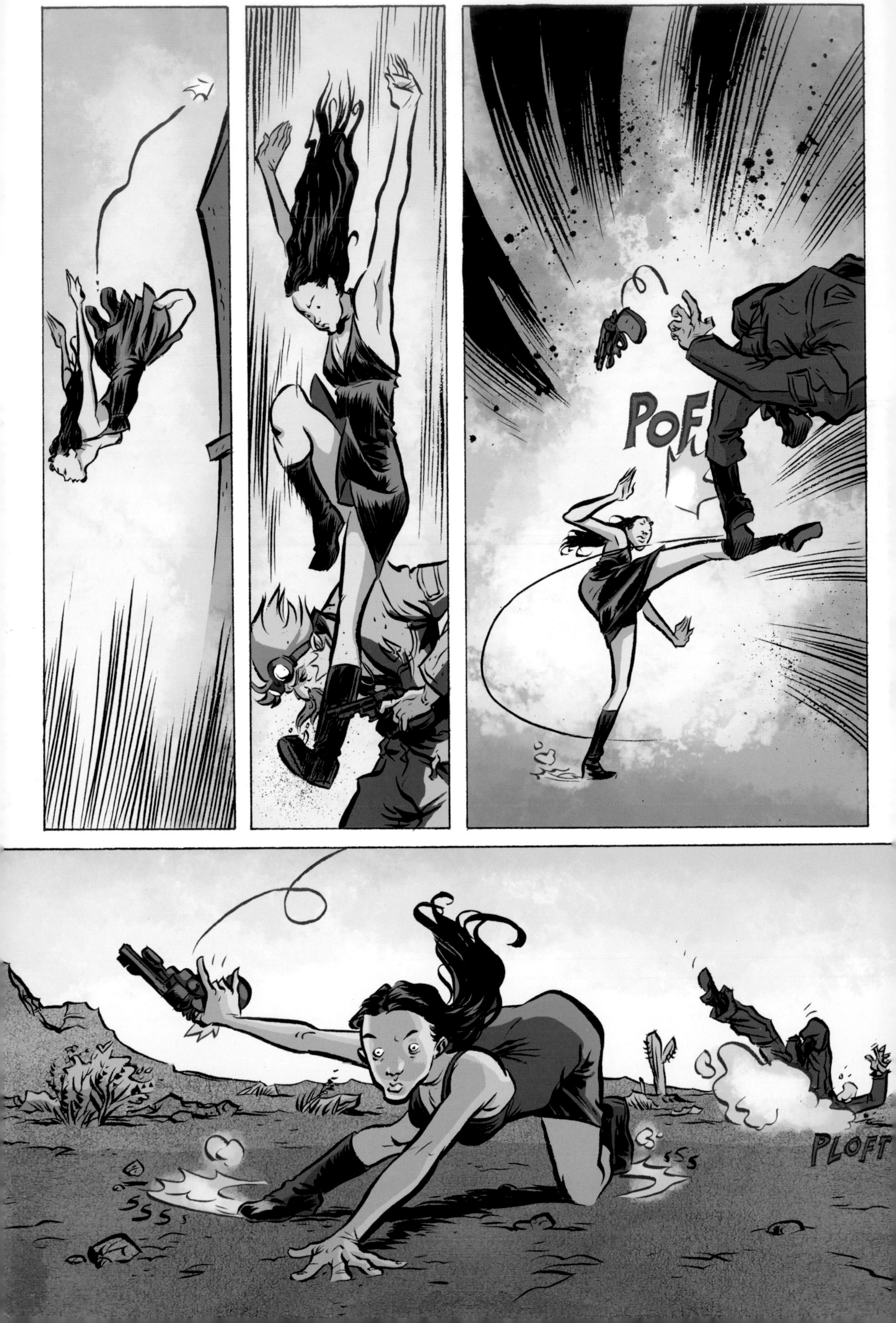
POF
PLOFT

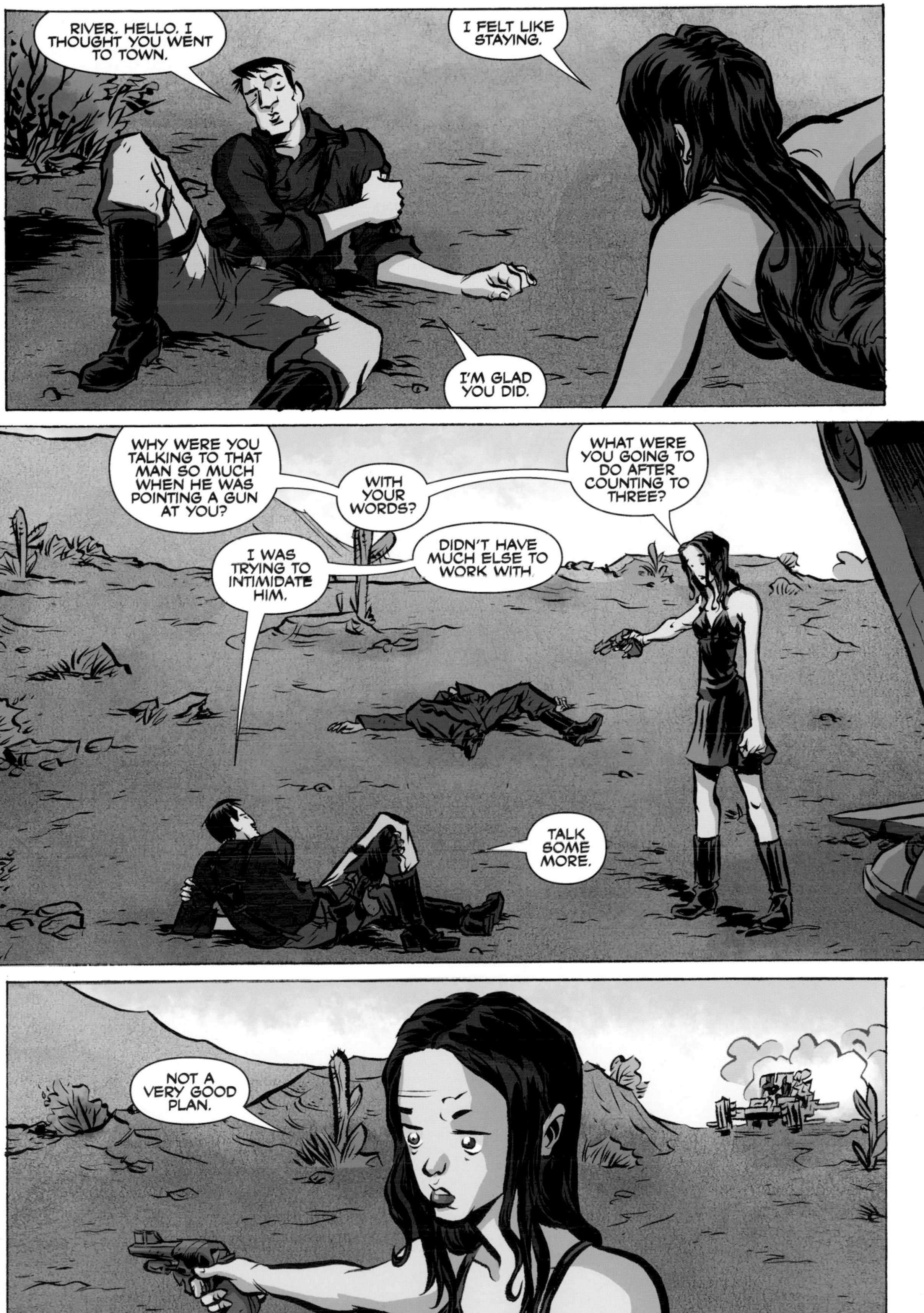
RIVER. HELLO. I THOUGHT YOU WENT TO TOWN.
I FELT LIKE STAYING.
I'M GLAD YOU DID.
WHY WERE YOU TALKING TO THAT MAN SO MUCH WHEN HE WAS POINTING A GUN AT YOU?
WITH YOUR WORDS?
WHAT WERE YOU GOING TO DO AFTER COUNTING TO THREE?
I WAS TRYING TO INTIMIDATE HIM.
DIDN'T HAVE MUCH ELSE TO WORK WITH.
TALK SOME MORE.
NOT A VERY GOOD PLAN.

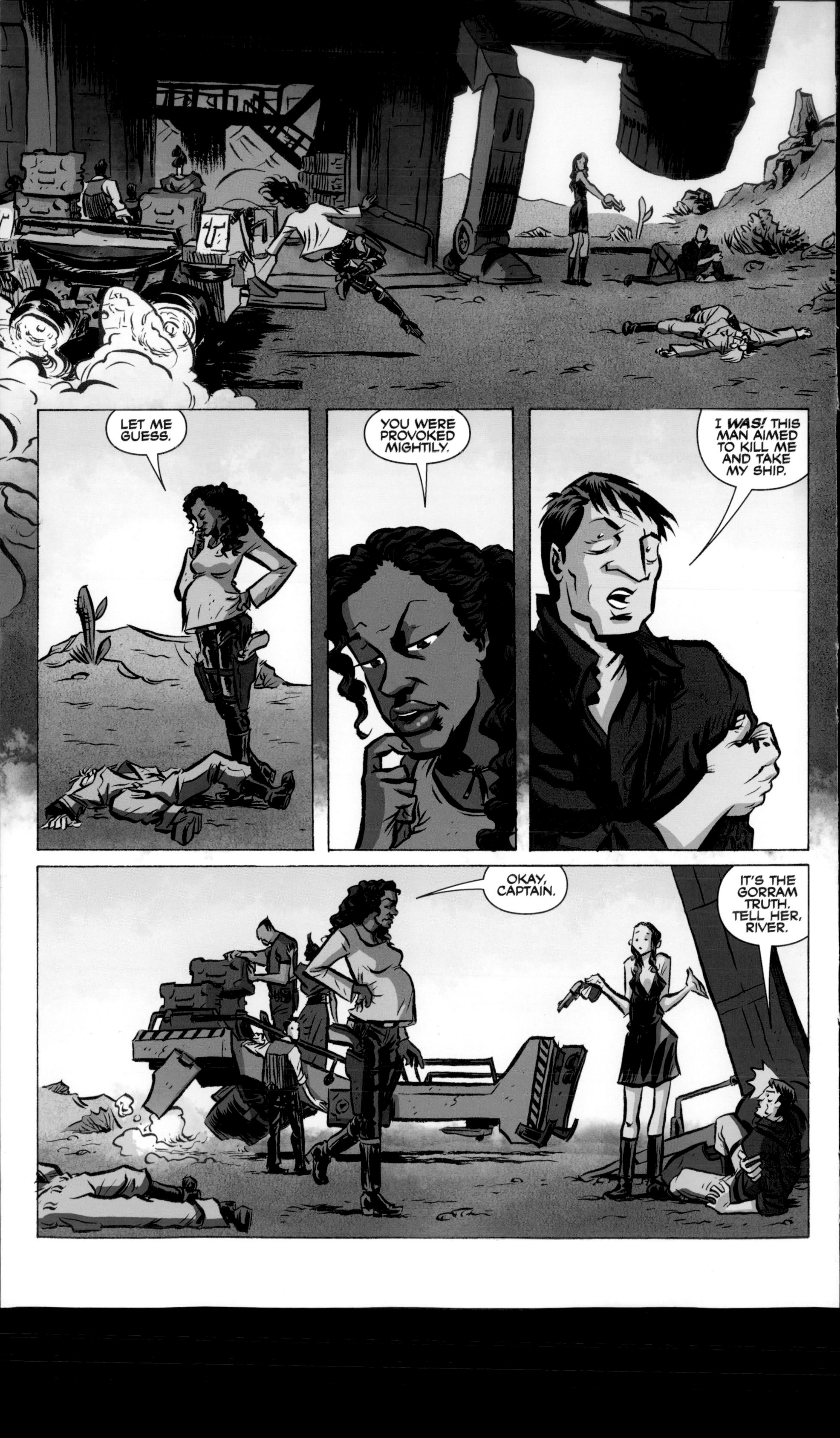
LET ME GUESS.
YOU WERE PROVOKED MIGHTILY.
I WAS! THIS MAN AIMED TO KILL ME AND TAKE MY SHIP.
OKAY, CAPTAIN.
IT'S THE GORRAM TRUTH. TELL HER, RIVER.

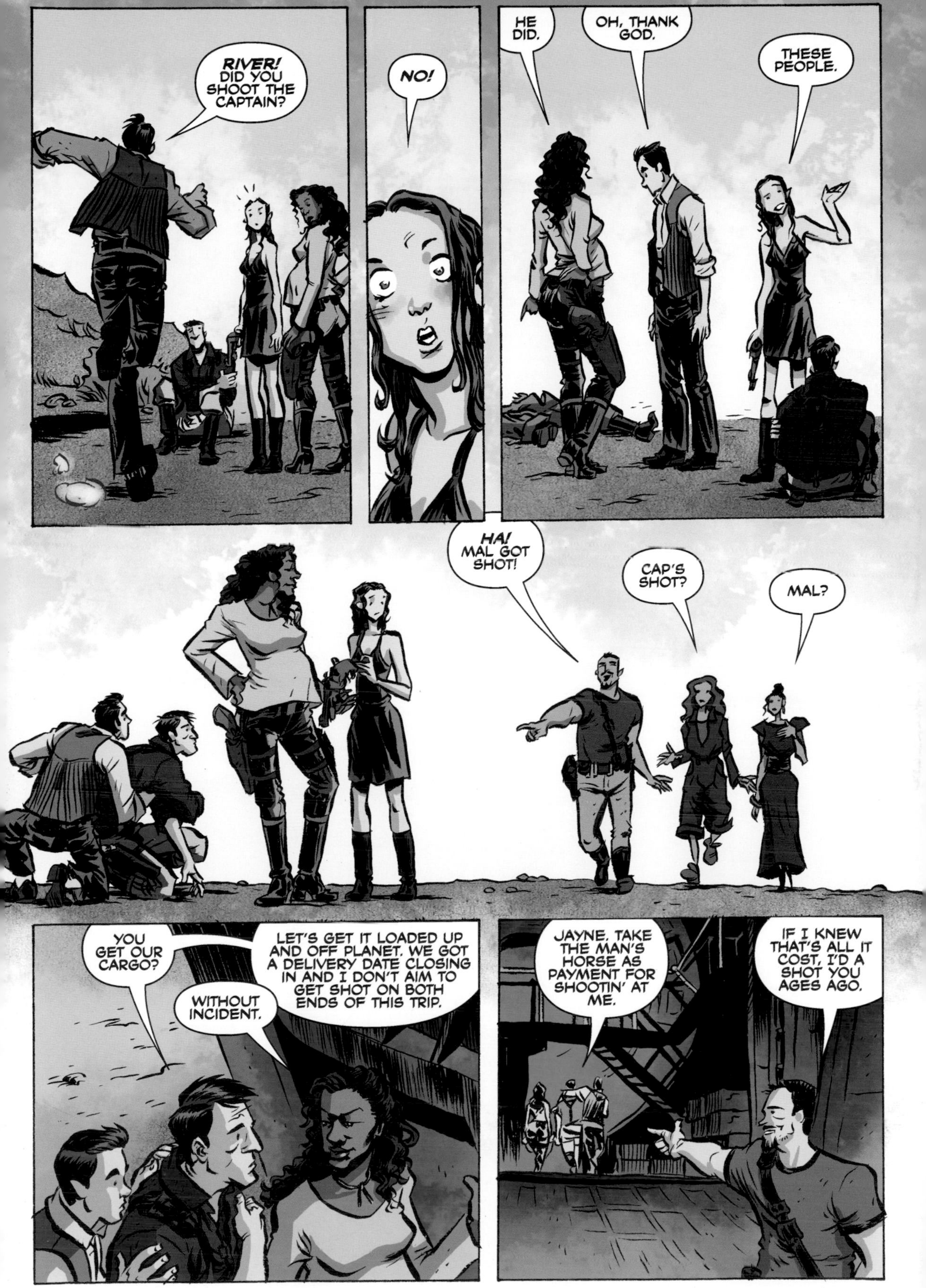
RIVER! DID YOU SHOOT THE CAPTAIN?
NO!
HE DID.
OH, THANK GOD.
THESE PEOPLE.
HA! MAL GOT SHOT!
CAP'S SHOT?
MAL?
YOU GET OUR CARGO?
WITHOUT INCIDENT.
LET'S GET IT LOADED UP AND OFF PLANET. WE GOT A DELIVERY DATE CLOSING IN AND I DON'T AIM TO GET SHOT ON BOTH ENDS OF THIS TRIP.
JAYNE. TAKE THE MAN'S HORSE AS PAYMENT FOR SHOOTIN' AT ME.
IF I KNEW THAT'S ALL IT COST, I'D A SHOT YOU AGES AGO.

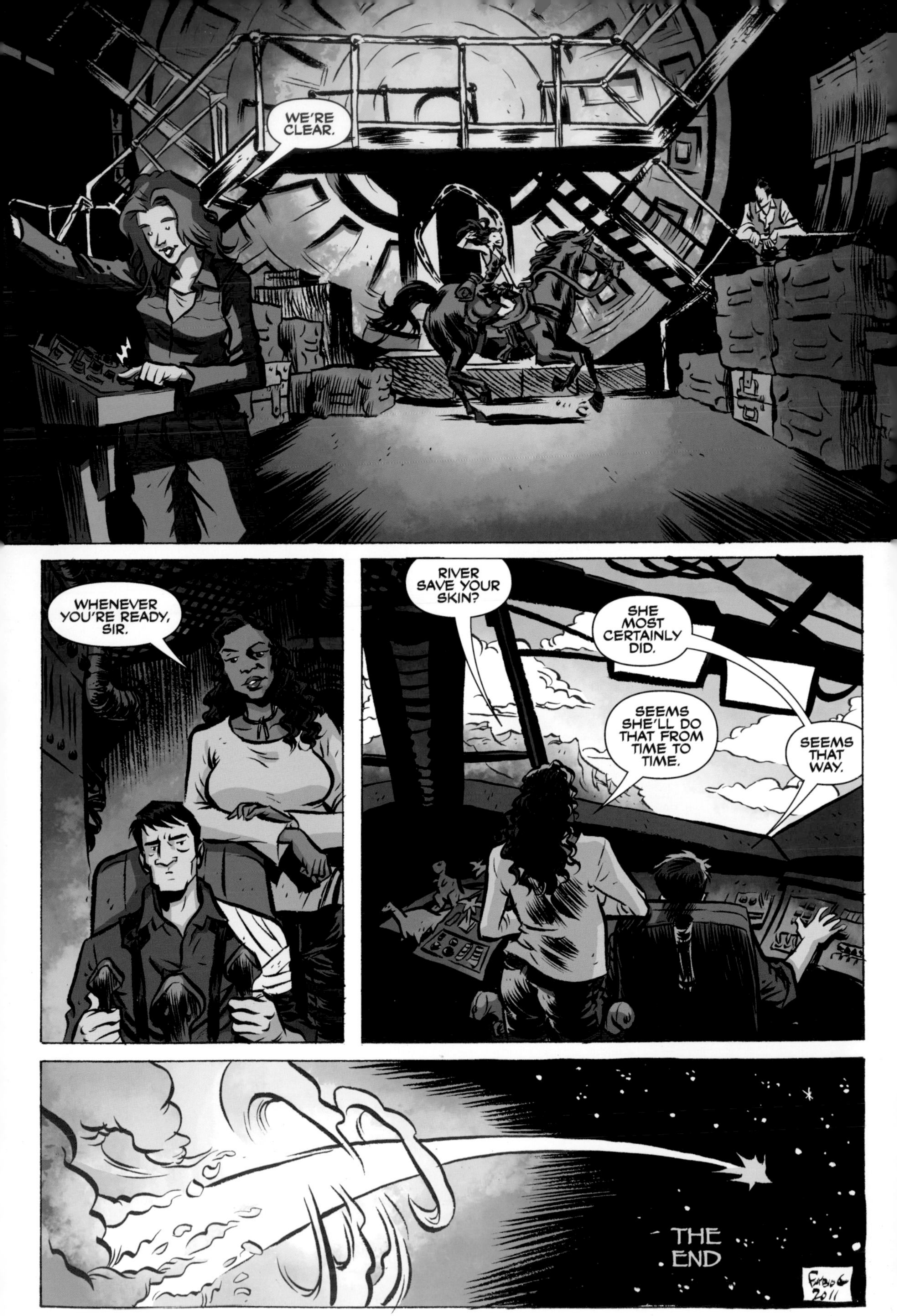
WE'RE CLEAR.
WHENEVER YOU'RE READY, SIR.
RIVER SAVE YOUR SKIN?
SHE MOST CERTAINLY DID.
SEEMS SHE'LL DO THAT FROM TIME TO TIME.
SEEMS THAT WAY.
THE END
FABIO C 2011

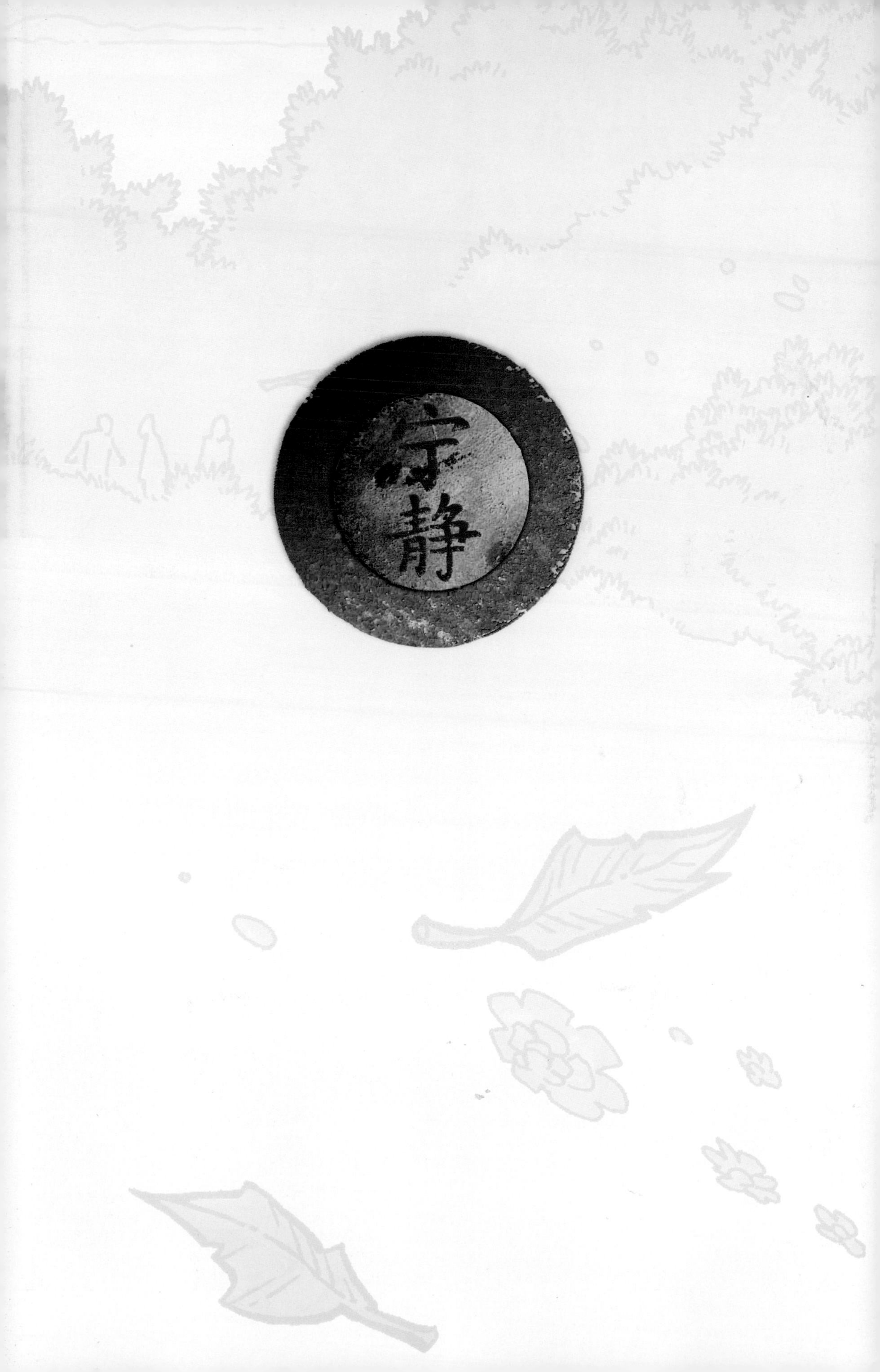
守静

ALSO FROM

JOSS WHEDON

Serenity
宁静 FIREFLY CLASS 03-K64
THOSE LEFT BEHIND

DR. HORRIBLE
ELE
AND OTHER HORRIBLE STORIES BY ZACK WHEDON
with Eric Canete, Farel Dalrymple, Jim Rugg, Joëlle Jones, and Scott Hepburn

JOSS WHEDON'S
dollhouse
EPITAPHS

Buffy
the vampire slayer
OMNIBUS
VOLUME 1

SERENITY VOLUME 1: THOSE LEFT BEHIND
Joss Whedon, Brett Matthews, and Will Conrad
978-1-59582-914-6 | $17.99

SERENITY VOLUME 2: BETTER DAYS AND OTHER STORIES
Joss Whedon, Patton Oswalt, Zack Whedon, Patric Reynolds, and others
978-1-59582-739-5 | $19.99

SERENITY VOLUME 3: THE SHEPHERD'S TALE
Joss Whedon, Zack Whedon, and Chris Samnee
978-1-59582-561-2 | $14.99

DR. HORRIBLE AND OTHER HORRIBLE STORIES
Joss Whedon, Zack Whedon, Joëlle Jones, and others
978-1-59582-577-3 | $9.99

DOLLHOUSE: EPITAPHS
Andrew Chambliss, Jed Whedon, Maurissa Tancharoen, and Cliff Richards
978-1-59582-863-7 | $18.99

TALES OF THE SLAYERS
Joss Whedon, Amber Benson, Gene Colan, P. Craig Russell, Tim Sale, and others
978-1-56971-605-2 | $14.99

TALES OF THE VAMPIRES
Joss Whedon, Brett Matthews, Cameron Stewart, and others
978-1-56971-749-3 | $15.99

BUFFY THE VAMPIRE SLAYER: TALES
978-1-59582-644-2 | $29.99

ANGEL OMNIBUS
Christopher Golden, Eric Powell, and others
978-1-59582-706-7 | $24.99

BUFFY THE VAMPIRE SLAYER OMNIBUS
Volume 1 978-1-59307-784-6 | $24.99
Volume 2 978-1-59307-826-3 | $24.99
Volume 3 978-1-59307-885-0 | $24.99
Volume 4 978-1-59307-968-0 | $24.99
Volume 5 978-1-59582-225-3 | $24.99
Volume 6 978-1-59582-242-0 | $24.99
Volume 7 978-1-59582-331-1 | $24.99

BUFFY THE VAMPIRE SLAYER: PANEL TO PANEL
978-1-59307-836-2 | $19.99

SPIKE VOLUME 1: A DARK PLACE
978-1-61655-109-4 | $17.99

WILLOW VOLUME 1: WONDERLAND
978-1-61655-145-2 | $17.99

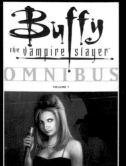

JOSS WHEDON

741.597
W

Whedon, Zack.

Serenity Firefly
Class 03-K64 Leaves
on the wind

DUE DATE	MCN	11/14	19.99
NOV 2 6 2014			